ISLAM, CHRISTIANITY AND TRADITION

Other books by Ian Richard Netton

Across the Mediterranean Frontiers (ed. with D. A. Agius)

Allāh Transcendent: Studies in the Structure and Semiotics of Islamic Philosophy, Theology and Cosmology

The Arab Diaspora: Voices of an Anguished Scream (ed. with Z. S. Salhi)

Arabia and the Gulf: From Traditional Society to Modern States (ed.)

Encyclopaedia of Islamic Civilization and Religion (ed.)

Al-Farabi and his School

Golden Roads: Migration, Pilgrimage and Travel in Mediaeval and Modern Islam (ed.)

Hunter of the East, vol. 1 (ed.)

Middle East Materials in United Kingdom and Irish Libraries: A Directory (ed.)

Middle East Sources (ed.)

Muslim Neoplatonists: An Introduction to the Thought of the Brethren of Purity (Ikhwān al-Ṣafā')

A Popular Dictionary of Islam

Seek Knowledge: Thought and Travel in the House of Islam

Ṣūfī Ritual: The Parallel Universe

Text and Trauma: An East–West Primer

ISLAM, CHRISTIANITY AND TRADITION

A COMPARATIVE EXPLORATION

◆ ◆ ◆

IAN RICHARD NETTON

EDINBURGH UNIVERSITY PRESS

Edinburgh University Press Ltd
22 George Square, Edinburgh

Typeset in Goudy by
Koinonia, Manchester, and
printed and bound in Great Britain by
Cromwell Press, Trowbridge, Wilts

A CIP Record for this book is available from the British Library

ISBN-10 0 7486 2391 4 (hardback)
ISBN-13 978 0 7486 2391 4 (hardback)
ISBN-10 0 7486 2392 2 (paperback)
ISBN-13 978 0 7486 2392 1 (paperback)

Published with the support of the Edinburgh University
Scholarly Publishing Initiatives Fund.

CONTENTS

PREFACE AND ACKNOWLEDGEMENTS

This is not an Introduction to Islam, nor is it a textbook. There are many excellent introductions and textbooks in the marketplace already. One notes in particular David Waines, *An Introduction to Islam* (Cambridge: Cambridge University Press, 1995), Gerhard Endress, *An Introduction to Islam* (Edinburgh: Edinburgh University Press, 1988), Sachiko Murata and William C. Chittick, *The Vision of Islam: The Foundations of Muslim Faith and Practice* (London and New York: I. B. Tauris, 1996) and John L. Esposito (ed.), *Oxford History of Islam* (Oxford: Oxford University Press, 1999). All of these, in their diverse and very attractive ways, play a significant and important role in introducing student and scholar alike to one of the world's major religions.

This book is a research monograph which aims to do much more than that. It operates generally within the sphere of comparative religion and is, specifically, a comparative exploration of the role of tradition/Tradition within two distinct faiths, Islam and Christianity. Specific leitmotivs include the roles of authority, fundamentalism, the use of reason, *ijtihād*, and original comparisons between Islamic Salafism and Christian Lefebvrism. 'Salafism' refers to that strain in Islam which looks backwards to the thought, practices and traditions of the *Salaf* (pious ancestors); 'Lefebvrism' is a reference to the traditionalist thought and practices of the schismatic Archbishop Marcel Lefebvre (1905–91) who rejected much of the teaching of the Second Vatican Council (1962–65) and what he perceived as that Council's overthrow of tradition/Tradition. It is recognised in my text that the word 'tradition/Tradition' in both Islam and Christianity has a variety of senses and definitions.

While this volume is not an Introduction to Islam, it does aim to be accessible to the serious non-specialist as well as to the seasoned scholar in the field. It aims to make connections; it aims to add immediacy to the text by its use, among a variety of primary and secondary sources, of contemporary newspaper and journal articles, documents, letters and encyclicals. It aims to present a lucid and stimulating text which can be read with pleasure and profit by the scholar as well as by the serious, interested, non-specialist. It does so by drawing on the author's intensive study of Islam and Christianity over a period of nearly forty years.

Methodologically, this volume recognises from the outset that Islam is not a monolith, and it seeks to explore at first some of the worn methodologies and vocabularies by which this faith has been articulated in the past, and to suggest new ones. Some of the originality of this volume lies in its proposal of a new vocabulary for the articulation of Islam, rather as M. G. S. Hodgson in *The Venture of Islam* (3 vols, Chicago, 1974) did many years ago, but in a more attractive form.

Islam is not, I repeat, a monolith. Vartan Gregorian, *Islam: A Mosaic, Not a Monolith* (Washington, DC: Brookings Institution Press, 2003, pp. 112, 134), is at pains to stress this:

> The fact is that there is no unified 'Muslim World' or unified Muslim ideology ... Muslim diversity and division is a historical fact ... Islam, like other religions, cannot be categorised or stereotyped because it is brimming with nuances, exceptions, divisions, contractions, and ambiguities.

This volume investigates certain aspects of that mosaic. It recognises that both Islam and Christianity, via their contemporary and diverse traditionalist adherents, have cleaved at times to a supposedly 'golden age' of tradition from the past. Like Sophocles, they have believed that 'sometimes you have to wait until the evening to see how glorious the day has been'. The variegated splendours of the mosaic are unveiled in this volume with particular reference to the concepts of *object* (cf. Edmund Husserl, 1859–1938, and Martin Heidegger, 1889–1976), *sign* (Umberto Eco, b. 1932) and *the sacred* (Mircea Eliade, 1907–86). In other words, I deploy a triple methodological sieve of phenomenology, semiotics and what might be loosely termed '*sacral science*'. The overall structure is that of comparative tradition, the comparison being with Christianity. To the best of my knowledge, this kind of comparative focus, *done in this way* with the underlying substratum being that of tradition, has not been attempted before – though there have, of course, been many volumes of comparative religion published in the past which deal with the two faiths. These range from J. W. Sweetman' s multi-volume classic *Islam and Christian Theology* (London and Redhill: Lutterworth Press, 1945–67) to James A. Bill and John Alden Williams, *Roman Catholics and Shiʿi Muslims: Prayer, Passion and Politics* (Chapel Hill and London: University of North Carolina Press, 2002) and Anthony O'Mahony, Wulstan Peterburs and Mohammad Ali Shomali (eds), *Catholics and Shiʿa in Dialogue: Studies in Theology and Spirituality* (London: Melisende, 2004).

While sharing in the concerns and *some* of the subject matter of all of these books, my present volume differs profoundly from all of them in aim, theme, orientation and presentation. It articulates and illustrates a fundamental *silsila* or chain whose members have a common interest in *ijtihād*, independent judgement, or something like it. That chain, whether of discipleship, influence or study runs from the jurist Aḥmad b. Ḥanbal (780–855) through the Ḥanbalī theologian and jurist Ibn Taymiyya (1263–1328) through the Arabian reviver of Ḥanbalism and propagator of the ideas of Ibn Taymiyya, Ibn ʿAbd al-Wahhāb (1703–92) to the firebrand Jamāl al-Dīn al-Afghānī (1838/9–1897), who strongly influenced the Chief Muftī of Egypt and apostle of *neo-ijtihād* Muḥammad ʿAbduh (1849–1905), at whose feet sat the Syrian intellectual Rashīd Riḍā (1865–1935), who taught the founder of the Ikhwān al-Muslimūn, Ḥasan al-Bannā' (1906–49), who 'mentored' the ideologue of the Muslim Brotherhood in Egypt, Sayyid Quṭb (1906–66). In a magisterial article entitled 'Was the Gate of Ijtihād Closed?' (*International Journal of Middle East Studies*, 16 (1984), pp. 3–41; repr. Ian Edge (ed.), *Islamic Law and Legal Theory* (Aldershot: Dartmouth Publishing Co., 1993), Wael B. Hallaq argued powerfully that it was not (see idem, *Authority, Continuity and Change in Islamic Law* (Cambridge: Cambridge University Press, 2001), p. 56 n. 143). This present volume of mine works within the framework of that denial drawing on past and present evidence, and highlights seemingly paradoxical, but very real, contrapuntal harmony between tradition/Tradition in Islam and *ijtihād*. Christian tradition/Tradition serves as a focus for contrast and comparison.

Finally, this volume is conscious of a yearning on the part of some movements in both Islam and Christianity for a 'golden age', whence all good traditions now derive, which some would claim never actually existed. Just as, over 1,500 years ago, St Augustine of Hippo (354–430) famously seemed to detect a goal just out of reach in his lament that *nondum amabam, et amare amabam* ('I did not love but yearned to love') (*Confessions*, Bk III, 1 (i), so many traditionalists and traditionists today – Muslim and Christian alike – yearn for the revival of an age in which all will be well once again. This volume, finally, is an articulation and lucid illustration of that yearning. It is an exploration of the imagination of tradition/Tradition and the *Traditional Imagination* in Islam.

I must acknowledge once again a profound debt of gratitude to my wife, Sue, and my family, who have had to put up with the vagaries of an author in full spate! I am grateful, too, to my excellent editors at Edinburgh University Press, especially Nicola Ramsey and Stuart Midgley, together with James Dale and Eddie Clark, for their care and help which lasted from first commissioning through to the final product. It has been a continued pleasure to work with EUP. Finally, I must pay a most warm tribute to my superb copy-editor, Ivor Normand. He has an eagle eye *sans pareil*!

ABBREVIATIONS

ARCIC	Anglican–Roman Catholic International Commission
CCA	*The Cambridge Companion to Augustine*
CCSL	*Corpus Christianorum Series Latina*
CIH	*Corpus Inscriptionum Semiticarum IV, Insciptiones Sabaeas et Himiariticas continens*, vols I–III, 1889–1927
DAS	*Divino Afflante Spiritu*
DV	*Dei Verbum*
EI[2]	*Encyclopaedia of Islam*, 2nd edn
EIS	*Shorter Encyclopaedia of Islam*
HG	*Humani Generis*
ISIM	The International Institute for the Study of Islam in the Modern World, Leiden
PD	*Providentissimus Deus*
Q.	The Holy Qur'ān
reg.	*regnavit* (reigned)
SOAS	The School of Oriental and African Studies, University of London

To the Memory of my beloved mother, Olive Christine Netton

CHAPTER

1

PREPARATION FOR A THREEFOLD SIEVE

1.1 Whose Agenda for the Twenty-first Century?

We live in an age when the tired paradigms of public perception reign supreme. Stereotype is all. In this respect, the new millennium is no different from the old. Samuel P. Huntington famously talked of the potential clash of two civilisations, a Western Christian and an Eastern Islamic.[1] The Kosovan crisis of 1999 provided an interesting example of that within the former communist Yugoslavia, with Serbian forces of the Christian Orthodox faith conducting a policy of ethnic cleansing against Kosovan Albanians.[2] The profound irony of this particular conflict, in the light of Huntington's prognostication, was that 'the West' in the form of the NATO Alliance, allied with, rather than fought against, Kosovan Albanian Islam.

Much more omnipresent is that paradigm of public perception whose essence is the clash of two seemingly immovable and invincible stereotypes, rather than civilisations: that beloved in Europe and the USA, especially since 11 September 2001, of a fanatically terrorist Islam,[3] and that beloved by some 'fundamentalist'[4] Muslims of an utterly corrupt and morally bankrupt West. Both stereotypes are fostered and fed by a press hungry for scandal and saleable copy, but the Western stereotype, at least, is part of an ancient tradition.[5]

While rejecting such stereotypes, this volume will explore other paradigms and vocabularies, more firmly based in reality, often with particular reference to the concepts of tradition and authority in Islam. As it does so, frequent comparisons will be made with Christian concepts of tradition and authority by way of illuminating the Islamic dimension. In this respect, a major comparative focus will be the Roman Catholic branch of Christianity because of that Church's strong emphasis on both these key *topoi*. One thinks especially of the Roman Catholic dogma of Papal Infallibility. Our purpose is that of Bill and Williams: 'By comparing two religious traditions that at first sight appear to be quite different and distinct, [one may seek] to advance our understanding of both faith systems'.[6] Our hope is that these new paradigms and vocabularies will serve to replace what we have characterised as the tired paradigms of public perception.

Islamic authority on earth is pragmatically 'grounded'[7] in what Julian Baldick calls 'orthopraxy'[8] and what I will term here 'sacred multipraxis 'or 'sacropraxis' for short. For certain scholars, 'right authority' in mediaeval Islam is seen as having followed an almost *jāhilī* (pre-Islamic) paradigm of variegated custom, force and power.[9] 'Right authority', articulated in reality, derived not from religious 'orthodoxy', 'heterodoxy' or any other such 'dead' category[10] but, according to this thinking, from a mixture of practices, political and legal,[11] which with luck might be graced with a veneer of the religious or the sacred. It is true that the Ka'ba was, and is, perceived as a semiotic key to the fundamentals of Islamic dogma: it is 'a single site' towards which 'on Friday throughout the world the faithful bow' and 'this attachment of every space on earth, as if to a magnet, by the spiritual center sustains the centricity of the infinite oneness of God'.[12] That is the Islamic *tradition*. But many hold that the locus of real authority over the Islamic community, the *umma*, lay elsewhere. The mediaeval *bay'a*, the oath of allegiance, offered by the nobles to an incoming ruler, and other such human devices, provided an essential cloak of sacred order which is at the heart of what we have termed sacred multipraxis. This volume aims to explore and lay bare that multipraxis by a comparative analysis of its objects, signs and sacredness, with a central focus on Islamic tradition and authority. And these twin *topoi* are as relevant to our new millennium as they were in mediaeval times.

Several questions arise: how will tradition and authority be articulated in a future age? Whose agenda will dominate the new millennium? To what extent, if any, will modern perceptions and categories of Islamic tradition and authority depend on past, mediaeval paradigms? Whose agenda will design and sanction solutions to problems neither encountered in the Qur'ān nor prefigured in the Sunna of the Prophet Muḥammad (AD c. 570–632)? To what extent will *ijmā'*, consensus either of the learned scholars or the whole *umma*, and *qiyās*, reasoning by analogy, play a role in the future elaboration of jurisprudence in Islam? And whose Islam? Not for nothing did one modern scholar entitle a book *Islams and Modernities*.[13] The double plural is highly significant for our discussions.

It is a cliché that, classically, Islam is an entire way of life in which there is no divide, a seamless robe in which religion, politics and law, for example, are one. The historical reality has, of course, differed profoundly from this classical model: Islam is not, and never has been, a monolith.[14] This truism, then, returns us to our initial questions: whose Islam? Whose agenda? Let us briefly survey six possible scenarios. They are by no means exhaustive, nor mutually exclusive.

Digital Islam[15]

Will it be an Islam clothed in the fashionable garbs of the new technology? Certainly, the Qur'ān, ḥadīth and *sīra* literature have survived for over 1,000 years without computers and will continue to do so.[16] Computer applications to sacred and related texts will enhance accessibility; but this is not really the essence of the matter. What we are on the brink of is an epistemological revolution in the Islamic domain which may, or may not, have serious consequences for such foundational themes as tradition and authority.

Profound questions arise demanding answers.

> The phenomenal popularization and transnational propagation of communications and information technologies ... in recent years has generated a wide range of important questions in the context of Islam's sociology of knowledge. How have these technologies transformed Muslim concepts of what Islam is and who possesses the authority to speak on its behalf? Moreover, how are they changing the ways in which Muslims imagine the boundaries of the *umma*?[17]

The Internet, especially the World Wide Web, has rightly been compared to 'an enormous bazaar' where 'the hawkers are many and the inf-goods, at first glance, seem to address every imaginable need'.[18]

In terms of the sociology of knowledge, a revolution has taken place akin to that precipitated by the introduction of the printing presses in the fifteenth century by Johannes Gutenberg and William Caxton. What might be characterised as a liberation of élite knowledge combined with a fostering of new political discourses has occurred.[19] Observing the use of 'book, pamphlet and newsletter' in the nineteenth century by a body of the *'ulamā'* (the Islamic scholars) appalled at the advance of European imperialism, Mandaville notes that an ineluctable by-product was 'the demise of the stranglehold' of those same *'ulamā'* 'over the production and dissemination of religious knowledge'.[20] But the result of today's new information technologies has been to accelerate that demise to a staggering and, for the modern *'ulamā'*, uncomfortable degree as they find their custodianship of specialist, and sometimes élite, knowledge both challenged and threatened.[21] Mandaville quotes Sa'ad al-Faqih, 'leader of the London-based "Movement for Islamic Reform in Arabia" and another keen advocate of information technology', as suggesting 'that the average Muslim can now revolutionize Islam with just a basic understanding of Islamic methodology and a CD-ROM'.[22] The sometimes cherished gulf between the religious or legal scholar and the ordinary Muslim is bridged at the click of a button and the production of 'relevant texts' at a stroke.[23]

There are, of course, obvious dangers in this kind of instant and, perhaps, previously unstudied, knowledge for the lay surfer of the Net: how reliable are the texts and sources placed instantly at one's disposal?[24] Will the age of the e-mail *fatwā* signal an intellectual free-for-all?[25] But there are epistemological advantages too: a deeper questioning may be provoked as to what it really means to be Islamic. This may result in a sharper set or variety of foci, emphases or definitions.[26] The mediaeval search for authenticity, with its inevitable politics and rubrics, has revived and continues into the present.[27] Mandaville summarises the modern position very neatly: 'the changing connotations of authority and authenticity in digital Islam appear to be contributing to the critical re-imagination of the boundaries of Muslim politics'.[28]

Crisis Islam

Will the Islam of the future be a faith which is in perpetual crisis as it confronts, and perhaps attempts to absorb, varying modes and articulations of 'modernity'? That term, of course, itself requires proper definition; many have been offered.[29] It is used loosely to provide a simple but striking rhetorical antithesis, as in Muqtedar Khan's statement that

> Muslim women are caught in the struggle *between the imperialism of modernity and the intransigence of tradition*. At times, they are victims of those who seek to protect them and, at other times, they are oppressed by those who seek to emancipate them. For Muslim women, tragedy and irony are the two dominant themes of their existence.[30]

Here the simple motif of modernity, simply understood, is used as a powerful but fundamental counterpoint to that of tradition, in a statement which also encapsulates the underlying complexities of both positions.

Modernity has been characterised as 'a particularly organised and insidious form of worldliness ... the collection of practices, processes, structures and values which have characterized European expansion' and something which 'was associated with the establishment of the European empires.'[31] The rationalism and individualism which formed part of the agenda were, and are, perceived by the Muslim world as both alien and threatening,[32] though several aspects of the modern European experience, especially Europe's superiority in technology, maintained a perennial appeal and attraction.[33] According to this understanding, the clash of modernity and tradition at the beginning of a new millennium may be perceived as yet another calque of the antique conflict between revelation and reason,[34] a clash which for many Muslims reifies the need to construct 'a narrative of equal power to counter the corrosive effects of modernity upon the authorities that validate a distinctively Muslim identity'.[35]

Of course, the debate about and between tradition and modernity is by no means limited to the single religion of Islam. Tradition and modernity have been defined as 'two separate outlooks by which to judge the state of the contemporary world', with tradition being characterised as '*sophia perennis* or primordial wisdom, which is not limited to any specific cultural or religious tradition', and modernity having, as its defining aspect, '*a loss of the sense of the sacred*' and representing an outlook which is essentially ambivalent and rudderless. This is 'the malaise of modernity'.[36] It is to be contrasted, as a term, with the more neutral 'contemporary', which designates 'that which is of the present age, be it traditional or modern', shorn of the pejorative overtones which the words 'modern' and 'modernity' have for many traditionalist scholars.[37]

For the Swiss mystic Frithjof Schuon (1907–98), the question of how to act, and react, in a perilous modern world was bound up with what he termed 'antecedent certainties'.[38] In addition, for him, tradition had to be articulated in comprehensible language, and its abandonment in our own age indicated more an unwillingness to understand rather than an inability.[39] Seyyed Hossein Nasr described Schuon as 'without doubt the foremost expositor in the latter half of this century of the *philosophia perennis* as well as the *sophia perennis*'.[40]

From all this, it is clear that several modern scholars have linked the concept of tradition, as contrasted with modernity, with a primordial *sophia perennis* which transcends individual religions, cults and cultures and which becomes a *sine qua non* in the armoury of the 'traditionist' today.

However, modernity, too, has both its moment and its champions. In discussing tradition, there can be a tendency towards a 'certain transcendental idealism' in which the ground of the eternal is unduly romanticised by the rejection of modernity's 'now'.[41] David Appelbaum has drawn attention to René Descartes (1596–1650) as the 'father of modernity'[42] and quotes from that author's *Meditations on First Philosophy* as follows: 'I realized that for once I had to raze everything in my life, down to the very bottom, so as to begin again from the first foundations, if I wanted to establish anything firm and lasting in the sciences'.[43] Ultimately, however, for Appelbaum, to posit a contrast between tradition and modernity is to posit a false dichotomy: 'What then is the quintessentially modern if not an adaptation of an ancient approach?'[44]

This brief survey of attitudes and approaches to tradition and modernity which we have just adumbrated is designed to illustrate both the contemporary nature and the vitality of the debate which, though it might assume a certain individual poignancy at times for Islam, nonetheless transcends the formal boundaries of all the major world religions.[45] It is a debate which will not go away; in response, groups as diverse as the Islamic Fiqh Academy and the Berlin-based *Working Group Modernity and Islam* have realised the importance of its articulation and study.

The Islamic Fiqh Council, which comes under the aegis of the Organisation of the Islamic Conference (OIC), formally recommended that 'on the question of Islam vis-à-vis modernism … the OIC should form a committee of Muslim intellectuals who would tackle the phenomenon of modernism and its effects and study it both scientifically and objectively'.[46] Speaking during the 11th Session of the Islamic Fiqh Council, in November 1998 in Manama, Bahrain, the Secretary-General of the Muslim World League, Dr Abdullah Saleh al-Obeid, stressed the need to understand exactly what was meant by such terms as modernism. It required rigorous definition. There was nothing wrong with such terms if they implied using new methodologies and techniques which could be used to implement the key goals of the *umma* (the worldwide Islamic community). However, if modernism implied a rejection of 'religion and ethics, a concept that has come from different disciplines in arts, humanities and literature', then it required careful evaluation and study: the implications of such subjectivity and the individualism associated with it were unacceptable and, indeed, un-Islamic.[47]

The Working Group Modernity and Islam, which is 'hosted by the Wissenschaftskolleg zu Berlin',[48] has as its mission the fostering of 'a deeper understanding of Muslim cultures, their histories, and their social structures with the two-fold aim of revealing their complexities and of offering deeper insights into the phenomena of "modernity" and "modernization"'.[49] The Group does not start from the premise that there is what might be termed 'a fundamental polarity' between the world of Islam and the other areas of the world which have embraced modernity so enthusiastically. It recognises that there is 'an inherent crisis', one from which the West with its modernising instincts is by no means immune.[50] In a very real way, then, there is an overlap with the interests, if not with the same solutions and enthusiasm for the traditional, which motivate and stir Ali Lakhani and his journal *Sacred Web*,[51] on the one hand, and those which provoke the apprehensions of the Secretary-General of the Muslim World League on the other.[52]

Ḥijāb Islam

Will the Islam of the new millennium be what I will term here '*ḥijāb*' Islam? In other words, will it be an Islam which feels that its major task is to confront the spectre, in every way possible, of what it perceives to be an advancing *secularism*? That awful, and awesome, spectre in Western suit and Eastern *gallabiyya* has, for the Muslim, an irresistible and ineluctable twin: globalisation.[53] In his worst nightmares, will he see the two slowly advancing to rob the *umma* of its children – and the *da'wa*, or missionary call to embrace the Islamic faith, of its fruits?

For the Islamic Fiqh Academy, recognition and confrontation of the menace of such secularism made it imperative that the Muslim religious scholars, the *'ulamā'*, should redouble their efforts at *da'wa*, both exposing and warning against such secularism.[54] Education was the key to showing a united front against that evil, together with a need to train more workers in *da'wa*.[55] In such statements, of course, the Academy merely recognises once again a venerable debate – Islam versus secularism – which has lasted for more than 100 years, and in which the protagonists 'are apparently locked in a stalemate and an endless "war of positions"'.[56] It is the question of *compatibility* between Islam and secularism which is raised more and more, by contrast with the parallel question of *happening* with reference to Christian European societies, where the emphasis appears to be much more on 'how secularization happened in some European societies at some time, and how it influenced their functioning'.[57]

For Islam, secularism was – and is – perceived as irreligious, negative and alien,[58] even though, as Filali-Ansary insists, 'it is easy to observe that secularization has found its way to Muslim societies, and has *deeply* and *irreversibly* permeated their ordering and the prevailing conceptions within them'.[59] The dominance of secular state law over most areas of *Sharī'a* law (except in the realms of family law), in most countries which call themselves Islamic, is a notable illustration of this.[60] Only in the Kingdom of Saudi Arabia does *Sharī'a* law hold perfect sway to the exclusion of all other.

Perhaps nowhere in recent times have the semiotics of the debate between secularism and Islam been articulated more lucidly, more bitterly and more publicly than in the European/Middle Eastern state of Turkey. Here, to wear an Islamic headscarf in public may be interpreted as making a political statement against the state and, indeed, against the reforms of the founding father and guru of modern, post-Ottoman, secular Turkey, Kemal Atatürk (1881–1938) himself. As Chris Morris put it succinctly: 'Turkey's secular elite regards the scarf as the symbol of political Islam and *hidden fundamentalism*'.[61] It is no surprise, then, that when Merve Kavakci, having been elected an (Islamist) Virtue Party deputy for Istanbul, decided to enter the Turkish Parliament wearing a headscarf on Sunday 2 May 1999, a massive furore ensued. The then Prime Minister, the secularist Bulent Ecevit, protested vehemently, but Ms Kavakci alleged attempted discrimination 'against the female relatives of soldiers killed in action against the Kurdish rebel movement in Eastern Turkey'.[62] In such simple, poignant and yet dramatic ways have the forces of secularism collided and clashed with those of militant Islamism.

The revulsion against the headscarf exhibited in this incident was, of course, not just another duel between secularism and the insurgent forces of Islam. It was a revulsion against one who, by wearing such a scarf, seemed to challenge in her actions the very foundation of a state which was pleased to have overthrown Islamic Ottomanism. The latter had profound connotations of corruption, backwardness and inferiority in the face of Western technology and arms. The Caliphate had been abolished with the last Ottoman Caliph Abdül Mecit II (reg. 1922–4) being forced into exile in 1924.[63] Also abolished had been the role of Şeyhülislam and the Ministry of Şeriat, while religious medreses and ṣūfī tekkes were closed.[64] Most significant though, in the light of what Merve Kavakci did in May 1999, was the fact that Kemal Atatürk, more than seventy years before, had pilloried the fez as a sign *par excellence* of the backwardness of the Muslim way of life. Freely quotes Atatürk's speech of October 1927:

> Gentlemen, it was necessary to abolish the fez, which sat on the heads of our nation as a symbol of ignorance, negligence, fanaticism, and hatred of progress and civilization, to accept in its place the hat, the headgear used by the whole civilized world, and in this way to demonstrate that the Turkish nation, in its mentality as in other respects, in no way diverges from civilized social life.[65]

On 25 November 1925, the fez was outlawed, as were other items of traditional Islamic clothing.[66]

Anthony Giddens holds that tradition 'defines a kind of truth'. He adds that, 'for someone following a traditional practice, questions don't have to be asked about alternatives'.[67] However, globalisation means that more traditional societies around the world are becoming 'detraditionalised'.[68] What we encounter in the whirlpool of modern Turkey in its secularist–Islamist confrontation is a clash of two paradigmatic traditions. The first, signified by the wearing of the scarf, defines, in Giddens' vocabulary, the truth of Islam which may not and should not be questioned. *For Islamists, there is no alternative to Islam.* The second, signified by the vehement rejection of all religious clothing, whether fez or veil or headscarf, devises and epitomises a new secular stance; in turn, this reifies and defines the truth of Kemalism. This too may not and should not be questioned. *For the Kemalist, there is also no alternative.*

Ms Kavakci did much more than just wear a headscarf in Parliament: she also questioned the New Kemalist Tradition, ensured that the debate would continue and set herself up as a defiant symbol of Islamism in the face of rampant, state-approved secularism. And many will characterise what has been called 'liberal Islam' as a cousin of such secularism, since the juxtaposition of such terms as 'liberal' and

'Islam' is perceived as a contradiction in terms.[69] Will secularism, as articulated today in such lands as Turkey, ever view 'liberal Islam', with its three tropes,[70] as a possible ally? Or will such a species of Islam nonetheless continue to be perceived by Kemalists and other secularists as the enemy, the Ottoman 'other', from which they were all rescued by Kemal Atatürk in the first decades of the twentieth century? The question is posed here, not to answer it with simplistic solutions, but merely to indicate the scale of the secularist–Islamist confrontation at the dawn of the new millennium.

The three tropes put forward by Charles Kurzman were as follows:

> The first trope of liberal Islam holds that the *sharīʿa requires* liberty, and the second trope holds that the *sharīʿa allows* liberty. But there is a third liberal Islamic trope that takes issue with each of the first two. This I call the 'interpreted *sharīʿa*'.[71]

The arch-proponent of the latter view is ʿAbd al-Karīm Soroush (born 1945), whom Kurzman quotes as insisting:

> Religion is divine, but its interpretation is thoroughly human and this-worldly … The text does not stand alone, it does not carry its own meaning on its shoulders, it needs to be situated in a context, it is theory-laden, its interpretation is in flux.[72]

Political Islam

Will the Islam of our new age be a thoroughly political, or politicised, Islam, pursuing the classical but oft-abused theory that politics and religion are a seamless whole, and the ensuing, ineluctable stance that the only Islam worthy of the name is that which pursues an offensive, as opposed to a defensive, *jihād*?[73] Would such an Islam, mirrored in the Afghānī Ṭālibān[74] on the one hand, and the Iranian Ayatollah Khomeini (1902–89)[75] with his *fatwā*[76]-toting propensity, on the other, wholeheartedly embrace what has been described as a 'Theo-Fascist ideology'?[77] To what extent is the horrific destruction of the twin-towered World Trade Center in New York by the airborne followers of the Saudi dissident Usama b. Laden, on Tuesday 11 September 2001,[78] to be the paradigm of political Islam for the twenty-first century?

Calls for moderation and a 'middle way' are many. ʿAbd al-Hakim Murad, for example, writes as follows:

> At this critical moment in our history, the umma has only one realistic hope for survival, and that is to restore the 'middle way', defined by that sophisticated classical consensus which was worked out over painful centuries of debate and scholarship. That consensus alone has the demonstrable ability to provide a basis for unity.[79]

Yet another scholar, Pandita, perceives

an international agenda before the extremist Islamists the world over to destabilise civil societies and regimes against whose interests they work in one way or the other and to create Islamic theocracies. They want to achieve world domination of radical Islamists, through force of arms if and where necessary.[80]

The case of Indonesia is instructive. That state, as is very well known, has the largest population of Muslims in the world.[81] The Islam which reigns within the archipelago has always been extremely tolerant and welcoming, with a few rare exceptions, perhaps due to its peaceful and gradual introduction into the Indonesian islands in the Middle Ages by Arab traders.[82] Yet, in May 1998, riots brought down President Suharto, with the fall-out hurting mainly ethnic Chinese Buddhists or Christians.[83] In October 1999, the 'moderate Islamic teacher and scholar, and the leader of one of the country's biggest Muslim groups', Abdurrahman Wahid (universally called Gus Dur), was elected President of Indonesia.[84] He was supported by many Muslims of a much more conservative hue, one of whom immediately called for the introduction of Islamic law. Another proclaimed: 'We expect the new government will promote Islam, which was discriminated against for so many years'.[85]

Richard Lloyd Parry commented at the time: 'The chances of Indonesia becoming an Islamic state are remote – but the election of Gus Dor is a vivid demonstration of the way in which religion has re-entered the political mainstream in Indonesia after decades in the margins'.[86]

Analysts of the political and religious thought of Gus Dur could well be forgiven for thinking that the new President's views would truly place him on a collision course with his erstwhile or opportunist followers.[87]As Mujiburrahman put it: 'Abdurrahman Wahid, who is popularly called Gus Dor, is often considered controversial, not only because his public statements are frequently against the mainstream of public opinion, but also because his "unusual" activities anger many Muslim activists'.[88] Liddle is quoted as observing: 'Abdurrahman is perhaps the most "secular" contemporary Indonesian Islamic leader', in the sense that he aspires to a future democratic Indonesia without a religion-based party system'.[89] The reference to 'secularism' is intriguing and provocative here, in the light of our earlier survey of the clash between secularism and Islamism.

Mujiburrahman acknowledges that Gus Dur's ideas, like the use of *maṣlaḥa* (judging according to public welfare), were not particularly original if placed beside those of the Islamic reformers. However, their real originality lay in Gus Dur's 'endeavour to put Islamic ideals in Indonesian context'.[90] And Mujiburrahman detected a strong link between the theology and. the political thinking of Gus Dur.[91]

Gus Dur was born in East Java on 4 August 1940 and grew up among the Indonesian equivalent of the Arab *'ulamā'*. His very sobriquet 'Gus' signalled this, for it was a title in Java given to 'the sons of prominent Islamic scholars called Kiai'.[92] ('Dur', of course, was simply an abbreviated form of his first name, Abdurrahman.[93]) His early awareness of his position as a member of the Indonesian *'ulamā'* was confirmed and strengthened by the tragic death of his father, a Religious Affairs Minister, in 1953, when the youthful Abdurrahman was only 13 years old.[94] Later studies in Indonesia,

Cairo and Baghdad were combined with a private but deep immersion in Western culture, texts and languages.[95] Like a latter-day Ṭāhā Ḥusayn (1889–1973),[96] he returned to his native country with a good knowledge of the West as well as the East.[97] Like Ṭāhā Ḥusayn, he studied at al-Azhar University[98] but, while Ḥusayn was also able to undertake formal doctoral study at the Sorbonne,[99] lack of European recognition of his Baghdad degree prevented Gus Dur from undertaking graduate study in Europe in the early 1970s.[100] Nonetheless, his unusually varied intellectual training and development,[101] which must have sat uneasily on his shoulders in the eyes of many other contemporary traditionalists, in view of Gus Dur's family background, clearly played a key role in the formation of his theological and political thought.

Comparisons between the Indonesian Gus Dur and the Egyptian Ṭāhā Ḥusayn are instructive and illuminating. These lie not only in the early, total blindness of the latter,[102] and the later near-sightedness of the former,[103] together with the fact that both achieved high political office in their respective countres,[104] but also in their atttudes towards the traditionalist forms of education to which they were exposed in their extreme youth, suffered at the venerable al-Azhar University in Cairo. This institution clearly symbolised for both all that was wrong with Islamic education in particular, and education in general.

Mujiburrahman tells us that Gus Dur 'found the intellectual atmosphere at al-Azhar unsatisfactory. The method was based on memorisation and reminded him of his experience at the Pesentren [the Islamic boarding school at Magelang which he attended from 1957 to 1959]'.[105] In the second volume of his autobiography *al-Ayyām* (*The Days*), Ṭāhā Ḥusayn also relates how he became increasingly unhappy at the Azhar: 'The young man became more and more disgusted with the Azhar, where he was committed to a life he loathed, and cut off from all that he longed for'.[106] And, just as Gus Dur sought solace in the library of the American University in Cairo (AUC),[107] so Ṭāhā Ḥusayn haunted, and enrolled at, the new Egyptian University.[108] It was a very welcome contrast to the teaching which he had encountered at the Azhar, a style which Cachia characterises as 'dogmatic' and 'lifeless', and 'carried [out] from generation to generation by men whose liveliest interest was in petty intrigues against one another'.[109]

In 1993, Gus Dur was awarded what has been described as 'Asia's equivalent of the Nobel prize'.[110] This was a Ramon Magsaysay Award, and Mujiburrahman says that it was given 'for his significant role in promoting religious pluralism in Indonesia'.[111] This was, then, an extraordinary award for an extraordinary man. Islamically, his politics were founded on a trinity of concepts: 'Islamic universalism, cosmopolitanism and *pribumisasi Islam* (contextualisation of Islam)'.[112] Yet, despite the award, the latter were not to be regarded as syncretism. They meant, rather, that local needs and customs were deserving of consideration in the implementation of Islamic law.[113]

Attention has been drawn to three main facets of Gus Dur's political thought. Firstly, his preferred political strategy was what was called 'integrative', that is, the sharīʿa was only applied in terms of its 'substantive principles'.[114] (There is a strong contrast here with the different strategies operated in Malaysia on the one hand, and in Saudi Arabia, Pakistan and Iran on the other[115]). Secondly, classical *sharīʿa* could be accepted and, indeed, implemented provided that no harm was done to the national Indonesian interest. If there was a perceived clash between the two, then an attempt should be made to draw out 'the moral purposes of the Sharī'a'.[116] And Indonesian Parliamentary laws may have 'religious power as Sharī'a'.[117]

It is clear from all this that Gus Dur furnished a kind of straitjacket for the more draconian aspects of Islamic law and, by the use of his own independent judgement (*ijtihād*), both sanctioned the use of *Sharī'a* law in some form *and* set clear boundaries for its implementation. Ultimately, for him, the Islamic law should be interpreted in the light of the national interest and not vice versa.

Thirdly, Gus Dur was at pains to stress that the values of democracy were in harmony with the fundamental principles of Islam.[118] He argued that 'if the process of democratisation works smoothly in Indonesia, then Muslim interests will be automatically satisfied'.[119] Furthermore, he insisted on the need for inter-religious dialogue between Muslim and non-Muslim.[120]

Dur is more usefully labelled a 'neo-modernist', rather than a 'secularist'.[121] He did not want an Islamic state to develop in Indonesia, but he did use the tradition to bolster his own ideas.[122] His political doctrine was a unique combination of *maṣlaḥa* (taking into account the public good) and Indonesian state ideology.[123]

It is not the intention here to suggest that the religious and political thought of Gus Dur derived in any way from that of the Egyptian Ṭāhā Ḥusayn. There are, however, some interesting intellectual contrasts to be made between the two, at least insofar as the clash between traditionalism and modernism in Egypt and Indonesia is concerned. For example, in the 1920s struggle between the forces of conservatism and modernism, Ṭāhā Ḥusayn was recognised as a leader of the latter in Egypt.[124] Indeed, the very struggle was, for him, 'a sure sign of vitality'.[125] And Ḥusayn called not for an 'imitation of the West' but for a borrowing which would strengthen Egypt itself.[126] However, going much further than Gus Dur after him, Ḥusayn developed the idea that religion was a purely personal affair best kept out of politics and science. At one point, he argued that 'the Azhar confine itself to producing religious teachers and preachers'.[127] While the state should recognise the religious consciousness – Islamic and Coptic – of its peoples, it should adopt a *Western* mode of government.[128]

It is possible to characterise both the Egyptian Ṭāhā Ḥusayn and the Indonesian Gus Dur as 'modernists' or 'neo-modernists'. But perhaps, in the final analysis, their life stories have more elements in common than the political, religious and intellectual solutions which they proposed for the age-old dilemmas thrown up by the clash of tradition and modernity in their respective countries and times.

Gus Dur himself will ultimately be judged by history in terms of his politico-religious thought, rather than his political deeds. His twenty-one-month career as President of Indonesia was held to be a spectacular failure at the time of his overthrow on 23 July 2001.[129] As a London *Times* leader succinctly put it the following day:

> Applause, tears and relief greeted the election in Indonesia's parliament yesterday of Megawati Sukarnoputri to succeed Abdurrahman Wahid [Gus Dur], the elderly, obstinate and ineffectual President dismissed for incompe-

> tence after 21 chaotic months in office. His capricious rule has brought his sprawling country to the brink of disintegration … Mr Wahid, appointed as a compromise candidate largely because he was untainted by the corruption of the Suharto years, never came to grips with his job.[130]

As Sukarno's daughter took power,[131] the manner of Gus Dur's going was undignified and a sad end for one who originally had much to contribute intellectually: 'The ousted Indonesian leader, Abdurrahman Wahid, remained resolutely in the Presidential palace last night in a stand-off with the new President, Megawati Sukarnoputri, who has already been sworn in'.[132]

The view of political Islam in Indonesia as a mainly tolerant, adaptive, contextualised and moderate growth down the ages (at least into very recent times), which might serve as a possible paradigm for other Islamic states, was borne out by the 2001 Nobel Laureate for Literature and eminent British novelist, Sir Vidia Naipaul (born 1932), when he visited Indonesia in 1979.[133] However, when he revisited the Archipelago in 1995,[134] he discovered a slightly more tense situation[135] and indications that the age-old 'laid-back' style of Islam was changing.[136] A paradigm shift was under way.[137]

On that first momentous visit in 1979, Naipaul had been impressed by the 'pre-Islamic past' – the *jāhilī* period, as Arabs would have called it – of Indonesia,[138] and had been reminded vividly, wherever he went, of the civilisation of that past which predated by 1,400 years the arrival of Islam in the fifteenth century and which had deep roots in tribal Buddhist and Hindu cultures and religions.[139] Naipaul recognised an unsystematised substratum below the formal surface level of Islam in which the remains of a pre-Islamic past lurked and sometimes flourished.[140] And even in 1979 the author recognised a new impulse to purge Islam of such things and live according to a strict theology and Islamic law.[141] A composite, or syncretic and eclectic religion, in which Qur'ān, *Ramayana* and *Mahabharata* merited equal or, at least, some attention and respect, was anathema to the newly devout.[142]

Although the ideas of Gus Dur were light years away from this kind of village syncretism, it is not surprising that the more intellectual theories of Gus Dur should have attracted the ire of his more 'fundamentalist' brethren. Gus Dur encapsulated, by his very ideas and presence, the dilemmas and contradictions of Islam in modern Indonesia: peasant versus intellectual, the new versus the old Islam, liberalism versus 'fundamentalism', ancient syncretism versus modern religious purification.[143] Whether or not political Islam is to be regarded as an innovation in Indonesia today, or a re-articulation of a classical paradigm,[144] there is no doubt that Gus Dur's heady *mélange* of *maṣlaḥa* and state ideology[145] has provided one model which cannot be ignored in the twenty-first century.

Dialogic Islam

Can the new century look forward to a dialogic Islam centred on a radical Christian–Islamic, or other, interfaith dialogue which goes below surface hospitality and encounter, exploring and comparing divergent theologies in an atmosphere of mutual trust and absence of recrimination over past wrongs and hostilities?[146] The semiotics of such a putative scenario are often difficult to read.[147]

At the end of his book *Muslims in Western Europe*,[148] Jørgen Nielsen wrote a final chapter entitled 'European Muslims in a New Europe?' The question mark is significant. The mutual adjustments necessary for a successful integration or assimilation of large bodies of Muslim migrants in Europe have not been easy. The multicultural ethos to which all Europeans are supposed to subscribe in such matters as religion may be more optimism than reality.[149] This was particularly obvious in the 2003 decision by France to ban the wearing of *ḥijāb* in its state schools, under a more general ban on the public display of ostentatious religious symbols in such schools.[150]

The 1985 British *Swann Report* denied that Europe was 'multicultural in the sense which is usually intended'.[151] The later report by the Runnymede Trust into Islamophobia in Britain appeared to confirm this.[152] Professor Nielsen makes a highly significant point: 'When the talk is of integration or assimilation, it is applied to the minority group – it is not the Swiss, Dutch or German who is going to integrate with the minority'.[153] Indeed, that minority may be perceived as a real threat to the very nationhood of the host country, as the intemperate outbursts by the Roman Catholic Cardinal Archbishop of Bologna, Giacomo Biffi, in 2000 and 2001 against Muslim immigration into Italy demonstrated.[154] Such remarks only served to reinforce the sense of 'foreignness' and 'otherness' among both newly arrived and more established Muslims and Muslim communities in Europe. and elsewhere.[155] Academic journals such as *Islam and Christian–Muslim Relations* (JICMR), *Islamochristiana* and *Encounter*[156] have striven for an eirenic and dialogic position; but, as the Rushdie Affair showed[157] the omens on the ground for even a 'dialogue of charity' have not always been good.

Nielsen reminds us that 'differences and plurality, especially of a religious kind, have historically been more destructive than constructive'.[158] This was painfully obvious beyond the immediate frontiers of Europe at the end of the twentieth and the beginning of the twenty-first centuries: an Islamic desire to build a mosque with a tall minaret next to the Church of the Annunciation in Nazareth in 1999 sparked widespread Christian–Muslim riots among a population estimated at 18,000 Christians and 42,000 Muslims.[159] Reporting on the affair, the *Times* columnist Christopher Walker cited an Israeli journalist who wrote that, were the mosque plans to proceed, 'the Pope, when he comes in 2000, will see directly how Jesus of Nazareth has been humiliated by Muhammad and Shihab el-Din'.[160]

When the Israeli government decided to permit the building of the mosque, the Christian hierarchy announced that all churches and other religious sites would be closed for two days in November 1999 as a protest. In an effort to express their frustration, they had decided to target the Israeli tourist industry.[161]

Elsewhere in the Islamic world, things have been no more peaceful from the perspective of interfaith dialogue. Archaeology has assumed an unlikely – and probably unlooked for – religious role in the holy town of Ayodhya. Anubha Charon explains:

> Never before in Indian history has a team of archaeologists been under such close scrutiny, or handled such a sensitive assignment, on whose conclusion

> rests not only the historical documentation of a nation, but also the scripting of its future. Ayodhya, in the Northern Indian state of Uttar Pradesh, is a site holy to both Hindus and Muslims, and has been a constant source of religious clashes. Now the Archaeological Survey of India (ASI), under directions of the High Court, is trying to settle the dispute over whether a Hindu temple once existed there. The disputed site houses the remains of the Babri Masjid, a sixteenth-century mosque built by Mir Baqi, commander to Mughal emperor Babar [*sic*] but destroyed by Hindu fundamentalists in 1992. Hindus believe that the mosque stood on the ruins of an earlier temple that once marked the birth-place of Lord Rama, one of the most revered deities in the Hindu pantheon.[162]

Elsewhere in the Indian subcontinent, Christians have suffered persecution in some areas of Pakistan, whose three-million-strong Christian community have a 'fragile place in a now volatile society'.[163] It is alleged that 'across the Punjab, where the vast majority of Christians live, communities that had lived together for decades are now divided by religion'.[164] The Catholic bishop of Faisalabad, Bishop John Joseph, who spearheaded an international campaign for the release of a Christian named Ayub Masih on death row in Sahiwal Central Jail, shot himself nine days after the death sentence had been passed on Ayub.[165] At the beginning of the new millennium, Michael Binyon wrote that 'from Egypt to Indonesia, Nigeria to Lebanon, an upsurge in intercommunal violence has already marked the new millennium as one of the worst periods of global conflict between Christianity and Islam for generations'.[166] He calculated that in the Moluccas Islands capital, Ambon, over 1,500 Muslims and Christians had been killed in 1999, the horrific, escalating result of a quarrel between a drunk and a taxi-driver. He commented: 'The islands were once held up as a model of religious tolerance'.[167]

A final example of fragile interfaith relations must suffice: the visit by the Israeli Likud Party leader, Ariel Sharon, in October 2000 to Temple Mount in Jerusalem provoked widespread rioting and bloodshed between Israeli Jew and Palestinian Muslim; the episode came to be called 'the Jerusalem *intifada*'. This could just as easily be interpreted in terms of religious hegemony as the working out, and restating, of a territorial imperative.[168] However one chooses to interpret this visit, it cannot be denied that it did not contribute to the cause of interfaith harmony.

Such events are far removed from the paradigmatic eirenicism espoused by the murdered Cistercian Prior of the Monastery of Our Lady of Atlas at Tibhirine, near Médéa, in Algeria. His name was Dom Christian de Chergé. Abducted with six of his fellow Cistercian monks on the night of 26–7 March 1996, his dead body, together with those of his brethren, was finally found on 30 May 1996. In his testament, dated Algiers, 1 December 1993 and Tibhirine, 1 January 1994, Dom Christian foresaw his own death at the hands of fundamentalist Muslims and wrote:

> I know the contempt that some people have for Algerians as a whole. I also know the caricatures of Islam that a certain (Islamist) ideology promotes. It is too easy for such people to dismiss, in good conscience, this religion as something hateful by associating it with violent extremists. For me, Algeria and

> Islam are quite different from the commonly held opinion. They are body and soul. I have said enough, I believe, about all the good things I have received here, finding so often the meaning of the Gospels, running like some gold thread through my life, and which began first at my mother's knee, my very first church, here in Algeria, where I learned respect for the Muslims.[169]

He concludes with these words of love and forgiveness for his future killer:

> And to you, too, my friend of the last moment, who will not know what you are doing. Yes, for you, too, I wish this thank-you, this 'A-Dieu', whose image is in you also, that we may meet in heaven, like happy thieves, if it pleases God, our common Father. Amen! Insha Allah![170]

Renaissance Islam

Our sixth and final scenario is this: could the Islam of the future be what might be termed 'Renaissance Islam' with the Ayatollah Khomeini cast in the role of a latter-day Luther?[171] This 'elderly, irascible Muslim cleric'[172] of popular mythology wrought a revolution in Iran so profound that its reverberations are still felt.[173] As the *Times* leader starkly, if simplistically, put it in 1999:

> No corner of the Islamic world was unaffected by the radical return to theological fundamentalism as a reassertion of Islamic identity and ideals. Two decades later, it still reverberates with the aftershocks of a convulsion comparable to that initiated by Martin Luther.[174]

It is, of course, true that diverse factors beyond the immediate charisma of the Ayatollah had paved the way for his return: there was the extraordinary arrogance of a Westernising Shah with his contempt for the role of traditional Islam; there was the corruption of an élite ruling class; there was the failure to see the danger of the developing equation between secularisation and modernisation; there was a profound underestimation of Islam's perceived role as the natural counterweight to an imposed Western tyranny.[175] But none of these factors in themselves explains the almost preternatural appeal of Khomeini as man, Imām and Spiritual Leader. 'The force of Khomeini's preaching was its uncompromising rejection of everything secular and everything emanating from the West.'[176] This rejection had a magnificently simple appeal for very large numbers among both the *'ulamā'* and the lower middle classes who, in various ways, had missed out on the prosperity brought to Iran under the Shah. However, the *Times* also concluded that 'twenty years on, Khomeini's shadow [inhibited] a necessary debate'.[177] Writing of the extraordinary scenes of frenzy which surrounded the funeral of the Ayatollah, Baqer Moin concluded that, from whatever perspective we viewed the Imām, we could not describe him as 'an ordinary man'.[178]

This theme of Khomeini as 'Islam's Luther' is worth developing briefly a little further. Luther was a major factor in a Protestant Reformation whose consequences are very much apparent and with us today. Islam's retreat from secularism and its increasing unwillingness to tolerate at least a *modus vivendi* with the diverse aspects of modernity and modernism, much less integrate happily within multifaith or pluralistic societies, are similarly all too apparent, according to one world view.[179] Theologically, Martin Luther too, retreated from secularism:

> The life of the Christian – as forgiven sinner – embodies precepts of the law and promises of the gospel. The interplay of church and society (or state) generally follows Luther's teaching on the two realms: the realm on God's right, the church; and the realm on God's left, the state – both are accountable to God.[180]

Just as Khomeini made it clear that he abhorred innovation and corruption in state and religion,[181] so too, in his different ways, did Martin Luther.[182] Both suffered profoundly in consequence.[183] Finally, both men needed, and sought, political influence if ever their theological world-views were to succeed. Khomeini's development of the doctrine of *wilāyat al-faqīh* ('government by the jurist') is too well known to require further elaboration here.[184] Martin Luther, too, craved political support and power:

> More difficult than doctrinal change and liturgical reform was the problem of organisation ... Luther's teaching therefore preserved the medieval principle of the universal *res publica Christiana*, even if organised in separate entities; he had no time for sectarian notions which confined the true church to the self-known chosen of God. In addition, the question of public order was always very much in Luther's mind, as it was in that of the civil authorities with whom he had to deal. All this demanded uniformity – the existence of one organisation and general conformity to it. But in trying to secure this Luther was thrown back upon the territorial ruler who alone could support ecclesiastical discipline with physical power. When Frederick the Wise, never a Lutheran, was succeeded by the Elector John (1525–32), Luther had to hand a prince willing to follow his lead.[185]

If the Imām Khomeini *is* perceived in the fullness of time by future historians to have been Islam's Luther, will the twenty-first century of the Common Era produce a Counter-Reformation in Islam akin to that undertaken in Western Christian Europe by Pope Paul III (1468–1549; reg. 1534–49), the Council of Trent[186] and such luminaries of the Western Counter-Reformation as St Ignatius of Loyola (1491–1556),[187] St Cajetan (1480–1547)[188] and St Charles Borromeo (1538–84)?[189] If it does, what form will Islam's Counter-Reformation take? Will it engage in definitive style with the twin spectres of modernism and secularism in a way acceptable to the whole of the Islamic *umma*?

1.2 The Twentieth Century Revisited: Surveys and Approaches

The twentieth century found scholars and interested observers alike deploying a multitude of approaches to the often intransigent narrative of the Middle East in general and the faith of Islam in particular. Three of these approaches will be surveyed briefly in the pages which follow. They are not intended to be exclusive or conclusive, or to indicate in any way that there were no other worthwhile approaches to our subject. They are merely intended to be illustrative of a diversity which embraced structuralism and semiotics[190] on the one hand and post-modernism[191] on the other.

I shall therefore survey three ways: (1) The Way of the Historian of Religion, illustrated by *The Islamic Threat: Myth or Reality?* by John L. Esposito[192] and *Islam in Modern History* by Wilfred Cantwell Smith;[193] (2) The Way of the Anthropologist, illustrated by *Recognizing Islam: An Anthropologist's Introduction* by Michael Gilsenan,[194] *Moroccan Islam: Tradition and Society in a Pilgrimage Center* by Dale F. Eickelman[195] and *Islam Observed* by Clifford Geertz;[196] and, finally, (3) The Way of the Traveller, illustrated by two works from the pen of the Nobel Laureate Sir Vidia Naipaul, in which he describes his forays into the Islamic world: *Among the Believers: An Islamic Journey*[197] and *Beyond Belief: Islamic Excursions Among the Converted Peoples.*[198] These brief surveys are designed as a form of prelude or overture by which to highlight the approaches which will be attempted in *this* volume.

1.2.1 The Way of the Historian of Religion

Esposito's *Islamic Threat*

In his seminal work, *The Clash of Civilizations and the Remaking of World Order*, Samuel P. Huntington likened what he characterised as 'the Islamic Resurgence' both to Marxism and, more usefully in his view, to the Protestant Reformation.[199] The former was textually based and looked forward to 'the perfect society' which would be achieved through a process of change and rejection of key elements of the *status quo*. The latter inveighed against corruption and stagnation, and espoused purification and reform of religion.[200] Huntington saw only one major difference between the Islamic Resurgence and the Protestant Reformation: while the latter, in the main, was a phenomenon which affected Northern Europe, the former had become a marked feature of virtually every country with a substantial population of Muslims over the last fifteen years.[201] For Huntington, this rise in Islamic awareness and identity posed one of the major threats to the world order in the twenty-first century. If the solution that is Islam proves not to be the universal panacea envisaged by its more passionate, so-called 'fundamentalist' followers, then the West may be blamed for Islam's failures.[202] In Huntington's world-view, the theme of ineluctable clash is the *leitmotiv* of first choice.

John L. Esposito begs leave to differ. Identifying Huntington's thesis of 'a clash of civilisations', originally adumbrated in article form,[203] as one of two pieces which had a particular influence[204] – the other was Bernard Lewis' article 'The Roots of Muslim Rage'[205] – Esposito undertakes a masterly demolition of the Huntington/ Lewis view:

> A sensationalized monolithic approach reinforces facile generalizations and stereotypes *rather than challenging our understanding of the 'who' and the 'why' of history*, the causes or reasons behind the headlines. This selective analysis fails to tell the whole story, to provide the full context for Muslim attitudes, events, actions and fails to account for the diversity of Muslim practice.[206]

An undifferentiated fear of Islam, whereby the actions of the few are used to judge the many, seems to have replaced the Western atavistic Cold War fear of communism.[207] For Esposito, Huntington's emphasis on seeing history in terms of 'sources of conflict' inevitably emphasises difference and otherness.[208]

The Islamic Threat: Myth or Reality? incorporates a question mark in its title, and its contents are themselves structured neatly between two question marks: after an Introduction,[209] Chapter 1 is entitled 'Contemporary Islam: Reformation or Revolution?',[210] while the concluding Chapter 6 bears the title 'Islam and the West: A Clash of Civilizations?'[211] In between these two key chapters, Esposito examines the twin themes of 'Islam and the West: Roots of Conflict, Cooperation and Confrontation'[212] and 'The West Triumphant: Muslim Responses'[213] on the one hand, and a contrasting pair of themes, 'Islam and the State: Dynamics of the Resurgence'[214] and 'Islamic Organization: Soldiers of God',[215] on the other. The whole work is brilliantly and succinctly conceived and structured and provides a welcome epilogue and update to Norman Daniel's classic volumes *Islam and the West: The Making of an Image*[216] and *Islam, Europe and Empire*.[217] In the words of the critic in the *Times Higher Education Supplement*, 'we hear the authentic voices of Islam, sense the genuine mood of the Muslims and even share their fears and hopes'.[218]

In his book, which the author 'never intended to write',[219] Esposito answers the two seminal questions posed in the two chapter headings mentioned above: instead of the Western, value-laden term 'Islamic fundamentalism', he prefers to speak in terms of Islamic revivalism, activism and reform, as well as social transformation and, thus, reformation;[220] and he mentions in his extensive concluding chapter that 'the challenge of political Islam need not always result in a threat to regional stability or Western interests'.[221] In short, Esposito's volume, even though it was published several years before what is termed in America '9/11', provides a constant prophylactic for the doom-mongers, Eastern and Western, who are imbued with an overarching sense of the 'otherness' of Islam and who perceive that religion as totally inimical to all but its most fundamental interpreters and adherents. The spectre of the Ottoman Turk at the gate of Vienna,[222] in other words, despite 9/11, is not the essential, or even the only, paradigm for the twenty-first century in the eyes of modern historians of religion like Esposito.

While neither advocating nor articulating a particular historical method or approach, Esposito wrote his book in 1992 (with a new edition in 1995) in response to what he perceived as the need 'to address the issue of an Islamic threat and *to place it in historical perspective*'[223] as well as from a desire 'to initiate a dialogue among scholars and policymakers'.[224] The book may thus be said to have a foot in several camps ranging from modern histories of Islam through international relations and dialogic Islam to the spheres of religious revival or 'fundamentalism'.'[225]

The Islamic Threat: Myth or Reality? endeavours to place what has been perceived as 'the challenge or threat of Islam in perspective, and discuss the vitality of Islam as a global force and the history of its relations with the West'.[226] The horrific events of 9/11 have not rendered its basic arguments ineffective or invalid. This is because it discusses, above all, the 'variegated nature of Islamic resurgence,[227] although there are many recurring themes as well.[228] Esposito's volume remains an excellent example of a certain scholarly eirenic tendency towards Islam among several historians of religion in the pre-9/11 period.

Cantwell Smith's *Islam in Modern History*

Wilfred Cantwell Smith's volume is an altogether more old-fashioned, but nonetheless, readable account of Islam, produced in the middle years of the twentieth century. Unlike Esposito's book, it did not seek to respond to a contemporary pressing issue but intended, rather, to be a modern continuation of those histories of classical Islam which had preceded it. It was published in 1957 in an age when Islam could not have been perceived as a potential supplanter of communism as the arch-rival of the West; thus its priorities and emphases are somewhat different from those outlined in Esposito's volume. Nonetheless, there are several points in common: Cantwell Smith (who died in 2000) characterises his study as that 'of a people in the turmoil of the modern world'.[229] It recognises the clash with modernity and the transitional nature of the *umma*.[230]

Cantwell Smith offers his work as 'a politico-economic-social study' and 'fundamentally [as] a study in religion, comparative and contemporary. It seeks to discover and expound the nature and present significance of a community's faith.'[231] It also aspires to have a deep interfaith appeal and understanding, in an age when interfaith matters were far less clearly articulated and supported.[232] This all the more remarkable in the era which predated the Second Vatican Council.[233]

In support of these objectives, Cantwell Smith begins his Introduction, classically, with a survey of 'Islam and History'.[234] For him, Islamic history was, in theory, 'the fulfillment, under divine guidance, of the purpose of human history. It is the Kingdom of God on earth.'[235] However, he recognises that the reality could indeed fall short of this lofty ideal.[236] The Faith (*al-dīn*), while ultimately transcending the material world, nonetheless had a solicitude for that world (*al-dunyā*); and the *dunyā*, under the rule of a secularly inclined caliph, might dictate to the *dīn* a more subordinate or peripheral role.[237] All students and scholars of Islamic history, for example, will be well aware of the clichéd accusation levelled at the Umayyad Dynasty (661–750) that most of its rulers were *mulūk*, kings, rather than *khulafā'*, caliphs.[238]

Cantwell Smith identifies a religion in crisis rather than a religion as threat.[239] As he puts it in an early chapter: 'The fundamental *malaise* of modern Islam is a sense that something has gone wrong with Islamic history'.[240] This then is a lament with echoes of the late nineteenth century from within *dār al-Islām* itself: where 'the earlier reformers had preached that the Muslims' social condition was wrong',[241] later thinkers like the 'firebrand agitator'[242] Jamāl al-Dīn al-Afghānī (1839–97) 'insisted that it was feeble'.[243] The Muslim world had to look to its own salvation and be responsible for itself without seeking an outside saviour. This was a profoundly Qur'ānic sentiment.[244] These and similar ideas were articulated in the Journal *al-'Urwa al-Wuthqā* (*The Strongest Link*), which al-Afghānī published with Muḥammad 'Abduh (1849–1905).[245]

Cantwell Smith identifies what he calls 'the three outstanding new tendencies of modern Islam'. They are 'nationalism, apologetic, and dynamism'.[246] It is the middle element of this mid-century paradigm, apologetics, which is of particular interest here because it underscores profoundly the gulf between Esposito's audience's perception of Islam, some decades later, and Cantwell Smith's. The latter states baldly: 'Most books and speeches on the faith by those within it today are defensive'.[247] Much energy, in Cantwell Smith's view, has been expended by modern Muslims in the 'intellectual defence' of the *dīn*.[248]

In a number of extensive case studies, the author examines 'The Islamic crisis' which he perceives afflicts the Arabs,[249] asks whether there has been an 'Islamic Reformation' in Turkey[250] and surveys the 'Islamic State' of Pakistan.[251] His principal four case studies conclude with an examination of Islamic involvement in India.[252] Here, the three key elements of Cantwell Smith's initial paradigm of nationalism, apologetics and dynamism make occasional appearances; but they are not used as rigid parameters throughout by which to judge the state of Islam in the Arab world, Turkey, Pakistan or India.

After a very brief foray into 'Other Areas',[253] incorporated by the author on the grounds that 'Islam is in principle a universal religion',[254] Cantwell Smith attempts some prediction of the future in his Conclusion.[255] He believes that 'something is being brought to birth',[256] and he briefly alludes to the monster of the late twentieth-century Western European and American imagination against which Esposito inveighs: 'Will [Muslims] perhaps emotionalize [Islam] into a closed system, by which they retreat from modernity into a fanaticism of crippling isolationist violence?'[257] It is, however, a brief allusion; and, in his tentative looking to the future, Cantwell Smith is neither deliberately seeking objects to fear nor identifying future systems of hate.

1.2.2 The Way of the Anthropologist

Gilsenan's *Recognizing Islam*

Gilsenan's classic and immensely readable *Recognizing Islam* was the product of much 'material drawn from personal experience of Islam' and an attempt 'to recreate the surprise of the moment when my work really began, that moment when realization collided with illusion in South Arabia'.[258] His themes range classically and widely from 'the formation and transformation of power and authority within Muslim societies' through an assessment of the *'ulamā'* to 'the sense of a world turned inside out'.[259]

Many of the principal *topoi* of the anthropology of religion are here: learned custodians of authority,[260] theodicy,[261] miracle-working[262] and the relationship of the latter to 'worldly power'[263] as well as the secret and the pure,[264] the cultural and political articulation of religion,[265] sacred space,[266] the mystical dimension of religion,[267] and semiotics.[268] In an Afterword, Gilsenan describes his book as 'a kind of excavation and a wandering'.[269] This should not lead us in any way to suppose that he has written a superficial book. On the contrary, despite its lightness of touch and anecdotal style, the whole volume richly deserves the plaudits showered upon it: 'Rarely has a Western orientalist so convincingly seized the subtle interrelationships between people, their perceptions of themselves and their neighbours, or the ways these are changing in our day … this is a profound and original book.'[270]

Gilsenan writes from a well of deep anthropological experience and knowledge of Islam, and, though he does not disparage the 'trained innocence' of one such as Jonathan Raban, the travel writer[271] (particularly with reference to the latter's well-written and intriguing *Arabia Through the Looking Glass*[272]), Gilsenan stresses that such experience and knowledge as he himself has are clearly foundational for a really deep understanding of Islamic religion, societies and cultures.[273] Jonathan Raban, early in his book, characterises 'British Arabism' as 'an old romantic love affair in which a faint glimmer of the perverse is never far from the surface'.[274] His is akin to an amateur Arabist approach which is innocent of formal anthropology: it works well only to a superficial degree. Gilsenan's volume shows what is possible with the reverse approach.

A brief comparison of Gilsenan's volume with Fiona Bowie's *Anthropology of Religion: An Introduction*[275] is useful. Like Gilsenan's, this is designed to be an 'introductory' work, but it is written from a far less specific perspective. Bowie 'combines discussion of the origin and development of ideas and debates within the anthropology of religion with a look at where the subject is going today – the interests and preoccupations of current practitioners'.[276]

In an initial chapter on 'Theories and Controversies', it is wisely acknowledged 'that there is no one anthropological approach to the study of religion'.[277] However, Bowie, while recognising the potential pitfalls and weaknesses of the method, cites with approval the definition of the anthropologist's role given by one of the giants of twentieth-century anthropology, E. E. Evans Pritchard (1902–73), whose name is ineluctably associated with his studies of the Nuer tribe of the South Sudan[278] and the Azande tribe of that area and the Eastern Congo:[279]

> What I have said does not imply that the anthropologist *has* to have a religion of his own, and I think we should be clear on this point at the outset. He is not concerned *qua* anthropologist, with the truth or falsity of religious thought. As I understand the matter, there is no possibility of his *knowing* whether the spiritual beings of primitive religions or of any others have any existence or not, and since that is the case he cannot take the question into consideration. The beliefs are for him sociological facts, not theological facts, and his sole concern is with their relation to each other and to other social facts. His problems are scientific, not metaphysical or ontological. The method he employs is that now often called the phenomenological one – a comparative study of beliefs and rites, such as god, sacrament, and sacrifice, to determine their meaning and social significance.[280]

Bowie goes on to look at 'The Body as Symbol,[281] religious identity and the whole arena of ritual purity,[282] 'Sex, Gender and the Sacred'[283] with some particular reference to the role of women,[284] the cultural and environmental aspects of religion,[285] theories of ritual, ritual violence and rites of passage,[286] Shamanism[287] and witchcraft.[288]

Bowie's book illustrates the broad boundaries of contemporary anthropological study. If we compare it with Gilsenan's, we note a different series of emphases at work in both. Gilsenan has a specific focus, while Bowie paints a very broad canvas.

Gilsenan has a particular interest in power and authority and the custodians of each; Bowie has a particular interest in the role of women. This is not to say, however, that each scholar ignores the other aspect. And we may note that both *are* interested in purity and cultic purity, though Bowie includes Mary Douglas's classic *Purity and Danger*[289] in her bibliography whereas Gilsenan does not. The latter covers neither Shamanism nor witchcraft, though Gilsenan does devote an entire chapter to 'Miracles and Worldly Power'.[290] Both Gilsenan and Bowie, like numerous anthropologists before them, are intrigued by the boundaries and overlap between magic and religion.

Bowie notes that both Bronislaw Malinowski (1884–1942) and Sir James Frazer (1854–1941) made a distinction between magic and religion:[291]

> A religious act aims at something beyond itself. Its object is not performance of the rite. A mortuary ritual, for instance, is intended to release the soul and prevent it from returning to haunt the living. In magic, the end is the efficacious action itself. Both magic and religion, however, serve the same psychological function, the alleviation of anxiety in the face of life's uncertainties.[292]

Bowie, believes, nonetheless, that Malinowski's distinction may have been a little simplistic in the sense that, in reality, it may be less easy to distinguish between magic and religion. She asks whether a rain dance, for example, should be categorised as 'an efficacious magical act' or the invoking of a divinity to act for the interceder.[293] She notes perceptively that most acts of magic 'involve the action of an intermediary power between the performer of the rite and its intended result',[294] and cites the words of consecration in the Roman Catholic Mass as capable of being seen as 'an end in themselves'.[295]

Gilsenan prefers to concentrate on the word 'miracle' rather than 'magic'. For him, the religion of Islam speaks the language of miracles – indeed, is infused by, and built upon, the miraculous in a very fundamental sense with the divine miracle of the Qur'ān to mankind.[296] Here, for the Muslim, the miraculous language of the Divine is mediated to humanity in an inimitable text. And, for the ṣūfī, the language of miracles may be further articulated on earth through the mysterious and mystical powers and actions of a ṣūfī saint or shaykh.[297]

In a superbly lyrical but apposite vein Gilsenan characterises miracles as 'the vital proofs, the sudden transfixing moments in which the "ever-present" reveals its otherwise veiled purposes in life, re-establishing the sense of the vividness of the Divine and the power of holy men as well as offering an assuring and triumphant experience of blessing'.[298] He devotes a whole chapter in *Recognizing Islam* to what he terms 'The Operations of Grace'.[299] Miracles validate the truth of a saint's sanctity and authority and, as an obvious challenge to an established order, may be perceived as dangerous.[300] And there is a vital intermediary role to be played by the eponymous *walī* (Friend, i.e. of Allāh) from the ṣūfī order: it is he who is the sole channel of *baraka* (blessing) from God.[301] *Baraka* is the bridge between the ephemeral temporal world of humanity and the spiritual sacred world of the Divine.[302]

It comes as no surprise, then, that the earthly custodian of this bridge may, on occasion, achieve some considerable temporal power, allowing an ambitious shaykh to function as an efficient and deadly opposition to a ruling bey:[303] 'The sheikh can vividly demonstrate the other, "underlying" reality by being even more forceful than the lord', using his miraculous powers against that lord.[304] Gilsenan neatly concludes that, while *baraka* may indeed be 'a vital part of the religious *bricolage* [Claude Lévi-Strauss's term] of the poor', it can also 'be the language of domination'.[305]

Eickelman's *Moroccan Islam*

Eickelman's volume also now ranks as a major modern classic of Islamic anthropology. It has been much admired. The *Times Literary Supplement* described the work as 'a very thoroughly researched, sensitively interpreted, elegantly and readably presented case study'.[306] It was the product of fieldwork undertaken in the Moroccan pilgrimage centre of Boujad and its surrounding areas from October 1968 to June 1970.[307] As a study of 'popular' or 'folk' Islam, it focuses in particular on the North African phenomenon of marabouts: 'They are persons, living or dead, to whom is attributed a special relation towards God which makes them particularly well-placed to serve as intermediaries with the supernatural and to communicate God's grace (*baraka*) to their clients'.[308] This articulation of some of the 'popular' dimensions of Islam is, of course, rejected by 'formal' Islam[309] but Eickelman (born in 1942) notes:

> As I discovered early in my fieldwork, the supporters of marabouts are fully aware, at least in outline, of the interpretations of Islam offered by the scripturalists; yet they continue to regard maraboutic Islam as a meaningful religious representation of reality.[310]

The chapters of Eickelman's volume follow a somewhat unorthodox pattern, at least from an anthropological perspective.[311] The first two chapters provide a basic historical grounding in the coming of Islam to Morocco, the phenomenon of maraboutism and the Sherqawa *zāwiya*, ṣūfī house, in Boujad which was founded by the sixteenth-century marabout Sīdī Mḥammed Sherqi (d. 1601). The Sherqawa was the name given to his descendants.[312] The author then goes on to provide a survey of Boujad[313] and an examination of the social structure of the Sherqawa.[314] This is followed by an investigation of 'The Ideology of Maraboutism'.[315] In a highly significant statement, the author notes that 'the key to understanding the ideology implicit in Maraboutism is in the cultural conception of *baraka* as a form of causality and the means by which it can be appropriated to sustain one's own activities'.[316] Here, we are clearly not far from the realms of *baraka* adumbrated so lucidly by Gilsenan in *Recognizing Islam*, to which we alluded earlier. Because of the *baraka* to be gained, there is a 'symbolism of closeness' whereby groups, and even individuals, assert and claim a kind of 'closeness' with the Sherqawa.

Eickelman concludes with an examination of Sherqawi identity and the fragmentation of maraboutism.[317] He observes that a small number of the well-educated in Boujad have begun to reject maraboutism as they become attached to 'Islamic Reformism'. Others embrace the novelties of the latter but cling to the 'myths' of the marabout.[318] His final words are instructive:

> The hierarchical conception of man–God relations represented by maraboutism is now in eclipse [his book was first published in 1976], but there is no reason to suppose that it will necessarily remain so. Islamic reformism, now ascendant, is self-consciously less compromised by the social order. But Islam, like other major world religions, constantly must face anew cycles of compromise and noncompromise with the social order. [319]

Geertz's *Islam Observed*

Geertz's book is subtitled *Religious Development in Morocco and Indonesia* and thus focuses almost totally on those two countries. The four chapters which comprise Geertz's short book were initially a series of lectures, the Terry Foundation Lectures on Religion and Science which were given at Yale University in 1967.[320] The author's intention was to provide a theoretical substratum which would allow a comparative examination of religion and an analysis of Islam in Morocco and Indonesia.[321] In his chosen method, the author showed that he was well aware of the scholarly problems and dangers of extrapolating from the particular to the general, and of reading what he poetically calls 'the contours of a whole civilization' from micro-systems to be found in a small village or town.[322] He justified his approach by highlighting the need for understanding and knowledge: it was licit for the scholar and anthropologist to see whether the understanding born of the study of a micro-system, the village or small town, might contribute to understanding the macro-system, the whole civilisation of which that micro-system was a tiny cog.[323]

Geertz's principal theme was religious change in the two countries where he did much anthropological research, Indonesia (1952–4, 1957–8) and Morocco (1964, 1965–6).[324] He admits that they make an odd pair for comparison at first sight, but he insists on the usefulness of the comparison: they have much in common while being very different in other respects, Each thus constitutes a useful form of 'commentary' on the other,[325] a mirror wherein are reflected those differences and similarities. Geertz reminds us that, while 'both incline towards Mecca ... they bow in opposite directions'.[326] The author goes on to contrast the tribal ethos of Morocco with the peasant society of Indonesia. The latter, for him, was most obvious in Java.[327] He draws attention to the highly syncretic and heterodox nature of Indonesian Islam, an Islam not always underpinned by a Qur'ānic ethos. Unlike many countries in the early spread of Islam, the archipelago encountered the religion as a result of trade rather than the usual conquest paradigm.[328] The middle, peasant and mercantile classes developed, in different ways and styles, an Islamic syncretism which contained elements of gnosticism, folklore and animistic beliefs and practices.[329] Geertz underlines in a striking and succinct way the gap which he believes has always existed between popular and theological Islam. He insists that this was becoming more and more obvious in both the Morocco and Indonesia of which he wrote when he presented his analysis of their 'Islams' in 1968.[330]

How was this gap to be bridged? The problem was the same; the approach was radically different. Geertz perceived, on the one hand, a centuries-old attempt to enforce a pure and rigid uniformity in Morocco, an attempt which was by no means always successful; on the other hand, he saw an Indonesian Islam whose mainstays were pragmatism, inclusivism and compromise.[331]

The author identifies what he calls 'Classical Styles' of religion in both Moroccan and Indonesian Islam. Both are marked by, or infused with, mystical elements.[332] Each style is epitomised by very different spiritual leaders who, nonetheless, share a common mysticism.[333] The 'Islams' developed by their respective peoples had, however, very different characteristics, the Indonesian reflecting introversion, patience and selflessness, the Moroccan being more extroverted, assertive and individualistic.[334]

Geertz reflects, too, on what he characterises as 'The Scripturalist Interlude'. He concentrates on three factors which have had a profound impact on the histories of both Morocco and Indonesia: Western imperialism, the rise of a legalistic, 'scriptural' Islam, and finally the struggle for, and rise of, the independent nation state.[335] (All three, we may note, are of increasing significance in these, the early years of the twenty-first century.) In a prescient concluding chapter, Geertz identifies the scripturalist tendency as the main factor in both Morocco and Indonesia in producing what he calls 'the ideologization of religion'.[336]

Geertz's short book was an important volume of comparative anthropology in its day and, in its stark analysis, still has something to teach those who study the anthropology of his two central foci, Indonesia and Morocco. His work has not been without its critics, however. 'All was not a matter of quietistic conversion … as implied in Geertz's *Islam Observed*', states Robert W. Hefner.[337] The latter, citing Marshall Hodgson, notes the 'too casual' nature of some of Geertz's work:

> Among other things, as Marshall Hodgson has observed, he applied so narrow and 'modernist' a perspective on Islam that he ended up identifying many of the practices and beliefs of Indonesian Muslims as 'Hindu–Buddhist' rather than as subaltern streams in Southeast Asian Islam.[338]

1.2.3 The Way of the Traveller

Naipaul's *Among the Believers* and *Beyond Belief*

In October 2001, Sir Vidia Naipaul was awarded the Nobel Prize for Literature.[339] Nalpaul speaks with a unique voice, whether it be in his fiction or his travelogues. He once observed that 'I am the kind of writer that people think other people are reading'.[340] Jason Cowley assessed his work as follows:

> His books are haunted by solitude and disciplined by a need to understand the anxieties of the decolonised world. Long ago, dissatisfied with the limitations of fiction, Naipaul liberated himself, as he saw it, from borrowed forms, from mechanical patterns of behaviour and ways of seeing. Hence his repeated pronouncements that the novel is dead, by which he means the novel as it is practised by most professional novelists as a preformed mould of plot, character and event into which one pours his or her cheap slurry of words. Naipaul's own novels are novel in the true sense of the word: new, mould-

> breaking, experimental, a hybrid of autobiography, social inquiry, reportage and invention.[341]

Cowley concluded that Naipaul definitely deserved the Nobel Prize:

> His work may, at times, be characterised by irritable misanthropy, sexual disgust and by rage; but in the canon of contemporary British writing he is without peer: a scourge of sentimentality, irrationalism and lazy left-liberal prejudices.[342]

As we have already noted, two of his travelogues deal with his perceptions of Islam. *Among the Believers: An Islamic Journey* describes his own successive impressions of Iran ('The Twin Revolutions'),[343] Pakistan ('The Salt Hills of a Dream'),[344] Malaysia ('The Primitive Faith')[345] and, finally, Indonesia ('Usurpations').[346] The author labels his conclusion 'Reprise: The Society of Believers'.[347] Naipaul is the anthropolgist of the word *par excellence*. He enjoys, and records, conversations with all whom he meets: the conversation is the medium which conveys the message. *Among the Believers* was written between August 1979 and February 1981.[348] In the light of the catastrophe which hit the USA on 11 September 2001, his concluding words have a raw prophetic quality and span the two decades between 1981 and 2001 with a terrible quiet urgency:

> It was the late twentieth century that had made Islam revolutionary … and increasingly now in Islamic countries there would be [those] who, in an inversion of Islamic passion, would have a vision of a society cleansed and purified, a society of believers.[349]

Naipaul freely confesses that, though there had been Muslims in the Indian community in which he had been raised in Trinidad, he knew little of Islam, nor, indeed, of his own Hinduism.[350] Watching television news at the time of the Iranian Revolution had caused Naipaul to ask himself some fundamental questions about Islam such as the treatment of women, the nature of a truly Islamic state and the attraction of Islamic law.[351] All these questions had sown the seeds of a journey to the classical lands of Islam in the author's mind.[352]

Naipaul came, he saw and he reached certain summary conclusions: in *Iran* the nation's confusion arose from its perception that the present looked back to a 'high medieval culture' and forward to 'oil and money' while surrounded by a Western civilisation which could not be beaten, should be rejected but, at the same time, was needed.[353] In *Pakistan*, fundamentalism feared contamination by alien ideologies. Naipaul recognised the sterile quality of this excessive fundamentalism. 'It offered,' he said, 'a political desert.' But he wondered whether an Islamic transformation might be born from the burden of excess.[354] In *Malaysia*, he met those who yearned for a 'restructuring' of the country perhaps led by an *alter* Khomeini.[355] He encountered a longing among some young Malays to live as 'old Arabs', as it were, as in the days of the Prophet Muḥammad himself.[356] And in *Indonesia* Naipaul found a revolutionary current flowing again as it had done in 1965, but Islamicised.[357]

Naipaul made a similar 'journey of enquiry into faith', visiting the same four countries over five months in 1995. *Beyond Belief* is the record of that visit, a direct sequel to *Among the Believers*. Naipaul characterised the later volume as 'a book of stories' and 'a book about people'.[358] In it, he also tries even harder to filter out his own presence[359] and illustrate further what he calls 'the crossover to Islam'.[360] There is no neat summary conclusion at the end of this volume as there was at the end of the first. And the chapter sub-headings are much more cryptic: 'Indonesia: The Flight of the N-250';[361] 'Iran: The Justice of Ali';[362] 'Pakistan: Dropping Off the Map';[363] 'Malaysian Postscript: Raising the Coconut Shell'.[364] Naipaul detected a world 'full of ghosts' in Indonesia;[365] a 'new nihilism' threatened Iran;[366] a 'cultural desert' undermine Pakistan;[367] there was conflict between Malays and Chinese in Malaysia. It seemed to Naipaul that, to be a real Malay, you had to embrace Islam.[368] And, on this second visit to Indonesia, Mr Wahid (Gus Dur) makes but a scant impression on Mr Naipaul when they meet.[369]

Beyond Belief is an impressive, indeed brilliant, *tour de force*, like its predecessor. In the manner of a latter-day Ibn Baṭṭūṭa[370] but without sharing the latter's Islamic faith, Naipaul made two major journeys through some of the heartlands of Islam, including its most populous region, Indonesia. Although he does not confess directly to such a feeling, an air of growing pessimism is communicated to the reader, and, in the light of such seminal events of the early twenty-first century as 9/11, an air of gentle apprehension about the futures of the lands which he visits seems to tinge the text. That said, Naipaul is an unfailingly courteous and punctilious observer of what he sees, with a genius's eye for the quirky as well as the profound. His two-volume account of his *riḥla* into Islam has deservedly become recognised as a classic account of personal exploration as well as popular anthropology.

His 'public pronouncements on Islam' have not been universally free from criticism.[371] He has been accused of proposing 'the broad idea of Islam as the worst kind of imperialism, which condemned Muslim societies to neurosis and nihilism'.[372] Thus he is alleged, quite wrongly in my view, to 'provide much comfort to Islamophobes' and sometimes 'to blur the crucial distinction between Islam as an often harshly imposed ideology and as a private and diversely followed faith'.[373] But his critic here acknowledges that 'his books on Muslim societies' do in fact maintain this distinction 'as they quickly outgrow their narrow theoretical frameworks, and become vivid, sympathetic portraits of individuals trying to accommodate themselves to an inhospitable world'.[374]

1.3 *Methodologies for a New Millennium*

In the above pages, we have surveyed briefly just three ways in which the raw subject matter of our discussions, Islam, was tackled in the twentieth century. We stressed earlier that our choice of these three ways was merely illustrative rather than prescriptive or indicative; randomly selective rather than exclusive. There are, and were, many other ways and methodologies by which this subject might be approached.

In what follows, it is intended to try to operate a threefold sieve or methodology deploying the concepts of object, sign and the sacred. These may at times be perceived to create, or alternatively disclose, an intertext.[375] Whether that occurs or not, the aim in any case is to make connections. Each of these three concepts is historically embedded in a particular author or set of authors. Our concept of *object* derives from the phenomenology of Husserl and Heidegger; the concept of *sign* flows in this volume from the semiotics of Umberto Eco; and we have drawn on Eliade's treatment of theology and the sacral for our concept of the *sacred*. Together these three elements of object, sign and the sacred combine to create a methodological sieve or paradigm which I will here term *the paradigm of sacred multipraxis*. The great doyen of the French *Annales* School of History, Fernand Braudel (1902–85), deployed a threefold 'method, in which history is viewed and studied on three levels of (i) enduring geographic and economic structures, (ii) social structures and "conjunctures" and (iii) events'.[376] It is not proposed to replicate Braudel's precise structure here but, under his inspiration, to parallel it with another, perhaps more suitable for the study of one of the world's great faith traditions.

1.3.1 Phenomenology, Husserl and Heidegger: Object

Phenomenology is one of the slipperiest of philosophical methods. It can also be one of the most complex. Modern phenomenology is ineluctably bound up with the names of Edmund Husserl (1859–1938) and his successor in his Professorship at the University of Freiburg, Martin Heidegger (1889–1976).[377] And, as Paul Ricoeur insists, while Husserl's thought does not constitute the sum total of phenomenology, it lies at the very heart of that philosophical method.[378]

Husserl's phenomenology has been characterised as seemingly bizarre[379] and also the result of his opposition to psychologism.[380] In the author's first edition of the *Logical Investigations*, Husserl calls phenomenology 'descriptive psychology'.[381] We may share, perhaps with some feeling, Ricoeur's view that, by itself, the word 'phenomenology' is not very helpful or lucid.[382] The word is, however, usefully defined as the 'science of appearances or of appearing'.[383] In answer to the question of reaching an understanding of Husserl's approach to philosophy and evaluating what Husserl was really trying to do, Jaakko Hintikka suggests that one way is to characterise Husserl's phenomenology as 'a theory of *i*ntentionality'.[384]

The Cambridge Companion to Husserl provides one of the simplest definitions: phenomenology is 'the study of "phenomena" in the sense of the ways in which things appear to us in different forms of conscious experience'.[385] However, Husserl believed that philosophy could be transmuted into 'a rigorous science'.[386] This was no less true of his philosophical method, phenomenology. The latter for him had three sequential key elements, technical terms which appear in a variety of guises through his various writings: *epoché*, eidetic reduction and cognition. These terms were expounded in a series of five lectures which Husserl gave at the University of Göttingen between 26 April and 2 May 1907.[387]

(1) *Epoché* has been translated as 'bracketing-out'[388] from a phenomenological perspective or, as Ricoeur puts it, an abstention from pronouncing on the ontological aspect of what appears; one should concern oneself only with what appears *qua* appearance.[389] (2) *Eidetic reduction* or abstraction implied a focus on the essence.[390] In the perception of a chair, for example, the pure perception becomes a universal.[391]

The object of 'nonsensory intuition' is pure essence, and it is the job of eidetic reduction to separate that which is general (essence) from that which is particular in the realms of intuition.[392] (3) The third step in this sequential process for Husserl's phenomenology is to see how the 'objects of cognition are *constituted* in cognition'.[393]

Martin Heidegger followed Husserl at Freiburg and built upon the latter's thought, as Heidegger himself acknowledged.[394] He stressed powerfully in one of his greatest works, *Sein und Zeit* (*Being and Time*), that phenomenology was primarily a philosophical method and concerned itself with the *modality* of research rather than dealing with the objects of that research from the perspective of *what* they actually are or were.[395] For Heidegger, a phenomenon was 'the self-showing in itself', and the word referred to a distinctive manner in which something might be met.[396] 'Phenomenology' itself was encapsulated in the maxim 'To the things themselves!'[397] Heidegger held that phenomenology was the gateway to ontology. The latter was only possible because of the former.[398] Indeed, philosophy itself can be designated as 'universal phenomenological ontology'.[399] Phenomenology unveils or uncovers that which is veiled, hidden or covered in terms of phenomena. And Heidegger identifies 'being covered up' as phenomenon's 'counterconcept'.[400]

This brief survey of the beginnings of modern phenomenology, a movement which coincided neatly with the start of the twentieth century,[401] is not intended to be an exercise in philosophical archaeology. Phenomenology still has much to offer, whether it be at the surface level of empathy and the total suspension of all value judgements, on the one hand, or the much deeper and profoundly rigorous insights of a Husserl or a Heidegger. Sokolowski believes that there is still a huge attraction in the idea of 'the isolated consciousness'. And, for him, there is much more to be unearthed in phenomenology for those who want it.[402] This volume will attempt to deploy and apply some of the more general insights articulated by the great phenomenologists of the twentieth century.

Phenomenology, then, is a particular way of 'looking' or 'seeing'. Its positive purpose is to focus on clarification and restoration rather than the negativity of doubt and rejection.[403] It can neatly be applied to a religion such as Islam: a phenomenology of Islam would discuss what Sokolowski calls 'the manifolds of appearance proper to religious things'.[404] Identity can be structured in a myriad ways.[405] Thus a cube has many different facets but it also has an individual, recognisable identity regardless of the sides, angles and profiles by which it is perceived.[406] Three different expressions, one perhaps in a foreign language, can convey a single meaning.[407] Similarly, a single religion such as Islam, Christianity or Judaism may have a single phenomenological identity but manifest that identity in manifold ways.

The modern phenomenologist is a spectator, a 'detached observer' an onlooker.[408] The Husserlian tool of *epoché* still has profound meaning and substance in our own age: we refrain from judgement, neutralise our 'natural intentions' and, with the suspension of belief, 'we *bracket* the world and all the things in the world'.[409] We also strive to have some insight into the essence of the things we see and encounter. *Eidetic intuition*, then, is a vital and living possibility in twenty-first-century phenomenology and no more an aspect of an antique philosophical archaeology than *epoché* itself.[410]

We note, by way of concluding this section, the comments of Hubert Dreyfus, Professor of Philosophy at the University of California, Berkeley. He suggests that 'Husserl was important in a reactionary way'. He stood at the end of the Cartesian tradition which defined the relationship of man to his universe 'in terms of subjects knowing objects'. Husserl himself believed that the philosophical tradition which culminated in himself stretched back as far as Plato.[411] We can note and refute. After Husserl came Martin Heidegger, Jean-Paul Sartre (1905–80) and Maurice Merleau-Ponty (1908–61), who in 1945 produced a major work entitled *The Phenomenology of Perception*.[412] Edward Husserl may thus be considered more accurately as a Janus figure whose philosophy looks both backwards and forwards: back at least as far as Descartes; forwards towards our twenty-first century. Some of his valuable insights will be used in broad outline in this volume to illuminate certain aspects of Islam in our own age.

1.3.2 Semiotics and Eco: Sign

Professor Umberto Eco (born in 1932), Professor of Semiotics at the University of Bologna, is the primary architect and high priest of semiotics in contemporary times.[413] He has a huge intellectual range. His novels – *The Name of the Rose*,[414] *Foucault's Pendulum*,[415] *The Island of the Day Before*,[416] *Baudolino*[417] – have become as popular on airport bookstalls as his more serious philosophical works on semiotics have in the intellectual atmosphere of the academy. His essays and pieces of collected writing – *Travels in Hyperreality*,[418], *Serendipities*,[419] *Kant and the Platypus*[420] – reach out alluringly in paperback to that wider popular audience. In short, Eco is a popular as well as an intellectual phenomenon.[421] Perhaps this should not surprise: his field literally partakes of a universe of signs.[422] And his world of signification embraces subjects as diverse as football[423] and philosophy of language.[424]

Definitions of semiotics and semiology are many and various. Only a brief flavour will be provided here. They include the following:

- *Semiotics*. The study of patterned human behaviour in communication in all its modes … semiotics can also mean the study of sign and symbol systems in general; for which an alternative term is SEMIOLOGY.[425]
- *Semiology*. The general (if tentative) science of signs: systems of signification, means by which human beings – individually or in groups – communicate or attempt to communicate by signal: gestures, advertisements, language itself, food, objects, clothes, music …[426]
- Semiotics as a discipline is simply the analysis of signs or the study of the functioning of sign systems.[427]

Terence Hawkes succinctly reminds us that man has a primary role of communication: he sends and receives messages by verbal and linguistic as well as non-verbal and non-linguistic means. Flashing lights and attractive smells *signify*.[428]

Building on, and continuing, the seminal work of Ferdinand de Saussure (1857–1913)[429] and Charles Sanders Peirce (1839–1914),[430] Umberto Eco adumbrated a complex theory of semiotics in his volume entitled A *Theory of Semiotics*.[431] Terence

Hawkes described this work as 'a re-working and revision by the author, in English, of previous work ...[432] A formidable attempt at a unified theory: not for beginners, but valuable to work through.'[433] In the Introduction to his book, Eco proclaimed it as his intention and aim

> to explore the theoretical possibility and the social function of a unified approach to every phenomenon of signification and/or communication. Such an approach should take the form of a *general semiotic theory*, able to explain every case of sign-function in terms of underlying systems of elements mutually correlated by one or more codes.[434]

He believes that a general theory of semiotics should embrace 'a theory of codes' and 'a theory of sign production', but his book is only intended to be 'a preliminary exploration'.[435]

He divides it into five major sections entitled 'Introduction – Toward a Logic of Culture',[436] 'Signification and Communication',[437] 'Theory of Codes',[438] 'Theory of Sign Production'[439] and 'The Subject of Semiotics'.[440] Eco concludes his whole volume with the following penultimate paragraph:

> Semiotics recognizes as the only testable subject matter of its discourse the social existence of the universe of signification, as it is revealed by the physical testability of interpretants – which are, to reinforce this point for the last time, *material expressions*.[441]

Eco is aware of the 'dangers' of holding to a theory of 'unlimited semiosis'.[442] To read a text is to attempt to decode the signs embedded in that text.[443] There is the final possible goal of 'a Final Interpretant'.[444] Intention is paramount, and Eco tries to distinguish between authorial, readerly and textual intention.[445]

Perhaps one of the most enjoyable and accessible modes of entry into the world of semiotics in general, and Eco's often complex semiotics in particular, is to read his first novel *The Name of the Rose*. The *New York Times Book Review* had this to say, *inter alia*, about the novel:

> A learned Franciscan who is sent to solve the mystery [of a number of murders occurring in a mediaeval Benedictine monastery] finds himself involved in the frightening events ... a sleuth's pursuit of the truth behind the mystery *also involves the pursuit of meaning – in words, symbols, ideas, every conceivable sign the visible universe contains*.[446]

Brother William of Baskerville, one of the leading protagonists in the novel, makes a very illuminating statement towards the end: 'The good of a book lies in its being read. A book is made up of signs that speak of other signs, which in their turn speak of things.'[447]

Lois Parkinson Zamora regards the main characters in both *The Name of the Rose* and *Foucault's Pendulum* as 'detectives, semioticians whether they know it or not'.[448] For her, the former is a 'modernist' novel while the latter is Eco's 'postmodernist' novel.[449] Such labels may not be particularly helpful, but they do serve to situate each novel in a stereotypical set of 'lit crit' references and frames. In *The Name of the Rose*, she detects a shift from an idealised Neoplatonic faith by the young Benedictine novice of Melk, Adso, in metaphysical levels of meaning to a state of mind in which the older Adso, narrating fifty years after the events in which he has participated, begins to doubt the validity of such faith. Adso seems to have become a nominalist and to be questioning 'the existence of any level of transcendental signification, to wonder whether there is any meaning beyond the name of things'.[450] But the end of the novel shows that a belief in the significance of all past events holds sway.[451]

Every semiotician is, perforce, a detective, though perhaps not as obviously as in the clear parallelism engineered by Eco between Adso in *The Name of the Rose* and Watson in the Sherlock Holmes novels.[452] David Richter intriguingly points out something that most of Eco's readers will miss. It is a vital textual 'sign':

> The narrator's name, Adso, is the middle four phonemes of 'Watson' (as close as one could come in a Latinized name), and though a cloistered monk, Adso shares Watson's unascetic gusto for the pleasures of the table and his predilection for romance, along with a talent for muddling up the clues.[453]

But, however muddled, if one looks carefully at the world of signs, the clues are all around. Some may be for our enlightenment; others, at first, may share in the darkness of the night. As the Qur'ān puts it:

> We have made the Night
> And the Day as two
> (Of Our) Signs: the Sign
> Of the Night have We obscured,
> While the Sign of the Day
> We have made to enlighten
> You; that ye may seek
> Bounty from your Lord,
> And that ye may know
> The number and count
> Of the years: all things
> Have We explained in detail.[454]

Thus the worlds of *The Name of the Rose*, the Sherlock Holmes novels and the Holy Qur'ān all breathe forth, and spin in, a whole Universe of Signs.

1.3.3 Theology and Eliade: The Sacred

The great historian of religion, Professor Mircea Eliade (1907–86), is best known for editing a massive multi-volume *Encyclopedia of Religion*.[455] However, his list of other publications is huge, and his influence has been correspondingly extensive.[456] At the end of an extraordinarily varied career, Eliade rejoiced in the title of Sewell L. Avery Distinguished Service Professor (later Emeritus) in the Divinity School, and Professor in the Committee on Social Thought, of the University of Chicago.[457]

In Eliade's lifetime, Thomas J. J. Altizer characterised him as 'the greatest living interpreter of the whole world of primitive and archaic religion'.[458]

Romanian in origin, Mircea Eliade was born in Bucharest on 9 March 1907. His early studies in that city's university, culminating in an MA dissertation on Italian philosophy in 1928, were followed by a spell in India studying Indian philosophy and Sanskrit at the University of Calcutta. His 1933 Romanian Ph.D. allowed him to take up a junior teaching post at the University of Bucharest. The years of the Second World War saw him as a cultural attaché, first in London and then in Lisbon. From 1957, he was a Professor of the History of Religions in the University of Chicago, and in 1962 he became the Sewell L. Avery Distinguished Service Professor.[459]

John A. Saliba has stressed that, like other phenomenologists and historians of religion, Eliade strove to understand the religious beliefs and practices he studied and encountered, and to make some kind of sense out of it all, 'to construct an image of religious man in the light of this understanding'.[460] There could be problems: as a committed Christian, writing 'primarily as a believer who looks on religion as a manifestation of the divine or the holy',[461] Eliade's impartiality has been questioned.[462]

Saliba notes also that he omits to cover Islam and the Chinese religions.[463] However, Saliba's 1976 volume predated Eliade's famous trilogy of 1978–85 entitled *A History of Religious Ideas*, which does provide ample coverage of those faiths.[464] Saliba's criticisms were thus somewhat premature.[465]

Finally, Saliba notes that Eliade was no longer concerned with finding the origin of religion but that his 'two principal aims [were] integration and generalization'.[466] In the latter, he is held to have succeeded: 'His works probably contain the most comprehensive generalizations of religious man in contemporary literature'.[467]

For Eliade, 'the essence of religion' was the aim of the phenomenological enterprise.[468] This was his 'eidetic' endeavour, to deploy Husserl's own term, his attempt to reduce religious phenomena to their defining or essential characteristics.[469] Eliade insisted that religion was to be studied *qua* religion, and Saliba notes that this was in perfect harmony 'with the phenomenological approach which concentrates on the essentials of religious beliefs and practices'.[470] Furthermore, as a historian of religion, he espoused the classic tendency to stress *similarities* between religious beliefs, experiences, structures and meanings.[471] In this, he diverged from the anthropologists of religion, who placed a greater stress on *differences*.[472]

It has been noted that three *leitmotivs*, or concerns, underlie all Eliade's writing about such matters as symbolism, myth and ritual. They are the idea of the sacred, the idea of death and resurrection, and the spiritual degeneration of man through the course of history.[473] It is with the first of these *leitmotivs* that we shall be primarily concerned in this book when we come to consider our material through an Eliadean lens. For 'The Sacred' was a favourite motif of Eliade which imbued many of his books in one form or another.

In *Patterns in Comparative Religion*, Eliade created and discussed a morphology of the sacred.[474] Elsewhere, insisting that '*every* manifestation of the sacred is important to the historian of religions',[475] he gave us, in his magisterial trilogy *A History of Religious Ideas*, 'the manifestations of the sacred in chronological order'.[476] In *Patterns*, he provides a very simple definition of the sacred as 'the opposite of the profane'.[477] While contemporary man may find comfort in life in 'a desacralized world',[478] that which is sacred or holy 'manifests itself in the context of a personal total life-experience which is intimately related to the social and physical environment'.[479]

For Eliade, the sacred has certain characteristic features: we have already seen that, speaking apophatically, it is that which is not profane. Furthermore, it can have a certain ambivalent quality, both attracting and repelling.[480] Although the manifestation of the sacred is, perforce, in the profane world, it 'is qualitatively different from the profane'.[481] And religion itself must be studied and analysed in terms of the sacred.[482]

However, the sacred itself can easily be degraded. Mircea Popescu translates Eliade as follows:

> Everything that is 'fantastic', everything that belongs to the extrarational – religion, magic, myth, legend – begins to degrade itself as soon as it enters 'history', as soon as it participates in 'becoming' ...[483]

Popescu insists that the problem of this 'desecration' or 'degradation of the sacred' in the fields of folklore is one to which Eliade alludes often and to which he wants us to pay particular attention.[484] Eliade provides the striking example of the degradation of symbols which may lose their initial cosmological or other charge and degenerate into base superstition.[485] There is an applicability of all this across arenas other than that of pure folklore: in the field of liturgy, for example, the Roman Catholic traditionalist followers of Archbishop Marcel Lefebvre continue to proclaim loudly that their beloved pre-Vatican II Latin liturgy has been desecrated and degraded.[486]

Perhaps the most powerful illustration in modern times of the desecration and degradation of a 'sacred' symbol – in this case one sacred to Mammon but attacked with profoundly religious motives – is that event which has become known in contemporary history as '9/11'. On 11 September 2001, the twin towers of the World Trade Center in New York were attacked and destroyed by hijacked suicide airliners.[487] About 3,000 people were killed. This is neither the field of folklore nor that of the sacred in any institutionalised religious sense but rather that of grim reality, and Eliade's concept of degradation has an eerie applicability. Here was one mighty symbol of power and mercantile wealth, the World Trade Center, built by the mightiest nation on earth, deliberately destroyed by another symbol, the airliner, symbol of man's scientific advancement, willingness and ability to bridge the space, the void, between nations in terms of travel, trade and general goodwill.

The media of the day was well aware of the powerful symbolism of all this. As the *Observer* put it on 18 November 2001:

> The twin disasters of 11 September and 12 November [2001: the crash on New York of American Airlines Airbus 300 Flight 587] have left the global travel industry confronting the worst crisis in its history. The romance and thrill of taking to the skies for business or simply a week or two away from

> it all, which began with the Wright Brothers and saw aircraft such as the Boeing 747 and Concorde become *symbols of progress, freedom and glamour*, is over. With 526 passengers and crew killed in five air crashes in the past nine weeks, the public would now rather do anything, it seems, than fly.[488]

A more theological element, which was powerfully 'degraded', to use Eliade's term once again, was the Islamic symbolism and doctrine of *jihād*. No longer was it a case of the greater *jihād* against the evil inclinations and ambitions of the *nafs* ('the self' or the ego), nor even a case of the lesser *jihād* in defence of an Islam under threat of imminent assault or extinction. It was rather, to deploy a suitably ṣūfī gloss, the spectacular victory of that unchained *nafs*.[489]

1.3.3.1 *The Sacred and the Profane*

Eliade's volume entitled *The Sacred and the Profane* had as its subtitle *The Nature of Religion*. In this important work, he examined the ways in which the sacred has manifested itself under the four headings of sacred space, sacred time, sacred nature and sacred cosmos.[490] As a portmanteau word by which to embrace the concept of the '*act of manifestation* of the sacred', Eliade proposes that we use the term *hierophany*. He likes the neatness of this neologism because it does not transcend its fundamental etymology, which is the showing of something sacred. He observes that in each hierophany

> We are confronted by the same mysterious act – the manifestation of something of a wholly different order, a reality that does not belong to our world, in objects that are an integral part of our natural 'profane' world'.[491]

Stating that 'the first possible definition of the *sacred* is that it is *the opposite of the profane*', Eliade proclaims that his aim in writing *The Sacred and the Profane* 'is to illustrate and define this opposition between sacred and profane'.[492]

Eliade analyses the attempt by *homo religiosus* to live within a sacred universe and tries to compare this attempt with that of 'the man without religious feeling', as Eliade puts it, whose desire is to inhabit a 'desacralized world'.[493] And, while in the act of hierophany any object can be transmuted into something quite different, and yet preserve its essence or ipseity, and while 'all nature is capable of revealing itself as cosmic sacrality' and 'the cosmos in its entirety can become a hierophany', all this takes place in a world which has become fundamentally desacralised in modern times.[494] The contrast, then, for Eliade, is between a potentially – and often actually – sacred cosmos and man's desacralistion of that cosmos into a profane arena.[495] For primitive man, the sacred was 'saturated with *being*'.[496] The *sacred* was 'equivalent to 'a *power* and, in the last analysis, to *reality*'.[497]

Eliade's three-part paradigm of *sacred*>*power*>*reality*[498] is articulated in the context of sacred stones, but it may have a modern applicability as well, as with the Islamic concept of *jihād*: warfare, offensive or defensive, becomes clothed with an aura of the sacred by being undertaken 'in the path of God' (*fī sabīl Allāh*: see Q.2:190, Q.4:84). It assumes a 'divine' *power* or momentum in the eyes of its proponents which can then result, *in extremis*, in the *reality* of a 9/11. The cosmos portrayed by Eliade exhibits the dual pathways of the sacralised and the desacralised,[499] adumbrated under his four headings of sacred space,[500] sacred time,[501] sacred nature[502] and sacred life.[503]

For Eliade, there is an overt war between the sacred and the profane, the sacralised and the desacralised. The profane result or reality may bear no relation to the initial sacred impulse. A metamorphosis comes into play. Thus we learn from the black box of one of the doomed suicide airliners on 11 September 2001 that the last cry of one of the hijackers, as his plane was about to smash into the World Trade Center, was *Allāhu Akbar*.[504] Yet the profanity of that action itself breathes a return to the sacred: Ground Zero becomes a 'sacred space'; 9/11 enters the living memory of man as 'sacred time'. It becomes a sacred *indelible* memory which, like the famous Massacre of St Bartholomew's Day in 1572, when thousands of Huguenots were slaughtered in Paris,[505] will live on for centuries in the collective and individual recollections both of those who deplore and those who support the trauma of 9/11.

1.3.3.2 Mircea Eliade, the Sacred and Islam

Mircea Eliade was certainly aware of the religious and political significance of the founder-Prophet of Islam, Muḥammad (c. 570–632). Indeed, the subtitle of the third volume of his *A History of Religious Ideas* is *From Muhammad to the Age of Reforms*. It is in this work that he provides one of the closest and most extensive insights into his thinking about Islam and the sacred.[506] His sources are varied but, by the date of publication in 1985, already somewhat dated. They range from A. J. Arberry' s translation of the Qur'ān[507] to W. Montgomery Watt's *Muhammad at Mecca*[508] and Tor Andrae's *Mohammed: The Man and His Faith*.[509]

Eliade begins his presentation of Islam by characterising Allāh in his initial heading as '*deus otiosus* of the Arabs'[510] which seems an odd way of speaking about the Sacred! Dictionary definitions of the English word 'otiose', which may directly translate the Latin *otiosus*, are not very helpful: 'Not required, serving no practical purpose, functionless ... indolent or futile'.[511] The classical Latin usage of *otiosus* does not greatly improve our understanding: 'At leisure, without occupation ... free from public duties or *occupied in literary work only* ... calm, quiet ... indifferent, neutral ... free, quiet, undisturbed'.[512] One wonders at first whether Eliade intends his usage to be a reference to Allāh in His capacity as originator of the Qur'ān, where the latter may be regarded as the mind of God made textual, thereby tying in with the classical authorial definition cited above. However, it transpires that Eliade's designation refers to Allāh's role in the pre-Islamic 'Age of Ignorance', the *Jāhiliyya*, where, although 'Lord of the Ka'ba', He had 'already become a *deus otiosus*: his cult had been reduced to certain offerings of first fruits (grains and animals), which were brought to him conjointly with various local divinities'.[513]

Eliade applauds what he perceives as the 'rich historic documentation' for the life of Muḥammad.[514] He characterises the religious milieu of pre-Islamic Central Arabia as imbued essentially with 'the structures of Semitic polytheism' unmodified by the impact of Christianity or Judaism.[515] Its centre is identified as Mecca, and

Eliade goes on to focus on aspects of sacred *ḥajj* ritual in the *jāhilī* period, as well as the pre-eminence of the three goddesses Manāt, al-Lāt and al-'Uzzā. He accepts without further question the story of the Satanic verses.[516] In Eliadean terms, this was a profane but temporary aberration. So, in a nutshell, for Eliade, religion in pre-Islamic Arabia 'resembled the popular religion of Palestine in the sixth century BC'.[517]

Eliade goes on to seek the elements of the sacred and the mystical in this 'new' religion of Islam with a *deus*, previously considered to be *otiosus*, now supplanting all other gods. He notes the lack of a formal priesthood in pre-Islam, by contrast with Judaism and the presence of those non-Christian and non-Judaic monotheists known as *ḥanīfs*.[518]

He dwells at some length on the mystical experiences of Muḥammad as the latter received the first revelation of the Qur'ān (Q.96:1–5) according to the tradition of Ibn Isḥāq.[519] And, as an anthropologist and historian of religion, Eliade is interested in human responses to the mystical, whether mental or physical; for him, there was a mystical 'intertextuality'

> Muhammad's initial resistance recalls the hesitation of shamans and numerous mystics and prophets before assuming their vocation. It is likely that the Quran did not mention the oneiric vision in the cavern in order to avoid the accusation that the Prophet had been possessed by a *jinn*. But other allusions of the Quran confirm the veracity of the inspiration. The command to 'recite' was often accompanied by violent trembling, attacks of fevers, or chills.[520]

In identifying the themes of the Qur'ān, Eliade dwells on God's power and mercy[521] and the eschatology of the sacred text.[522] In surveying the latter, Eliade appears to identify Muḥammad as the author[523] rather than adopting the preferred phenomenological approach of modern Western, non-Muslim scholarship, which is to emphasise Muslim belief in the divine provenance of the Qur'ān.

Given Eliade's intellectual and mystical interests, it comes as no surprise that he is captivated by the story of the *mi'rāj*, Muḥammad's ascension into Heaven. Eliade characterises this, not in the more normal Arabist and Islamicist terminology of *isrā'*, night journey, and *mi'rāj*, ascension through the heavens to Paradise, but, interestingly, as Muḥammad's '*ecstatic* voyage to Heaven and the Holy Book'.[524] The intertextual dimension interests Eliade, and he draws parallels with other prophets and messengers in other faith traditions who have experienced an ascension into a Heaven and received therein a text of divine revelation.[525]

After briefly surveying the *hijra* to Medina and the ultimate reconquest of Mecca in a virtually bloodless fashion, Eliade concludes: 'The history of religions and universal history know of no enterprise comparable to that of Muḥammad'.[526] Islamic morphology is identified as encapsulating 'the purest expression of absolute monotheism'.[527] It is noted that early rituals are presented and represented, interpreted and reinterpreted in an effort to provide a ritual intertext between the three Abrahamic faiths.

When it comes to Islamic theology and Ṣūfism, Eliade freely acknowledges that he grounds his interpretation in that of his friend, the great Iranologist Henry

Corbin, who died in 1978.[528] In his survey of both *kalām* (Islamic scholastic theology) and Ṣūfism, Eliade follows a fairly traditional route, one that has been elaborated upon many times by scholars before and after him.[529] However, Eliade manifests a particular fascination for the 'symbolism and function' of the *dhikr*, the ṣūfī litany, and the *samāʿ*, the 'spiritual concert' of the ṣūfīs.[530] He draws the expected parallels with the Eastern Christian prayer, the *monologistos*, as well as with Indian mystical practices.[531] Such is Eliade's fascination with Ṣūfism that he concludes his survey of the great theologians, philosophers and mystics of Islam with a lament that Islamic mysticism was not better known in the mediaeval West.[532] It is clear that, at the end of two full chapters on the doctrines and rituals of Islam, in which are highlighted elements of the sacred and the mystical, Eliade best locates Islam's sacred dimension within its mystical spaces.

1.4 *Case Studies*

1.4.1 Case Study Ground Zero: Object

If, in the months following the terrorist attacks on America on 11 September 2001, one had asked a very simple question, namely, 'what lies beyond Huntington's thesis?', the almost universal answer, from scholars and the ill-informed alike, might have been: *The Paradigm Spectre of Ground Zero*. The following survey and analysis is based on contemporary media records.

As we have already noted, on 11 September 2001 two suicide airliners smashed into the twin towers of the World Trade Center in Manhattan, New York, thereby precipitating in the ensuing hours the total destruction of those buildings. A third airliner plunged into the Pentagon, while a fourth was brought down near Somerset, Pennsylvania. The world media headlines, regional, national and international, were huge, stark and apocalyptic, as the following examples illustrate:

- A declaration of war (*Guardian*)[533]
- US on war footing as thousands die in hijack jet outrage (*Guardian*)[534]
- 'We got down to the outside and it was like an apocalypse' (*Guardian*)[535]
- America in flames (*Yorkshire Post*)[536]
- Terror from the sky (*Yorkshire Post*)[537]
- *Dhuʿr fi Amrīkā* [Terror in America] (*al-Quds al-ʿArabī*)[538]

The constant *leitmotivs* were war, apocalypse, flame and terror. Devotees of Nostradamus (1503–66), the sixteenth-century Provençal seer, sought confirmation of what was happening in his quatrains.[539] Innocent Muslims, and many of Asian appearance, were attacked; some were murdered.[540] At one stroke, the twenty-first century was inaugurated as The Age of Terror.[541]

1.4.2 Case Study Ground Zero: Sign

Some cities give birth to a unique semiotics: one thinks, for example, of Mecca and the *ḥajj* in which the semiotic focus is both travel to, and arrival at, the *Kaʿba*.[542] Jerusalem, too, is another sign of religious desire and pilgrimage, tragically labelled

'Slaughterhouse of the Religions' in recent times.[543] Now, like the city of Jerusalem, the fundamental semiotics of New York breathe a threnody of terrorism and death whose memory will linger for hundreds of generations.

Of Jerusalem, that paradigm city *par excellence* of hope, despair, conflict and death, Ben Macintyre had this to say:

> This is where the story starts and this is where it will probably end. To understand why men still kill in the name of God, come to Jerusalem, holy of holies, the 'slaughterhouse of the religions', in the words of Aldous Huxley, the oldest, hottest crucible of belief, holy nationalism boiled down into an area of less than one square mile.[544]

On 9/11, New York became a 'New Jerusalem', but it assumed that mantle in a sense quite different from that intended by the English poet William Blake (1757–1827):

> I will not cease from Mental Fight
> Nor shall my Sword sleep in my hand,
> Till we have built Jerusalem
> In England's green and pleasant land.[545]

The twin towers of the World Trade Center may have been perceived as 'dark Satanic mills'[546] by the enemies of America, but their destruction heralded an age of fear rather than the kind of Jerusalem promised by Blake. For well over a century, the city of New York had stood as a beacon of enterprise, opportunity and hope for Arab economic migrants such as the Lebanese writer and poet Jubrān Khalīl Jubrān (1883–1931).[547] The assault on one of the primary symbols in modern times of that enterprise, opportunity and hope by dissident Arabs is one of the many poignant ironies of the semiotics of the city of New York as they dramatically unfolded at the beginning of the twenty-first century.[548]

Ben Macintyre stresses the symbolic nature of Jerusalem: 'Jerusalem is not just the holiest of holy cities, but a metaphor, an idea, a symbol'.[549] He believes that 'it is no accident that the most patriotic English hymn speaks of building Jerusalem, our own Jerusalem, in England's green and pleasant land. The Taleban built their brutal Jerusalem in Kandahar. *New York is America's Jerusalem*, which is why the terrorists destroyed its twin temples.'[550] The World Trade Center was a *sign* of US commercial might; the Pentagon was, and is, a *sign* of US military might. Both now participate in a bizarre semiotics of death.

An aspect of all this is the misuse or even perversion of vocabularies by those who fail to perceive the cultural or theological baggage which such vocabularies bear. The original name dreamed up by the Western *Alliance against Terrorism* in 2001 was Operation Infinite Justice. Professor Clive Holes commented soon afterwards:

> The expression was accurately and literally translated into Arabic as *adala ghayr mutanahiya*, a phrase whose implication of divine retribution being arrogated to itself by an earthly power would strike any ordinary Muslim, let alone a zealot, as bordering on the blasphemous.[551]

And while it is true that many words in English have long since lost their religious connotations and resonance, President George W. Bush's use of the word 'crusade' roused many unhappy memories in the Islamic world.[552] Adel Darwish observed:

> President Bush's unfortunate phrase 'Crusade against terrorism', which led the White House to apologise on Wednesday, caused a storm of angry responses from columnists, even in Kuwaiti papers that once sang the praises of his father. 'Mr Bush's Freudian slip says it all', said a columnist for the Kuwaiti daily *Al-Watan*, 'as [Bush] and other Westerners hold in their hearts the dream to replay the Crusades launched against Islam 800 years ago. But his ancestors were defeated then, so he had better watch out this time.[553]

Such words as 'crusade' in the volatile aftermath of 11 September 2001, have become an integral part of the semiotics of conflict and death. Jonathan Phillips put it in a nutshell: 'For Bush to cast himself as the leader of a modern crusade is to fulfill one of militant Islam's most charged and dangerous descriptions of the US and Western powers'.[554]

1.4.3 Case Study Ground Zero: The Sacred

'Fundamentalists', J. J. G. Jansen reminds us, 'select a limited number of the precepts of their religion and make these absolute.'[555] Not only do they make them absolute; they anoint them as sacred. 'Abd al-Salām Faraj, one of those who assassinated President Anwār Sādāt of Egypt (1918–81), made the position extremely clear:

> To carry out God's prescripts [is] an obligation for the Muslims. Hence, the establishment of an Islamic State is obligatory ... *If such a state cannot be established without war*, then *this war is an obligation as well.* The laws by which the Muslims are ruled today are [not the laws of Islam but] the laws of unbelief. The rulers of this age are [hence] in apostasy from Islam. *An apostate has to be killed even if he is unable to carry arms and go to war.*[556]

K. N. Pandita detects 'an international agenda before the extremist Islamists the world over to destabilise civil societies and regimes against whose interests they work in one way or the other'.[557]

The 'problem' of Islamic fundamentalism has been viewed as a response to diverse phenomena which range from alienation and globalisation to exclusion from a particular society. Scott Thomas does not believe that it is any of these.[558] Its true definition for him is much starker and far less simplistic: 'It is a cultural and religious response to secular materialism'.[559] As such, it chooses to sacralise and hold sacred not just its perceived *telos*, who is God Himself, but also the means to that end.

Modern scholars have endlessly debated the origins of such a passionate and focussed dwelling upon, and articulation of, contemporary Islamic fundamentalism. Robert Irwin, Middle East editor of the *Times Literary Supplement*, identifies the Egyptian Sayyid Quṭb (1906–66) as a leading contender for the title of 'Father of Islamic Fundamentalism'.[560] The latter held that it was legitimate for Muslims to resist by force those supposedly Islamic regimes which fell short of the ideal.[561] (The 'sign' of perfection is part of the modern semiotics of Islamic fundamentalism.) His political trajectory is very well known, his life being terminated by hanging on 29 August 1966 under the Egyptian Nasserist regime.[562]

His literary trajectory achieved equal prominence and significance. Sayyid Quṭb wrote one of the most famous *tafāsīr*, exegeses, of the Qur'ān of the twentieth century, a multi-volume work under the title of *Fī Ẓilāl al-Qur'ān* (*In the Shadows of the Qur'ān*).[563] In these volumes, he insisted over and over again on the idea that the demands made upon the Muslim community are non-negotiable. The inescapable conclusion was that corrupt Muslim regimes should command no obedience; rather, they were to be outlawed in any possible way.[564] Sacred goal and intransigent means became thus merged in a sacred whole.

It is a truism that both the ordinary and the extraordinary can become sacralised by ritual.[565] Prominent among such sacralising rituals are those which pertain to ritual purity. In both Judaic and Islamic society, for example, menstruation is considered to render women unclean.[566] The Book of Leviticus puts it thus:

> Whenever a woman has a discharge and the discharge from her body is of blood, she will remain in a state of menstrual pollution for seven days. Anyone who touches her will be unclean until evening.[567]

Sexual intercourse is prohibited during menstruation.[568] A modern commentator on Leviticus 15 notes that 'the kinds of impurity here dealt with include not only contagious venereal disease but also normal seminal discharge and menstruation. *Everything connected with conception and birth is sacred and mysterious.*'[569]

Islam embraces a similar ethic:

> They ask thee
> Concerning women's courses.
> Say: They are
> A hurt and a pollution
> So keep away from women
> In their courses, and do not
> Approach them until
> They are clean.[570]

The distinguished anthropologist Mary Douglas held that the diverse rituals concerning purity and impurity practised in various societies were responsible for fostering a sense of unity of experience. They could make an actual contribution to such concepts as atonement and become a public display of the 'symbolic patterns' inherent in any social or religious system.[571] Places and objects which are held to be sacred must be preserved from that which is impure.[572] It follows that anyone bent on what is deemed a sacred mission will have a similar care about cleanliness and purity rituals. W. Lloyd Warner in 1937 suggested that 'masculinity is inextricably interwoven with ritual cleanliness, and femininity is equally entwined with the concept of uncleanliness, the former being the sacred principle and the latter the profane'.[573] Whether or not one chooses to espouse such an extreme view, it is interesting to note the obsession with cleanliness and ritual purity exhibited by

Mohammed Atta, one of the '9/11' suicide bombers, who wrote in his will: 'I don't want pregnant women or a person who is not clean to come and say goodbye to me because I don't approve of it. I don't want women to go to my funeral or later to my grave.'[574]

War may also be sacralised, by the concept of the Just War in the West and that of Jihād in the East.[575] After 11 September 2001, journalists analysed the usage of the 'Just War' concept by politicians who sought to justify a military response and bombing of the Tālibān in Afghanistan. Quoting the American Civil War general William Sherman that 'war is cruelty and you cannot refine it', Michael Gove showed, nonetheless, that many had tried to do just that.[576] Their fountain of inspiration, of course, was St Thomas Aquinas (1225–74).[577] And for 'refine' we can also read 'sacralise'.

Gove noted, however, that 'Aquinas' theory has since been honoured as much in the breach as in the observance. Many wars, including those of religion, such as the Thirty Years' War, have encompassed great brutality towards civilians.'[578]

Writing on 13 October 2001, barely a calendar month after the 9/11 attacks, a former Permanent Under-Secretary at the British Ministry of Defence observed that 'the legitimacy of taking military action is beyond dispute by most of these [classical Just War] criteria: Just cause, Right intention, Proper authority, Proportionality, Last resort'.[579] Not only did such criteria, for their proponents, serve to justify war ('*jus ad bellum*: the justice of going to war'[580]) but they served to cleanse and sacralise what was proposed.

Not everyone was convinced. The view that the journalist and famous commentator on Middle Eastern affairs, Robert Fisk, heard aired in Pakistan ran as follows: 'If, as Mr Bush claims, the attacks on New York and Washington were an assault on "civilization", why shouldn't Muslims regard an attack on Afghanistan as a war on Islam?'[581] *Jihād* may be shown to have a sacred character as well.

1.5 *Samuel Huntington Revisited*

Asked, in the wake of 9/11, whether this was 'the clash of civilizations you have been warning about for nearly a decade', the now renowned Harvard political scientist, Samuel Huntington, responded that it was clearly *intended* to be viewed as such.[582] There was a danger, he admitted, that further US attacks by way of response on other perceived terrorists could precipitate just that kind of clash of civilisations.[583]

However, he went on to stress that violence was not inherent in Muslim theology and that, as with all other religions, the sacred texts of Islam were open to diverse interpretations.[584] Huntington also noted the fragmented character of the Muslim *umma* and insisted that no civilisation, whether Islamic or European, was a unitary monolith.[585]

Of course, Huntington's stark analysis has not gone unchallenged. Thomas Meyer, for example, Professor of Political Science at the University of Dortmund in Germany, argues

> Huntington's approach reveals the hallmarks of the ideologies of which it is so critical. It is selective in its real world examples, moulding them to its

> needs, drawing general conclusions and deliberately omitting anything that does not fit its argument ... Huntington treats civilisations as though they consist of nothing but fundamentalism.[586]

Meyer perceives Huntington's thesis to have gained some plausibility in the light of the 9/11 attacks and other terrorist activities. But he believes that its prominence helps 'to promote the concept of fundamentalism'.[587]

Meyer does not deny the existence of fundamentalism of various kinds in all cultures but refuses to accept that such fundamentalisms can ever characterise or define the culture, of which they are a part, as a whole.[588]

Arab politicians, too, have not been slow to enter the 'Huntington debate'. In June 2003, Sheikh Hamdan bin Zayed, Minister of State for Foreign Affairs of the United Arab Emirates, commenced an article in the London *Times* as follows:

> Ever since September 11, 2001, a dangerous view has taken hold in many Western countries. A view fuelled by ignorance and misunderstanding, a view which could destabilise many parts of the world. It is this: that the Muslim and Western worlds are locked in a clash of civilisations. It is a good slogan, but far from the truth. The Arab and Muslim world's dispute with the West is not religious. It is political- and focussed on one issue alone [i.e. the Arab-Israeli problem].[589]

This whole debate, precipitated by Huntington, begins to resemble that earlier one over Edward Said's famous text *Orientalism*, published in 1978:[590] a basic thesis with some sound and useful points is transmuted into an overblown and exaggerated polemic which then accrues an influence out of all proportion to its initial or actual worth.[591]

1.6 Conclusion

On 11 September 2001, the terms 'secular', 'profane' and 'sacred' assumed a certain fluidity. For the suicide bombers, the profane signs were the World Trade Center (sign of US commercial might) and the Pentagon (sign of US military might). Their sacred object, that from which they derived sacrovalence or sacred value, was their interpretation of *jihād* in the hope of Paradise, a *jihād* physically articulated in the form of four airliner suicide missions.

For the USA, and most (but not all) of a horrified world, the profane sign was, to deploy the Eliadean term, the catastrophic degradation of the sacred, the attack upon the twin 'secular-sacred' shrines of the WTC and the Pentagon, erected to honour Mammon and Mars respectively.

The three Eliadean motifs of the *sacred, the degradation of the spiritual* and *death and resurrection* assume a vibrant poignancy when applied to 11 September:

- A sacred space (Ground Zero) was created by both sides, the one willingly, the other forced.
- A sacred time (11 September 2001) was created for all time to rank beside St Bartholomew's Eve, the Glencoe Massacre and other memorial dates, but on a far grander scale.

- The spiritual Islamic concept of *jihād*, whose twin aspects involve a fight against inner sinful tendencies (the greater *jihād*) as well as a fight in defence of Islam against her external enemies (the lesser *jihād*), was degraded in the eyes of many moderate Muslims.
- The nature of man was sacralised through death in the eyes of both perpetrators and victims. The purificatory rituals of the bombers contrast with the heroism, and multiple deaths, of the many New York rescuers, especially among the city's fire fighters.
- The post-9/11 cosmos was sacralised and sanctified in the eyes of many in the US government by the initiation of a purificatory war on terrorism and terror.

And while the degradation of the spiritual did indeed harvest a monstrous crop in the deaths of thousands, New York *rose* again, as Eliade would have noted, even though much unease remained.[592]

CHAPTER

2

ORTHODOXY AND HETERODOXY: A WORN VOCABULARY EXPLORED

2.1 *Rejecting the Terms: Baldick* contra *Popovic and Veinstein*

Earlier Western commentators on Islam have had few problems in deploying such terms as 'orthodoxy' and 'heterodoxy' with complete freedom, as if they were immediately self-explicable. Thus we find Professor Sir Hamilton Gibb, writing originally in 1949, stating in an initial chapter:

> By this time the pressure of Muslim doctrine and practice had mastered most of the resistances that had, at an earlier time, sought an outlet in *heterodox* and subversive movements. But this did not lead to stagnation. On the contrary, the devotional feeling of the townsmen, grinding a channel of its own, burst the bonds of the *orthodox* disciplines and found a new freedom in the ranges of mysticism.[1]

Elsewhere in the same volume, he entitles a chapter 'Orthodoxy and Schism',[2] which discusses 'the elaboration of orthodox theology'.[3] He notes that 'it would have been difficult for a contemporary to prophesy which of all these multifarious forms would emerge as the definitively orthodox or "official" version of the Islamic faith'.[4] He goes on to recognise that 'the establishment of an orthodox system was thus a gradual process, in which political considerations and political action played a large part (as always in the establishment of orthodox systems)'.[5] In all this, there is little, if any, introspection on the part of Gibb as to the validity, or otherwise, of using the term 'orthodox', though he does admit that it carries with it the cultural baggage of 'official', as we have seen above. Furthermore, he suggests that the persecution of 'the most heretical forms of Islam and more especially the gnostic and dualistic perversions' led to 'the definition of orthodoxy ... being tightened up'.[6]

Gibb goes on to note that many of the great medieval Islamic philosophers, like al-Kindī (died after AD 866), al-Fārābī (870–950) Ibn Sīnā (979–1037), Ibn Bājja (1106–38) and Ibn Rushd (1126–98), 'were far from orthodox',[7] 'despite their sublime intellectual achievements. Above all, it is Sunnī Islam for Gibb which stands for all that is 'orthodox'.[8] This is his fundamental criterion in a book which is surprisingly deep, as well as wide-ranging, given its introductory nature, but also (unconsciously?) glib in its use of such terminology.

Tied, of course, to that which is regarded as 'orthodoxy' or 'official' in a given age are the domains of authority, text and entitlement to interpret those texts or bodies of text. The *'ulamā'* came to be considered as custodians, not just of intellectual power, but of political power as well; custodians not just of the intellectual development of Islam as a system of theologico-legal thought but, because of the classically articulated, unbroken bond between the 'secular' and the 'sacred', of political Islam as well. The trained *'ulamā'* guard and interpret the sacred texts, produce commentaries upon them, and 'the text becomes an instrument of authority and a way of excluding others or regulating their access to it'.[9] Thus it is that some scholars perceive that an authoritarian 'orthodoxy' is created, maintained by textual or intellectual hierarchs. The problem, as Gilsenan recognised, is that when the 'common people' are shut out from an élitist educational system or style of learning, then they may appoint their own textual guardians, interpreters and men of religious authority: 'Heterodoxies might flourish".[10]

'Orthodoxy' is a notoriously slippery term. For the Christian Orthodox Churches, the term 'Orthodoxy' means both 'right belief' and 'right glory' or 'right worship'.[11] The various branches of the Orthodox Church believe that they are 'the custodians of 'true [Christian] belief about God'.[12] Indeed, the nineteenth-century Russian theologian Alexis Khomiakov described the Pope as 'the first Protestant'.[13]

For the lexicographer, the definition of 'orthodox' can be equally lacking in final, concise and monovalent definition, even in *The Concise Oxford Dictionary*:

> *orthodox* a. Holding correct or currently accepted opinions esp. on religious doctrine, not heretical or independent-minded or original; generally accepted as right or true esp. theology, in harmony with what is authoritatively established, approved, conventional.[14]

The definition of 'heterodox' by contrast, in the same source is infuriatingly brief:

> *heterodox* a. (of person or opinion) not orthodox.[15]

In Arabic, there is no precise, single word to render the English term 'orthodoxy' except for the direct transliteration *urthūdhuksiyya* and the *jāhilī*-derived term *ḥanīfiyya*, which, of course, has its own linguistic and cultural baggage. The paraphrase *tatmīm al-wājibāt al-dīniyya* (completion [or fulfillment] of religious obligations) carries no value judgements of 'rightness' or 'correctness' such as is explicit in the Oxford Dictionary definition cited above.[16] However, the phrase *al-Khulafā' al-Rāshidūn*, usually translated into English as 'The Rightly-Guided Caliphs', is rendered by Doniach as 'the orthodox caliphs'.[17] In Arabic, it is perhaps within the framework of such diverse words as *sunna* or *ṣaḥīḥ* that one comes slightly closer to some of the multifarious senses of 'rightness' in the English word 'orthodox'.[18] Both the words *sunna* and *ṣaḥīḥ*, however, have a multi-layered Arabo-Islamic linguistic and religious baggage in the field of ḥadīth studies which the English word 'orthodox' cannot begin to approximate.

In their volume entitled *Les ordres mystiques dans l'Islam: cheminements et situation actuelle*, the editors, Alexandre Popovic and Gilles Veinstein, say in their *Avant-propos* that their volume will speak of 'un autre Islam':

> C'est un autre Islam donc, mais qui en général ne se veut pas opposé au premier, se présentant plutôt comme complémentaire. Aussi ne doit-il pas être confondu avec les schismes rejetant l'Islam sunnite, la Shī'a en particulier, point de mire de notre actualité – même s'il s'en rapproche sur quelques points; il reste au contraire, le plus souvent, *au sein de l'orthodoxie*, bien que de tout temps tenu à l'oeil par les Docteurs de la Loi et cible favorite des intégristes.[19]

In the same volume, Marc Gaborieau states that his intention is not to write a history of the ṣūfī orders in India. Rather,

> mon but est seulement d'en présenter une nomenclature en retraçant brièvement les étages de leur implantation. Trois critères sont utilisés ... Le troisième critère sépare, parmi les ordres mineurs, ceux qui sont orthodoxes, *bā-shar'*, de ceux qui sont hétérodoxes, *be-shar'*.[20]

All this is anathema to Julian Baldick, reviewing the work in the *Times Literary Supplement*. While admiring the academic dedication and industry of the various contributors to the volume, Baldick deplores their 'peculiarly old-fashioned overview' which causes them to identify an 'official' or 'orthodox' Islam on the one hand, and a parallel, alternative or heterodox Islam on the other.

He maintains that Ṣūfīs have been part of the 'establishment' in the East for centuries and suggests that 'the abuse of the word "orthodox" here must be seen as a classic illustration of the futility of its use in the study of religions' Ṣūfīs, he stresses, have for the most part over the years been as keen on 'Islamic legality' as anyone else. Furthermore, the sheer diversity of 'orthopraxy' or 'orthopraxies' means that simplistic dualist divisions into 'orthodox' and 'unorthodox' are simply untenable.[21]

In fairness to the book under review, Baldick does note that Veinstein's

> postscript to the volume contrasts oddly with his preface. In the latter he confidently predicts that the book will consider not 'official Islam" but an 'Islam *parallèle*'. In his concluding survey he is obliged to admit that several of his colleagues have insisted upon the absence of a particularly clear opposition between 'legal Islam' and the 'Islam of the brotherhoods'.[22]

The above debate very clearly shows that the old vocabulary of 'orthodoxy' and 'heterodoxy', articulated in stark dualistic terms as a single pair of antagonists, is no longer tenable. This chapter will therefore eschew any dwelling on *single* paths of orthodoxy or heterodoxy, whether in Islam or Christianity, and focus instead on a *diversity* of what were perceived as *right doctrines* in both faith traditions, acknowledging the possibility of doctrinal, legal or other contradiction within a single tradition. Stress will be laid on the plurality of religious and doctrinal experience and its custodians, whether they be the *'ulamā'* (religious leadership), the *fuqahā'* (jurisprudents) or the ṣūfīs. The old vocabularies and stark dualisms of orthodoxy and heterodoxy, coherence and incoherence, will be abandoned in favour of treating both Islam and Christianity as bodies of *diversity in unity*. The chapter will, of course, note what those intellectual and religious custodians themselves believed to be *right doctrines*, but it will not indulge in the false dichotomies condemned above by Baldick whereby one doctrine, or set of doctrines, is characterised externally for all time as true or false, orthodox or heterodox. Ours is a phenomenological approach. It is also neater in that it allows a more fluid and versatile approach to diversity within a single tradition without the perpetual need to compartmentalise into the orthodox and the unorthodox or heterodox. Throughout our discussions and explorations, a primary *leitmotiv* will be that of authority and how such authority derives, or is derived, from what one custodian of knowledge or another – *ʿalim*, *faqīh* or *ṣūfī* – deems to be true.

2.2 *Christianity: Sources of Authority and Right Doctrines*

Both Christianity and Islam teach obedience to God's authority and man's properly constituted and delegated authority. From the former spring what the theologians will construe and articulate as *right doctrines* in all their glorious diversity; from the latter spring what the statesmen and politicians will establish as *right order*. The fundamental paradigm in both Islam and Christianity is that man's authority should flow from God's authority.[23] (Practice does not always follow theory!)

In Christianity, obedience to God is primal. As the Swiss theologian Hans Urs Von Balthasar (1905–88) showed, the whole of history may be interpreted in terms of fidelity and infidelity to the Deity.[24] Sin is specifically a stark 'No', to the covenanting God of the Old Testament. Adam's disobedience in the face of God's sublime authority sought to refashion his relationship with God without the latter's authority and 'outside the grace and the space given him by God'.[25] That primal negative of Adam is a direct challenge to an 'as yet unveiled, unalienated face of the God of grace'.[26] By his disobedience, Adam engineers the incomprehension about, and alienation from, God of himself and subsequent generations.[27] Lack of respect for God's Order and Authority results in the terrestrial disorders consequent upon the Original Sin.

Etymologically, the English word 'authority' implies 'growth'.[28] But that growth within the Christian framework of the development and exercise of authority was neither easy nor straightforward. Its ideal exercise is *pro bono populorum*,[29] or what the Islamic jurists would term *maṣlaḥa* (common good, public interest or weal).[30] However, the dispute over authority in Christianity was one of the earliest to vex the nascent religion.[31] In this, too, there are marked parallels with early Islamic history and the quarrels over leadership and governance between Sunnīs and those who became characterised as Shīʿites.[32] Major cracks appeared in the body politic of Christianity; some may be characterised as epistemic breaks in the sense beloved by Michel Foucault,[33] for they were profound, wide-ranging in consequence and long-lasting in effect:

> By 800, popes had been telling people for centuries that they were the successors of St Peter, the prince of the Apostles, and, as such, were the supreme arbiters of God's will on earth ... Where Charlemagne's view of the descent of religious authority went God–Charlemagne–pope, the papacy's went God–pope–Charlemagne.[34]

The year AD 1054 saw a major break between the Eastern and Western branches of Christianity. The causes were complex and diverse but included, *inter alia*, the *filioque* clause in the Nicene Creed and, perhaps even more significantly, the refusal by the East 'to recognize the universal authority and jurisdiction of the pope'.[35] It was politics and, in particular, the Crusaders' sack of Constantinople in 1204 during the Fourth Crusade[36] that cemented the divide between *ex patre et filio* and *ex patre per filium*.[37] Politics and doctrine supped from a similar cup of discontent and produced, from the separate authoritarian stances taken by the East and the West, scandal and disorder rather than right order and agreed doctrine.

> Later in the Middle Ages, moreover, popes such as Gregory VII (1073–85) and Innocent III (1198–1216) developed further the papal view of who exercised divine authority on earth, inventing the concept of secular authority as a means of emasculating kings and emperors of the religious powers which their predecessors, after late-Roman models, had all claimed.[38]

Leaving aside the various major and minor heresies which had afflicted the early Christian Church, it is 1054, rather than the European Protestant Reformation[39] several hundred years later, which constitutes the definitive, classical or archetypical fracture in Christian unity and authority. It is this which, in its age, called into question, with the mutual anathemas and excommunications,[40] the ancient concepts and definitions of orthodoxy and heterodoxy for that Church. And if 1054 was the defining event for that fracture, then 1204 was the validating fact: 'The occupation of the Byzantine empire by colonists was a direct consequence of the crusading movement, but there was nothing religious about it'.[41]

The great doyen of Crusader historians, Sir Steven Runciman, characterised the Fourth Crusade as 'The Crusade against Christians',[42] and made this the title of an entire book's chapter within a section designated 'Misguided Crusades'. On the significance of this crusade, he wrote eloquently; modern Crusader historians consider Runciman to be somewhat dated in the light of the huge quantity of original new research which has been produced on the Crusades over the last few decades, but his narrative is worthy of quotation here for its very eloquence and style which nobly emphasise the importance of this fracture in Christendom:

> The sack of Constantinople is unparalleled in history. For nine centuries the great city had been the capital of Christian civilisation ...[43] There was never a greater crime against humanity than the Fourth Crusade ...[44] In the wide sweep of world history the effects were wholly disastrous ... Meanwhile hatred had been sown between eastern and western Christendom. The bland hopes of Pope Innocent [III reg. 1198–1216] and the complacent boasts of the Crusaders that they had ended the schism and united the Church were

> never fulfilled. Instead their barbarity left a memory that would never be forgiven them. Later, east Christian potentates might advocate union with Rome in the fond expectation that union would bring a united front against the Turks. But their people would not follow them. They could not forget the Fourth Crusade. It was perhaps inevitable that the Church of Rome and the great eastern Churches should drift apart; but the whole Crusading movement had embittered their relations, and henceforward, whatever a few princes might try to achieve, *in the hearts of the east Christians the schism was complete, irremediable and final.*[45]

The divisions were reflected in the exercise of authority, with an authoritarian and centralised West confronting a more collegial East. And, in the West, matters crystallised at the Reformation, with the disputes over authority assuming 'strictly doctrinal significance'.[46] While the Protestant reformers agreed that human authority was necessary for good ecclesial order and mission, it was not directly derived from Jesus Christ in the manner taught by the Roman Catholic Church, nor did it have the same possible consequence of infallible dogmatic proclamation.[47]

The Orthodox Churches preserved a kind of *via media* between these two poles, accepting the magisterium of the episcopate and inerrancy but tying this kind of authority to the *synaisthesis* or '"general consciousness" of the church', placing a particular emphasis on conciliar infallibility, discerned in a *post facto* fashion.[48]

On the one hand, then,

> the Reformation churches generally reject the idea of an ecclesial magisterium in the name of the principle that scripture is its own interpreter and always produces anew its own correct interpretation. Doctrinal authority in the church is simply human and is judged by its fidelity to 'the sovereign authority of the holy scriptures'.[49]

By contrast, the Roman Catholic Church teaches that Christ bestowed on the leaders of His Church 'the charism of infallibility in matters of faith and morals'.[50]

The Fathers of the Second Vatican Council (1962–5) put it thus in their *Dogmatic Constitution on the Church*, known as *Lumen Gentium*:

> The Roman Pontiff, head of the college of bishops, enjoys this infallibility in virtue of his office, when, as supreme pastor and teacher of all the faithful – who confirms his brethren in the faith (cf. Luke 22:32) – he proclaims in an absolute decision a doctrine pertaining to faith or morals.[51]

It is, of course, a truism that the ability to enforce – spiritually, morally or even physically – a particular item of what was perceived to be 'right doctrine' was – and is – dependent upon the *acceptance* (or otherwise) of the legitimacy of a particular authority. Thus a diverse interpretation of the bounds of authority, and those who exercise it, unsurprisingly and logically bespeaks the possibility of a variegated development and interpretation of those traditional sources, guardians and accepted guarantors of Christian 'right doctrines' in a given age, scripture and tradition. Their manifestly diverse fruits and exegeses were and are the product of those fractured magisteria of which we have just spoken.[52]

J. N. D. Kelly confirms that by AD 450 the Bishop of Rome had achieved a position of Western episcopal dominance which had been precisely and formulaically articulated. History had helped in the process, as had the fame and antiquity of Rome itself.[53] One thinks, for example, of the role of Pope Leo I 'the Great' (reg. 440–61) in negotiating the release of captives held by Attila the Hun.[54] It was easy to see how a popular respect or admiration could clothe the papacy with a divine authority or aura. And, as Kelly points out, 'the student tracing the history of the times, particularly of the Arian, Donatist, Pelagian and Christological controversies, cannot fail to be impressed by the skill and persistence with which the Holy See was continually advancing and consolidating its claims'.[55]

The case of Arius and Arianism is particularly instructive in terms both of what was perceived to be 'right doctrine' and the exercise of authority: it is to this that we will turn in a short while. Two points, however, deserve to be surveyed here. The *first* is that the claim of primacy for the Apostle Peter and his successors has been subject to frequent challenge by those outside the Roman Catholic Church. A single, albeit antiquated, quotation will illustrate this neatly. A certain Dean of Canterbury, Dr Frederic W. Farrar DD FRS, wrote as follows in 1897:

> That St Peter was a leading Apostle – in some respects *the* leading Apostle – none will dispute; but that he never exercised the supremacy which is assigned to him by Roman Catholic writers is demonstrable even from the New Testament ... Peter had ... primacy of order, but not a supremacy of power. Such a supremacy our Lord emphatically discountenanced ... He was eminent among the Apostles; – *supreme* he never was.[56]

The historical and doctrinal consequences of such a view for the development of the Papacy and papal authority are obvious.

The real problem behind all this for those who adhered to the various forms of Christianity can be articulated very simply: did, or could, a 'fractured' authority lead to a 'fractured' (i.e. 'denied') salvation if the 'wrong' authority were chosen and the 'wrong' path were followed? And what, or who, ultimately, decided about the 'rightness' and the 'wrongness' of the path? How did the would-be believer identify what the Muslim would term *al-ṣirāṭ al-mustaqīm* (the straight path)?[57] An error over a temporal, temporary ecclesiological authority could lead to a permanent loss of infinite, eternal salvation. As Montgomery Watt put it, talking of the bitter, early disputes in Islam between the Khawārij and the Shīʿites:

> The Khārijites, not convinced of the infallibility of the [Shīʿite] leader, saw rather that he might make a mistake and thereby lead the whole community into a course of action which would cause them to forfeit their status as people of Paradise.[58]

In the Latin Roman Catholic Church, authority derived from, and depends upon, the following paradigm: *salvation* is pursued by an institutional *Church* which claims Jesus Christ as its direct founder and which is led by a human, papal 'successor' (one might compare here the Islamic *khalīfa*) possessed by the dual charisms of (1) a *silsila* (chain) of succession going back to the Apostle Peter himself and (2) infallibility:

Tu es Petrus et super hanc petram aedificabo ecclesiam meam (Matthew 16:18 'Thou art Peter, and it is upon this rock that I will build my church').[59]

In terms of pure soteriology, the paradigm at first espoused the exclusivist doctrine of *extra ecclesiam nulla salus* ('No salvation outside the church'), an axiom often attributed to the Council of Florence (1439) but predating that Council by more than 1,000 years.[60] The axiom was clearly a part of the Christian mediaeval tradition: it was mentioned, for example, at the Fourth Lateran Council (1215) and in the Bull *Unam Sanctam* of Pope Boniface VIII (reg. 1294–1303) of 1302.[61] Later, in more modern times, that axiom would be revised, revoked or, at least, reinterpreted, depending on one's stance.[62]

The paradigm, then, discloses a situation in which salvation depends on a Church, an institutional, divinely founded custodian of what are considered to be 'right doctrines', led by a Leader, an individual custodian of those doctrines who claims God-given authority. The logic of all this dictates that a 'flawed' or potentially 'flawed' leader, or one whose authority is questioned or whose credibility is undermined in any way, may be a positive danger and thereby preside over a 'denied' salvation. Instances of this range from the vicissitudes of the Avignon papacy[63] to the accusations levelled, in modern times against Pope Pius XII (1939–58) that he did little to help or protect the Jews from persecution, deportation or death during the Second World War.[64]

What is perceived as an unduly severe exercise of authority could also attract equal opprobrium from the Church's critics. Good examples from recent times in the Catholic Church include the prohibition on the ordination of women to the priesthood[65] and the wording of the Vatican document *Dominus Jesus*[66] (which described 'the followers of other religions' as being objectively 'in a gravely deficient situation'.[67] These factors contributed to an enfeeblement of personal papal authority in the twilight years of the Polish Pope John Paul II (1978–2005), a pontiff already enfeebled by the debilitations of Parkinson's disease in old age, as well as other ills whose origin went back to a failed assassination attempt in 1981.[68] Cornwall put it thus:

> Countless millions of Catholics are walking away from a Church that has lost touch with ordinary Catholics, their problems and spiritual aspirations ... the ultraconservative articulation of Catholicism's claims of exclusive truth, the papal demonisation of the West and the oppression of Catholic advocates of religious pluralism all signal an ominous rejection of history's leading proven experiment in the coexistence of religions under democratic auspices. That rejection encourages fundamentalism within Catholicism and within non-Christian faiths.[69]

In Cornwall's view, there is a true crisis of authority here. But the issue is broader than just the confines of an institutional and institutionalised Church. He points to the violence bred from Islamic fundamentalism and warns of parallel problems and dangers resulting from Christian and Judaic fundamentalism.[70] For him, the conclusions are logical and stark: a breakdown of authority *may* provide a vacuum for such fundamentalism and its confrères, extremism and violence.

Our *second* brief point, before we turn to Arius and Arianism, is the following: reading the above, the casual observer may be led to suppose that the differing concepts of authority, and thus differing interpretations of doctrine flowing from those authorities, are irreconcilable. Yet a genuine eirenicism has emerged, and some progress has been made by ecumenical theologians: in recent times, 'the dialogue which has advanced furthest towards agreement on the problem of authority is certainly the ARCIC [Anglican–Roman Catholic International Commission]'.[71] Related topics such as the Petrine verses in scripture and papal infallibility have also been studied; and, though no absolute convergence has been reached, a clarification of attitudes to the exercise of authority has been achieved.[72] Language clearly has a role to play: thus, while in the past the papal claim to universal primacy by divine law or right was not considered to be acceptable to the Anglican Communion, it is now possible to affirm such primacy as part of the divine plan '*in terms which are compatible with both our traditions*'.[73]

2.2.1 The Authority of the *ekklēsía* (I): Arius and Arianism

The case of Arius and Arianism is profoundly instructive in any study of the exercise of early Church authority and the establishment in that age of what were perceived to be 'right doctrines'. The Arian heresy bestraddled and challenged such concepts with powerful force.

Maurice Wiles has rightly drawn attention to the real difficulties inherent in any quest for the historical Arius: 'It may be that, in view of the nature of [the] sources, the historical Arius will always remain as elusive a figure as the historical Jesus'.[74] In a Preface to a book about the latter, E. P. Sanders notes that the majority of scholars who have written on antiquity have felt it necessary to warn their audiences that knowledge about the ancient world is never total and that we can rarely achieve certainty. He notes, furthermore, that New Testament scholars have fluctuated between stressing that hardly anything can be known of the historical Jesus to a reactive confidence which has produced a rash of unproven hypotheses.[75] Whatever the relevance and application of the last remark, it is certainly true that we need to treat the totality of our information on the life of Arius with caution. It is thus a brief and *cautious* biography which follows.

According to the evidence of Epiphanius, cited and accepted by one of today's most respected Arius scholars, Rowan Williams, Arius appears to have been born in Libya at a date before AD 280.[76] We know little of his philosophical education, but it is possible that he absorbed some of the contemporary trends in Aristotelianism and Neoplatonism.[77] However, from 313 we are able to write with a little more certainty about his life, focusing on his ministry in a major church in Alexandria, where he may or may not have become involved in the Melitian schism.[78] On balance, Rowan Williams believes that 'the Melitian Arius, beloved of several modern scholars, appears to melt away under close investigation'.[79]

A certain Alexander became Bishop of Alexandria in 313, and his episcopacy saw a major theological 'falling out' between Arius and Alexander, with public, mutual theological repudiations and a gradual schism.[80] Arius was formally excommunicated by a synod in Alexandria but launched an appeal to a variety of prelates, one of whom, Eusebius of Nicomedia, attempted to have Arius reinstated. A synod in Palestine supported Arius, and Bishop Alexander wrote an exposé of Arius's behaviour and alleged heresy.[81]

Finally, the Council of Nicaea met in 325: the Emperor Constantine I (reg. 306–37) himself presided over the Council, drawing unto himself a kind of dual secular and spiritual authority. Arius was excommunicated, and exiled by the Emperor.[82] Williams comments that this dual ecclesiastical and civil punishment set 'an ominous precedent' since 'it sowed the seeds of endless bitterness and confusion in the years that followed ... although the emperor could rescind his own legal decisions, he could not on his sole authority reverse ecclesiastical rulings. The two systems were to be seldom in step after 325.'[83]

During a chaotic and complex series of events between the end of the Council and the sudden death of Arius in 336, Arius returned from exile with an emended creed which was presented to, and accepted by, Constantine; however, he became embroiled with the successor of Bishop Alexander of Alexandria, the redoubtable Bishop Athanasius, who refused in 328 the Emperor's request to restore Arius.

Constantine, in receipt of Arius's complaints and yet another creed, then turned against Arius in 332 or 333, probably on the assumption that Arius was contemplating schism. But the emperor later changed his mind once again. The sudden death of Arius, which according to tradition occurred in a public lavatory, put an end to the Emperor's vacillating and wavering.[84]

Rowan Williams wryly concludes:

> Arius' death, like most of his life, is surrounded by uncertainties, and is yet at the same time an unmercifully public affair. His life and death were not easy material for a conventional hagiography, and (if we can judge by Philostorgius) he was never unequivocally a hero for the parties associated with his name.[85]

So what exactly *was* Arianism? Maurice Wiles puts it in a nutshell: following Athanasius, he states that the primary feature of this heresy was 'that the status of the Son is not one of essential Godhead. The Son is not eternal or immutable; he has no exact vision, understanding, or knowledge of the Father. Put more positively, he is a creature brought into being from nothing.'[86] Of course, as Wiles confirms, the logical corollary of all this is that the Father cannot always have rejoiced in that epithet.[87]

For Kelly, 'the fundamental premiss' of the system adumbrated by Arius 'is the affirmation of the absolute uniqueness and transcendence of God, the unoriginate source (*agénnētos apkhē*) of all reality'.[88] Athanasius proclaimed:

> Their heresy has no ground in reason and no clear proof in Holy Scripture, so they are always resorting to shameless subterfuges and plausible fallacies. And now they have ventured to slander the Fathers.[89]

Williams holds that Arius cited scripture to establish three fundamental theological points: (1) the Son is a created being and was produced by the will of God; (2) the actual word 'son' must be understood metaphorically rather than literally; (3) the very status of the Son, like the existence, is a product of the will of God.[90]

In Arianism we have not just a dispute about correct dogma and issues of religion but one which challenged both the ecclesiastical and secular authorities of the day. 'The fifth-century church historian Socrates thought that "all theological disputes were to be treated as a mere figleaf for contentions about power and authority".'[91] And there were in Arianism at least four major challenges to power, authority and what was perceived to be 'right doctrine' : there was the challenge to ecclesiastical and religious tradition; there was the challenge to the local Church and the Universal Church; there was the challenge to the authority of an ecumenical Council; and there was the (albeit often implicit) secular challenge to the authority of the emperor himself. The presence of the emperor at the Council of Nicaea in AD 325 is a marvellous semiotic indicator of the consolidation of all those ecclesiastical and secular points in the one powerful figure who was, nonetheless, much more than a mere *figurehead.*

The opponents of Arius, like Bishop Athanasius (who lived c. 296–373, and was Patriarch of Alexandria from 328), perceiving a challenge to the authority of tradition, *themselves appealed to tradition.* In the twentieth century, a would-be latter-day Athanasius by the name of Archbishop Marcel Lefebvre (1905–91) would later clothe himself in the same garb of tradition, as we shall see, in his energetic efforts to keep at bay those whom he regarded as the hounds of heresy and falsehood.

Athanasius claimed that the doctrine which he espoused 'had been handed down from father to father' whereas the Arians could not cite 'a single respectable witness to theirs'. The faith propagated by Nicaea was only what had been taught and accepted by Christianity from its earliest days. Nicaea was nothing but a ratification of Christ's teaching, preserved and handed down by the Apostles and Fathers of the Church. Deviants from the traditional Truths forfeited the right to call themselves Christians.[92]

Arianism challenged not just theological tradition but the *ekklēsía* itself and its magisterium. This second challenge was linked to the first by Kelly:

> Against the Arians [Athanasius] flung the charge that they would never have made shipwreck of the faith had they held fast as a sheet-anchor to the *skopòs ekklēsiastikós*, meaning by that the Church's peculiar and traditionally handed down grasp of the purport of revelation.[93]

Arius's quarrels with the custodians or propagators of that *skopòs ekklēsiastikós*, especially with Bishop Alexander of Alexandria in the early days, and later with Bishop Athanasius, have been much commented upon.[94] Yet Arius was well aware of the need for episcopal authority and support. He won the support, for example, of Eusebius of Caesarea, who was later provisionally excommunicated.[95] And scholars debate as to the exact number of the bishops who supported Arius at the commencement of the Council of Nicaea.[96]

Of course, Arius's opponents were not blameless in their exercise of due legal, canonical or theological authority. The latter could easily slip into pure authoritarianism – as happened with Athanasius, who must have alienated many by his severity, even if his opponents were not, strictly speaking, Arians in the sense that they identified *totally* with what Arius taught.[97] All in all, Williams's own reading of the sources emphasises a variety of conflicts in the early Alexandrian Church (and, one might add, in the broader Universal Church) which were not just theological but which carried a heavy – and heady – baggage of meditation on the nature of hierarchical authority and what that meant for a local (Alexandrian) Church as well as a Universal one (centred on Rome).[98]

The challenge to the Church's magisterium produced a major ecumenical Council, the Council of Nicaea in 325, which established what was to be regarded as 'right doctrine'. One could become Nicene and 'orthodox', or one could challenge both the Council and its stance and remain Arian and 'heterodox.' Nicaea itself became, within a few years, a living part of the established tradition. As Kelly so neatly and succinctly puts it: 'A century later ... the Nicene council and its creed enjoyed the prestige of unimpeachable authorities'.[99] Arianism was officially condemned;[100] Arius was 'officially excommunicated';[101] and the Nicene Creed, as a result, 'has come to be seen as the primary symbol of Christian orthodoxy'[102] and 'the primary norm of Christian orthodoxy'.[103]

Finally, Arianism constituted a challenge to, and a vexation for, the secular authorities, epitomised most especially in the person of the Emperor Constantine himself. Williams notes how the Arian crisis was bound up with issues of how far the ruler could or should interfere in matters ecclesiastical.[104] And interfere, for whatever secret or overt motivations, the emperor certainly did. It was clear to him that doctrinal disunity might very well be a prelude to political disunity.[105] Here, it is perhaps no exaggeration to say that Constantine had the mindset of an early Islamic *khalīfa* who wished to preserve the unity of the Islamic Community, the *umma*, and thus the Islamic Empire, whatever his own personal piety.

Thus the ecumenical Council of Nicaea met at Constantine's instigation,[106] and some of its credal and theological vocabulary owed something to the emperor himself.[107] With Christianity as the official religion of the Empire, the emperor became a kind of secular guardian of religious doctrine,[108] whether or not he was theologically minded and whether or not he was a supporter or opponent of the Nicene formulations.[109] Wiles notes: 'In the words of B. J. Kidd, when [the Emperor] Valens fell on the field of Adrianople [in AD 378], "Arianism fell with him".'[110]

It is interesting that the Emperor Valentinian II (reg. 375–92) clashed dramatically with Ambrose (c. 340–97) the Bishop of Milan, over a Basilica in 385–6 – and the clash illustrates an ongoing tension between civic and ecclesiastical authority which would vex many another age, whether that of Canossa[111] or Henry II[112] of England (reg. 1154–89) or, indeed, Henry VIII (reg. 1509–47). Valentinian claimed authority over all property, whether civil or ecclesiastical, which came 'under his jurisdiction'.[113] Ambrose's view, on which he based a flat refusal of the emperor's wishes, was that the churches over which he had ecclesiastical authority ultimately were God's and not the emperor's; he therefore declined to yield the basilica to the emperor. The latter unsuccessfully attempted the use of force. This later conflict over a basilica mirrors an earlier one between Ambrose and the preceding Emperor Gratian (reg. 367–83).[114]

How, then, should Arianism best be viewed and summarised from the comparative aspect of this volume? Certainly, there is a perennial danger of considering Arius and Arianism through the polemics engendered by Athanasius.[115] Indeed, with Rowan Williams, we may wish to be somewhat wary in our usage of the very term 'Arianism'.[116] Whatever our reservations, however, it is a useful portmanteau concept or category,[117] and it is with this in mind that the following concluding remarks are offered.

Following Williams, we note that Arius was a true son of Alexandria in his predilection for negative theology.[118] He cannot, and should not, be characterised as a real philosopher.[119] In theology, he must rightly be labelled a conservative.[120] But he followed a path which ineluctably led him into 'isolation'.[121] What he sought was 'for a way of making it clear that the doctrine of creation allows no aspect of the created order to enter into the definition of God'.[122] There are parallels of emphasis, at least, to be drawn here with the Islamic doctrine of the oneness of God, *tawḥīd*.

The traditional view of Arianism, implicit or explicit in the writings of many scholars, deploys the classical vocabulary of orthodoxy and authority. Thus Rowan Williams begins his magisterial work on Arius with the statement: '"Arianism" has often been regarded as the archetypal Christian deviation, something aimed at the very heart of the Christian confession'.[123] A scholarly stereotype has been perpetuated whereby Arius is perceived as an 'arch-heretic', someone who precipitated on purpose an oppositional trend to theological orthodoxy.[124] This tradition of conspiracy, blame and, indeed, paranoia goes right back to the fourth-century heresiographer, Epiphanius, who spoke of Arius and the Arians as having ignited a huge fire which devoured practically the whole Roman empire of the day.[125]

By contrast with this mainstream polemic, it is salutary to discover that some in eighteenth-century Britain, including many notable scientists like Sir Isaac Newton FRS (1642–1727), actually embraced Arianism, regarding 'Athanasian orthodoxy' as 'the archetypal heresy' and perceiving the 'Arianism' of antique horror and distaste as a genuine form of 'primitive Christianity'.[126]

Since, in scholarship, 'old certainties have given way to new lines of inquiry',[127] it may well now be opportune to jettison the label 'Arian' altogether and explore a new, perhaps more 'heterodox', vocabulary.[128]

In a tantalising comment in his *Postscript (Theological)* to the volume *Arius: Heresy and Tradition*, Archbishop Rowan Williams concludes: 'In many ways – and here is a still stranger paradox – [Arius's] apophaticism foreshadows the concerns of *Nicene* theology later in the fourth century, the insights of the Cappodocians, or even Augustine'.[129] And so it is to Augustine that we shall now turn.

2.2.2 The Authority of the *ekklēsía* (2): Augustine, Manichaeism and the Flesh Rejected

A cursory review of the chronology of Augustine's life (AD 354–430) shows that it was spent mainly in North Africa (354–83, 388–430), with an important Italian sojourn (383–8)[130] sandwiched between his two major African periods.

Aurelius Augustinus was born on 13 November 354 in Thagaste (Numidia

Proconsularis) in what is now eastern Algeria.[131] Here he began his early education before passing to the nearby town of Madauros and thence to Carthage.[132] He clearly disliked his schooldays, hating Greek literature though he did learn to love Latin.[133] Three aspects of his early life have precipitated much comment from scholars: his own much-repented lust, the notorious theft of the pears, and his taking a Carthaginian concubine at about the age of 17 or 18 who bore him a son whom they called Adeodatus.

He tells in his *Confessions* how, in his sixteenth year, he was swallowed up in a maelstrom of lust which he indulged at every opportunity, vying in sexual deeds with his peers and even boasting of sexual acts which he had not committed.[134] But, while Augustine clearly had a strong sexual drive, his actual sexual activity before his conversion was not particularly unusual or outrageous by the standards of his age.[135] Wills reminds us that he was faithful to his concubine for fifteen years – and, indeed, such concubinage was recognised in Roman law and even by the Church itself (at the Council of Toledo in 400).[136]

Augustine himself, even in his early years, seems to have valued fidelity:

> In those years I had a woman. She was not my partner in what is called lawful marriage. I had found her in my state of wandering desire and lack of prudence. Nevertheless, she was the only girl for me, and I was faithful to her. With her I learnt by direct experience how wide a difference there is between the partnership of marriage entered into for the sake of having a family and the mutual consent of those whose love is a matter of physical sex, and for whom the birth of a child is contrary to their intention – even though, if offspring arrive, they compel their parents to love them.[137]

Wills warns that, despite Augustine's own later sense of guilt exhibited throughout the *Confessions*, we must beware of exaggerating overmuch Augustine's early sexual adventures. For example, he believes that to suggest, as some scholars have done, that Augustine was perceived by his father either masturbating or with an erection in the public baths is to misinterpret totally Augustine's own phrase to the effect that 'when at the bathhouse my father saw that I was showing signs of virility and the stirrings of adolescence [*inquieta adulescentia*] he was overjoyed to suppose that he would now be having grandchildren'.[138]

The episode of the theft of the pears is more perplexing. With Garry Wills, the reader of the *Confessions* is amazed that more than half of Book Two is preoccupied with what many another writer might have ignored or passed over as a childish peccadillo.[139] Augustine tells us that, filled with wickedness, he stole something with which he was already plentifully supplied. The idea of theft and wrongdoing excited him, and so he and a group of fellow youths targeted a pear tree near his vineyard which was endowed with somewhat indifferent fruit. They seized a large haul of pears, ate some and threw the rest to the pigs. The real pleasure, Augustine submits, lay in having done something illicit.[140]

The memory of that childish deed grieved him sorely in later life. Introspectively, he asked himself what it was that he loved in that act of theft. He acknowledged the beauty of the fruit , because it was created by the hand of beauty Himself. Bleakly, he confesses that his 'feasting was only on the wickedness which I took pleasure in enjoying'.[141]

In this whole puerile incident, there is much scope for both the pop psychologist and the commentator who would attempt superficial comparisons with other religious figures known for their delicate consciences in other ages – for example, Martin Luther (1483–1546), an Augustinian in every sense of the word. This is not to deny, of course, the very real impact of Augustine on the young Luther.[142] What may be argued with some plausibility is that incidents such as that of the pears, together with his sexual peccadillos, created a sense of guilt and sin in Augustine which sought an outlet, firstly in what was considered to be heterodoxy and formal heresy, and, later, in purification of the intellect, faith and body in the authority and disciplines of the established Church.

The third aspect of Augustine's early life, to which we alluded earlier, was his cohabitation with a Carthaginian concubine for many years. Having remained faithful to her, he was then persuaded to abandon her, and she returned, heartbroken, to North Africa, even though she had borne him a much-loved son.[143]

This seemingly casual abandonment, and forced return, of the girl to Africa has shocked many observers. Henry Chadwick describes it as 'deplorable'.[144] The chief reason seems to have been snobbery: the lowly status of the concubine was an impediment to Augustine's social, financial and professional advancement and his burning ambition to do great things in Milan.[145] His mother, Monica, arranged for him to become engaged to a prepubescent heiress.[146] But was all this just snobbery mixed with ambition, or did it also betray a profound streak of cruelty in Augustine? Was it the need for a large dowry by a relatively impecunious male making his way in the world, or was Augustine merely a product of his own society?[147] The real answer is that it was probably a confused mixture of all these motives. Certainly, Augustine himself was deeply pained and upset, like his concubine, by what he nonetheless perceived as a necessary separation and dismissal of the girl.[148]

It is certainly true that Augustine did nothing by halves. His conversion in the summer of AD 386 has been characterised as 'an all or nothing affair'.[149] James J. O'Donnell observes that 'our last impression of Augustine is of a man who never made things easy for himself'.[150] He was clearly devoted to his concubine, whose name we do not know, and to their son Adeodatus, whose name we do.[151] The huge pain which both felt at the separation is recorded in the *Confessions*:

> The woman with whom I habitually slept was torn away from my side because she was a hindrance to my marriage. My heart which was deeply attached was cut and wounded, and left a trail of blood. She had returned to Africa vowing that she would never go with another man.[152]

In a poignant, and beautifully written, novel entitled *Vita Brevis: A Letter to Saint Augustine*,[153] Jostein Gaarder, who achieved international fame with his philosophical novel *Sophie's World*,[154] attempts to imagine the feelings of the rejected concubine, whom Gaarder names Floria Aemilia. She writes him a lengthy letter; and, through the medium of Gaarder's fiction, across the centuries, the girl expresses her terrible hurt, dwelling on the intimacy and near-marital closeness that they had shared for so many years which had produced their beloved son.[155]

The fiction of Gaarder expresses as clearly as the *Confessions* of Augustine that what had been sundered was indeed a marriage in all but name. In the end, though she has lived as a catechumen, she refuses baptism,[156] proclaiming that she fears not God but the theologians. She prays that 'the God of the Nazarene' will forgive Augustine for all the love and tenderness which he has rejected and banished.[157]

In the light of all this, it is perhaps unsurprising that Augustine's doctrine of sin should have had such a powerful, brooding and far-ranging influence on the Church down the ages, even though it might be interpreted with more reference to his early Manichaeism, and then his struggles against the Manichees, the Pelagians and the Donatists, rather than to his repentance for youthful sins of the flesh.[158]

It is true that feminist theologians have blamed Augustine for 'the scapegoating of women for sin, particularly sexual sin'.[159] However, Mary Grey reminds us that Augustine believed that both men and women shared a responsibility for sin[160] and that 'in both racism and sexism – the causal connection with the actual teaching of Augustine cannot be proved. It is the link between the penal character of sin and its societal expressions which has proved so damaging.'[161]

Henry Chadwick has rightly observed that 'Augustine's *Confessions* will always rank among the greater masterpieces of western literature'.[162] Yet we will go badly astray if we regard this autobiography as a mere chronicle of sexual indulgence followed by repentance. It may indeed be 'an unparalleled account of a spiritual struggle with sexual desire', in the words of Mary Grey,[163] but it is also much more than that. Garry Wills prefers to translate the Latin *Confessiones* as *Testimony* rather than the more usual *Confessions*. For him, the latter translation lacks 'theological resonance'.[164] This is because the word *confessio* in Augustine means not solely 'confession of sin' but also 'praise of God and profession of faith' together with an even broader semantic range according to which '*Confiteri* means, etymologically, to corroborate, to confirm testimony, and even inanimate things can do that'.[165]

For all these reasons, Wills prefers to translate *confessio* as 'testimony'[166] (Latin *testimonium*); he quotes Augustine as proclaiming '*Pulchritudo eorum confessio eorum* [Their beauty is their testimony]'.[167] The standard dictionaries confirm, or at least justify, Wills's own preference for *testimony* as the *mot juste*:

> *confiteor* -fiteri -fessus sum … (1) to confess, admit, acknowledge … (2) to reveal, make known: … *confessa deam*, manifesting her divinity …[168]

In a very real sense, then, the *Confessiones* of Augustine are by no means just a confession of sexual peccadillo; nor are they *just* a *testament*, in Wills's phrase. The *Confessiones* are a *manifestation* to the civilised Christian world, and beyond, of the truth, as Augustine perceives it, as well as a tribute to the *authority* of the established Church against the 'heterodoxies' of Manichaeism, Donatism and Pelagianism. Following Wills, then, and perhaps being slightly more daring, one might render the term *Confessiones* as *The Manifestations of Saint Augustine* or even *The Epiphanies of Saint Augustine*.

There is an interesting, and by no means unknown, psychosomatic association which may be made between poor health and worry or guilt. Just before his conversion, as well as during the process and its aftermath, Augustine had been in poor health with asthma and the loss of his voice.[169] In the *Confessions*, he mentions the acute state of anxiety in which he performed his routine duties;[170] he was keenly aware of how physically and mentally ill he had become;[171] his academic workload got the better of him and he suffered a weakness in his lungs, rendering breathing difficult. Chest pains prevented him from speaking clearly or at length.[172] In 386, he decided to abandon his prestigious teaching career as Rhetor, or Professor of Rhetoric, in Milan.[173] Francis Thompson's, 'Hound of Heaven'[174] had not only pursued him but overtaken him and won. He had held his teaching post for a mere two years.

In all this, there are many parallels which may be drawn between the life of Augustine of Hippo and that of the great Islamic scholar Abū Ḥāmid al-Ghazālī (1058–1111), whose career and significance will be dealt with at some length in a later section of this book.[175] Particular areas of affinity and comparison include al-Ghazālī's intellectual and spiritual crisis resulting in a number of similar psychosomatic symptoms, and the abandonment of his academic career in the Niẓāmiyya College in Baghdad for the peace of Ṭūs. The vocal afflictions suffered by both men and the mutual desire and search for peace after their respective abandonments of academe – by Augustine in Cassiciacum (near Como) in 386–7[176] and by al-Ghazālī in Ṭūs – make the two men particularly useful for comparative study. And al-Ghazālī, too, wrote his own species of *Confessions* under the title of *al-Munqidh min al-Ḍalāl*, usually translated as *Deliverance from Error*.[177]

The lives of Augustine and al-Ghazālī were theologically grounded in doubt, quest, spiritual crisis, mental anguish and physical trauma; the result was a quest for refuge in the security of what was perceived by each to be 'right doctrine' while at the same time attempting to preserve a measure of independent thought and action within the framework of what was deemed to be acceptable by the custodians of intellectual and theological power.

The rest of Augustine's life is soon told: after the beginning of his famous conversion in the garden in Milan[178] in July 386, and his Easter 387 baptism by Bishop Ambrose of Milan,[179] Augustine found himself back in Thagaste on his father's land in 388.[180] A shock was to follow: in 391, Augustine was unwillingly ordained priest by the Greek-speaking Italian Bishop of the seaport of Hippo Regius; the elderly prelate's name was Valerius. While such forcible ordinations were by no means uncommon,[181] the impact on Augustine was no less traumatic. Worse was to follow for one who had desired only solitude and peace. Bishop Valerius induced the Numidian Primate in 395 to consecrate Augustine as his coadjutor in Hippo. Canon law seems to have been ignored in this case.[182] And so it was that, for more than thirty years, until his death in Hippo on 28 August 430, Aurelius Augustinus wore a bishop's mitre. It is abundantly clear that, despite personal taste and unwillingness, a strong skein of obedience marks the man in all this. It was to be coupled with a predilection for defending the established Church by excoriating the three major heresies of the day: Manichaeism, Donatism and Pelagianism.

Arius had represented a challenge to the rule of ecclesiastical and lay authority, whether represented in tradition, Church, council or emperor. Augustine, in a language borne of spiritual suffering and intimate personal knowledge of what he attacked, at least in its Manichaean incarnation, championed in his sermons and writings the rights of those authorities. Athanasius had fought Arianism without any prior embracing of that heresy; Augustine had embraced Manichaeism before he fought it.

In an intriguing article entitled 'On the Function of Heresy' Paul Parvis observed: 'The Church is a city under siege, the orthodox an army under attack. In the history of the Church, then, it is the heretics who make all the running.'[183] Parvis uses the antique terminology of 'orthodoxy', but his meaning is clear. The task of theology may be perceived as the need to sail steadily on a course whose main direction is articulated by the rocks of heresy which are to be avoided.[184] Parvis concludes, magisterially:

> In the nature of the theological task, it must be by indirection that we find direction out. In that complex web of conflict which is the historical life of the Church, the running is made by those who care and those who see – those who can read the signs of the times – men like Arius and Athanasius, Nestorius and Cyril, Eutyches and Leo. And in that web of conflict, the heretics are those who lose. Indeed, the function of heresy is to lose. The function, the vocation, of heretics is to suffer defeat, that, through the failure of their attempts to speak, the words of others might find meaning.[185]

To paraphrase Parvis's initial words here, we might note that it was in the nature of Augustine's theological task, after the early 'indirection' of the Manichaeism in which he wallowed in his younger days, to find the 'right' direction in his mature years at Hippo. Like Athanasius and, indeed, Arius, he tried to read the signs of the times and produced a theological semiotics[186] which ultimately rejected, rather than embraced, the 'indirections' of Manichaeism, Donatism, Pelagianism and plain paganism.[187]

In *De Civitate Dei* (*The City of God*), Augustine signals, as John O'Meara reminds us, that 'the great lesson of the *City of God* is that out of all things comes good'.[188] Both Christianity and Rome could gain mutual benefit from each other's good. Christianity would benefit from the acceptance which assimilation into the Roman Empire would bring; Rome could benefit from a new birth and longevity of rule; the Greek intellectual tradition would spread, develop and expand. O'Meara believes that the key to reading the signs of *De Civitate Dei* is an emphasis on 'fulfilment not destruction', even though 'the practical problem with which Augustine had to deal was the problem of a spiritual Church in a secular world: the city of God in the city of this world'.[189]

Yet, at first, Augustine seems to have misidentified the true nature of this 'city of God'. Reading a now lost dialogue of Cicero entitled *Hortensius*, at the age of 19, he embraced Manichaeism.[190] In the *Confessions*, Augustine tells how he began to consort with a group of glib and voluble Manichees in whose mouths were 'the devil's traps and a birdlime' formed from their perverted mixture and interpretation of the names of God, Jesus Christ and the Holy Ghost into a Trinity in which Christ's humanity was rejected and 'the Paraclete is the other self of Mani'.[191]

J. N. D. Kelly notes that this Manichaean way of thought is often considered to be a Christian heresy but was, in fact, an independent, albeit highly syncretic, religion. Kelly identifies elements from Buddhism and Zoroastrianism, as well as Christianity. The Manichees claimed that Mani (who died c. AD 274) had brought a full and universal religion of which only parts had been previously known. Manichaeism, with its great mythical dramas, had much in common with Christian Gnosticism. Salvation was attainable by knowledge of a world in which two great forces, good and evil, opposed each other throughout eternity.[192]

This emphasis on salvation via knowledge had a particular appeal at first for the young Augustine: he was in love with learning and wanted to study what the classical texts had to say about eloquence when he chanced on Cicero's *Hortensius*.[193] He was studying hard with the goal of becoming a distinguished lawyer.[194] And, like al-Ghazālī at a later date, he too came to appreciate the hollowness of what he sought. The law courts where he sought distinction bestowed a reputation which was 'high in proportion to one's success in deceiving people'.[195]

Augustine would only finally break free from the doctrines of the Manichees when he learned 'to conceive of incorporeal reality'.[196] By developing, theologically, what MacDonald characterises as a doctrine of 'cosmological monism', Augustine was at last able to argue that 'since God is what truly *is*, Manichaean theological dualism must be false. There cannot be two independent divine principles.'[197]

Augustine proclaimed the supremacy of God's authority. Even if God commanded something that was contrary to a people's established laws or customs, they were obliged to do it.[198] God's ways may not be man's ways, but man's unquestioning obedience is always required. Augustine himself is the human paradigm of such Isaac-like obedience. He submitted to both sacerdotal and episcopal ordination when what he would really have liked was to embrace an eremitical or quasi-eremitical life.

For Augustine, there was also an obvious cascade of authority from God to both Church and text: the Bible is 'commended by the authority of your Catholic Church'.[199] Henry Chadwick notes how the problem of authority was centred in the arguments and debates which flared between the Manichees and the Catholics, and he also draws attention to the way in which Augustine believed that the truth could be gained by the parallel routes of authority and reason, the latter being Plato and the former being Christ.[200] However, Christ's authority is at the same time 'the highest reason. He is the very wisdom of God, identified with the Mind of Plotinus' supreme triad.'[201] Chadwick stresses how, for Augustine, the Bible was representative of 'the principle of authority ... the authority of Bible and Church rested on reciprocal support'.[202]

Not only did divine authority cascade from God to the institutional Church and the Text, but it could devolve further, in the human realm, both ecclesiastical and secular. Bishops were owed due obedience by other Christians because of the episcopal office.[203] In the secular field, Augustine admits that there can be merit in 'institutionalised force'.[204] He quotes approvingly *Romans* 13:1–8 in which it is stated that all are subject to 'higher authorities' whose ultimate source and confirmation is God Himself: 'Anyone who resists authority resists what God has established. But those who resist that, bring judgement on themselves.'[205]

However, Augustine was interested not so much in the forms that government should take as in the relationship between governor and governed. Some may need to exercise this authority by coercive means. This is the result of sin. Fallen man may need to be controlled by force, threat or coercion. It is clear that Augustine's preference is for a benevolent form of authority, the sort that a father or husband might exercise. Indeed, God is the arch-paradigm here.[206]

Augustine, then, is an upholder of authority in both the ecclesiastical and secular spheres. But any would-be authoritarianism – a grave temptation for any who hold episcopal office – is tempered by a tendency to mercy. He is willing, for example, to intercede with the secular authorities on behalf of Donatists who have murdered, and mutilated the bodies of, two Catholic priests.[207] In his letter to Marcellinus, brother of Apringius, Pro-Consul for Africa, Augustine begs that injustice should indeed be condemned but a common humanity should be noted and observed.[208] There should ideally be a symbiosis of justice and mercy: this, for Augustine, is the meaning and the framework of the proper exercise of authority. In *De Civitate Dei*, Augustine presents a paradigm for precisely this:

> This is where domestic peace starts, the ordered harmony about giving and obeying orders among those who live in the same house. For the orders are given by those who are concerned for the interests of others; thus the husband gives orders to the wife, parents to children, masters to servants. While those who are objects of this concern obey orders; for example, wives obey husbands, the children obey their parents, the servants their masters. But in the household of the just man who 'lives on the basis of faith' and who is still on pilgrimage, far from that Heavenly City, even those who give orders are the servants of those whom they appear to command. For they do not give orders because of a lust for domination but from a dutiful concern for the interests of others, not with pride in taking precedence over others, but with compassion in taking care of others.[209]

In an age of sects and heresies – Manichaeism, Pelagianism, Donatism – whose teachings, as Augustine knew from personal experience, could be particularly attractive, there was a profound need to maintain and respect the authority of the established Church. This is a *leitmotiv* of his work and is underlined in his numerous writings refuting the heretics of the day, and in his preaching, especially against the Donatists. After the June 411 Conference held in Carthage, the Commissioner Marcellinus, sent by the emperor, found in favour of Augustine's views and effectively sounded the death knell for Donatism in Africa.[210] The Conference was attended by both Catholic and Donatist bishops under the presidency of Marcellinus. Augustine's diplomacy and generosity won the day.[211]

Two aspects of the Conference are worthy of note: the interweaving of imperial, secular authority with ecclesiastical authority; and the fact that, although not a formal Council or Synod of the Church, Carthage conformed to the conciliar paradigm in its intention to resolve doctrinal and other ecclesiastical disputes.

Augustine lived through the sack of Rome by Alaric and the Goths in August AD 410; this event must have had a profound effect on him.[212] Pragmatically, Augustine as a Bishop had to deal with the perennial problem of a Church which was spiritually inhabiting a world that was overwhelmingly secular. It was 'the city of God in the city of this world'.[213]

Yet Augustine does not entirely write off the latter. After all, God had created it.[214] O'Meara is at pains to stress that Augustine has a generally positive attitude towards the secular states of Rome and Greece[215] even though Augustine acknowledges that the pagan gods could not, and did not, protect or save Rome.[216]

Augustine is a pragmatist who, perhaps because of his own spiritual wounds, is able to filter the language of authority and 'right doctrines' through his own peculiar, but powerful, scriptural and hortatory sieve without damage to anything except his own delicate conscence.[217]

2.3 *Readings: Christianity*

2.3.1 Reading the Phenomena of Christianity

Phenomenology may loosely, but lucidly, be described as the unadorned 'science of the Object'. We noted, earlier, useful definitions of the term as 'science of appearances or appearings', 'a theory of intentionality' and 'the study of "phenomena" in the sense of the ways in which things appear to us in different forms of conscious experience'.[218] We noted Heidegger's view that phenomenology was the gateway to ontology, and that the latter was only possible because of the former.[219] We surveyed, briefly, Husserl's terminological trinity of *epoché*, eidetic reduction and cognition.

Drawing together the threads, then, of what may be noted about the phenomena of Christianity, and employing the first Husserlian term of *epoché*, or refraining from subjective judgement or pronouncement on what is perceived – in other words, concentrating on 'what appears *qua* appearance' – we detect the existence of a Church which inhabits a universe of discourse comprising three distinct elements: it propounds a series of doctrinal propositions to its faithful; it deploys a series of validating sources or tools – scripture, tradition, magisterium; and it articulates the latter within a range of historico-religious roles and frameworks which may or may not be voluntarily embraced, and whose geographical locale or locus may vary from Rome to Avignon, or Jerusalem to Constantinople. Key factors include the roles of papacy and episcopacy, Synod and Ecumenical Church Council, the *filioque* controversy, the Crusades and the European Reformation, to name but a few.

Those phenomena which validate doctrine – scripture, tradition and magisterium – can be both sources and tools: they can be sources of the doctrines they propound, whether those be Christological, soteriological or Trinitarian, and they can be tools in that they serve to confirm what has been propounded, especially if the charism of infallibility is deployed. Some theological and methodological circularity may not be avoidable.

If we then put Christianity under the spotlight of eidetic reduction, and adapt the usage of the term slightly, we note how, for a Christian, obedience to God's authority and fidelity to his will, as portrayed in scripture and tradition and confirmed by magisterium, leads to 'right doctrines' and 'right order' whose essence, in turn, is salvation.

It is not mere word-play, therefore, to suggest that the essence of the proper observance of God's *authority*, and, indeed, that of man when properly delegated by God to him, is *soteriological.* Sin is epitomised by infidelity and disobedience, and the logical consequences are disorder, alienation and potential loss of salvation. For an Augustine, battling against the pounding waves of sects like Manichaeism and heresies like Donatism and Pelagianism, all of which threatened the lawful authority of both Church and state, the essence of any effective response had to be couched in severely eschatological and soteriological terms.

And if phenomenology is the gateway to ontology, then, from the perspective of Husserlian cognition and epistemology, we may ask two very simple yet difficult questions: what *is* the Christian Church and *how* is it constituted? The question is simply answered in terms of the numerous literal, metaphorical and mystical definitions which have been provided down the ages;[220] it becomes much more difficult when one takes into account the divisions within the Christian Church and the various inclusivist or exclusivist definitions of its various branches.

Furthermore, while it is useful to consider the phenomena of Christianity under the general heading of 'Church', it must always be recognised that the institutionalised Church, or Churches, by no means represent the entire body of Christian adherents. Indeed, the late 1960s saw a growing trend against institutionalised Churches in favour of Church Base Communities or Basic Christian Communities in the Third World and Europe.[221]

However, any consideration of Christianity as Church usually takes care to note that the Christian Church is both a divinely founded,[222] but humanly organised and run, community (*koinōnía*), as well as a historical structure and institution.[223] In terms of eidetic reduction then, and whether or not we refer to both 'institutional' and 'house' Churches, it is clear that a primary and *essential* sense or nature of 'Church' is *koinōnía*,[224] a word defined by the classical dictionaries as 'communion, association, partnership, fellowship'.[225]

Yet the eidetic reduction does not simply rest with the primary definition of 'Church' as 'community'. Tillard draws attention to the fact that

> the introduction to the final report (1981) of ARCIC [Anglican–Roman Catholic International Commission] I affirmed that reference to koinonia is fundamental to all reflection on the nature of the church and that, in consequence, it is the base on which the whole report rest ... [The latter] ... proceeded to demonstrate how the eucharist, episcope ... and primacy are all to be understood in terms of koinonia.[226]

In view of the profound importance of this further series of essential elements it is worth turning to the actual ARCIC document for further illumination. In the Introduction to *The Final Report* issued by ARCIC in September 1981, the authors reflect that the subjects which they were asked to study all deal with the actual 'nature of the Church' and that the idea of *koinōnía* (here translated as 'communion') lies at the heart of all that they have to say.[227] Although they note that the New Testament does not equate 'Church' with *koinōnía*, they believe that it is the term which most appropriately encapsulates the mystery behind the images of the Church in the Gospels.[228] There is a developing semiotics of *koinōnía* perceptible in the various ARCIC statements, and these will be adumbrated at greater length in the next section. Suffice it to say here that the Christian eucharist is conceived as the 'effectual' *sign of koinōnía*, the episcopacy has only one function and that is to *serve* the community, *koinōnía*, and primacy is perceived as the office which links the community and provides a powerful focus for it. 'Effectual sign', service and link: these are all semiotic indicators of, or attached to, eucharist, episcopacy and primacy, whose single eidetic reduction, purpose and focus is *koinōnía*. While the theological, structural and sacramental content and context will differ, comparisons are inevitably to be made here with the whole Islamic concept of the *umma*,[229] the community of worldwide believers.

2.3.2 Reading the Signs of Christianity

It is a truism that Christianity is a world of signs. In Roman Catholic Christianity, it is believed to be founded upon seven classical signs in its sacramental theology. The very definition of sacrament is semiotic in structure and orientation, as even the most elementary statement drawn from *The Penny Catechism* shows:

> Q. *What is a Sacrament?*
> A. A Sacrament is *an outward sign of inward grace*, ordained by Jesus Christ, by which grace is given to our souls.[230]

Other, more sophisticated, statements of the same theme support this basic definition:

> Q. What is a sacrament?
> A. A sacrament is a *sacred sign by which we worship* God, his love is revealed to us and his saving work accomplished in us. In the sacraments God shows us what he does and does what he shows us.[231]
>
> - The sacraments are *perceptible signs* (words and actions) accessible to our human nature. By the action of Christ and the power of the Holy Spirit they make present efficaciously the grace that they signify.[232]

Reminding us that the Latin *sacramentum* renders the Greek *mustḗrion*, Ludwig Ott sets out a variety of meanings of 'sacrament' which include secret (*mysterium*), 'sign, symbol, type of a sacred mystery'.[233] He reminds us, too, of Augustine's definition in *De Civitate Dei*, x, 5: '*Sacramentum, id est sacrum signum*'.[234] Ott continues:

> The Sacraments are neither purely natural signs, as a natural action can designate a supernatural effect only on the ground of the positive ordinance of God, nor purely artificial or conventional signs, as according to their inner composition, they are appropriate for vividly depicting inward grace. They are not merely speculative or theoretical signs, but efficacious or practical signs as they not only indicate the inner sanctification, but also effect it.[235]

In a few words, a sacrament effects what it signifies.[236] Furthermore, they function or act *ex opere operato* (i.e. by the very fact that they are undertaken) regardless of the virtue of either recipient or celebrant.[237]

It is noteworthy in Islam how the Qur'ān stresses the presence of God's signs in the World: *Sa nurīhim āyātinā fī 'l-āfāq wa fī anfusihim* (Q.41:53: 'We will show them Our signs on the horizons and in themselves'). A modern Christian catechism's disquisition on the sacramental economy similarly notes that human beings cherish signs and symbols which may facilitate the expression and perception of 'spiritual realities'. And just as each person uses signs and symbols for his or her communication with a fellow human being, so these are useful for communication with God, especially with regard to the human signs and symbols embedded in the liturgical worship of God. Sacramental signs confirm the antique signs of the Old Covenant as well as the later Christological signs articulated as part of the New.[238]

Hans Urs Von Balthasar stresses that the form of Jesus can only be understood within the historical contexts of time and space. He cannot, and should not, be divorced from either.[239] He brought 'manifest signs (*sēmeia*) of his divine power' as well as powerful verbal clues[240] which were all signalled or articulated for the Christian within a particular historical framework.

Robert Corrington reminds us that 'signs do not exist in a vacuum ... signs always have one or more contexts within which they obtain'.[241] Christ's signs for the Christian begin in a historic present – or, better, are *perceived* in a historic present – and stretch to infinity. They are articulated in Palestine and are relevant to a universe.

Of course, the Christian sacraments, whether counted as two or seven,[242] do not constitute the *entire* semiotic economy of Christianity, but they are a most powerful part of it.[243] How does all this link to a broader semiotic picture? The sacrament of the Eucharist, accepted as sacrament by both the Catholic and Protestant Churches (though interpreted differently), is the key.

Earlier, we examined the Christian Church in terms of *koinōnía*. What we can stress here now is that it is, above all, in the majority and diversity of its branches, a Eucharistic *koinōnía*.[244] There is thus an umbilical link between the Church as objective phenomenon and as a body of signs. And if, phenomenologically and semiotically, the Christian Church is articulated in terms of community, then the question of who exercises legitimate authority over that community becomes paramount – as we saw in our discussions of Arius and Augustine. This point is underlined by a modern *Catechism*:

> Since he has the ministry of Peter in the Church, the Pope is associated with every celebration of the Eucharist, wherein he is named as *the sign* and servant of the unity of the universal Church.[245]

The Eucharist today is held up by the Catholic Church as a symbol of unity to be aspired towards by others; it may only be received by its own faithful (except in certain specified cases of grave need), and it is denied to others on principle.[246] Thus the modern phenomenon that is divided Christianity embraces an aspirational unity whose semiotic indicators include Eucharist, *koinōnía* and, sometimes, a desire for a greater shared authority. Yet the separate, and separated, celebrations of the Eucharist are nonetheless regarded as witnesses and signs by both Anglicanism and Roman Catholicism:

> The Sacramental nature of the Church as sign, instrument, and foretaste of communion is especially manifest in the common celebration of the eucharist. Here, celebrating the memorial of the Lord and partaking of His body and blood, the Church points to the origin of its communion in Christ, himself in communion with the Father; it experiences that communion in a visible fellowship; it anticipates the fullness of the communion in the Kingdom; it is sent out to realise, manifest and extend that communion in the world.[247]

It will not go unnoticed that some of the issues which divide the Sunnī–Shīʿite Muslim world are those of authority, leadership (*khilāfa*) and mutual acceptance of each other's *umma*.

A sacrament, then, 'is both sign and instrument'. And 'the [Christian] Church as *koinonia* requires visible expression , because it is intended to be the "sacrament" of God's saving work'.[248] We have demonstrated the semiotic thread which links sacrament, authority and *koinōnía*. How does this marry with modern semiotic theory?

We surveyed earlier some modern definitions of semiotics and semiology and identified a plethora ranging from 'the study of patterned human behaviour in communication in all its modes' 'the study of sign and symbol systems' and 'the analysis of signs or the study of the functioning of sign systems'[249] to Umberto Eco's desire 'to explain every case of sign-function in terms of underlying systems of elements mutually correlated by one or more codes'. For him, a general theory of semiotics meant 'a theory of codes' and 'a theory of sign production'.[250]

If we take, then, Christianity, with the Church as its formal edifice or articulation, or, to use Eco's phrase, 'universe of signification',[251] deliberately constructed as such by Jesus Christ on the foundations of the sacraments,[252] then we find ourselves studying an interlocking universe of signs whose constituent parts include, as we have noted, the concepts of authority, *koinōnía* and *mysterium/sacramentum* which point 'heavenwards' to the Divine and 'earthwards' to the human. *Sacramentum* becomes a mediate link as well as a primary, efficacious *signum*. And as Augustine reminded us earlier, *sacramentum* is not just *signum* but *sacrum signum*.[253]

Hence it is to the arena of the sacred that we will now turn, remaining aware at the same time of the applicability of the words of the protagonist of Eco's novel, *The Name of the Rose*, Brother William of Baskerville, to the New Testament itself: 'A book is made up of signs that speak of other signs, which in their turn speak of things'.[254]

2.3.3 Reading the Sacred in Christianity

The word *sacred* is a commonplace in Christianity. It infuses both language and worship itself. In Catholic Christianity, a cult of worship of the Sacred Heart of Jesus developed which had its origins in mediaeval German mysticism and which was fiercely attacked by the Jansenists.[255] In words which, from the comparative perspective though not of course in terms of content, seem to echo the mediaeval Islamic debates about the nature and union of the attributes of God – were they an identical, intrinsic and essential aspect of the Deity or separate in some respect?[256]

– Pope Pius VI (reg. 1775–99) responded to the Jansenists: he underlined the utter sacredness of the Heart of Jesus, declaring that it was 'not separated or dissolved from the Godhead' (*cum separatione vel praecisione a divinitate*) but rather adored as 'the heart of the Person of the Word, with which it is inseparably united' (*cor personae Verbi, cui inseparabiliter unitum est*).[257]

A casual glance at one of the documents of the Second Vatican Council, *Gravissimum Educationis* (The Declaration on Christian Education), makes reference to 'the sacred ecumenical Council',[258] links 'the sacred sciences' and 'sacred learning' and 'sacred revelation' in one passage[259] and concludes with reference to 'the sacred Synod'.[260] Elsewhere, it is a commonplace to refer to 'Sacred Tradition and Sacred Scripture'.[261] It is clear from all this that the word 'sacred' is susceptible of a great variety of applications.

A simple dictionary definition of 'sacred' has the following: 'Consecrated or held especially acceptable *to* a deity, dedicated or reserved or appropriated *to* some person or purpose; made holy by religious association, hallowed'.[262]

Examining the phenomena of world religions, Ninian Smart, in his magisterial volume *Dimensions of the Sacred: An Anatomy of the World's Beliefs* (1996), identifies a total of nine such dimensions: (1) the ritual or practical; (2) the doctrinal or philosophical; (3) the mythic or narrative; (4) the experiential or emotional; (5) the ethical or legal; (6) the organisational or social; (7) the material or artistic; (8) the political; and (9) the economic.[263] These categories, or dimensions as Smart preferred to call them, have as their natural focus and 'object' of worship (formal or informal, private or public) 'a holy, numinous Being' who is perceived to be the sole fount of holiness and, thus, salvation itself.[264] The role of formal worship is inextricably bound up with the Sacred; indeed, changes to long-standing modes of formal worship in one Christian tradition or another have evoked in recent times a widespread fear of losing that which is perceived to be Sacred/sacred, either in the worship or in the Divine 'Object' of worship Itself.[265]

Ninian Smart concludes his 'taxonomy of the sacred'[266] by noting that, while some aspects of the sacred continue to flourish, others (for example, the ritual aspect) are fading away, having lost their old powers to attract or compel. But Smart's is essentially a message of hope: those fading sacred dimensions are being replaced by other, stronger ones, among which he notes the experiential.[267]

Ninian Smart's work both complements that of Mircea Eliade and illustrates the great diversity of emphases among scholars in the general field of Religious Studies. Eliade's own preferred *leitmotivs* which we noted earlier were threefold: the idea of the sacred, the idea of death and resurrection, and the way in which man has degenerated spiritually over the course of history. For Eliade, the sacred was that which was not profane, although it manifested itself in a profane world. However, he perceived that there was a very real danger of degradation of the sacred.

It is not difficult to apply these concepts to some of the selected details which we viewed earlier of the phenomenon which is Christianity. This claims to be a divinely founded institution[268] yet it has proved down the centuries to be only too capable of corruption and degradation. Under the iron rod of fallibility, the sacred may be transmuted into the profane, whether epitomised in a licentious Borgia pope,[269] a politically weak Pope,[270] a modern paedophile scandal[271] or a mediaeval romance such as that of Heloise and Abelard.[272] The world of late antiquity, inhabited by an Arius or an Augustine, was no more naturally inclined to moral or other perfection *as a whole* than is the secular world inhabited by contemporary Christianity. Certainly, then as now, it had its sacred spaces and places.[273] Then as now, it had its voids and moral vacuums. John O'Meara neatly notes that 'the practical problem with which Augustine had to deal was the problem of a spiritual Church in a secular world: the city of God in the city of this world'.[274]

Earlier, he observed:

> And yet, when Augustine was writing the *City of God*, his confident reading of the future cannot have seemed so justified to many of his contemporaries as it is to us now. The prospects of Christianity in the first quarter of the fifth century may have seemed bright, but we tend to forget that until that time the Church's history had been one, for the most part, of bare toleration and frequent persecution. Within Augustine's own lifetime there had been the pagan reaction under Julian the Apostate (361–363 A.D.). Even in the fifth century pagans had not lost all countenance. Again, the decline of the powerful and closely integrated Empire of Rome, evident to all and admitted by Augustine, must have struck its citizens with a chill as great as that which affects in our day the loosely and vaguely associated West.[275]

This Eliadean motif, where the Profane is the opposite or downside (or even logical successor, in terms of degradation or degeneration) of the Sacred will strike a powerful comparative chord in any student of the great North African historian and proto-sociologist Ibn Khaldūn (1332–1406), with his cyclical theory of history according to which, 'simplistically and crudely [stated], a nomad tribe struggles to achieve urban power, becomes corrupt and luxurious after a few generations having achieved that power, and is in turn overthrown by a rising and less effete tribe'.[276] Sacred authority, or authority which should be held as sacred, becomes degraded, corrupt and profane, and a worthier, purer, more 'sacred' power rises to prominence.

As Ibn Khaldūn himself put it:

> The (passing) days get the upper hand over the original group (in power). Their prowess disappears as the result of senility. (The duties of) the dynasty make them soft. Time feasts on them, as their energy is exhausted by well-being and their vigour drained by the nature of luxury … At that moment, the group feeling [*'aṣabiyya*] of other people (within the same nation) is strong … Their superiority is recognized, and, therefore, no one disputes (their claim to royal authority). They seize power.[277]

Other exemplars of this sort of paradigm are to be discovered in Western Christian Church history: the sack of Rome by imperial troops on 6 May 1527 and the subsequent flight of Pope Clement VII (reg. 1523–34) to the Castel Sant'Angelo and then Orvieto, placed the papacy at the feet of the Emperor Charles V: 'As for the city, the sack was rightly seen at the time as the end of a great age. The Rome of the Renaissance was no more.'[278] Thus did a sacred city yield to a profane invasion; and a series of sometimes weak and sometimes licentious papal despots,[279] representatives *par excellence* of the Sacred on earth – albeit armed and endowed with much land and wealth – capitulate in the face of secular armed might. The arena of the Sacred became that of the Profane.

Of course, one should not paint too stark or total a contrast between these two categories in an effort to fit an elemental Eliadean paradigm. The Sacred and the Profane mingled freely in the papal courts long before the 1527 Sack of Rome, in terms of licence, wealth, lands, armies and power.[280] What the Sack of Rome can do, however, is provide the historian with useful, albeit flawed, evidence of an epistemic break, to use a phrase beloved of Michel Foucault.

2.4 Islam: Sources of Authority and Right Doctrines

We stressed earlier that obedience to God's authority and man's lawful, God-given authority are fundamental *leitmotivs* in both Islam and Christianity. For the Muslim, the text of the Qur'ān is the divine *fons et origo* of doctrine suppemented by that part of the ḥadīth literature which is deemed to be wholly reliable. The sacred text of the Qur'ān is considered to be utterly incomparable and cannot be duplicated.[281] The text, and the God from whom it emanates (not in a Neoplatonic sense!) are eminently worthy of obedience if only because of the Deity's Creator-Lordship over the entire universe. As al-Ṭabarī put it: 'The whole of creation yields in obedience to Him, whether willingly or by force.'[282]

This Qur'ān is lauded by al-Ṭabarī as 'a brilliant light in the obscurity of ignorance, a lustrous star in the twilight of uncertainty, a sure guide against wandering in the ways of confusion, and a leader on the paths to salvation and truth'.[283] Obedience to God and His text is therefore a *sine qua non* for any Muslim who wishes to travel the *ṣirāṭ al-mustaqīm*, or straight path. And the Qur'ānic paradigm of obedience assumes a sharp and dramatic focus when we briefly consider examples of those who obeyed and those who disobeyed.

Ibrāhīm must rank as one of the foremost in the first category. He is willing to sacrifice his son Ismā'īl at God's command[284] and shows himself obedient to God in all things.[285] Iblīs, of course, is the arch-exemplar and prototype of all who disobey.[286] Al-Ṭabarī portrays Iblīs as a paradigm of those who refuse to give their obedience to God, like the Jews in Medina who refused to accept Muḥammad's prophethood.[287]

This fundamental Qur'ānic paradigm of obedience to the will of God may be, and has been, articulated in a multitude of ways. Here, we will examine it under the two headings of *theoretics* and *pragmatics*. The first will focus on four sets of Qur'ānic verses which may be characterised severally (but certainly not exclusively) as an injunction, a prescription, an invitation and a call to arms; the second will survey the pragmatics of Abū 'l-Ḥasan al-Māwardī (974–1058) as enshrined in his *magnum opus*, *al-Aḥkām al-Sulṭāniyya* (*The Rules of Government*).

Theoretics. The *injunction* is the well-known call to obedience enshrined in the Qur'ān:

> O ye who believe!
> Obey God, and obey the Apostle,

And those charged
With authority among you.

Yā ayyuhā 'llathīna āmanū:
Aṭī'ū Allāh wa aṭī'ū al-Rasūl
wa ulī al-amr minkum.[288]

The dictionary definition of *ulū 'l-amr* is 'rulers, leaders'.[289] Yusuf Ali defines the term as 'those charged with authority or responsibility or decision, or the settlement of affairs'.[290] He draws attention to the idea that, for the Muslim, 'all ultimate authority rests in God. Men of God derive their authority from him.'[291] He further remarks that, in view of the classical Islamic belief that there is no real divide between the sacred and the profane, governments should be 'imbued with righteousness'. Since such governments are *in loco Imām*, their authority merits respect and obedience.[292]

The *prescription* commands Muslims to ensure that the reign of good predominates and that evil is proscribed. Literally, there is to be a situation where 'right is commanded and wrong is forbidden': *Al-amr bi 'l-ma'rūf wa 'l-nahy 'an al-munkar.* Those who abide by this dictum are the believers in God and the Day of Judgement[293] as well as those who follow Muḥammad.[294] They rank as the best *umma* (*khayr umma*).[295] In the Qur'ān, the Aesop-like figure Luqmān advises his son to command what is good and forbid evil in the same breath as he enjoins the practice of the Islamic prayer.[296] *Al-amr bi 'l-ma'rūf* is an important characteristic of the united or unified *umma.*[297] Happiness will be their lot.[298]

As we can see, there is a variety of Qur'ānic verses, together with a variety of *tafāsīr*, which deals with the topic of *al-amr bi 'l-ma'rūf.*[299] Professor Michael Cook, in his magisterial and wide-ranging volume on the subject, observes:

> [The exegetes'] reading of scripture tends to be informed by an understanding of forbidding wrong which cannot be derived directly from the verses themselves. They understand the duty primarily as one to be performed by individual believers to each other, and not, say, by the community as a whole towards the world at large; and they see its scope as in the first instance response to specific misdeeds, rather than vague and general ethical affirmation ... The overall effect is to insert the duty into the daily life of the community in a far more concrete way than the Koran, read as naked scripture, would seem to require.[300]

Custom and practice, then, have sanctioned the obligation to command the doing of good and the prohibiting of evil far more than may have been intended by the original Qur'ānic verses which deploy the notion. The duty of *al-amr bi 'l-ma'rūf* has become 'a moral imperative to Muslims', but exactly how it should be implemented has been a matter of debate among the jurisprudents and theologians for numerous generations.[301] It must be clear, for example, that one's obligation to undertake *al-amr bi 'l-ma'rūf* has to be limited or defined by one's own knowledge and experience of what is good and evil, as well as one's capacity for such things.[302]

The third of our four selected themes from the domain of Qur'ānic theoretics, which serve to highlight the sources of authority and right doctrines in Islam, is *invitation*. This is embedded within the framework of one of Islam's most famous Qur'ānic *Prayer-Sūras*, *Sūrat al-Fātiḥa*, 'The Opening Chapter': Allāh is invited to show mankind the correct path to travel in life:

> Show us the straight way
> *Ihdinā al-ṣirāṭ al-mustaqīm*.[303]

Many centuries' worth of ink and intellectual labour have been expended by the exegetes on this short verse, and this will not be repeated here. We note, however, that, for the Muslim, God has already shown the *ṣirāṭ al-mustaqīm* in the form of the guidance provided by a *Qur'ān mubīn*.[304] Man therefore has no excuse for rejecting God's supreme authority and the guidance encapsulated in the sacred text. For the Muslim, the *ṣirāṭ* represents that which is 'orthodox' or, better, 'mainstream' and, therefore, necessarily true. And, while couched here as a metaphor, this *ṣirāṭ al-mustaqīm* has a very real physical opposite which is the bridge over the pit of Hell, the *ṣirāṭ al-Jaḥīm*.[305]

Abdel Haleem prefers to describe Q.1:6, which we have discussed above, in terms of *petition* rather than invitation, and this puts an equally acceptable gloss on the verse.[306] He reminds us that the *Fātiḥa* contains the Essence of the Qur'ān and that 'the request ,"Guide us to the right way" in this first *sūra* is answered immediately at the beginning of the second: "This is the book, there is no doubt about it, a guide for all the God-conscious" (2:2)'.[307]

With the Shī'a, of course, our three themes of injunction (key motif: *ulū 'l-amr*), prescription (key motif: *al-amr bi 'l-ma'rūf*) and invitation (key motif: *al-ṣirāṭ al-mustaqīm*) neatly combine in the single persons of the Imāms and their descendants. One text among a multitude is chosen here to illustrate this. In the *Kitāb al-Munāẓarāṭ* (*The Book of Discussions*) of Ibn al-Haytham, a ninth–tenth-century scholar and Ismā'īlī *dā'ī* from Qayrawān, such figures are lauded as having jurisdiction over affairs (*mālik umūrinā*) and are characterised, *soteriologically*, as the elongated thread or rope (*al-ḥabl al-mamdūd*) to which followers of the Imām are urged to cleave.[308] The latter image discloses an interesting complement to the many connotations of the classical *ṣirāṭ*. Unsurprisingly, the Imāms are endowed with *hudā* (right guidance);[309] tendentiously, Q.15:41, which reads *Qāla hādhā ṣirāṭ^{un} 'alayya mustaqīm^{un}* (and has been translated variously as 'Said He, "This is for Me a straight path"' (Arberry)[310] and '(God) said :"This (Way of My sincere servants) is Indeed a Way that leads straight to Me"' (Yusuf Ali)[311]), is provided by one of the protagonists in *Kitāb al-Munāẓarāt* with the sense of 'This is the straight path of 'Alī'.[312] His interlocutor is not slow to point out that the speaker has, in effect, fallen off the *ṣirāṭ al-mustaqīm* as far as Arabic grammar is concerned![313]

Finally, the Imāms and their descendants carry out the duty of *al-amr bi 'l-ma'rūf* by righting what has become corrupt (*ṣalāḥ mā qad fasada*) and uncovering what had been concealed (*kashf mā 'statara*).[314] Of course, the Imām also has the duty to fight in defence or advancement of the faith, and this will bring us neatly in a moment to the fourth and last of our Qur'ānic themes of obedience and authority, *the call to arms*. From the Shī'ite perspective, Ibn al-Haytham puts it thus:

[The son of the Imām = the future Fāṭimid Caliph al-Manṣūr (reg. 946–53)] with those are rightly guided fought against those who went astray until God made the religion mighty.[315]

Wa aṭfa'a nīrānahum wa jāhada man ḍalla bi-man 'htadā ḥattā a 'azza Allāh al-dīn.[316]

The emphasis in all these areas is very much on the sublime figure of the Imām. It would be for others such as the great Sunnī theologian and *ṣūfī*, Abū Ḥāmid al-Ghazālī (1058–1111), to remind the body politic of Islam that an infallible Imām was unnecessary.[317] The Qur'ān and Sunna sufficed.[318] And Muḥammad was the only real infallible teacher (*mu'allimunā al-ma'ṣūm (huwa) Muḥammad*).[319]

In effect, al-Ghazālī steers his interlocutor away from the idea of an infallible Imām towards that of an infallible Prophet (Muḥammad) and Text (the Qur'ān). And since Muḥammad is the vehicle, not the author, of textuality in mainstream Islam, we can say that here the move is away from the cult of person (as enshrined in the concept of the infallible Shī'ite Imām) to the cult of the Text. For the Sunnī Muslim, the Text is the Imām and the Imām is the Text.[320]

Fourth of our four themes from the domain of Qur'ānic (i.e. textual) theoretics (chosen to highlight the sources of authority and right doctrines in Islam) is *the call to arms*. This is, in effect, the Lesser *Jihād*, as opposed to the Greater *Jihād* which refers to man's perennial struggle against the sinful inclinations of his own soul.[321] The second edition of *The Encyclopaedia of Islam* provides the following thumbnail definition:

In law, according to general doctrine and in historical tradition, the *djihād* [*sic*] consists of military action with the object of the expansion of Islam and, if need be, of its defence.[322]

A first glance at the primary Arabic sources shows a diversity of confusing and conflicting views. Al-Nawawī, for example, cites Muḥammad as saying that he had been ordered to fight others (lit. *al-nās*, the people) until they proclaimed the *shahāda* that there was no god but God and that Muḥammad was His *Rasūl*.[323] Tyan identifies a four-stage developmnt in the Qur'ānic doctrine of *jihād* and war, with the later verses abrogating the earlier ones.[324] He notes the view of Sufyān al-Thawrī (born in AD 715), later adopted by Abū 'Uthmān 'Amr b. Baḥr al-Jāḥiẓ (776–868/9), that only *defensive jihād* was obligatory and that *offensive jihād* was merely recommended.[325] Finally, he reminds us that, for the Shī'a in the absence of the Imām, who is the lawful authority for the declaration of war, *jihād* should be suspended until such time as the Imām or a delegate appointed by him, reappeared.[326]

Vaunting the merits of jihād in his *Muwaṭṭa'*, Mālik b. Anas (716–95) wrote:

Yahya related to me from Malik from Yahya ibn Sa'id from Abu Salih as-Samman from Abu Hurayra that the Messenger of Allah, may Allah bless him and grant him peace, said, 'Had I not been concerned for my community, I would have liked never to stay behind a raiding party going out in the way of Allah. However, I do not have the means to carry them to it, nor can they

> find for themselves anything on which to ride out and it is grievous for them to have to stay behind from me. I would like to fight in the way of Allah and be killed, then brought to life so I could be killed and then brought to life so I could be killed.[327]

Overshadowing all such statements, of course, is the Qur'ānic injunction in Q.2:256 that there should be no force or compulsion in religion (*lā ikrāha fi 'l-dīn*). It is the Qur'ān that is one of the primary sources for the Islamic doctrine of war and peace.[328]

Abdel Haleem maintains that 'a thorough survey of the relevant verses of the Qur'ān shows that it is *consistent* throughout with regard to [its] rulings on the justification of war, and its conduct, termination and consequences'[329] even without recourse to the principle of abrogation (*naskh*).[330] He tries to show that a truly Islamic Just War theory may be derived from the sacred text, comparable to the classical Western paradigm in which such concepts as 'Righteous Intention', 'Discrimination and Proportionality', 'Cessation of Hostilities', and 'Humanitarian Intervention' all play a vital role.[331]

Finally, Abdel Haleem provides an eirenic *tafsīr* of the notorious 'Sword Verse' which classical *tafsīr* regarded as abrogating all previously revealed verses dealing with conflict between Islam and non-Muslims.[332] He notes that this verse is frequently taken out of context:

> But when the forbidden months
> Are past, then fight and slay
> The Pagans [*al-mushrikīn*] wherever ye find them. (Q.9:5)

He holds that the phrase about slaying the pagans, or killing the polytheists as he puts it, is often isolated by scholars in the West as representative of *the* attitude of Islam towards *jihād* and war. But to suggest this is to decontextualise 'a small part of a sentencec'.[333] The passage is directed at the contemporary polytheism with which the Prophet had to contend – in particular, those who broke agreements or instigated warfare against Islam.[334]

It is clear from Abdel Haleem's remarks that those in the West and the East who would establish an Islamic theory of war or *jihād* on the basis of this so-called 'Sword verse', and who maintain that this verse should abrogate all its predecessors in a bid to apply it to the modern age, have forgotten the fundamental concept of *asbāb al-nuzūl* (the reasons for revelation). That said, there are still many in the modern world who choose to endow this verse with the broadest of semantic ranges, thereby ensuring that *their* interpretation will provide dynamism for a variety of internal or external agendas.[335]

In sum, the fourth of our textual theoretics, the call to arms, drawn from the Qur'ān, requires interpretation, perspicacious application and recognition of context. The general 'call to arms' may indeed be an obligation of a kind, on an individual or a whole Islamic community, a *fard 'ayn* or a *fard kifāya*, to use the technical terminology[336] but that was never a dispensation from careful exegesis or judicious *ijtihād*.[337] The fundamental Qur'ānic theoretics of Q.2:256 and Q.9:5 may be reconciled by informed *tafsīr* and disclosed as two equal sides of the same coin of *the call to arms*.

It is also salutary at this point in our discussion to bear in mind the warning issued by Professor Fred M. Donner. He believes that we still know too little of the early texts, legal and theological, to establish a definitive canon of Islamic warfare texts. It is still difficult to say with precision who influenced whom. And in any case, he believes, we should not formulate a definitive 'Islamic' view purely from the available theological and juridical evidence. Attitudes to war, in Islam as elsewhere, are shaped by a huge and diverse range of factors.[338]

Finally, as Donner succinctly puts it: 'Deciding whether the Qur'ān actually condones offensive war for the faith, or only defensive war, is really left to the judgement of the exegete'.[339]

Pragmatics. By way of contrast – but not exclusive contrast – we move now to a major illustration from the Islamic Middle Ages of *how* Islamic authority and right doctrines were supposed to be discerned and implemented. The following section will survey the renowned corpus of 'Mirrors for Princes' in Arabic, which is the *Aḥkām al-Sulṭāniyya* (*The Rules of Government*) by Abū 'l-Ḥasan al-Māwardī.

Taking the headings deployed above in the Qur'ānic theoretics sectiom – *injunction* (obedience to rulers), *prescription* (commanding the good), *invitation* (showing the correct path)and *call to arms* (*jihād*) – we will survey briefly *how* al-Māwardī believed that these four *topoi* should be pursued in practice. As with the fourfold Qur'ānic theoretics, this is certainly not intended to be an all-embracing survey either of the pragmatics of authority and right doctrines in Islam or of the total corpus of al-Māwardī himself; it is simply intended as a gateway, one of many possible gateways, useful for comparative purposes, to a complex area.

It is al-Māwardī's *Kitāb al-Aḥkām al-Sulṭāniyya* which has established his reputation in the West. The book has been much valued as 'a classic work of public law'.[340] Gibb observed that 'it has been generally accepted as the most authoritative exposition of the Sunni Islamic political theory'.[341] Modern Muslim scholars have been equally complimentary: for example, Muhammad Qamaruddin Khan of the University of the Panjab in Lahore characterised the political theory section as 'the first attempt in Muslim history to evolve a comprehensive theory of the State, ... [which] has left an enduring influence on the course of Muslim political thought up to our own day'.[342] He concludes that

> al-Mawardi's great contribution to political thought was that he gave a detailed account of the administrative machinery of the government of his time and in formulating his political theory he took full cognizance of historical facts and, unlike the jurists and the scholastics, did not indulge in empty speculation.[343]

Furthermore, reason and revelation were considered to overlap rather than to be 'mutually exclusive'.[344]

Al-Māwardī's theories are explained by the spotlight of history and written in realistic response to it.[345] Fully aware that the reputation of the *khilāfa* (Caliphate) is at rock bottom, he proposes, as a legal *mujtahid*,[346] a theory of executive power which, nonetheless, establishes the Caliph as its linchpin.[347] And it is a theory of power specifically directed 'in an attempt to assert the authority of the Abbasid caliphs against the Buwaihid emirs who were in effective control of their state'.[348]

For al-Māwardī, *obedience to the ruler* will, or should, derive, or flow from, right choice of ruler, right qualifications held by that ruler, and the right practice and implementation of duties which are expected from that executive. Those in authority (*wulāt al-umūr*) have been divinely empowered to maximise the fruits of what has been foreordained;[349] the primary engine of that is the office of Imāmate.[350]

This leader whom God has given to His *umma* is a logical successor or substitute for the prophets previously sent to mankind by God,[351] and al-Māwardī stresses this again at the very beginning of his first chapter, which is entitled *'Aqd al-Imāma* (*The Contract of Imāmate*). He says that 'the Imāmate has been established to succeed prophethood as a device whereby the Faith (*al-dīn*) is guarded and the world (*al-dunyā*) is governed'.[352] Here, then, at the very heart of the classical antithesis of *dīn* and *dunyā* is the political locus for stability and right order in matters both religious and temporal. Al-Māwardī cites a group of jurisprudents who hold that men naturally accept leaders who are just and have the capacity for arbitration.[353] It is not long before our author is citing the key Qur'ānic text of Q.4:59, which insists that believers should obey God, His Prophet and those in authority.[354]

Of course, the Imām must be properly chosen by well-qualified electors and fulfil certain specific conditions. These criteria are clearly delineated by al-Māwardī.[355] In particular, the duly chosen Imām must be just, knowledgeable, able to hear, speak and see, sound in wind and limb, endowed with political and managerial perspicacity, brave to the extent of being able to undertake *jihād* and a member of the family of Quraysh.[356]

If all this occurs, and the Imām carries out, as best he may, a specific set of duties[357] – duties which Rosenthal points out 'are all religious, being directly related to God and likened to a walking in "the path of Allah"'[358] – then the conditions are ripe for the Caliph-Imām to demand obedience from his subjects.

Al-Māwardī puts it like this, succinctly but dogmatically, in his *al-Aḥkām al-Sulṭāniyya*:

> Provided that the Imām carries out what the *Umma* is entitled to [expect from him], as mentioned above, he will [also] discharge what Almighty God demands by right for and from [that] community. [In that event] the latter will owe him [the Imām] a twofold duty: *Obedience* (*al-ṭā'a*) and support (*al-nuṣra*) as long as his state remains unaltered [i.e. he continues to carry out his obligations to the *Umma*].[359]

Al-Māwardī goes on to underline those factors which will exclude one from holding the Imāmate,[360] the delegation of authority to *wazīrs*[361] and *amīrs*[362] and the post-facto 'encouragement of obedience' after an *amīr* has seized power unlawfully.[363]

A consideration of *how* the Māwardian Imām is to gain and compel obedience in the first place is not our concern here. What we want to stress is the fundamental point enshrined in al-Māwardī's text: provided that the Imām meets certain conditions and undertakes his set duties correctly, he is entitled to the obedience of the *umma*.

We turn now to the second in our select list of pragmatics, the *prescription* whereby good is to be commanded and evil is to be proscribed. Al-Māwardī institutionalises[364] this prescription, and its deployment, in the very practical office of *ḥisba* and its primary officer, the *muḥtasib*. These words have been variously translated into English. A *Popular Dictionary of Islam* provides the following concise definition and survey:

> *Muḥtasib* This term has been loosely translated as 'Market Inspector'. The *muḥtasib* was charged with the exercise of *ḥisba*, that is, making sure that the religious and moral injunctions of the Sharī'a were carried out, especially in the markets of Islamic cities and towns. The *muḥtasib* checked weights and measures and exercised a kind of quality control over cloth, brass etc. The concept and term do not appear in the Qur'ān.[365]

The second edition of *The Encyclopaedia of Islam* concurs:

> *Ḥisba* non-Ḳur'ānic term which is used to mean on the one hand the duty of every Muslim to 'promote good and forbid evil' and, on the other, the function of the person who is effectively entrusted in a town with the application of this rule in the supervision of moral behaviour and more particularly of the markets; this person entrusted with the *ḥisba* was called the *muḥtasib*. There seems to exist no text which states explicitly either the reason for the choice of this term or how the meanings mentioned above have arisen from the idea of 'calculation' or 'sufficiency' which is expressed by the root.[366]

The *Encyclopaedia* goes on to cite al-Māwardī's *Aḥkām* as an important juridical treatment of *ḥisba*,[367] and emphasises that, besides the formal office of *ḥisba*, every Muslim is obliged to command or promote good and proscribe evil 'by information and remonstrance, more particularly by legal intervention and, in special circumstances, in the case of absence of public authority, by constraint if he is able to do so'. But the ordinary Muslim may not unilaterally substitute himself for a lawfully constituted 'public authority'.[368]

In the formal office of the *Muḥtasib* himself, it seems that there may have been a merging of the Hellenistic *agoranomos* and the early Islamic *Ṣāḥib al-Sūq*.[369] However, whatever the general duties of *ḥisba* incumbent on every Muslim, or the specific ones assigned to the formally and legally appointed *Muḥtasib* himself, it is clear from a glance at the Arabic root of both words that the element of 'reckoning', both material and spiritual, was involved.[370] Of particular analogous interest are such classical meanings of *ḥisba* (plural *ḥisab*) as 'burying of the dead' and 'reward'.[371] Asadullah Yate's preferred translation for Chapter 20 of the *Aḥkām* is 'Public Order (hisbah)'.[372]

In the most magisterial treatment of *al-amr bi 'l-ma'rūf wa 'l-nahy 'an al-munkar* ever to be published in a Western language, Professor Michael Cook translates *muḥtasib* as 'censor' and *ḥisba* as 'censorship'.[373] This translation brings us closer semantically, if not in terms of real content, to the role of censor in secular society, as well as in faith traditions other than Islam. An example of the former is a film censor; an example of the latter would be the old Diocesan Censor in a Roman

Catholic diocese during the days of the Index of Forbidden Books.[374] This is not to suggest in any way a close harmony between the roles of the *muḥtasib* and the *censor librorum*, but merely some harmony of interest in moral order.

Slightly closer perhaps, is the example of a role drawn from the field of Roman Catholic Diocesan tribunals, that of the *Promoter of Justice*. Canon 1430 defines his role as follows: 'A promoter of justice is to be appointed in the diocese for penal cases, and for contentious cases in which the public good may be at stake. *The promoter is bound by office to safeguard the public good*.'[375]

The emphasis on *pro bono populorum* provides here a slghtly less tenuous link between Islamic *Muḥtasib* and Catholic Promoter of Justice; though the two are still quite different in *character* and *function*, they nonetheless both operate within the general field of public morality in a broad sense and are both governed by a religious perspective. The Promoters of Justice clearly have a quasi-judicial role and, while they may be clerical or lay, they should possess a JCL or JCD degree (i.e. a degree in Canon Law) and should be 'of proven prudence and zeal for justice'.[376]

Al-Māwardī's judge or *qāḍī*, however, differs in role and function from those of the *Muḥtasib*. For al-Māwardī, the activity of *ḥisba* is between that of the judiciary (*al-qaḍā'*) on the one hand and 'enquiry into wrongs' (literally, *aḥkām al-maẓālim*) on the other.[377] The latter function was exerised as an 'alternative jurisdiction' by an

> official known as the 'Master of Complaints' or *Ṣāḥib al-Maẓālim* ... Their duty was simply to resolve litigation in the most effective way and on the basis of the best evidence available. While the *qāḍīs* became identified as the servants of the Sharī'a law, the *maẓālim* officials were regarded essentially as the representatives of the political ruler's law. The distinction came dangerously close to a dichotomy between religious and secular jurisdiction ...[378]

Our final point of comparison, by way of highlighting the singular nature of the Islamic *Muḥtasib*, is the Dominican Inquisition, also called at various times the Holy Office. The latter 'was to dominate the Church's attempt to control error and disbelief'.[379] And indeed, whatever the very real differences between *ḥisba*, *qaḍā'* and the *maẓālim* courts, and between *muḥtasib*, *ṣāḥib al-maẓālim*, *qāḍī*, Dominican inquisitor, *censor librorum* and modern Promoter of Justice, there is no doubt that all represent in one form or another attempts at religious and/or secular control.

Cook stresses that in al-Māwardī's *Aḥkām* the author's 'primary concern' and interest is with the duties of the *Muḥtasib* rather than those of the individual Muslim, and he underlines how al-Māwardī adumbrates nine specific differences between the latter's duties and those of the official *Muḥtasib*.[380] Cook prefers not to dwell overlong on these differences; but, since the purpose of this section is to lay stress on the *pragmatics* of *al-amr bi 'l-ma'rūf*, as opposed to the *theoretics*, it is useful to refer to them, and enumerate them, here.

Al-Māwardī begins his chapter on *Ḥisba*, the twentieth and last chapter of the *Aḥkām*, with the classic quotation of Q.3:104 and follows immediately with the nine differences to which Cook refers:[381] they form a neat corpus of pragmatics for the execution of voluntary (individual) *ḥisba* and compulsory (official) *ḥisba*:

- The *Muḥtasib* acts by virtue of an official designation; the individual shares in a communal obligation. Here we have the classic legal distinction between *fard 'ayn* and *fard kifāya.*
- The *Muḥtasib* is obliged to act by virtue of his non-transferable office; individuals perform *ḥisba* voluntarily and may leave that performance to others.
- The office of *muḥtasib* is designed to be a focal point where people may seek assistance regarding unacceptable matters. The performer of voluntary *ḥisba* has no such function.
- The *Muḥtasib* must be responsive to those who seek his assistance; the layman has no such obligation.
- The *Muḥtasib* has a duty to seek out instances of evil, or occasions where good is no longer practised; the lay practioner of *ḥisba* has no such obligation.
- The *Muḥtasib* must have helpers; but it is not for the volunteer to appoint helpers.
- The *Muḥtasib* has some limited discretion to punish evil-doers; the voluntary practitioner of *ḥisba* has no such discretion.
- The *Muḥtasib* may receive payment from the Treasuy (*Bayt al-Māl*) for the practice of *ḥisba*, unlike the volunteer.
- Finally, according to al-Māwardī, the *Muḥtasib* may exercise *ijtihād* in matters of custom (*'urf*), though not in *sharī'a*; the lay practitioner of *ḥisba* has no such right.[382]

Moving now from *prescription* to *invitation*, we noted earlier that our rubric here was based on the invitation to God, encapsulated in verse 6 of the *Fātiḥa*, that He should show mankind 'the correct path' or 'the straight way' (*al-ṣirāṭ al-mustaqīm*) and guide the whole of humanity thereon. At the very end of *al-Ahkām al-Sulṭāniyya*, al-Māwardī asks God to grant success and help for the goals outlined in his volume.[383]

He has earlier shown that it is the duty of those in authority (*wulāt al-umūr*) – rulers, judges, *wazīrs*, *amīrs* – to share in the divine soteriological task, rooted in the *ṣirāṭ al-mustaqīm*, by their path of example which will 'maximise the fruits of what has been foreordained'.[384] Thus, bad example in the moral domain disqualifies a person from continuing as Imām.[385] The excellent qualities of the ideal *wazīr* (parallel, perhaps, in some respects to Plato's Philosopher-King?) are much vaunted by al-Māwardī.[386] An exemplar of such qualities provides a general benefit for all, but the *umma* will suffer from that *wazīr*'s deficiencies.[387]

The *qāḍī*, too, is required to provide an example of probity and impartiality.[388] In all these ways which, it has to be said, are often counsels of perfection, the just ruler, judge, *wazīr* or *amīr* will provide a perfect example and, by their actions, rulings and judgements, assist the *umma* to remain on the *ṣirāṭ al-mustaqīm*. Through such men of authority (*wulāt al-umūr*), God responds to man's request or invitation that he be shown the *ṣirāṭ al-mustaqīm*.

Finally, we turn to the fourth of our *topoi*, the *call to arms* or *jihād* in this selective overview of the pragmatics of al-Māwardī. Again our particular reference is to his most famous text, *al-Aḥkām al-Sulṭāniyya*. Al-Māwardī devotes two major chapters in his volume to the subject of warfare. They are entitled, specifically, 'Chapter Four: Authorising the Amīrate of Jihād' (lit. *Al-Bāb al-Rābiʿ fī Taqlīd al-Imāra ʿalā al-Jihād*)[389] and 'Chapter Five: The Governance of Wars Waged *Pro Bono Populorum*' (lit. *Al-Bāb al-Khāmis fī 'l-Wilāya ʿala Ḥurūb al-Maṣāliḥ*).[390]

In these two chapters, al-Māwardī identifies four different kinds of *jihād*: firstly, there is the fight against the *mushrikūn*;[391] then there are the other types of *jiḥad* or warfare to be waged against the *Ahl al-Ridda*, the *Ahl al-Baghy* and the *Muḥāribūn*.[392] Each of these will first be defined here, mainly according to al-Māwardī, before we note the 'word of war' used in its connection and, finally, discuss the pragmatics of al-Māwardī's opposition to them.

The *mushrikūn* are the easiest to define. They are the polytheists and al-Māwardī, in an early reference, takes it for granted that we know what a *mushrik* is without the need for formal defnition.[393] The *Ahl al-Ridda* are the apostates whom al-Māwardī defines as follows: they are those who renounce their Islamic faith having previously been considered to be Muslims in the eyes of the law, either by virtue of birth or conversion.[394]

The *Ahl al-Baghy* are those who do wrong by opposing the communal view (*ra'y al-jamāʿa*) with innovative doctrines of their own.[395] Finally, the *Muḥāribūn* are those 'belligerents' or 'warmongers' who take up arms, commit highway robbery, steal, kill and impede travellers (lit. *manʿ al-sābila*).[396]

How is each of these groups to be dealt with? Al-Māwardī specifically talks of 'fighting' (*qitāl*), though the fighting is clearly intended to be an aspect of an overall *jihād*, the latter word being used to introduce the groups.[397] The pragmatics are carefully articulated: among a multitude of other stipulations, our author emphasises that those *mushrikūn* who have not heard the call of Islam are not to be attacked before they have been thus called.[398] Apostates (*Ahl al-Ridda*) classically deserve the death penalty, in view of Muḥammad's pronouncements on the matter. The obdurate male or female apostate is to be executed.[399]

The 'Evil Dissenters' (*Ahl al-Baghy*) may be treated with some leniency according to the degree of their rebellion. Ultimately, they may be fought in order to compel their obedience.[400] However, al-Māwardī specifies a series of eight respects in which the fighting against such dissenters should differ from the fighting against polytheists and apostates.[401]

Finally, the *Muḥāribūn* are to be treated in accordance with Q.5:36, for which al-Māwardī cites several exegeses:

> The punishment of those
> Who wage war against God
> And His Apostle, and strive
> With might and main
> For mischief through the land
> Is: execution, or crucifixion,
> Or the cutting off of hands
> And feet from opposite sides,
> Or exile from the land.[402]

Al-Māwardī accepts a number of interpretations of this: those who are killers *and* thieves may be killed and crucified; the crucifixion should be for no more than three days, after which the corpse should be taken down from its cross. Killers who are not thieves can be killed but not crucified. Thieves who are not murderers will suffer amputation. Those who have wounded another will be subject to retaliation or the payment of blood money. With regard to the most minor of the crimes which come under al-Māwardī's heading of 'warmongering', namely intimidation or incitement, al-Māwardī specifies a rebuke or imprisonment. But no amputation or death sentence should be carried out on such a minor criminal. Repentance of any of the above-mentioned crimes removes the stain of their sins (*ma'āthim*) from their souls but leaves them still liable to a number of physical consequences, or obligations which may or may not be exacted.[403]

This concludes our examination of the *pragmatics* of al-Māwardī under our four chosen headings of *injunction*, *prescription*, *invitation* and *the call to arms*. We have attempted to match them with, or base them upon, the theoretics of the Holy Qur'ān. As with that latter text, al-Māwardī is concerned with certain kinds of right order – spiritual, moral and physical – which in his view will yield an ideal universe; we may draw analogies with Plato's *Republic* or St Thomas More's *Utopia*.[404] In al-Māwardī's ideal world, all will be safe to live freely,[405] to worship voluntarily and ultimately to arrive at the destiny forecast in the sacred text of Islam, having travelled with insight the *Ṣirāṭ al-Mustaqīm*.

For al-Māwardī, harmony is both a key and a goal. It is God-derived, and much of the *Aḥkām* is concerned to show how such perfect harmony may be achieved through God's agents on earth, the Caliph, the Imām and 'those in authority' (*wulāt al-umūr*).

2.4.1 The Authority of the Text (1): Ibn Ḥanbal and the Text Transcendent

When one considers the mediaeval group of theologians who sheltered under the umbrella term of Muʿtazila, the great Sunnī theologian Aḥmad b. Ḥanbal (AD 780–855) and the ninth-century *Miḥna* or Inquisition, one is reminded most vividly of two modern pugilists in a boxing ring. The perception of the nature of the Text – in this case the Holy Qur'ān – together with the religious and secular authority derived from that perception was the coveted prize for Caliph and *ʿulamā'* alike. The contest is of particular interest and poignancy here, since one of the five cardinal principles of the Muʿtazila was *al-amr bi 'l-maʿrūf wa 'l-nahy ʿan al-munkar*, a principle about which we have already had much to say.[406]

Briefly, these Muʿtazilite theologians comprised

> diverse scholars who were divided on a number of points but united on others. Among those on which many agreed were the doctrine of a created Qur'ān, God's absolute Oneness (which they believed the doctrine of a created Qur'ān reflected) where God's principal attributes were identical with His divine essence, God's justice and man's free will, and an allegorical attitude towards the *physical* attributes of God mentioned in the Qur'ān.[407]

The Mu'tazila have been variously discussed and interpreted by mediaeval and modern scholars. Certainly, they were rebutted by mainstream Sunnī theologians like Abū 'l-Ḥasan al-Ash'arī (873/4–935/6)[408] from the Middle Ages onwards. Al-Ash'arī was able to speak with an insider's knowledge, since he had been a Mu'tazilite himself before abandoning their dogmas in 912–13 as the result of a vision of the Prophet Muḥammad. Later, he would deploy the logical methods of the Mu'tazila to defend Sunnism.[409] W. M. Watt draws attention to the fact that 'in an account of [the Mu'tazila] published in 1865, Heinrich Steiner of Zurich spoke of them as "the free-thinkers of Islam"'.[410] Watt goes on to observe that, in the mid-nineteenth century, there was not a great deal known about *kalām* and its development and that, in consequence, 'the Mu'tazilites were seen as standing for freedom of the will and human responsibility'. There was a tendency to view them through the spectacles of nineteenth-century liberalism.[411]

George F. Hourani holds that, ethically speaking, the Mu'tazila espoused a theory of 'rationalistic objectivism'.[412] J. R. T. M. Peters notes: 'The difference between the Mu'tazila and their opponents is to be found in their theological methods: for the Mu'tazila, theologians who had come to know the Greek philosophical tradition, the human intellect itself was a source of real knowledge'.[413] Martin, Woodward and Atmaja underline the 'rigorous devotion' of the early Mu'tazila 'to a rational understanding of divine unity and justice'.[414] Earlier, Harry Wolfson had identified two types of Mu'tazilite *kalām* or scholastic theology: in the first, which he terms 'non-philosophical Mu'tazilite Kalam', lasting for about a century into the first part of the ninth century, there is an emphasis on 'the old Kalam method of analogy', manipulated in various ways. The second type, philosophical Mu'tazilite *kalām*, was inaugurated with the rise of the translation movement from Greek to Arabic in the early ninth century. It was characterised by new usages of analogy and the deployment of the syllogism.[415]

Michael Cook provides a final, concise and lucid orientation:

> If the bias of Ḥanbalite thinking was towards the concrete, that of Mu'tazilite thought was towards the abstract ... Mu'tazilism tended to represent something between a systematic body of substantive scholastic doctrine and an intellectual technique which ... even the Ḥanbalites were to find irresistible ... Mu'tazilism thus tended to become a tradition of socially and politically disembodied intellection.[416]

After analysing the views of three major classical Mu'tazilite authorities – Mānkdīm (died AD 1034), al-Ḥākim al-Jishumī (died 1101) and Abū 'l-Ḥusayn al-Baṣrī (died 1044)[417] – on the subject of *al-amr bi 'l-ma'rūf*, Cook identifies three general aspects: their analytical approach, their doctrinal homogeneity and their activism.[418] He shows that, for Mānkdīm, *al-amr bi 'l-ma'rūf* is an aspect of 'the business of the state' and, indeed, 'most of what falls under the duty can only be performed by rulerst'.[419]

In all the above surveys and discussions which have been alluded to above, it is clear that there was a growing strain of intellectualism and emphasis on the role of reason and logic in the historical development of Mu'tazilism. But that intellectualism did not abandon the text. Like the Ḥanābila, the Muʿtazila were still text-bound, that is, bound to the text of the Qur'ān in one form or another. And the two forms were both distinct and significant. Was the Qur'ān a Created or an Uncreated Text? The Muʿtazila, as we have noted earlier, adhered to a doctrine of a Created Qur'ān.

In two famous credal statements, Abū 'l-Ḥasan al-Ashʿarī proclaimed in no uncertain terms that those who followed the Islamic traditions and the *Sunna* believed that the Qur'ān was *the uncreated word of God* and that believers in the creation of the Qur'ān were to be accounted unbelievers. The actual verbal articulation of the Qur'ān was to be accounted as neither created nor uncreated.[420] The important point was that the Qur'ān itself was uncreated.

Aḥmad b. Ḥanbal (AD 780–855) has the distinction of being one of the most famous theologians and jurists in mediaeval Islam. He gave his name to the Ḥanbalī *madhhab*, the most rigorous of the four Sunnī law schools.[421] And, like the great theologian al-Ashʿarī, he held to a doctrine of an uncreated Qur'ān which brought him persecution, imprisonment and beating. *The Encyclopaedia of Islam* describes him as 'one of the most vigorous personalities of Islam, which he has profoundly influenced in its historical development and its modern revival'.[422] His refusal to follow the adoption by the 'Abbāsid Caliph al-Ma'mūn (reg. 813–33) of the Muʿtazilite doctrine of a created Qur'ān led to his being arraigned by al-Ma'mūn, summoned in chains to appear before him and then, on al-Ma'mūn's death, imprisoned and beaten under the new Caliph al-Muʿtaṣim (reg. 833–42). It was not until the abandonment of Muʿtazilism by the Caliph al-Mutawakkil (reg. 847–61) that Ibn Ḥanbal began teaching again, free from fear.[423]

The historian al-Ṭabarī (839–923) provides a vivid account of the whole affair: he relates how al-Ma'mūn sent a long letter to Isḥāq b. Ibrāhīm (died 849/50), the Ṭāhirid governor of Baghdad,[424] ordering him to question the judges about their belief, or otherwise, in a created Qur'ān,[425] and insisting that they should make a public declaration that they held the Qur'ān to be created.

This letter was sent in Rabīʿ al-Awwal 218/March–April 833 and was followed by a second similar letter, after which a variety of jurisprudents, judges and traditionists were summoned to appear before Isḥāq.[426] Among them was Aḥmad b. Ḥanbal, who refused to affirm specifically that the Qu'ān was created:[427] 'But Aḥmad b. Ḥanbal and Muḥammad b. Nūḥ persisted in their original profession and would not recant. Hence they were both loaded with fetters and sent to Tarsus …'[428]

Al-Ma'mūn died in AD 833[429] insisting in his last hours on the createdness of the Qur'ān.[430] But Aḥmad b. Ḥanbal underwent further interrogation and suffering under al-Ma'mūn's successor, al-Muʿtaṣim,[431] before whom he preferred to ignore the question as to whether the Qur'ān was created and to evince apparent ignorance.[432]

Michael Cook poignantly concludes:

> It was through no choice of Ibn Ḥanbal's that the state burst into his world and shattered its peace. First came what he called the 'religious ordeal' (*fitnat al-dīn*), in which he was imprisoned, interrogated and flogged for refusing

> to pay lip-service to heresy ... [Yet] Ibn Ḥanbal stood for unhesitating obedience to the ruler, except in disobedience to God ... He was ready to render unto Caesar the things which were Caesar's; beyond that, what he asked most of all was to be left alone, and in that lies a key to his doctrine of forbidding wrong.[433]

For a period of three Caliphates – al-Ma'mūn's (813–33), al-Mu'taṣim's (833–42) and al-Wāthiq's (842–7) – 'heterodoxy', became the mandatory 'orthodoxy'. Partisans of the latter, like Aḥmad b. Ḥanbal, suffered grievously. There are analogies here with the rise of Arianism, especially with regard to the issue of authority. For the opponents of Arianism, a major issue was the authority of the Uncreated Logos, Jesus Christ. For Aḥmad b. Ḥanbal, the issue was the authority of Allāh himself, whose eternal mind had been made textual in the revelation of the eternal Qur'ān. The concept of the eternal nature of the Qur'ān invested that text with the highest authority. M. A. Shaban stresses the secular, political dimension of belief in a created Qur'ān:

> At first [al-Ma'mūn] encouraged and took part in elaborate discussions with the intellectual elite about the fundamental principles of Islam and their relation to all the contemporary issues, but always with a constant focus on the political significance of these questions. Finally, his decision was for the official adoption of the Muʿtazilite dogma. However, the only tenet which was particularly emphasised was the Muʿtazilite insistence that the Qur'ān, the Word of God, was created and therefore could not be as eternal as God and was certainly less divine. In other words the authority of revelation was not as paramount as the conservative Ḥanbalites were claiming, and in accordance with the Muʿtazilites, *reason should be given its proper place* in order to allow religious thinking to develop without undue hindrance. *The logical political conclusion of this argument was that change was possible without a divinely guided ruler*.[434]

Aḥmad b. Ḥanbal thus stood for the Text Transcendent, Triumphant and Eternal. It is not, of course, suggested here that the Logos doctrine in Christianity, with Jesus Christ as the eternal Word of God (John 1:1–3), is an exact parallel of the Islamic doctrine of an uncreated Qur'ān (even though that is the mind of God made textual), or that the Arian heresy directly mirrors the Muʿtazilite view of the Qur'ān as created.[435] Where there is, however, a congruence of paradigm is over the issue of authority arising from the multifarious Arian and Muʿtazilite debates. The medieval Islamic dimension was further complicated by the intellectual conflict between those whom R. C. Martin identifies as 'traditionalists' ('reformist religious movements, primarily the Hanbaliya, the followers of Ahmad ibn Hanbal') and the 'rationalist' Muʿtazilites.[436]

2.4.2 The Authority of the Text (2): Al-Ghazālī and the Ismāʿīlī Imām

The Arabic text entitled *al-Munqidh min al-Ḍalāl* (*The Deliverer from Error*) by Abū Ḥāmid al-Ghazālī (1058–1111) ranks as one of the world's great pieces of confessional literature, despite its rather obviously artificial structure. It bears sustained comparison with Augustine's *Confessions* and John Henry Newman's *Apologia Pro Vita Sua*.[437]

Structurally, the *Munqidh* divides, all too neatly, into an examination of the belief systems of four distinct categories of seekers (*al-ṭālibīn*) after truth:

- The Scholastic Theologians (*al-Mutakallimūn*)
- The Ismāʿīlī Sect of Shīʿism (*al-Bāṭiniyya*)
- The Philosophers (*al-Falāsifa*)
- The Ṣūfīs (*al-Ṣūfiyya*)[438]

Al-Ghazālī insisted that the truth (*al-ḥaqq*) must lie within one of these groups; and, if it did not, he wondered what the point was in trying to identify the truth.[439]

Al-Ghazālī had intellectual problems with each of these groups: theology sought only to maintain the theological *status quo*;[440] the philosophers were infected with *kufr* (unbelief) and *bidʿa* (lit. innovation, popularly 'heresy');[441] and the essence of ṣūfism could only be apprehended by, literally, 'tasting' (*dhawq*), i.e. experience.[442] That left the Ismāʿīlīs, whom al-Ghazālī termed the Taʿlīmiyya, with their talk of knowledge via an Infallible Imām (*al-Imām al-Maʿṣūm*).[443]

Al-Ghazālī counters such a notion by insisting that the Islamic community, the *umma*, already has an infallible teacher who is Muḥammad (*muʿallimunā al-maʿṣūm (huwa) Muḥammad*).[444] One may use *ijtihād* in the absence of the text (*al-naṣṣ*);[445] but ultimately however, the text of the Qur'ān reigns supreme:

> The fundamental beliefs are contained in the Book [*al-Kitāb*] and the Sunna; in questions of detail and other disputed matters apart from these fundamentals the truth is known by weighing them in 'the just balance', that is, the standards set forth by God most high in His Book [*fī Kitābihi*]; and they are five in number as I show in *The Just Balance* [*Kitāb al-Qisṭās al-Mustaqīm*].[446]

In other words, the Text rules, not the infallible Imām of Ismāʿīlī dogma, and it is to the former rather than the latter that the *umma* should have recourse.

In the last passage which we have just quoted, al-Ghazālī directs us specifically to his earlier work *al-Qisṭās al-mustaqīm*. Here he tells us, in an interpretation of Q.17:35 ('and weigh with a balance that is straight' [*bi 'l-qisṭās al-mustaqīm*])[447] that this balance consists of 'the five rules of measurement which God has revealed in His Book and which He has taught His Prophets to use'.[448] Here again, then, is the clearest of all statements that it is the Text, the Qur'ān, which reigns supreme in al-Ghazālī's eyes. *This* is the final criterion by which all should be elucidated and judged, not a human being like an Ismāʿīlī Imām. For al-Ghazālī, 'your (true) Imām shall be Muḥammad, your guide shall be the Qur'ān'.[449] He goes on: 'I do not summon people to any Imām other than Muḥammad or to any book other than the Qur'ān. From the Qur' an I draw all the secrets of knowledge.'[450]

It is clear from all this that al-Ghazālī is concerned to degrade the authority of the Ismāʿīlī Imām. He does so by a massive stress on two primary sources of authority: there is that of the only real Imām, Muḥammad himself, but there is also that of the sacred text of the Qur'ān which, in a very real sense, becomes a kind of *alter*-Imām:

the eternal Words and Mind of God made textual on earth are, in effect, for al-Ghazālī an infallible Imām for the entire umma.

After a long and possibly exhausting debate, reported in *al-Qisṭās al-Mustaqīm*, al-Ghazālī treats his Ismāʿīlī interlocutor with scant respect, even though the latter has been worn down by al-Ghazālī's arguments.[451] It is almost as if al-Ghazālī wishes to underline the total truth of what he has been saying by his total contempt for his Ismāʿīlī companion:

> You are not suited to be my companion, nor am I suited to be yours. Depart from me, so that there is distance between us. I am preoccupied with ordering my own soul and cannot look after yours as well. I am too concerned with learning about the Qur'ān to instruct you too.[452]

Of course, al-Ghazālī did not deny that there should be earthly Caliph-Imāms as well, though these must clearly rank in status as lower than that of the Prophet Muḥammad and the Holy Qur'ān itself. Mitha stresses that in al-Ghazali's *Kitāb al-Mustaẓhirī*, written c. 1094/5 at the behest of the ʿAbbāsid Caliph al-Mustaẓhir (reg. 1094–1118),[453] Chapter Nine begins 'with a clear emphasis on the legal ideal, as expressed in the wording of the Chapter's title':

> On the Establishment of the Legal Demonstrations (*al-barāhīn al-sharʿiyya*) that the Imām charged with the truth whom all Men are Bound to obey in this Age of Ours is the Imām al-Mustaẓhir Billāh.[454]

Mitha goes on to note that al-Ghazālī 'argues that al-Mustaẓhir fulfils the conditions (*sharā'iṭ*) of the Imām, and hence he is God's *khalīfa* over mankind and obedience to him is a religious obligation (*fard*) incumbent on all mankind ... the caliph is an indispensable source of legitimacy'.[455] This observation is syllogistically validated in al-Ghazālī's text.[456]

In sum, one of al-Ghazālī's pressing concerns was to devalue the status of the Ismāʿīlī Imām.[457] For al-Ghazālī, the Proto-Imām, the Supreme Teacher, was the Prophet Muḥammad.[458] After that came the rightful *Imām-Khalīfa*. But beyond all was the eternal Text of the Qur'ān itself. That text, by virtue of its divine oigins, had to be the lodestar, ultimate Imām, Mentor and Teacher *par excellence* for al-Ghazālī.[459]

2.5 *Readings: Islam*

2.5.1 Reading the Phenomena of Islam

From the perspective of *epoché*, in which a deliberate attempt is made to abstain from pronouncing upon, and judging, the ontological aspect of what appears, a summary thumbnail sketch – which is also phenomenological – may be presented as follows: there are two dimensions: a historical and an intellectual.

Historically, one perceives a pre-Islamic Arabian framework or milieu, – the *Jāhiliyya* or Age of Ignorance, as it is known in Islam, comprising a mysterious, relatively unknown North Arabia and, by contrast, a better-known South at whose heart was Saba of the Sabaeans.[460] Assessing 'The Foundations of Greatness' of the

Prophet Muḥammad, W. Montgomery Watt evaluates time and milieu as follows:

> Circumstances of time and place favoured Muhammad. Various forces combined to set the stage for his life-work and for the subsequent expansion of Islam. There was the social unrest in Mecca and Medina, the movement towards monotheism, the reaction against Hellenism in Syria and Egypt, the decline of the Persian and Byzantine empires, and a growing realisation by the nomadic Arabs of the opportunities for plunder in the settled lands round them.[461]

The Persians and Byzantines had fought each other into the ground between AD 603 and 630, even though Heraclius (reg. 610–41), the Byzantine Emperor, claimed the final victory.[462]

The death of the Prophet Muḥammad in 632 left a very fluid situation: Abū Bakr (reg. 632–4), the first *khalīfa* after the Prophet, proclaimed on Muḥammad's death: 'O people, those who worshipped Muḥammad [must know that] Muḥammad is dead; those who worshipped God [must know that] God is alive [and] immortal'.[463]

The Prophet's death, from an intellectual perspective, did not leave an intellectual vacuum: his legacy was (1) a sacred text already memorised and, according to tradition, preserved in writing in various forms; and (2) the memory of the Prophet's speech and actions preserved in the minds of his companions, the *ṣaḥāba*. Intellectually, too, we are left with the existence of a young faith whose universe of discourse, like that of Christianity, embraced *inter alia* three important elements:

- *Doctrines*, enshrined in, and eternally emanating from, the eternal mind of God made textual in the Qur'ān .
- *Validating tools*, such as *tafsīr* (exegesis), traditions, *sharī'a* and *ijtihād* (exercise of independent judgement).
- A succession of *historico-religious frameworks*, ranging from the above-cited proclamation by Abū Bakr, through the *Ridda* or Apostasy War on the Prophet's death, the *Miḥna*, and the Ismā'īlī-Fāṭimid conquest of Egypt in AD 969, to the death of the last Caliph in 1258 as a consequence of the Mongol destruction of Baghdad.

Eidetic reduction, as we have seen, focuses on essences. What constitute the essences of Islam? The answer may be given in a twofold manner. In the first place, as every Muslim will avow, there are the doctrinal essences such as *tawḥīd* (the declaration of the oneness of God), *īmān* (faith, 'right belief') *nubuwwa* (prophethood), the belief in angels and the Last Day. Then there are the raw 'validating tools' from which, or within which, all these aspects or fundamentals of Islam have their origins, namely *text* (Qur'ān), *tradition* (*ḥadīth*), law (*sharī'a*), authority (*khalīfa, imām*), *school of law or madhhab* (*Mālikī, Ḥanafī, Shāfi'ī, Ḥanbalī*) and *sect* (Sunnī, Shī'ite of one kind or another). There may be some overlap between some of these and the 'validating tools' discussed under the heading of *epoché*.

The text of the Qur'ān, that shrine of *tawḥīd*, visibly reveals that it is intended for all time in that it looks backwards, surveys the present (i.e. the period of revelation during the Prophet's life) and looks forwards. It looks backwards, for example, in its graphic references to the unsuccessful attack on Mecca by Abraha in AD 570, delineated in the 105th *Sūra* of the Qur'ān, *Sūrat al-Fīl* (*The Chapter of the Elephant*). Other Qur'ānic references to an *essential* past, which bind it to the present, include that to the sixth-century AD bursting of the Ma'rib Dam in Saba (*sayl al-ʿarim*)[464] and the reference to the Byzantine–Persian War in the seventh century in the 30th *Sūra* of the Qur'ān, *Sūrat al-Rūm* (*Chapter of the Byzantines*):

> The *sūra* belongs to the Meccan period and has 60 verses. Its title is taken from the 2nd verse which reads: 'The Byzantine Greeks have been defeated'. This is probably a reference to the Persian capture of Jerusalem … from the Byzantines in AD 614. This is one of the very few references in the Qur'ān to contemporary history.[465]

The Qur'ān surveys the present in terms of the essential motif of *umma*, community:

> Thus have We made of you
> An *Ummat* justly balanced
> [*Wa kadhālika ja' alnākum*
> *Ummat*^{an} *wasaṭ*^{an}]
> That ye might be witnesses
> Over the nations.
> And the Apostle a witness
> Over yourselves.
> [*Wa yakūna al-Rasūl*
> *ʿalaykum shahīd*^{an}].[466]

Umma, and the prophethood of Muḥammad, are thus neatly, and *essentially*, linked in a single verse. Later, Abū Ḥāmid al-Ghazālī would seek in his writings

> to connect the Prophet's *ta'līm* [teaching) with that of a living, historical community, so that the cumulative experience of the Sunni community [became] the repository and continuing guarantor of truth for every individual believer … Al-Ghazālī affirms the necessity of both a teacher and a community. In the K. *al-Mustaẓhirī*, the necessity of the community is articulated in terms of al-Ghazālī's recurrent emphasis on the centrality of the law as the *raison d'être* of the Muslim community …[467]

Finally, in numerous eschatological verses, the Qur'ān looks forward to a distant era in which the end of the world, the *Yawrn al-Qiyāma*, will arrive:

> When the Sky
> Is cleft assunder;
> When the Stars
> Are scattered;
> When the Oceans
> Are suffered to burst forth;
> And when the Graves
> Are turned upside down; [468]

On that day mankind will be gathered together in a group for judgement,[469] an eschatological *umma* as it were, comprising this time *all* mankind. (The event is prefigured annually by the *wuqūf*, standing, at ʿArafāt during the *ḥajj*.[470]) On the Last Day, of course, judgement will be uniquely individual.[471] However, the Prophet Muḥammad himself will intercede for the believers beside the Pool (*al-ḥawḍ*) in Paradise on that Day of Reckoning, as one greater individual for a lesser.[472]

From everything we have said, then, it is clear that, eidetically, essential salvation in Islam is to be gained through an essential text, an essential Prophet and an essential *umma*. Islamic eidetic reduction yields a fundamental religious core of Book, Chosen Messenger and Community.

From the final, phenomenological perspectives of *cognition and epistemology*, we turn to two final, very broad questions, related both to what has gone before and to each other: (1) What is Islam? (2) How is it constituted? A variety of statements will be surveyed in answer to the first question; a variety of structures will be examined in answer to the second.

The Qur'ān itself has no doubts about its definition of Islam and Muslims:

> Ye are the best
> Of Peoples [*khayr Ummat*^{in}] evolved
> For mankind,
> Enjoining what is right,
> Forbidding what is wrong
> And believing in God.[473]

Here, the motifs of *umma*, *al-amr bi 'l-maʿrūf* and *tawḥīd* all combine succinctly in a single verse.

The famous ḥadīth of Gabriel, known as Jibrīl in the Islamic tradition, recorded by the Syrian traditionist al-Nawawī (1233–77), defines Islam in terms of its principal beliefs, especially those encapsulated in the Five Pillars (*arkān*):

> Islam is to testify that there is no god but Allāh and Muḥammad is the Messenger of Allāh, to perform the prayers, to pay the zakāt, to fast in Ramaḍān, and to make the pilgrimage to the House [i.e. the Kaʿba in Mecca] if you are able to do so.[474]

A modern Islamic Student Catechism provides the following succinct definition:

> The word Islam means submission to the will of God and obedience to God's law. The will of God is defined by the Koran as good and compassionate, and His law as the most beneficient and equitable. Any human being who so submits and obeys is, therefore, a Muslim in a moral state of Islam.[275]

Finally, a modern anthropologist writes:

> The fundamentals can be set out quite simply. Islam which means submission to God, is constructed upon what Muslims believe is a direct Revelation in Arabic from God: the Quran. This recitation or reading, for that is what the word *Quran* means, is the miraculous source of the umma, the Islamic community. It is the Word.[476]

In these various definitions, ancient and modern, the universal Islamic themes shine through; many of them have been surveyed earlier above. Islam is known by its text, by its *umma* and, above all, by its self-definition as submission to the will of God. So much for cognition and elementary epistemology.

How are Islam's objects of cognition 'constituted in cognition'?[477] Islamic structures are manifold. A weak, indeed possibly apocryphal, ḥadīth records that 'difference [of opinion] in my community is a sign of the mercy of Allāh'.[478] An antique Arabic proverb also states that 'the person who does not understand divergence in doctrine has not caught the true scent of jurisprudence' (*Man lā yaʿrif al-ikhtilāf lam yashumma rāʾiḥata ʾl-fiqh*).[479]

Islamic structures bear a real witness to the ancient ideas of unity in diversity and diversity in unity. While the fundamental doctrines (*ʿaqāʾid*) remain constant, they are articulated within a framework of widely differing, and culturally conditioned, structures, hierarchies, patterns and intellectual milieux: there are, for example, in *Sharīʿa* law, four Sunnī *madhāhib*, law schools; Islam itself divides into the two major branches of Sunnism and Shīʿism (with the latter dividing and subdividing into a plethora of smaller groups); a whole variety of schools of mediaeval theology developed like Muʿtazilism, Ashʿarism and Māturīdism. The diversity of articulation deriving from an *umma* united upon its central tenets (*ʿaqāʾid*) was well observed by the astronomer-poet of Nishapur, ʿUmar Khayyām (c. 1038–c. 1132), in his pithy *Rubāʿiyyāt* (*Quatrains*) which Edward Fitzgerald famously paraphrased as follows:

> The grape that can with Logic absolute
> *The Two-and-Seventy jarring Sects confute*:
> The subtle Alchemist that in a Trice
> Life's leaden Metal into Gold transmute.[480]

In citing this verse, my emphasis is not, of course, on 'the grape' but on the reference to theological and sectarian diversity in mediaeval Islam.

2.5.2 Reading the Signs of Islam

Everything Signifies:[481] Umberto Eco's dictum allows us to identify at least six important semiotic fields in any attempt at reading the signs of Islam. They may be successively termed (1) the Textual, (2) the Foundational, (3) the Terrestrial, (4) the Proclamative, (5) the Eschatological and (6) the Celestial. This listing, which is progressive, is by no means intended to be exclusive. Many other semiotic fields might have been cited, but we will restrict our attention to these six as a summary guide to reading the signs of the Islamic religion. It is to be stressed that the six constitute a logical progression: the first arena of the textual leads ineluctably to the sixth arena of the Celestial, with its twin dimensions of the Salvific and the Damnatory, via the four stated intermediate fields.

Textual semiotics. Earlier, we identified one of the principal sign systems or structures of Christianity as its system of sacraments. We also noted the comment of Brother William of Baskerville, hero of Umberto Eco's novel *The Name of the Rose*, that 'The good of a book lies in its being read. A book is made up of signs that speak of other signs, which in their turn speak of things.'[482]

This is as true of the Qur'ān as it is of the New Testament. The text of the Qur'ān constantly proclaims the signs *(āyāt)* of God.[483] And the Qur'ān is indeed made up of verses/signs (*āyāt*) which speak of other signs, which in turn speak of a multiplicity of things throughout the sacred text. That multivocal wealth of signs includes the heavens and the earth (*al-samawāt wa 'l-arḍ*), night and day (*al-layl wa 'l-nahār*), the rain (*mā anzala Allāh min al-samā' min mā'*[in]), beasts (lit. *dābba*) and clouds (*al-saḥāb*) – all are signs which bespeak and signify not only the direct manifold mercies of God 'for a people that are wise' (*li-qawm*[in] *ya'qilūna*) but other things such as sustenance and climate which flow indirectly from these major aspects of the divine creation.[484] And we see the truth of Eco's protagonist's first statement that 'the good of a book lies in its being read' paralleled in the Qur'ān's injunction to 'recite the Qur'ān, in slow measured, rhythmic tones'[485] for it contains 'a healing and a mercy (*shifā' wa raḥma*) to those who believe'.[486] Indeed, the very text and content of the Qur'ān itself are a striking sign:

> Yet they say: 'Why
> Are not Signs sent down
> To him from his Lord?'
> Say: 'The Signs are indeed
> With God: and I am
> Indeed a clear Warner'.
> And is it not enough
> For them that We have
> Sent down to thee
> The Book (*al-Kitāb*) which is rehearsed
> To them? Verily, in it
> Is Mercy and a Reminder
> To those who believe.[487]

Foundational semiotics. Islam has no sacraments nor direct concept of such rituals. Thus it was clearly impossible for it to develop any form of sacramental theology. However, it does have an alternative, quasi-parallel, semiotic structure, the five *arkān* or Pillars of Islam, namely, *Shahāda* (The Declaration of Faith), *Ṣalāt* (The Prayer Ritual), *Zakāt* (Almsgiving), *Ṣawm* (Fasting in the Month of *Ramaḍān*) and *Ḥajj* (Pilgrimage to Mecca in the Islamic Month of *Dhū 'l-Ḥijja*).[488] No other faith tradition embraces such a precise listing, and so it is original as well as foundationally important for Islam.

The five *arkān* are important from such diverse perspectives as the phenomenological, the anthropological and the theological as well as the semiotic, the sociological, the eschatological, the ritual and the liturgical.[489] All derive from the sacred text of the Qur'ān, with data supplemented by the ḥadīth literature on occasion. And, indeed, it is the famous Ḥadīth of Gabriel which constitutes one of the most vivid articulations of these foundational semiotics, the universe of the *arkān*.[490]

Terrestrial semiotics. The first verses of the first book of the Bible, the Book of Genesis, describe God in the beginning creating heaven and earth, night and day, the sun, the moon and the stars, the beasts of the earth and, finally, a man and a woman. After each moment of creation, the text observes that God ' found it good'. The chapter concludes: 'And God saw all that he had made, and found it very good'.[491] The text here signals that He who is the essence of goodness itself perceives His creation to be 'good' in unequivocal and lucid terms. As one pair of commentators, Richard J. Clifford and Roland E. Murphy, put it:

> God pronounces the light good, beautiful; the phrase will be repeated six times of created elements, climaxing in the seventh climactic occurrence for the whole universe (v. 31). The declaration is not a deduction from human experience but a divine declaration that all of creation is good ... There is no evil, only beauty, in the world that God makes.[492]

In the Qur'ān, a similar paradigm is in operation: Allāh is characterised as the One 'Who has made Everything which He has created Most Good' (*alladhī aḥsana kulla shay' khalaqahu*).[493] Among the many meanings of the basic adjective *ḥasan* are 'excellent', 'good' and 'exquisite'.[494] Even if one takes Arberry's slightly less powerful translation of the above Qur'ānic phrase as 'Who has created all things well',[495] it is clear that both the Book of Genesis and the Qur'ān share a common field of discourse with regard to God's pleasure in His creation.

In addition, the Qur'ān vaunts the truth, reality and rightness (*bi 'l-ḥaqq*) of God's creation,[496] as well as its intrinsic and ubiquitous order and beauty.[497] All these things are signs for the believer.[498] And these terrestrial signs of God are a constant motif in the Qur'ān, ranging from the creation of the heavens and the earth[499] and the existence of the night, the sun and the moon[500] to the presence of camels, sky, mountains and earth.[501] All are signs of the mercies and blessings of God which have been revealed in and to the depths of their hearts as well as the farthest horizons.[502]

Proclamative Semiotics. Can Islam be said to have a semiotics of proclamation and dialogue akin to that espoused in Christian interfaith and ecumenical circles? To pose this question is to invite a brief study of Qur'ānic *da'wa*, a word which may literally be translated as 'call' but which translates better in this context as 'mission', 'missionary work' or even 'propaganda' and 'prayer'.[503]

The second edition of *The Encyclopaedia of Islam* notes:

> In the religious sense, the *da'wa* is the invitation, addressed to men by God and the prophets, to believe in the true religion, Islam: Kur'ān XIV.46 [44].
>
> The religion of all the prophets is Islam, and each prophet has his *da'wa* ... Muḥammad's mission was to repeat the call and invitation: it is the *da'wat al-Islām* or *da'wat al-Rasūl*. As we know, the infidels' familiarity with, or ignorance of, this appeal determined the way in which the Muslims should fight against them. Those to whom the *da'wa* had not yet penetrated had to be invited to embrace Islam before fighting could take place.[504]

It is clear from this, then, that a major aspect of *da'wa* semiotics must be *nubuwwa*, prophethood.[505] The response will also signal whether a certain country is to be considered *Dār al-Islām* (House of Islam), *Dar al-Ḥarb* (House of War) or *Dar al-*

Ṣulḥ (House of Truce); each of these terms signals in a very precise way a particular relationship with Islam. The companion sign of *nubuwwa* in Islam, of course, is the Text of the Qur'ān itself.[506]

While recognising the difficulties that may arise in interfaith dialogue, and the sometimes apparent contradiction between dialogue *and* proclamation, branches of the Christian Church have felt the need to stress that no one should be forced to become a Christian.[507] Q.2:256 articulates a similar message for Islam, deploying the phrase that there should be no compulsion in religion: *la ikrāha fī 'l-dīn*. Neither Muslim nor Christian would have any quarrel with the idea that

> in the works of mission and *da'wah* (summons), our actions must be founded upon a respect for the inalienable dignity and freedom of the human person created and loved by God. Both Christians and Muslims are called to defend the inviolable right of each individual to freedom of religious belief and practice.[508]

Semiotic indicators of true da'wa, then, on both the Muslim and Christian fronts would include tolerance, mutual understanding and mutual respect, together with a pressing need to learn as much as possible about the position of the other person. This is, of course, ideal *da'wa*, and it is recognised that the reality has sometimes fallen short of the ideal.[509]

Each side, however, will impose limits on its reception of the other's *da'wa*. The death penalty is classically prescribed in Islam for apostasy (*irtidād*),[510] while Christianity, in all its talk of proclamation and dialogue, has also taken care to signal its aversion to a false eirenicism[511] or indifferentism.[512]

A final semiotic indicator of *da'wa* can therefore be said to be *tension*, within the framework of dialogue and proclamation. On the one hand, the International Islamic Committee for Relief has been responsible for the creation of an International Islamic Committee for Dialogue, which resulted from Catholic contacts. This consultation committee meets to discuss 'the promise and peril of contact with non-Muslims'. The former President of the Vatican Pontifical Council for Inter-Religious Dialogue (*Pontificium Consilium pro Dialogo Inter Religiones*), Archbishop Michael Fitzgerald M.Afr.,[513] observes of this Committee that 'it offers a forum in the Islamic world that did not previously exist ... and in itself represents a new level of commitment to dialogue'.[514]

The al-Azhar University also has

> a permanent committee for dialogue with monotheistic religions. ... Fitzgerald noted that the Vatican and Al-Azhar have established a joint committee for on-going relations that meets annually and officials at Al-Azhar have asked that the meeting take place each year on Feb. 24 – the anniversary of John Paul's visit to Al-Azhar .[515]

Fitzgerald also drew attention to the Pakistan Association for Inter-Religious Dialogue which, he said, 'is doing impressive work bringing Christians and Muslims together despite a very difficult social and political situation'.[516]

On the other hand, sources of tension and potential hostility are omnipresent in attempts at *da'wa* on either side of the Muslim–Christian divide. On 6 January 2003, Cardinal Severino Poletto of Turin informed his congregation that they should not 'allow good manners to deter them from evangelizing new arrivals in Italy, especially Muslims'. It has been observed that

> nothing Poletto said is inconsistent with respectful dialogue. Yet even if the tension isn't a logical one, some Muslims will doubtless be irked by the suggestion that they should consider changing religions in order to avoid threatening the identity of a historically Christian nation. The delicate balance between evangelization and tolerance will need constant pastoral attention especially given the already tense atmosphere.[517]

Pursuing this theme that one of the key signs of *da'wa* in any religion must inevitably be *tension*, we note also a case which complements what has already been outlined above. An Italian-Scottish convert to Islam, Adel Smith, received much Italian TV coverage 'by asserting the superiority of Islam and predicting doom for Christian infidels'.[518] Two of his appearances on Italian TV were so incendiary as to precipitate a fight.[519]

The fact that the remarks by such men as Poletto and Smith have been rejected and disowned by others among their own religious compatriots does not prevent us from recognising that the delicate concept of *da'wa* may easily be hijacked by extremists on all sides and that *tension*, potential or actual, is a semiotic indicator of real *da'wa*, proclamation and dialogue.[520]

Eschatological semiotics. When the *éskaton*, final judgement, is about to be realised, the emphasis in Islam will shift semiotically from the guiding *arkān* to the Signs of the Hour (*ishārāt al-sā'a, ashrāṭ al-sā'a*) . The second edition of *The Encyclopaedia of Islam* puts it like this:

> The materialisation of the Ḳur'ānic *Sā'a* will be preceded by a cataclysmic catastrophe. The moon will be split (LIV, 1), the earth will quake, and the people will be terrified (XXII, 1–2). The preceding signs (*ashrāṭ*) of the *Sā'a* are already manifest (XLVII, 18). The Hour is already 'heavy' in the heavens and in the earth (VII, 187).[521]

The Hour will be preceded by a series of natural disasters as well as the breakdown of human society and the natural and normal order of things. There will be wars and civil wars; 'Īsā will fight the Islamic anti-Christ, al-Dajjāl; and Gog and Magog, semiotic indicators of chaos *par excellence*, will be loosed to foster mayhem. The Mahdī will appear.[522]

Among the many commentators and delineators of the Signs of the Hour was the great collector of traditions, Muḥammad b. Ismā'īl al-Bukhārī (AD 810–70). In the *Book of Discords* (*Kitāb al-Fitan*) of his famous tradition collection entitled *al-Ṣaḥīḥ* (*The Authentic*), he forecast, *inter alia*, the following signs of the coming Hour of judgement and doom: fire will come forth from the Ḥijāz lighting up the necks of the camels in Busrā (Syria);[523] two great bands or parties (*fi'atāni*) will fight each other with many casualties, even though they both follow one doctrine (*da'wa*); about thirty lying *dajjāls* (literally, anti-Christs, imposters, charlatans) will arise, each claiming to be the prophet of God (*rasūl Allāh*); there will be earthquakes and disorder (*al-harj*); people will build high structures; and people will be unable to eat or taste the food which they raise to their mouths.[524] There will be many other signs of the approaching Hour, but the emphasis in al-Bukhārī's scenario on fire, war, lies, earthquakes, civil disorder and an inability to taste (or eat) are semiotic indicators that the days preceding the end of the world will indeed be dire, appalling to man and beast alike.

It was not only the great collectors of traditions like al-Bukhārī who dwelled on such matters. The Signs of the Hour were an important aspect of the Qur'ānic exegetical literature, the *tafsīr*, as well. In Q.43:61, we read the following:

> And (Jesus) shall be
> A Sign (for the coming
> Of) the Hour (of judgement):
> Therefore have no doubt
> About the (Hour), but
> Follow ye Me: this
> Is a Straight way.[525]

Like Yusuf Ali above, the famous Qur'ānic exegete before him, al-Bayḍāwī (died c. 1291) interpreted these verses as referring to Jesus ('Īsā) as a herald of the Day of Judgement. Reflecting on this verse, he notes that Jesus may rightly be identified here with the sign mentioned, since it is well known in Islam that his appearance will signal that the Judgement Day is close. He will descend through a mountain pass carrying a spear with which he will kill the anti-Christ (*al-Dajjāl*). He will then perform the morning prayer in Jerusalem, destroy the crucifixes, churches and synagogues and kill those Christians who do not acknowledge him according to Islamic belief.[526]

Celestial Semiotics. Any consideration of eschatological semiotics leads, logically, to a consideration of the semiotics of the final destinations of mankind; these might usefully be termed here the celestial. Thus we have come full circle, from the *textual* which proclaimed the semiotics of the two worlds of mercy and warning (and thus rewards and punishments), through the unfolding articulation of the semiotics of the foundations of Islam, their terrestrial deployment, their proclamation and their eschatology, to the final semiotics of these two worlds themselves, *al-Janna* and *al-Nār*. Indeed, each of these two words, meaning literally *The Garden* and *The Fire* and standing as the classical Arabic words for Heaven and Hell respectively, enshrine a whole world of signs *in extenso*.

There is a logic in viewing these celestial signs in Islam as bound up with the whole concept of God's justice or theodicy. God does not punish people in Hell fire without first signalling in His sacred text the existence of that Fire and the need for repentance; nor does He grant anyone reward in the eternal garden of bliss without first signalling the existence of that Garden and what mankind must do in order to enter it and dwell therein for all eternity.

Divine justice thus decrees and *signals* reward for *tawḥīd* and a consequent fruitful observance of Islam on earth:

Verily those who say,
'Our Lord is God',
And remain firm
(On that Path), –
On them shall be no fear,
Nor shall they grieve.
Such shall be Companions
Of the Garden, dwelling
Therein (for aye): a recompense
For their (good) deeds.[527]

If any do deeds
Of righteousness, –
Be they male or female –
And have faith,
They will enter Heaven,
And not the least injustice
will be done to them.[528]

The abode of Hell Fire is clearly signalled as the destination of those who reject the signs of God: in a powerful set of verses, this theme of rejection is clearly spelled out:

The Companions of the Fire [*aṣḥāb al-Nār*]
Will call to the Companions
Of the Garden [*aṣḥāb al-Janna*]: 'Pour down
To us water or anything
That God doth provide
For your sustenance'.
They will say: 'Both
These things hath God forbidden
To those who rejected Him; –
Such as took their religion
To be mere amusement
And play, and were deceived
By the life of the world'.
That day shall We forget them
As they forgot the meeting
Of this day of theirs
And as they were wont
To reject Our Signs.[529]

The message from the Qur'ān is crystal clear: if man rejects God and the ubiquitous signs that God has manifested, then God will 'forget' man. And such divine 'forgetfulness' implies an eternal spiritual death for the sinner who has been warned over and over again:

This is the Hell
Of which ye were
(Repeatedly) warned![530]

The Unbelievers will be
Led to Hell in crowd:
Until, when they arrive there,
Its gates will be opened,
And its keepers will say,
'Did not apostles come
To you from among yourselves,
Rehearsing to you the Signs
Of your Lord and warning you
Of the Meeting of this Day
Of yours?' The answer
Will be: 'True: but
The Decree of Punishment
Has been proved true
Against the Unbelievers!'
(To them) will be said:
'Enter ye the gates of Hell,
To dwell therein:
And evil is (this)
Abode of the arrogant!'[531]

In any reading of the Signs of Islam, one must identify and stress the primary semiotic register of the *Ma'ād*, literally the Return, especially with reference to Celestial Semiotics. While there were those who interpreted Platonically such Qur'ānic verses as 'Come back thou / To thy Lord – / Well pleased (thyself), / And well-pleasing / Unto Him!',[532] seeing such verses as a sign or evidence of the pre-existence of the soul before the divine creation of the body,[533] mainstream Islam has usually interpreted the *ma'ād* as a reference to 'the hereafter' or 'the life to come'.[534] The word is a synonym of *al-ākhira* and *al-dār al-ākhira*.[535] *Ma'ād* itself has connotatons both of 'place to which one returns' and '(place of) destination',[536] and it is clearly in the latter sense that *al-ma'ād* has come to mean 'the Hereafter'.

If, however, one also examines the implicit connotations, and fundamental meanings of *ma'ād* in the sense of 'return', there are some interesting parallels to be drawn with the Neoplatonic concept of return consequent upon the basic Plotinian themes of emanation, yearning or longing, and return.[537]

Everything does indeed signify. The six semiotic fields which we have surveyed confirm the omnipresence of the Signs of the Deity throughout the universe. Rejection of these signs logially is itself a sign of *kufr*, unbelief. As we have stressed, Allāh in the Qur'ān confirms that He will respond to the sign of rejection, the sign of *kufr*, with his own special sign of 'forgetfulness'. Of course, since Allāh possesses the divine attribute of perfection, no defect can be regarded as implicit in this word.

Yusuf Ali explains:

> 'Forgetfulness' may be involuntary, from a defect of memory, or figuratively, a deliberate turning away from, or ignoring of, something we do not want, as when we say in an argument, 'you conveniently forget that so-and-so is so-and-so'. Here the latter kind is meant. If men deliberately ignored the Hereafter [*the Ma'ād*] in spite of warnings, can they be expect[ed] to be received by God, Whom they themselves rejected?[538]

The exegetes Jalālayn interpret 'That day shall We forget them' as 'We will leave them in Hell' (*Natrukuhum fī 'l-nār*).[539]

A final sign of God's mercy for Islam, which attempts to prevent that human rejection and its terrifying divine consequence of 'forgetfulness', is the sending of a *mujaddid*, a Renewer of the Faith, at the beginning of every Islamic century. For example, the great Abū Ḥāmid al-Ghazālī (1058–1111) became persuaded that he was the 'Renewer' for the sixth Islamic century:[540]

> My resolution was further strengthened by numerous visions of good men in all of which alike I was given the assurance that this impulse was a source of good, was genuine guidance, and had been determined by God most high for the beginning of this century; for God most high has promised to revive His religion at the beginning of each century.[541]

And al-Ghazālī carefully recorded the signs of the coming *Ma'ād*.[542] This is the essence of his *magnum opus* the *Iḥyā'* (*Revival*).

In many sign systems – Islam is no exception – there is a need for a guide and an interpreter. Islam cleaves to a Revelation revealed through the final guide or interpreter, Muḥammad, the Seal of the Prophets. But other guides, interpreters and prophets had come before and attempted in their own ways, as the Qur'ān many times shows, to draw attention to the ubiquitous signs of God. After Muḥammad, there could be no more prophets: for Islam, he ranks as the very last prophet. But lesser beings than Muḥammad, in the shape of a *mujaddid*, a Ghazālī, could attempt to unravel and exhibit that universe of signs which is Islam and its revealed text, the Holy Qur'ān. Such men as al-Ghazālī were both the disclosers of signs as well as being signs themselves.

2.5.3 Reading the Sacred in Islam

We saw earlier[543] that Mircea Eliade defined the sacred as 'the opposite of the profane'. The sacred is subject to degradation, and there is perpetual war between the sacred and profane, the sacralised and the desacralised. And 'secular' can be an acceptable synonym for 'profane'.[544] Drawing, then, on Eliade, we find three key motifs in any discussion of the sacred: non-secular, degradation, conflict.

A casual glance at a typical English–Arabic dictionary yields the following Arabic words for 'sacred': *muqaddas* and *ḥarām*.[545] Both these Arabic words carry a huge cultural and linguistic baggage. As well as 'sacred', *muqaddas* means 'hallowed, sanctified, dedicated, consecrated, holy'.[546] 'The Holy Land' in Arabic is *al-Arḍ al-Muqaddasa* and *al-Bilād al-Muqaddasa*. One of the names for Jerusalem in Arabic is *al-Bayt al-Muqaddas*,[547] a name with a profound resonance in Islamic history, past and present.[548] The Christian Bible is called in Arabic *al-Kitāb al-Muqaddas*[549] which contrasts interestingly with the Qur'ān's preferred designation of itself as a *Qur'ān Mubīn*, that is, a Qur'ān 'that makes things clear'.[550] We may compare it also with the normal Muslim mode of reference to *al-Qur'ān al-Karīm*, *The Noble Qur'ān*.[551]

Yet, whatever their precise designations of their scriptures, both these textual religions, Islam and Christianity, worship a 'holy numinous being', as Smart puts it,[552] and the sense of the sacred in both is bound up with formal worship. Yet, while major changes in traditional styles of liturgical worship have precipitated much angst in Christian circles, Islam has largely escaped such traumas and continued to adhere to antique liturgical traditions whose very simplicity may have helped them to remain constant.

The Arabic word *ḥarām*, that other word which we also noted earlier meant 'sacred', bears further meanings as well which resonate in Islam. *Ḥarām* also means that which is 'forbidden, interdicted, prohibited, unlawful … cursed'. An *ibn ḥarām* is a 'bastard'. However, the Ka'ba in Mecca is designated *al-Bayt al-Ḥarām*, The Holy House, and the Holy Mosque in Mecca is *al-Masjid al-Ḥarām*.[553] The many connotations of *ḥarām* in Islamic law are too well known to need repetition here.

The Arabic word *ḥarām*, then, displays a Janus face of 'the forbidden' and 'the sacred'. The word evokes conflicting feelings of fear and obedience on the one hand, as Muslims strive to avoid that which is classified as forbidden in their daily lives, and feelings of awe, reverence, respect and love on the other, as they pray five times a day towards God's own house on earth, the *Bayt al-Ḥarām*, the Ka'ba in Mecca.[554]

It is a truism that, classically, in Islam there is no division between secular and sacred, profane and non-profane. The Islamic path is one seamless whole. This *leitmotiv* of classical thought has been adopted in our own age, even though, practically, an actual division may in fact be present:

> The Fundamentalists assert that the believer and unbeliever alike are a subject of state jurisdiction, because the Prophet founded a state and a religion to go with it. That makes the 'sacred 'and 'secular' one and the same thing and what distinguishes them is a matter of public will and religious interest.[555]

Contemporary Islamic political theory may, then, exhibit a classical theory of wholeness where ideal should merge with praxis and where no division is to be permitted, or even entertained, between the sacred and the profane. Islamic reality often exhibits a praxis where the sacred is divorced from the secular, even while one political state or another may invoke the former to bolster a shaky political edifice. And it cannot be stressed too strongly here that Islam is not a monolith. There are many kinds of Islam, as numerous distinguished scholars have stressed.[556]

Two very different cases may serve to illustrate the sort of division of the secular from the sacred which has occurred in history:

> The Turkish revolution of 1920–4 was as momentous as the Russian one of 1917–21, but Western historians and social scientists have given it much less attention. For it was a defining moment in the relationship between Islam

> and the state. It brought into being the first avowedly secular state in the Muslim world, and it forced former subject peoples of the Ottoman empire, the Arabs in particular, to rebuild their political identity.[557]

If it is argued that this is an unfair, indeed extreme, illustration, on the grounds that it represents a *replacement* of the sacred by the secular, rather than a division between the two, then the mediaeval Islamic Caliphate (*khilāfa*) is perhaps a more apt example. It was this religio-political phenomenon over which al-Māwardī agonised; while it lasted, it was the 'potent symbol of Islam's global spiritual identity' and 'bearer of Islam's imperial impulse'.[558]

In surveying the phenomena of Islam, we earlier identified two dimensions: the historical and the intellectual. In each of these dimensions, there is what we might term here 'sacred tension'. By this, we indicate Eliade's overt (but sometimes covert) conflict between the sacred and the profane. The Qur'ān records the creation of ideal *khulafā'*, caliphs, like Adam in Q.2:30. Later the Qur'ānic ideal and paradigm becomes muddied, not only in the future career of Adam himself but also in the careers of the Umayyad and ʿAbbāsid Caliphs. Secularism intrudes, and the accusation is levelled that rulers have become *mulūk*, kings, rather than *khulafā'*, caliphs.[559]

There is, then, to use Eliadean terminology, a degradation or dilution of the sacred, in this case the sacred office of the Caliph. This dilution is accompanied by a dilution of empire, consequent upon the dilution of the Caliph's spiritual and religious authority and the concomitant rise of partisanship and sectarianism. The fall of Baghdad to the Mongols in AD 1258 effectively signalled the final end of the ʿAbbāsid Caliphate, the ultimate dilution of power and the final degradation of an office which, theoretically at least, embraced both the secular and the profane.

Yet some awe of the sacredness of this Caliphal office appears to have remained, even among the profane invading infidels. The last ʿAbbāsid Caliph in Baghdad, al-Mustaʿṣim (reg. 1242–58), was murdered by the Mongols. This is not unsurprising but the manner of his demise was. Here is G. E. von Grunebaum's striking description of his end:

> After overthrowing a feebly conducted defence the Mongol army pressed into Baghdad on January 17, 1258. The city was spared, the caliph taken prisoner and forced to hand over his treasures, but a few days later he was executed. It is said that he was wrapped in a carpet and shaken to death; for had a drop of his blood touched the earth, the world would have begun to shake.[560]

Today, as Lamin Sanneh notes, 'the sovereign secular state ... will not countenance a challenge to the sacred/secular distinction'.[561] The great North African proto-sociologist, Ibn Khaldūn (1332–1406), long ago not only recognised that distinction between the secular and the sacred but also supported it. Otherwise we might 'patch our worldly affairs by tearing our religion to pieces. Thus, neither our religion lasts nor (the worldly affairs) we have been patching.'[562]

2.6 *Conclusion*

Even in the earliest days of Christianity and Islam, there was not a simple, single monolithic model of *The Faith*. Rather, there were different, and sometimes competing, nascent theological registers. The early Council of Jerusalem, on the one hand, and the Battle of Ṣiffīn (AD 657) on the other, provide excellent examples of incipient diversity.

The Christian 'paradigm of early dispute and attempted resolution' is neatly viewed in chapter 15 of The Acts of the Apostles: the debate was over the continuance of circumcision, and the so-called Council of Jerusalem (AD 49) was convened to discuss the matter:

> But now some visitors came down from Judaea, who began to tell the brethren, You cannot be saved without being circumcised *according to the tradition of Moses*. Paul and Barnabas were drawn into a great controversy with them; and it was decided that Paul and Barnabas and certain of the rest should go up to see the apostles and presbyters in Jerusalem about this question … When the apostles and presbyters assembled to decide this matter there was much disputing over it …[563]

The issue was eventually resolved in favour of the newly converted gentiles, who were not, thenceforwards, to be subject to the Jewish tradition of circumcision.[564]

The whole affair is of particular interest in its initial linking of ancient Judaic custom and tradition to the theological concept of salvation, and the later abandonment of this custom and tradition at the Council, and thus the 'decoupling' of an ancient tradition and salvation. As Richard J. Dillon puts it: 'The Lucan argument which began with the emergence of "the Hellenists" at [Acts] 6:1 is now brought full circle as their church's representatives return to Jerusalem to seek the legitimacy of the mission to the uncircumcised'.[565]

This presence from the earliest days of different theological registers is confirmed by Brown, Osiek and Perkins:

> By the late [AD] 40s, the Gentile issue had produced at least four different attitudes within the Christian *koinōnia*, reflecting theological differences – attitudes attested in varous NT witnesses.[566]

The end result is a certain permissible plurality[567] which is clearly at odds with any idea of a monolithic paradigm of Judaised Christianity. The gate for further reassessments of antique traditions, and examination of the necessity or otherwise of such traditions for the sustenance of dogma, is thrown wide open.

In Islam, the Battle of Ṣiffīn provides a comparable model of conflict followed by diversity, in this case the nascent establishment of what will later characterise themselves as the Sunnī and Shīʿite branches of Islam. The following stark outline reveals what happened.

In AD 657, ʿAlī b. Abī Ṭālib, the fourth *khalīfa*, confronted the army of the Syrian governor, Muʿāwiya. The latter sought the punishment of the murderers of ʿUthmān b. ʿAffān, the third *khalīfa*, who had presided over the Islamic community from 644 to 656. ʿAlī, for his part, sought Muʿāwiya's oath of allegiance. After an inconclusive, three-month stand-off, battle was finally joined properly in Ṣafar 37/July–August 657, only to be halted by a Syrian plea for arbitration. This was accepted, but the agreement dealt a death blow to ʿAlī's power base. A group who became known as *khawārij* seceded, and ʿAlī was assassinated in Kūfa in 661. Those who continued to adhere to his cause began to be referred to as the *shīʿa* or party of ʿAlī.[568] The theological dimensions of the political fall-out, in the development and establishment of both Khawārij and Shīʿa, are very well known, as are the plurality and diversity engendered as an ultimate result of the Battle of Ṣiffīn.

It is a truism that dogma and tradition, especially when enshrined in a revealed text, require exegesis. A plurality of exegetes *may* yield a plurality of views; new, competing and even conflicting exegeses may be born. Early Sunnī Islam developed a plurality of law schools (*madhāhib*) – Mālikī, Ḥanafī, Shāfiʿī and Ḥanbalī – popularly sanctioned by the useful (but possibly 'weak' (*ḍaʿīf*) or 'invented' (*mawḍūʿ*)) ḥadīth which insisted that difference of opinion in the Islamic *umma* was a sign of God's mercy. Coulson comments

> Arising as it does out of the search to discover the ideal law of the Sharīʿa, the phenomenon of unity and diversity in legal doctrine goes to the very heart of Muslim jurisprudence. There is an old Arab proverb to express this: 'The person who does not understand divergence in doctrine', it runs, 'has not caught the true scent of jurisprudence' (*Man lā yaʿrif al-ikhtilāf lam yashumma rāʾiḥata 'l-fiqh*).[569]

All this is confirmed and compounded by the plurality and diversity of different theological registers in mediaeval times, as well as in our own age, which have ranged from Muʿtazilism, Ashʿarism and Māturīdism to Wahhābism, Deobandism, Barelwism and Ṣūfism.

A classical tradition of Western scholarship, which may be termed here 'critical antonymy', had no problems until fairly recently in deploying the neat but simplistic terminology of 'orthodoxy' and 'heterodoxy', with all the connotations of 'right' and 'wrong' implicit in such absolute terms – which were, in any case, assumed to be self-explanatory. As we have noted earlier, Professor H. A. R. Gibb was the distinguished epitome of such scholarship. That which was 'orthodox' or 'official' – and the two were not necessarily always coterminous – was seen to be underpinned by a text, interpreted according to one light or another in a correct fashion. And, whereas Popovic and Veinstein spoke of 'un autre Islam', Baldick inveighed against what he perceived to be the old-fashioned divisions of 'official' and 'orthodox' Islam on the one hand, and 'parallel', 'alternative' or 'heterodox' Islam on the other. For him, the sheer diversity of Islam rendered this simple, though convenient, dualism untenable.

There is clearly a need for other vocabularies which reflect the reality of the diverse interpretations of text-bound faiths like Islam and Christianity throughout history. It is no longer sufficient to observe that 'heterodox' Muʿtazilism became 'official' for a certain period of time in mediaeval Islamic history, while challenging the authority of the state, like Arianism in the Christian West, at others.

For Sir Isaac Newton, 'Athanasian orthodoxy', was 'the archetypal heresy'. St Augustine's *Confessions* were a manifestation of the truth as he saw it, a statement of his belief in the authority of the prevailing Church and its teachings, against the pluralism of Manichaeism, Donatism and Pelagianism. But Augustine was a Manichee first!

Like Christianity, Islam, as we have shown, had – and, indeed, has – a diversity of phenomena, signs and dimensions of the sacred. Like Christianity, with its emphasis on revealed text, oral and written tradition and *koinōnía*, Islam places great store on deriving divine authority from text, tradition and *umma*. In both Christianity and Islam, history shows that enforceable terrestrial authority may help to sustain a particular doctrine. The battle within the Christian Church for and against Arianism, and the establishent of the Muʿtazilite inquisition, the *Miḥna*, provide ample evidence of that.

My argument is not that the great faith traditions like Christianity and Islam have failed to develop sustained and coherent bodies of doctrine down the centuries. It is rather that, in order to reflect the plurality and diversity of the interpretations of those doctrines, the true phenomenologist should eschew the value judgements implicit in the classical vocabulary of 'orthodox' and 'heterodox', with all that they imply in our own age of 'rightness' on the one hand and 'wrongness' on the other.

Historical diversity and plural exegeses are better reflected in such neologisms as '*pluridoxy*' as a replacement for 'orthodoxy'. Here, the combined classical roots would serve to indicate several, or more, *exegetical* opinions. *Orthopraxis* might yield to *multipraxis*, and *monovalence* to *multivalence*. A fundamentalist or exclusivist monoglot reading of a sacred text, *monolexis*, might be supplanted by a term such as *multilexis*, denoting a plenitude of intertextual readings or interpretations.

Finally, *in the light of the sacred*, we might venture to propose a new vocabulary for deployment in this ever important field. Using the ablative singular of the Latin word *sacrum* (holy thing, place, rite), after the manner of the English word *sacrosanct*, it is suggested that a reading of seminal texts which claim to have been revealed be characterised as *sacrolexis*; the appreciation of sacralised values becomes *sacrovalence*; and the praxis of authority which derives from, or accompanies, our textual reading becomes *sacropraxis*. Then perhaps the old 'orthodoxies' of 'orthodox' and 'heterodox' will wither on yesterday's semantic vine.

CHAPTER

3

THE FLIGHT TO TRADITION: A PARADIGM OF RETURN AND DENIAL

3.1 *Christian Tradition: Definitions and Distinctions*

Lexically the word 'tradition' has several facets. *The Concise Oxford Dictionary of Current English* provides four fundamental definitions:

1. Opinion or belief or custom handed down; handing down of these, from ancestors to posterity esp. orally or by practice.
2. (Theol.) Doctrine etc. supposed to have divine authority but not committed to writing, esp. (1) laws held by Pharisees to have been delivered by God to Moses, (2) oral teaching of Christ and Apostles not recorded in writing by immediate disciples, (3) words and deeds of Muhammad not in Koran.
3. Artistic or literary principle(s) based on accumulated experience or continuous usage …
4. (Law). Formal delivery.[1]

Etymologically, the word 'tradition' derives from the Latin *trado–tradere–tradidi–traditum* meaning 'to hand over, give up, surrender' in the sense of 'to hand down as any kind of inheritance to posterity'.[2]

Theologically, tradition may embrace in Christianity both the practice of the faith as well as the faith itself, including scripture; or, more narrowly, 'tradition may be distinguished from scripture, and taken to mean the teaching and practice of the church, not explicitly recorded in the words of the Bible, but handed down from the beginning within the Christian community'.[3]

More *mystically and eschatologically*, Kallistos Ware has observed:

> While Tradition is indeed the dynamic movement of God in history, it is to be seen also in a metahistorical or eschatological perspective. It is not so much a long line stretched out in time as the gathering of time itself into God's eternity, the irruption into this present age of the eschaton, or age to come.[4]

Catechetically 'the handing down of the word and sacraments by the Church is called tradition'.[5] Elsewhere, tradition for the Christian is defined as being 'distinct from Sacred Scripture, though closely connected to it'.[6] Revealed truth depends on both scripture and tradition.[7] Indeed, David Brown stresses that 'tradition, so far from being something secondary or reactionary, is the motor that sustains revelation both within Scripture and beyond'.[8] Tradition *can* imply that which is reactionary and conservative, but it can also 'be imaginative and innovative.[9] Above all, it can be illuminative, casting a spotlight on, and extending, the basic materials of revelation.[10]

Scripturally, we note Paul's 'dependence on early Church tradition'.[11] Fitzmyer draws attention to Paul's usage of such Greek terms as 'handing on' ,'*paradidonai*, of what he has 'received' (*paralambanein*). There is a direct parallelism here with 'the technical vocabulary of tradition ... in the rabbinic schools'.[12]

Many other definitions of tradition, from widely differing perspectives, could be given; but it is quite clear from the above that one of the overriding *leitmotivs* of tradition is the concept of 'handing on' or 'handing down', that is, of a corpus of information distinct from revealed scripture.

All this is of much more than pure academic interest and curiosity for the twenty-first century. If, as Anthony Giddens maintains, tradition's distinctiveness derives from the fact that 'it defines a kind of truth' and, 'in tradition, the past structures the present through shared collective beliefs and sentiments', then we may agree with him that 'fundamentalism is beleaguered tradition; it is tradition defended in the traditional way in a globalising world that asks for reasons'.[13] In other words, the antique debate between revelation and reason in both Christianity and Islam may be read, alternatively, as one between tradition and reason where the former is characterised, rightly or wrongly, as 'mindless', and the latter, in a similar way, is deemed 'insensitive'.

The fruits of tradition are as diverse as its definitions: tradition may be deemed by some to equate with, or produce, fundamentalism and a species of Christianity which is deeply conservative and lacks progressive growth.[14] In other quarters, it may produce deep conflicts of loyalty which may or may not be resolved. Thus, Sir Thomas More proclaimed, before he was beheaded on 6 July 1535, in deep adherence to the traditions of his faith, that he was 'the King's good servant but God's first'.[15] He had defended the old 'orthodoxy', the old 'tradition' of papal supremacy. But the new 'orthodoxy which mattered most to the regime [of Henry VIII] was adherence to the new doctrine of royal supremacy.'[16]

The Bull of excommunication and deposition of Queen Elizabeth I (reg. 1558–1603), entitled *Regnans in Excelsis*, issued by Pope Pius V (reg. 1566–72) in February 1570, severely tested the real loyalties of many.[17] Traditional beliefs and practices could no longer be fudged or compromised. As G. R. Elton puts it: '[The Bull] involved the English catholics in a dreadful dilemma by ending the long years of compromise. The pope's claim to be able to absolve subjects from their allegiance struck at the core of the national state.'[18]

However, the hideous dilemma of tradition and papal authority versus conscience was cheerfully resolved, at least for one man, by Cardinal Henry Newman (1801–90) in the nineteenth century: in a typically anti-ultramontane moment, he famously declared that, if 'obliged to bring religion into after-dinner toasts' he would drink to conscience first before the pope.[19]

Tradition, then, may embrace a sense of age-old 'orthodoxy' versus state autocracy. It may be associated with fundamentalism, too – for fundamentalists worldwide, of all faith persuasions, claim to be the guardians *par excellence* of the fundamentals, the traditions, the 'eidetic images' of their religions as they perceive them. Those who would espouse change or progression or liberalisation are anathematised:

> Fundamentalists begin as traditionalists who perceive some challenge or threat to their core identity, both social and personal. They are not frivolous, nor do they deal with peripheral assaults. If they lose on the central issues, they believe they lose everything. They react, they fight back with great innovative power.[20]

In his Foreword to Yves M.-J. Congar ' s wide-ranging volume entitled *Tradition and Traditions*,[21] Jeff Cavins draws attention to St Paul's *Second Epistle to the Thessalonians* (2:14),[22] in which the apostle urges: 'Stand firm, then brethren, and hold by the traditions you have learned, *in word* or in writing, from us'.[23] There is a clear concern here to embed in the consciousness of the recipients of the letter a 'Christian (Pauline) tradition' and this is done with reference to the 'addressees' experience, even its dangers, as part of an ultimately salutary divine process, countering diabolical deception'.[24] Human tradition, however, must not be at the expense of God's commandments.[25]

Tradition, then, may be verbal or written down – and, as we noted earlier, the whole concept is infused with the twin ideas of 'that which is handed down' and that which is *entrusted* by someone to someone else.[26] The twin *leitmotivs* here are *transmission* and *entrustment*. And Congar reminds us that the early Fathers of the Church made frequent use of the Greek and Latin vocabulary of 'handing on' and 'tradition' (*parádosis*, *traditio*).[27] Despite the antique and commonplace antithesis of Scripture and Tradition, the former could be viewed as part of the latter, as attested by 2 Thessalonians 2:14. 'Scripture itself is tradition – it is part of the greater category of Tradition.'[28] Both Sacred Scripture and Sacred Tradition are in intimate union with each other, sharing the common *télos* of transmitting 'the sacred deposit of faith'.[29]

All that said, however, it cannot be denied that the word 'tradition' embraces a slippery and fluid concept. Its meanings can be pluriform and multivalent, specific or broad, mediated by a diversity of sometimes antithetical Christian Churches, theologies or structures. Our discussion will continue to embrace the concept in all its slipperiness and fluidity while noting, for example, that specific divisions have been made at various times within the broad concept of tradition into 'social traditions, traditions of the Church and *The Tradition*'.[30] There is theological tradition with a small 't' and a capital 'T'. But perhaps the most important Tradition is the Apostolic Tradition. Cavins defines this as follows:

> The apostolic Tradition, however, comes from the apostles as they received it from Jesus' teaching, from His example, and from what the Holy Spirit revealed to them. It is this apostolic Tradition that is referred to when the Church speaks of Scripture and Tradition , making up the deposit of faith.[31]

Of course, the idea that Scripture and Tradition are not rivals, or in opposition, reflects a mainly Catholic Christian understanding of the respective roles of these two sources of faith.[32] They were never of equal weight, however, since Scripture had authority and sovereignty over Tradition.[33] (Here, we might compare the debate which took place in mediaeval Islam over the relative merits of Qur'ān and *Sunna* and the ultimate subordination of the latter to the former by al-Shāfiʿī (767–820), the Father of Islamic Jurisprudence.)[34]

The Protestant Reformation critique of the role of Tradition/tradition, however, chose to underline and stress the mainly Biblical orientation of mediaeval times,[35] and reject all but Scripture as a source of divine revelation.[36] Scripture alone (*scriptura sola*) became the criterion, and Martin Luther made scripture exclusive.[37] Catholic Tradition, according to the Protestant theologians, appeared to establish the Catholic Church and its pontiff as sole arbiters in matters doctrinal and even set Tradition up as superior to Sacred Scripture itself. In all these matters, the role of the Catholic magisterium, or 'teaching church', was seen to have a solipsistic link with Tradition/tradition running from the Council of Trent (1545–63) to the First Vatican Council (1870–1).[38]

It is clear, then, that, from Apostolic times onwards, Tradition/tradition had a sometimes uneasy relationship with Scripture, at least in the view of some branches of the Christian Church as they developed. This had obvious repercussions for the whole question of obedience and authority, particularly when that authority was exercised by a 'teaching church' which claimed to be founded upon Tradition, to preach Tradition and to be led by Tradition.

In some of what follows, we shall illustrate these points further by taking one aspect of Tradition, i.e. traditional scriptural exegesis, and survey how this particular aspect became metamorphosed from the middle of the twentieth century onwards. By way of comparison, after defining and distinguishing different kinds of Islamic *Sunna*, we will focus on the deployment of neo-*ijtihād*.

3.2 *Shadow and Spirt: The Second Vatican Council*

3.2.1 Pre-Conciliar: *Pascendi* and *Divino Afflante Spiritu*

Pope Pius X (reg. 1903–14) famously characterised 'Modernism' as *cumulatio omnium haeresium* (the synthesis of all heresies);[39] he went on to say:

> Undoubtedly, were anyone to attempt the task of collecting together all the errors that have been broached against the faith and to concentrate into one the sap and substance of them all, he could not succeed in doing so better than the Modernists have done. Nay, they have gone further than this, for, as We have already intimated, their system means the destruction not of the Catholic religion alone, but of all religion. Hence the rationalists are not wanting in their applause, and the most frank and sincere amongst them congratulate themselves in having found in the Modernists the most valuable of all allies.[40]

The suspicion expressed here of 'the rationalists' is significant and characteristic, reflecting as it does the ancient battle between revelation and reason which pervaded mediaeval scholastic thought in both Christianity and Islam. The 'Modernism' condemned by Pius X consisted *inter alia* of a variety of what might be termed 'neo-Arian' tendencies.[41] But what exactly was the essence of Modernism? Certainly, according to Pius, it was something which was hostile to the classical Apostolic Tradition:

> The Modernists pass judgement on the holy Fathers of the Church even as they do upon tradition. With consummate temerity they assure the public that the Fathers, while personally most worthy of all veneration, were entirely ignorant of history and criticism, for which they are only excusable on account of the time in which they lived.[42]

Modernism, furthermore, according to Pius, was guilty of what we might characterise as a neo-Averroism[43] as well as a distinctly methodological schizophrenia.[44] His Encyclical *Pascendi Gregis* (8 September 1907) was, of course, part of a theologically conservative trend, aimed at the preservation of traditional norms of thought as well as the Apostolic Tradition itself. It had been preceded by Pius X's own decree *Lamentabile Sane* (3 July 1907)[45] and, of course, by the notorious *Syllabus of Errors* (8 December 1864)[46] issued by Pope Pius IX (reg. 1846–78). In the Anti-Modernist Oath (*Sacrorum Antistitum*) instituted by Pius X on 1 September 1910, and required 'to be sworn to by all clergy, pastors, confessors, preachers, religious superiors, and professors in philosophical-theological seminaries'[47] the swearer was obliged to state:

> I sincerely hold that the doctrine of faith was handed down to us from the apostles through the orthodox Fathers in exactly the same meaning and always in the same purport. Therefore, I entirely reject the heretical misrepresentation that dogmas evolve and change from one meaning to another different from the one which the Church held previously.[48]

The stress in the whole oath is on 'the invariable character of Catholic tradition'.[49] And, reflecting a particular fear of the Modernists, the oath-taker was obliged to say:

> Likewise, I reject that method of judging and interpreting Sacred Scripture which, *departing from the tradition of the Church* [my italics], the analogy of faith, and the norms of the Apostolic See, embraces the misrepresentations of the rationalists and with no prudence or restraint adopts textual criticism as the one and supreme norm.[50]

Such oaths are the product of intellectual fear. We see parallels, albeit focusing on a completely different subject, in the *miḥna* (inquisition) instituted by the ʿAbbāsid Caliph al-Ma'mūn (reg. 813–33) – and there is a further Islamic parallelism, which we shall develop later, with the Islamic focus on the views and opinions of the 'pious ancestors', the *Salaf*. Among those Muslims who adhered – or who adhere – to the views of the *salaf*, there is the same visceral affinity with Tradition as we find in the writings and locutions of Pius X.

The Anti-Modernist Oath reflected a profound fear of the prevailing method of historico-critical and textual criticism which had been developing in scholarly Biblical exegetical circles during the nineteenth century.[51] The true believer was to reject the idea that

> a professor lecturing or writing on a historico-theological subject should first put aside any preconceived opinion about the supernatural origin of Catholic tradition or about the divine promise of help to preserve all revealed truth for ever; and that they should then interpret the writings of each of the Fathers solely by scientific principles, excluding all sacred authority, and with the same liberty of judgement that is common in the investigation of all ordinary historical documents.[52]

Finally, the swearer of the Oath was obliged to oppose the Modernist notion that there was 'nothing divine in sacred tradition'.[53]

It is abundantly clear from all this that Pius X, in his writings, believed that he was trying to hold back the floodwaters of heresy'– indeed, all heresies – and that the vehicles of heresy included historico-critical textual exegesis, 'modern' ideas about sacred tradition and a general attitude of scholarly independence which sat awkwardly with the unchanging nature of Church, Scripture and Tradition as envisaged and articulated by Pius.

Yet, years later, it would become apparent that the historico-critical approach did not have to be considered automatically as a vehicle for heresy: the Anti-Modernist Oath was finally abolished in 1967; the Encyclical of Pope Pius XII, *Divino Afflante Spiritu* (30 September 1943) permitted and espoused historico-literary criticism; and Pope John XXIII 'stressed that, while old traditional dogmas could never be changed in their essences, they could be interpreted or rewritten in new words'.[54]

The contrast between all this and the *dicta* of Pius X could not be greater, and it is not surprising that old-guard traditionalists, who had continued to welcome the strictures of a previous, more authoritarian and certain age, felt undervalued and betrayed. It seemed that the Apostolic Tradition itself, as well as many other aspects of much loved Traditions/traditions – scholarly, ritual and other – were under attack in a sea of liberalism, lack of ecclesiastical discipline and uncertainty.[55]

Thus was inaugurated a chain reaction which led, almost ineluctably, to a neo-traditionalism, best epitomised in the thought, spirit and practice of Archbishop Marcel Lefebvre. A perceived post-Conciliar, post-Vatican II Anti-Tradition movement within the Catholic Church – whether actual or apparent – was confronted by an opposition of fervent neo-traditionalists. The history of the Church had come full circle.

One of the keys to so much of this was that famous Encyclical of Pius XII to which we have already alluded, *Divino Afflante Spiritu*. And the moment moulded the man. So, who *was* Pope Pius XII?[56] The life, and its conflicting interpretations, have sometimes overshadowed the thought and the theology. (1) Was he a conservative traditionalist? (2) Against the backcloth of the Second World War, was he a conservative, 'timid', ineffectual and silent pontiff, hidebound by the manifold traditions of his Office, or was he a 'bold' pragmatist whose Roman circumstances under Nazi occupation dictated a need to work in strict secrecy *pro bono populorum* and, in particular, *pro bono Judaeorum?*(3) And if he was, politically, a careful but bold pragmatist, did the same spirit of pragmatic adventure imbue his theology and thought?

The following paragraphs attempt some answers to these three questions. Taken *in toto*, the answers provide a broad assessment of Pius XII's role in the development of Christian and, in particular, Roman Catholic Tradition. The life bespoke the thought in terms of both courage and pragmatics.

The future Pope Pius XII (reg. 1939–58) was born in Rome on 2 March 1876 and given the name Eugenio Maria Giuseppe Giovanni Pacelli. Exactly twenty-three years later, he was ordained priest; and, after a brief stint of parish work, he took up a post in the Vatican Foreign Office in 1901. Possessed of a brilliant mind, he had been awarded his Bachelor's and Licentiate degrees *summa cum laude*, and in 1902 he gained a doctorate in canon and civil law, also with the highest grade of *summa cum laude*.

Advancement was swift: 1912 saw Pacelli as Acting Secretary of the Vatican Foreign Office; and, after the outbreak of the First World War in 1914, Pacelli was advanced to the position of Secretary of the Vatican Congregation of Extraordinary Ecclesiastical Affairs. Pope Benedict XV (reg. 1914–22) consecrated him Archbishop on 13 May 1917, and he became Apostolic Nuncio to Germany in 1920. On 16 December 1929, he was created a Cardinal by Pope Pius XI (reg. 1922–39), and in 1930 he became the Pope's Vatican Secretary of State.

After Pius XI died on 10 February 1939, Cardinal Eugenio Pacelli was elected Pope on 2 March 1939 at the following conclave – one of the shortest in history – taking the name of Pius XII. The Second World War which followed very soon afterwards, and lasted from 1939 to 1945, provided the backdrop against which most contemporary historians have judged him, defensively or harshly. Towards the end of that war, on 30 September 1943, Pius XII issued his Encyclical *Divino Afflante Spiritu* (*On the Promotion of Biblical Studies*). He died on 9 October 1958.[57]

In his assessment of Muḥammad, the Founder Prophet of Islam, W. Montgomery Watt wrote: 'Of all the world's great men none has been so maligned as Muḥammad'.[58] Now, it is certainly not suggested here that comparisons should be sought and drawn between the lives of Muḥammad and Pope Pius XII. Yet it is salutary to reflect on the stream of venomous criticism which has adhered to the name of Pius XII, a historical figure whose reputation has suffered much.

The trend began with Rolf Hochhuth's play *Der Stellvertreter* (*The Deputy*), which opened in Berlin in February 1963 and severely criticised the 'silence' of Pius XII during the Jewish Holocaust under Nazi Germany. This hostile trend, which seeks to castigate Pius for an alleged silence, has continued into our own age with the publication of John Cornwall's *Hitler's Pope*.[59]

So, had Pius XII asked in our own age 'Who do men say that I am?' in echo of Mark 8:27 (tr. Knox), he would have received a bewilderingly mixed response.[60] John Cornwall would have accused him of demonstrating a clear antipathy towards the Jews from early on in his diplomatic career, of having learned nothing from Nazi Germany and of having been 'silent' in the face of the Holocaust.[61] Others, by contrast, would have lauded his goodness, his sanctity and his saving of nearly one million Jews.[62] Pius XII 's death in 1958 was mourned by the then Israeli Foreign Minister, Golda Meir, who praised 'a great servant of peace' and one who *had* spoken out in defence of the Jews.[63]

And, whether as an act of gratitude, as many believed, for all that Pius *had* done for the Jews, or for other reasons, the Chief Rabbi of Rome, Rabbi Israel Zolli, converted to Roman Catholicism in 1945, taking Pius's first name of Eugene.[64] He too, in our own age as in his, would have esteemed Pius XII most highly.

Ronald J. Rychlak sums up the evidence for the defence as follows:

> Efforts to portray Eugenio Pacelli (Pope Pius XII) as an anti-Semite are contradicted by an abundance of evidence – beginning with the fact that, in the critical six months between his election as Pope (March 1939) and the outbreak of the War (September 1939), he made six public appeals to prevent the catastrophe that was about to claim millions of innocent victims ... His first encyclical, *Summi Pontificatus*, released just weeks after the outbreak of war, expressly mentioned Jews and urged solidarity with *all* who profess a belief in God.[65]

In the light of all this, let us now return to our three questions which we earlier posed concerning the life of Pius XII: was he a conservative traditionalist? Or was he a closet moderniser? His critics see him as a 'Roman Catholic of his time, formal and disabled by traditional theological anti-Judaism that fed the "underside" of Christian Theology for centuries'.[66] They see him as a product of the cry of the New Testament Jewish crowds at the time of Christ's condemnation to death, which has reverberated down the ages: 'His blood be upon us, and upon our children' (Matthew 27:25, tr. Knox). There was, then, a *traditional* anti-Semitic, anti-Judaic milieu.[67]

Coupled with this was a liking by the Vatican in the 1930s for *traditional* conservative political regimes and a loathing and fear of communist ones.[68] In addition, the spirituality of Pius XII was itself ardently *traditional*, formed as it was by a reading of Thomas à Kempis's *Imitation of Christ*,[69] a deep faith in the power of prayer,[70] devotion to the Eucharist[71] and an immersion in the concept of 'suffering as redemption and purification' together with the *traditional* Biblical concept of punishment for sin.[72] Furthermore, it is clear that Pope Pius XII enjoyed – or at least desired – the *traditional* trappings and pomp of the papacy.[73]

Taking all these factors into account, he may then be characterised as a traditionalist, a man of his times raised in a traditional milieu and mould. Could he change? The answer to our two other questions posed at the beginning of this section will also provide an answer to that. Tradition *could* be ameliorated or even changed.

Our second question asked whether, against the backcloth of the Second World War, Pius XII was a 'timid', 'ineffectual', silent pontiff, hidebound by the *traditions* of his office, or 'bold' pragmatist who did what he could, *when* he could, for the Jews. I suggest that the evidence is in favour of the latter.

There is a substantial body of evidence to show that Pius did as much as he possibly could, pragmatically, to save as many Jews as possible from the Nazi Holocaust, without incurring the military wrath of the Nazi regime[74] and thus, inadvertently, precipitating further Jewish deaths.[75]

Dom Kilian McDonnell OSB comments as follows: 'Pius was not silent, but restrained. Pius himself said that when he spoke he weighed each word "with profound seriousness in the interest of those who suffer"'.[76]

Two examples of Pius XII's bold 'pragmatism'-cum-charity must suffice here. Most interestingly for our discussions of tradition, the first took place only a few days before the issue of the Encyclical *Divino Afflante Spiritu* (30 September 1943). On 20 or 26 September 1943, the Gestapo chief in Rome, Lt-Col. Herbert Kappler, demanded fifty kilos of gold from the Jewish community in Rome. Otherwise a large body of Jews would be taken hostage and deported from Rome to certain death. The Vatican offered to loan to the Jewish community any deficit in the sum collected by its members. The money was delivered to the Gestapo on 28 September without the need, however, to take up the offer of the papal loan.[77]

Secondly, when the Nazi round-up of Jews in Rome began in the middle of October 1943, Pius instructed his bishops 'to lift the enclosure from convents and monasteries, so that they could become refuges for the Jews'.[78]

This brings us to our third question, acutely relevant in any discussion of the changing roles and states of tradition: did Pius manifest the same spirit of cautious but pragmatic 'adventure' in his theology and thought? To ascertain this, and contextualise the revolution that was *Divino Afflante Spiritu*, we need to remind ourselves briefly how scripture was traditionally read and appreciated in the centuries leading up to the Encyclical, especially by the early Fathers. In short, their traditional reading may be characterised as multi-layered and multivalent: it was, firstly, 'sapiential'. The Bible was considered to be a 'total wisdom' reflecting the 'unique wisdom' of God Himself.[79] Secondly, it could be typologcal and allegorical.[80] Thirdly, it might also be both Christological and ecclesial.[81] Most importantly, however, we may emphasise that these early Fathers were less concerned to stress a *historical* tradition of reading scripture.[82]

Scholars have identified a pre-critical period of Biblical exegesis, lasting up to about the middle of the seventeenth century, in which the Bible was considered as a simple, heaven-bequeathed narrative divorced from its historical and cultural context.[83] The age of modern Biblical criticism is said to have begun with the Oratorian priest Richard Simon (1638–1712) and his three-volume *Histoire critique du Vieux Testament* (1678), in which he concluded, *inter alia*, that the Pentateuch had other authors apart from Moses.[84]

Textual criticism and the rise and growth of the historical method followed. Literary and historical criticism combined in what was to be characterised as 'historical-critical method'.[85] In all this, Roman Catholic Biblical scholarship lagged far behind, preferring to 'play it safe' with a 'severely traditional exegesis'[86] which eschewed, and was indifferent or even hostile to, the developing critical tradition.[87] In the meantime, Protestant Biblical exegesis, incarnated perhaps most vividly in the person of the Lutheran form critic and theologian, Rudolf Bultmann (1884–1976), explored the highways of a 'demythologised' New Testament.[88]

Roman Catholic exegetes, prior to *Divino Afflante Spiritu*, were not *all* totally opposed to the new criticism. Augustin Cardinal Bea, for example, who played such a decisive role in the implementation of the Second Vatican Council, did see 'in form criticism an ally against rationalistic exegesis'.[89] But he exercised an expected and traditional caution. Furthermore, the proscriptions resulting from the desire to quell the Modernist Heresy under Pope Pius X cast a deep blight over any really acceptable developments in Roman Catholic Biblical exegesis.[90]

Yet it is now admitted on all sides – Protestant and Catholic alike – that the most significant advance in Biblical exegesis since the pre-critical period to AD 1650 was the development and application of the historical-critical method. And it was the Encyclical of Pius XII, *Divino Afflante Spiritu* of 1943, which fell like a great stone into the pool of RC Biblical scholarship and produced the change on the Catholic side (though that has never officially gone to the lengths of Bultmann's demythologising). Brown and Collins describe Pius's Encyclical as 'a Magna Charta for biblical progress'.[91]

The path to that golden *telos* of general RC reception and acceptance of the historico-critical method had proceeded by leaps and setbacks.[92] Firstly, some of the groundwork for *Divino Afflante Spiritu* had been done by Pope Leo XIII (reg. 1878–1903) in his Encyclical Letter *Providentissimus Deus*, issued on 18 November 1893. The title of this Encyclical has been translated as *On the Study of Sacred Scripture*.[93]

In effect, this Encyclical stands as an early blueprint for future Catholic Biblical studies.[94] It is admitted that 'sacred scripture is not like other books. Dictated by the Holy Spirit, it contains things of the deepest importance, which in many instances, are most difficult and obscure.'[95] The informed modern exegete must be on his guard against the successors of the old heretics, the Rationalists, who 'deny that there is any such thing as revelation or inspiration, or Holy Scriptures at all; ... they set down the Scripture narratives as stupid fables and lying stories'.[96] Good teachers of Scripture are required to prepare beginners in exegesis, using as their primary text the Vulgate sanctioned by the Council of Trent.[97]

In an appeal to tradition, Leo noted: 'And this is the existing custom of the Church'.[98] Furthermore, in an additional such appeal, he noted that 'the Holy Scripture was safely interpreted by those who had the apostolic succession'.[99] No one is allowed to interpret sacred scripture in a manner which contradicts 'the unanimous agreement of the Fathers'.[100]

In all this, then, traditional exegesis rides paramount. However, the informed and well-trained exegete, in suitable cases and with just cause, may 'push inquiry and exposition beyond what the Fathers have done; provided [that] he carefully observes the rule so wisely laid down by St Augustine – not to depart from the literal and obvious sense, except only where reason makes it untenable or necessity requires'.[101]

This is an immensely important paragraph of *Providentissimus Deus*: it shows the permissibility of an informed exegesis, whose bonds to the prior exegetical tradition have been considerably loosened. In effect, it paves the way for *Divino Afflante Spiritu*.

Leo XIII emphasises that the study of Oriental languages and 'the art of true criticism' will facilitate proper scriptural exegesis,[102] as will a knowledge of natural science.[103] However, he stresses that one is not obliged to accept every opinion which has come down from the Patristic Age but only those which are *de fide* and have inspired unanimity.[104] The scriptures themselves are, *in toto*, the product of divine inspiration, and so they are to be characterised as inerrant. This is part of the tradition of the Church[105] to which Leo XIII appeals directly: 'This is the ancient and unchanging faith of the Church, solemnly defined in the Councils of Florence and of Trent'.[106] Biblical exegetes are to work with the knowledge that 'nothing can be proved either by physical science or by archaeology which can really contradict the Scriptures'.[107] If Catholic exegetes work within this framework, they will perform a valuable service to the scriptures themselves and the Church.[108]

Leo XIII 's Encyclical *Providentissimus Deus*, much less well known than Pius XII's *Divino Afflante Spiritu*, provided a kind of prototype for that later work. It encouraged, rather than stultified or cut off, Biblical scholarship. It loosened the bonds to Patristic exegesis but at the same time stressed the value of tradition/Tradition. It permitted a limited form of private exegesis provided that that was compatible with the norms and parameters also outlined. Above all, it acknowledged that modern Biblical scholarship did not, and could not, stand still. And though Pope Pius X's later Encyclical, *Pascendi Dominici Gregis*, issued on 8 September 1907 to counter what was termed 'the Modernist Heresy',[109] constituted a major setback for Catholic Biblical exegesis, inspiring fear of novelty and stressing 'orthodox' tradition over what was perceived as exegetical error, Leo XIII's earlier Encyclical provided the model for a way forward and, in particular, for *Divino Afflante Spiritu* itself.

Even the opponents of Pius XII, like John Cornwall, have professed a sneaking admiration for *Divino Afflante Spiritu* – though, in the light of an equally famous Encyclical issued by Pius XII (*Humani Generis*, 'given at Rome' on 12 August 1950), Cornwall characterises *Divino* as 'a false spring'.[110] Scripture specialists, however, were in no doubt about the significance of this text.

We have already noted the characterisation by Raymond E. Brown and Thomas Aquinas Collins of this Encyclical as 'a Magna Charta for biblical progress'.[111] They went on: 'Although the pope saluted the encyclicals of his predecessors, he announced that the time for fear was over and that Catholic scholars should use modern tools in their exegesis'.[112]

Brown and Collins hailed *Divino Afflante Spiritu* as completing much of the teaching in Leo XIII's *Providentissimus Deus*.[113] The emphasis in *Divino*

> on recognizing different types of literature or different literary forms in the Bible was probably the greatest single contribution of *Divino Afflante Spiritu* for it offered the Catholic scholar an intelligent and honest way of facing up to the obvious historical problems present in the Bible.[114]

Divino begins by praising the work and memory of Leo XIII and drawing attention to *Providentissimus Deus*.[115] It draws attention to the light that archaeological excavations have been able to throw on scriptural understanding as well as the discovery of relevant written documents and 'ancient codices of the Sacred Books' which 'have been found and edited with discerning thoroughness'. In addition, there has been a far ranging examination of Patristic exegesis.[116]

The importance of textual criticism is stressed 'for its very purpose is to insure that the sacred text be restored, as perfectly as possible, be purified from the corruptions due to the carelessness of the copyists and be freed, as far as may be done, from glosses and omissions'.[117] It is also important to analyse the mode of writing, and the exegete should, therefore, be concerned to 'determine ... to what extent the manner of expression or the literary mode adopted by the sacred writer may lead to a correct and genuine interpretation'.[118] Difficulties, if as yet unsolved in the sacred texts, must be treated with patience, but their existence should not inhibit a constant exegetical grappling in an attempt to reach solutions.[119]

Pius draws attention, towards the end of his Encyclical, to the value of scripture amid the raging of the Second World War 'when almost all peoples and nations are plunged in a sea of calamities, when a cruel war heaps ruins upon ruins and slaughter upon slaughter'.[120]

Although *Divino Afflante Spiritu* proceeds firmly from a bedrock of past traditional exegesis, and deploys numerous caveats, it was, nonetheless, a revolution in Catholic scriptural interpretation. So, did the later 1950 Encyclical, *Humani Generis*, represent the backward step which, in Cornwall's words, rendered *Divino* 'a false spring '?[121] Do we have here an example of 'the flight to tradition' and the 'paradigm of return and denial' (the twin *leitmotivs* of this chapter) *on the Christian side*? Did the *Pastor Angelicus*, the 'Angelic Pastor', as the prophecy of the twelfth-century Irish monk Malachy, centuries earlier, had allegedly designated Pius,[122] turn into a *Pastor Recidivus*, a theological clone of Pius X who had smitten the Modernist Heresy with his famous *Encyclical Pascendi*?[123]

Cornwall would certainly have us believe that this was the case. For him, *Humani Generis* 'froze creative scholarly endeavour and prompted an intellectual witch-hunt comparable to the anti-Modernist campaign in the first decade of the century'.[124] Brown and Collins hold a more conciliatory view: 'It is worth noting that in this predominantly monitory encyclical there is virtually no chastisement of biblical scholars. Seemingly to his death Pius XII remained firm in his faith in modern criticism.'[125]

The primary intention of *Humani Generis* was to discuss and condemn 'some false opinions which threaten to undermine the foundations of Catholic Doctrine'.[126] These errors included those which have always 'existed outside the fold of Christ',[127] errors among Catholics,[128] theological errors,[129] errors about the Magisterium, i.e. the teaching authority of the Church,[130] errors about the authority of Sacred Scripture,[131] errors in the field of philosophy[132] and errors which result from the positive sciences.[133]

For the purposes of comparison with *Divino Afflante Spiritu*, the errors identified above in *Humani Generis* which concern us most here are those concerning the authority of the scriptures: there was the refusal to acknowledge that God is fully the author of sacred scripture; the idea that a human sense of scripture covers a hidden, infallible, divine sense; the notion that 'the analogy of faith and *the Tradition of the Church*' [my emphases] may be ignored in exegesis; and the view that a symbolic or spiritual exegesis is superior to a carefully articulated literal sense. All this, says Pius, is foreign to the interpretive norms of *Providentissimus Deus* and *Divino Afflante Spiritu*, and a correct exegetical spirit.[134] None of the condemnations in *Humani Generis* is incompatible with *Divino Afflante Spiritu*, despite the other condemnations, caveats and cautions, however.

The answer to our third question, then, must assuredly be that Pope Pius XII *did* manifest a spirit of cautious but pragmatic 'adventure' in his exegetical method and thought. In sum, he may be classified as a careful moderniser who worked *with* tradition but, in his method, paved and smoothed the way for the 'modernisers' of the Second Vatican Council (1962–5). It was he, not Pope John XXIII (reg. 1958–63), who was the true architect of that Council and who assumed the role of a John the Baptist or precursor figure to the *Christus* of Pope John. He did not allow an innate caution to stifle the pragmatic impulse, whether politically or theologically. In theology, as in political life, he could be bold and take risks. *Divino Afflante Spiritu* was a bold and innovative document in the history of Catholic scriptural exegesis issued in 1943 at the height of a world war when bold, albeit covert, actions were similarly demanded and not eschewed.

Pius's dual *objects* were Truth and Humanity; *semiotically*, his life was a sign of contradiction; his Church for himself and others was the contemporary incarnation of 'the *Sacred*'.[135] *Humani Generis* might have seemed to represent a return to an age of caution and unchanging tradition in its manifold, *Pascendi*-like condemnations, but it did not represent a 'denial' or overthrow of the methodologies espoused and sanctioned in *Divino Afflante Spiritu*. In what follows, it will be salutary and instructive to bear the method and thought of Pope Pius XII in mind (by way of comparison) as we examine the views of contemporary Muslim proponents of *ijtihād*.

3.2.2 Intra-Conciliar: *Dei Verbum* and John XXIII

Angelo Giuseppe Roncalli (1881–1963) came to the papal throne in 1958 and assumed the name of John XXIII. He was born in Sotto il Monte near Bergamo, in Italy, on Friday 25 November 1881, at 10:15 am.[136] His early life of poverty [137] gave no hint of that conclave seventy-seven years later when he would boldly assume and sacralise a name supposedly made unusable by Baldassare Cossa, 'John XXIII' (reg.1410–15), an anti-pope, *condottiere* 'ex-pirate who had massacred, cheated and perjured his way to the papacy'.[138] Roncalli's life, actions, spirituality and, most of all, his *Journal* provide ample indication that he was the very opposite of a Cossa.[139]

After studies in the seminaries of Bergamo and the main seminary in Rome, the Apollinare, he received his STD (Doctorate in Sacred Theology) on 13 July 1904. The invigilator for the written exam was Eugenio Pacelli, the future Pius XII.[140] On 10 August 1904, Roncalli was ordained priest by Bishop Giuseppe Ceppetelli, the titular Patriarch of Constantinople.[141]

After war service during the First World War as a hospital orderly and military chaplain, Roncalli's career became stratospheric: he served extremely briefly as Professor of Patrology at the Pontifical Lateran University in Rome (Pontificio Ateneo Lateranense) from November 1924 to 3 March 1925, before being appointed Apostolic Visitor in Bulgaria with the rank of Archbishop and the titular See of Areopolis.[142] Diplomatic appointments to Istanbul[143] (1934) and Paris (1944)[144] followed.

On 15 January 1953, Angelo Roncalli was created Cardinal and Patriarch of Venice.[145] In such wise was he now, physically and historically, in place for that all-important conclave which, on 28 October 1958, elected him Pope John XXIII[146] (reg. 1958–63). That conclave would, in effect, precipitate the 'turning upside down' of tradition/Tradition and traditionalism in the Roman Catholic Church while rejecting neither.

Firstly, John decided to call a Council of the whole Church: 'Without any forethought, I put forward, in one of my first talks with my Secretary of State, on 20 January 1959, the idea of an Ecumenical Council'.[147] The *leitmotiv* of both pontificate and Council would be *aggiornamento*,[148] an Italian word which may be translated faithfully as 'update' or 'updating',[149] but which encapsulated notions of 'reform' and 'renewal'.[150] This word was to become inextricably linked in several minds with liturgical update, reform and renewal: thus the then Roman Catholic Archbishop of Birmingham in England, George Patrick Dwyer, on 23 October 1967 observed: 'The liturgical reform is in a very deep sense the key to the *aggiornamento*. Make no mistake, this is the starting point of the *revolution*.'[151]

Yet the *aggiornamento* of the traditional liturgy, and especially the replacement of the so-called Tridentine Mass by the *Novus Ordo* of Pope Paul VI (reg. 1963–78), John's successor, was to prove a horrendous Trojan horse for the traditionalists: 'This much is certain, therefore, that revolution and modernism [that ancient *bête noire* of Pius X][152] have penetrated the City of God by way of the liturgy. The Liturgical Movement has been [a] Trojan horse...'[153]

It was not just the liturgy which, in the eyes of the traditionists, seemed to be under attack. Some feared that even the traditional theology of the Church might be susceptible to change in the light of – or in spite of – John XXIII's extremely significant declaration to the effect that 'the substance of the ancient deposit of faith is one thing, and the way in which it is presented is another' (*Altra è la sostanza dell'antica dottrina del depositum fidei, ed altra è la formulazione del suo rivestimento*).[154] Would any *continuity* from the lengthy pontificate of Pius XII be left, or was all to be changed?[155]

The Dogmatic Constitution on Divine Revelation (*Dei Verbum*), promulgated by the Second Vatican Council on 18 November 1965, was a landmark, albeit a compromise one, for Catholic Biblical scholarship and studies.[156] From the time of the Council of Trent, and up to the Second Vatican Council, Roman Catholic discussions of tradition had tended to be dominated by a 'two-source' language: 'Tradition was usually treated as distinct from scripture and it was held that teachings not contained in the Bible may be gathered from Tradition alone'.[157] *Dei Verbum* brought Roman Catholics, Orthodox, Anglicans and Protestants closer in their understanding of the relationship between scripture and tradition.[158]

The chapter in *Dei Verbum* that concerns us most for this discussion is chapter 2. The fundamental question was whether there were two distinct sources of revelation, Scripture and Tradition, or just one source, that is, Scripture *interpreted by Tradition*. The Dogmatic Constitution did not settle the question, but it brought the two polarities into a harmony which had not hitherto existed: it stressed the close bond between Sacred Tradition and Sacred Scripture and the way in which the one, over time, communicated with the other. It stressed that both flowed 'from the same divine well-spring' and had the same goal. Both were worthy of acceptance and honour 'with equal feelings of devotion and reverence'.[159] However, the same paragraph stressed that not all revelation came from scripture alone,[160] a statement which many Protestant Christians would wish to reject.[161] *The Dogmatic Constitution* went on to underline the unity of Tradition and Scripture: 'Sacred Tradition and Sacred Scripture make up a single sacred deposit of the Word of God, which is entrusted to the Church'.[162] Tradition, Scripture and the Church's Magisterium were inextricably linked, and the one could not stand without the other.[163]

Kallistos Ware comments:

> Since Vatican II most Catholic theologians have taken the view that Tradition and Scripture, while different in form, are identical in content, so that Tradition is only formally, but not materially, independent of scripture. But this is not actually stated in the Constitution on Revelation; Vatican II deliberately left the question open.[164]

3.2.3 Post-Conciliar: The Spirit and Practice of Marcel Lefebvre

The Second Vatican Council, the 21st Council of the Catholic Church, lasted from 1962 to 1965. It provoked an intellectual, theological and, perhaps above all, insofar as it affected tradition/Tradition, *liturgical* convulsion. The very brief survey of *Dei Verbum* above is important on two counts: firstly, it is an example of developing attitudes in traditional exegesis. Secondly, the gloss by Bishop Kallistos Ware which we have just cited indicates how the 'spirit' of Vatican II was to be invoked and interpreted by the progressives to the fury of the traditionalists. Prime among the latter was Archbishop Marcel Lefebvre (1905–91).[165]

In the fourth century AD, the Patriarch of Alexandria, Athanasius, had stood, sometimes virtually alone, against the assaults of the Arian heresy.[166] Many modern traditionalists in the twentieth and twenty-first centuries held that Marcel Lefebvre was a new Athanasius.[167] Athanasius 'in times of similar general "blindness in heresy" (Arianism) was excommunicated but subsequently exonerated and eventually canonized'.[168] In 1988, Marcel Lefebvre provoked his own excommunication (and that of his clerical followers) after performing the unauthorised consecration of four traditionalist priests to the Roman Catholic episcopate on 30 June 1988.[169]

Marcel Lefebvre was born into a politically conservative family on 29 November 1905 in the north of France. After ordination on 21 September 1929, he joined the missionary order of the Holy Ghost Fathers, which he later headed, and served in French Equatorial Africa. In 1947, Pope Pius XII consecrated him a bishop, and in 1962 he received the rank and title of Archbishop of Synnada in Phrygia. He was involved in the preparations for the Second Vatican Council, where he emerged as an arch-conservative and champion of tradition.

After the Council, fearing that the Catholic Church had yielded to the infection of Modernism – that synthesis of all heresies, as Pius X had famously described it – he founded a traditionalist seminary in Écône in Valais, Switzerland, in 1970, and a traditionalist priestly society, the Fraternité Sacerdotale de Saint Pie X. Its traditionalism and its repudiation of the *aggiornamento* fostered by the Second Vatican Council, especially the reformed liturgy epitomised in the *Novus Ordo Missae* or

New Rite of Mass, incurred the wrath of the Vatican. The situation developed ineluctably through his public censure by Pope Paul VI (reg. 1963–78), his suspension *a divinis* (which deprived him canonically of his right to function as a priest) on 22 July 1976 to his final excommunication in 1988. Archbishop Marcel Lefebvre died on 25 March 1991 in Martigny, Switzerland, still excommunicated and still at odds with the Church whose antique traditions he so cherished and which had raised and fostered him.[170]

It is certainly a truism that, in the words of William D. Dinges, 'Catholic traditionalism does not present a completely uniform ideology, although it stands united as a worldview opposed to theological modernism'.[171] It is equally true, however, that one of the aspects of the Conciliar *aggiornamento* most detested by the Archbishop and his traditionalist followers was the reform of the liturgy, especially the apparent abolition of the so-called Tridentine Rite of the Mass and the imposition of the vernacular *Novus Ordo Missae* in 1970.[172] And, while it is true that 'Catholic traditionalism is not a campaign motivated by nostalgia for bygone ritualism', what I earlier characterised as 'the tired paradigms of public perception' did establish the Tridentine Mass as an arena of semiotics which signalled an adherence to all that was traditional and pre-Vatican II. Dinges himself admits this public, if incorrect, perception.[173] In the common mind, pre-Vatican II liturgy *was* tradition, and tradition *was* pre-Vatican II liturgy.

Archbishop Marcel Lefebvre, in the course of a long and often turbulent life, inveighed against many things which he regarded as abuses of doctrine or liturgy. For his first-year seminarians in the Écône Seminary, he devised a special syllabus on the *Acts of the Magisterium*:

> His life's great sorrow was to see the Church, with Vatican II – which he referred to many times as the Third World War – infected with … errors, and its key posts occupied by enemies. He saw the Conciliar and post-Conciliar popes turn their backs on the teachings and warnings of their predecessors. It was also with great sorrow that he saw the priesthood in ruins, the religious life fall to pieces, and Catholic states laicized in the name of the Council's teaching on religious liberty.[174]

Lefebvre's purpose in giving this special course on *The Acts of the Magisterium* was

> not so much a systematic study of the errors [besetting the modern Church], but a guided tour of the encyclicals themselves, especially those in which the popes made an in-depth study of the truths denied by these errors, or gave a detailed analysis of the errors themselves.[175]

In his desire to defend, expound and *sacralise* his carefully chosen selection of encyclicals, which range from Pope Leo XII's (reg. 1823–9) Encyclical *Quo Graviora* of 13 March 1826 (condemning secret societies, especially freemasonry)[176] to the Encyclical of Pope Pius XI of 19 March 1937 on communism entitled *Divini Redemptoris*,[177] Marcel Lefebvre made the following powerful point, against the Second Vatican Council and in favour of the chosen encyclicals: 'If, then, there are things in the Council which disagree with or which contradict what previous popes have said, how can we accept them? There is no room for contradictions; *the popes teach, and the matter is settled.*'[178] He goes on to accuse Popes Paul VI and John Paul II (reg. 1978–2005) of teaching error.[179]

In his desire to abide by tradition, 'to resist [errors] by relying on the constant teaching of the Church throughout the centuries',[180] Lefebvre is prepared to accuse two modern popes of heresy and, although he himself does not say so in *most* cases, virtually endow chosen papal encyclicals from the past 300 years, which agree with his own position, with the charism of infallibility. He does, however, believe that one of the encyclicals which he cherishes, Pope Pius IX's (reg. 1846–78) *Quanta Cura* (8 December 1864), *is* an infallible document.[181]

Underlying the overt issue of whether most Roman Catholic theologians would agree with Lefebvre, or not, on this issue, are the much deeper issues of ultimate ecclesial authority, divine sanction – real or claimed – and the binding nature or otherwise of past authority as expressed in papal encyclicals.

If one were to make comparisons with the device of the *isnād*, the 'chain of authorities' in ḥadīth literature, one would note that, in Islam, for the chain to be valid or sound (*ṣaḥīḥ*), certain quite rigorous conditions were to be met, including the direct knowledge of one transmitter of his predecessor and successor. The past is connected approvingly to the present.

Lefebvre, however, clearly felt it sufficient to cite a few 'encyclical authorities' from the past, who agree with him and each other, while ignoring 'Council authorities' (i.e. Vatican II) who might proclaim differently. Thus, in *Quanta Cura*, Pope Pius IX 'confirms the same condemnation [of Naturalism in politics] pronounced by Pope Gregory XVI [reg. 1831–46] [in the latter's Encyclical *Mirari Vos* of 15 August 1832]'.[182] Lefebvre is thus happy to look backwards for *his* 'chain of authorities' (Gregory XVI , Pius IX), but he is generally far less happy with contemporary ecclesial authorities on many subjects (e.g. John XXIII).[183]

The Tradition of the Church is presented by Archbishop Lefebvre as unchanging, and the culture and history against which the chosen set of encyclicals is articulated and proclaimed are not perceived as factors for comment or debate. Tradition is all. Lefebvre himself observed:

> The criterion of truth, and, moreover, of the infallibility of the Pope and of the Church, is its conformity to Tradition and to the deposit of faith ... *To separate oneself from Tradition is to separate oneself from the Church. It is because it is in the nature of the Church to be a tradition that she has always instinctively had a horror of novelty, of change, of mutation, under any pretext whatsoever.*[184]

So, while *The Syllabus of Errors* of Pope Pius IX (8 December 1864), which condemned, *inter alia*, absolute rationalism, is discussed approvingly in a lengthy chapter,[185] that seminal document of Pope Pius XII, *Divino Afflante Spiritu* (1943), which, as we have seen, gave official approval to the historico-literary exegesis of scripture, is totally ignored.

The whole of Lefebvre's first-year seminary course, *Acts of the Magisterium*, may be characterised as anti-*aggiornamento*, anti-Council and anti-ecumenism.[186] '*Extra*

Ecclesiam nulla salus ... must be preached', though the Archbishop does concede that salvation is possible for Protestants, Muslims, Buddhists, and others – but only 'by [= via] the Church'.[187] Archbishop Lefebvre is presented by his publishers as a second Irenaeus (died AD 202), who fought against the gnostic heresies:

> This work [the published seminary course *Acts of the Magisterium*, under the title *Against the Heresies*] is consequently of no less importance for the end of the 20th century than the *Adversus Haereses* of St Irenaeus was for the second century. The errors are different. The solution is the same. Catholic *Tradition* [my emphasis]. The deposit of the Faith. The *authority* [my emphasis again] of the Holy See.[188]

The comparison between Archbishop Marcel Lefebvre and Irenaeus is interesting: Irenaeus was a powerful proponent of a living, oral, public apostolic tradition as well as a written one. And Scripture, for him, confirmed the Apostolic Tradition.[189] In the Roman Catholic Church, the theological and liturgical movement seemed to have moved away – via the pendulum of *aggiornamento* – from the certainties of tradition and traditional articulation and then – in one sector at least – moved back again, clinging on to the lure of Lefebvrism and the return to the alleged certainties and rituals of the pre-Vatican II age.

In much of the debate, liturgy – traditional or modern, Tridentine or *Novus Ordo* – has played a key role. We noted earlier Archbishop George Patrick Dwyer's remark that the key to *aggiornamento* was liturgical reform. But, for the traditionalists, the traditional Tridentine liturgy, pre-Conciliar in form and content, became equated with that which was *sacred*. It is asserted, furthermore, that 'the liturgical implementation after the Second Vatican Council *was not in continuity with the tradition*' (my emphasis) and that 'there is today among the faithful a significant loss of belief in the Real Presence of Christ in the Eucharist', resulting from 'the implementation of the liturgical documents after Vatican II'.[190] In other words the *sacred* was disappearing or had, for many, already departed.

Liturgically and theologically, the sacred walks hand in hand with transcendence and mystery.[191] Modern papal allocutions have urged the need to rediscover 'the sense of mystery' in the liturgy: 'The liturgy ... is a means of sanctification; it is a celebration of the Church's faith, and a means of transmitting the faith. Together with Sacred Scripture and the teachings of the Fathers of the Church, it is a living source of authentic and sound spirituality.'[192]

Attempts to seek a greater freedom for the celebration of the so-called 'Tridentine Rite' of Mass continue.[193] It is as if there has been a dawning realisation of the 'loss of the sacred'[194] as a direct consequence of the liturgical reforms of Vatican II. 'Many of the criticisms which have occurred reflected an anxiety about the loss of the transcendent and sacred in liturgy, in the light of its more deritualised anthropocentric concerns.'[195]

In a striking passage, David Torevell suggests that the pre-Conciliar Roman rite 'embedded within its highly ritualised structure a reconfiguration of time and space in relation to the eschaton. Liturgical time occupied a distended period before this eschaton and the sacred spaces of ritual had assumed an analogical relationship to the heavenly realm.'[196] The liturgical reform destroyed this traditional perception.[197]

David Torevell talks in terms of 'losing the sacred'. Others, anguished and outraged at the reforms of Vatican II – and especially their interpretation – have accused the Conciliar reformers of holding that

> everything that was done before Vatican II must be forgotten at all costs; the entire spiritual and sacred patrimony that was built up during the centuries that preceded the Council must be gotten rid of. The excess baggage includes sacred chant, liturgical vestments, altars, processions, incense and so on.

Thus, for example, does Dr Denis Crouan STD characterise the way in which some identified pre-Conciliar traditional liturgy with *The Sacred.*[198]

However, Crouan goes on to stress that there was never a 'liturgical rite' created by Pope Pius V (reg. 1566–72), although that pontiff did make certain revisions to the Roman missal.[199] The real betrayal and crime, for Crouan, is that the necessary liturgical reforms espoused by the Council, and propagated in the *Constitution on the Sacred Liturgy* (*Sacrosanctum Concilium*) on 4 December 1963, have never been properly implemented.[200] This position is, of course, as much at odds with that of the Lefebvrists and pre-Conciliar traditionists as it is with that of the enthusiastic partisans of the *Novus Ordo Missae* of Paul VI. Crouan believes that the traditionalists, by invoking a 'Tridentine rite', with all the defensive baggage which they hoped would accompany that 'rite' as a bulwark against doctrinal error and as emotional and theological security, were really invoking a chimera.[201]

It is a truism that ritual and ritualised liturgy are important in any religion because they articulate and adumbrate in a vital semiotic way, and sometimes a splendidly visual way, the inner truths of that faith. One thinks of the *ḥajj* for Islam and the sacrifice of the Mass for Roman Catholics. A ritual or liturgy, anthropologically speaking, can be the frame for the scripture and doctrine of the religion.[202] Epistles and the Gospel are read during Mass, which presents, doctrinally and sacramentally, the sacrifice of Calvary itself. The Islamic *ḥajj* is a frame for both obeying and enacting the Qur'ān: 'And complete the *Ḥajj* or *ʿumra* in the service of God '.[203] It is also a re-memorialisation of the actions of Ibrāhīm and the Farewell Pilgrimage of Muḥammad.[204] Because of this bond between ritual, liturgy, doctrine and scripture as well as tradition, it is vitally important that there be a correct and acceptable exegesis or *tafsīr* of scripture.

However, traditionalists will hold to a traditionalist understanding and interpretation of scripture which, in the case of groups like the Lefebvrists, will castigate forms of exegesis deriving from the spirit of Vatican II.[205] For example, it is vehemently denied by traditionalists that Pius XII taught anything new regarding scriptural exegesis in *Divino Afflante Spiritu.*[206] And, in the traditionalist mindset, reformed liturgy is often linked to doctrinal error.

Thus we find Archbishop Marcel Lefebvre writing:

> If one studies well the New Mass, one finds that it is imbued with modernist ideas. It was drafted under the influence of the modernist spirit execrated and condemned by Pope St Pius X in his encyclical *Pascendi Dominici Gregis*, in

which he demonstrated the error and banefulness of Modernism, which he calls the synthesis of all heresies.[207]

If it is 'an essential function of the sacred to demonstrate the nature of a world that is in communion with God',[208] and the articulation of that which is sacred is perceived by the traditionalists to be fatally flawed, then a sacral *disjunction* will result in their eyes where tradition is overthrown[209] and innovation reigns supreme. Islamic fundamentalists had a similar concept with the idea of *bid'a*, literally 'innovation', the favoured word in the Islamic world for heretical novelty which might cause the unwary believer to diverge from the Straight Path, the *Ṣirāṭ al-Mustaqīm*, validated and sanctioned by antique Tradition.

3.3 Sunna: *Definitions and Distinctions*

As a linguistic *object* and theological 'ground', the Arabic term *sunna* in Islam is both ancient and multivalent. Numerous definitions are available, both succinct and extended. A few will be offered and outlined here.

For example, a modern glossary to a translation of Mālik's *al-Muwaṭṭa'* defines *sunna* (pl. *sunan*) as 'lit. a form, the customary practice of a person or group of people'.[210] The lexicographer Hans Wehr understands the term to mean 'habitual practice, customary procedure or action, norm, usage sanctioned by tradition'.[211] For Michael Cook, *sunna* is 'proper custom' or 'normative custom.'[212] *The Shorter Encyclopaedia of Islam* favours 'custom, use and wont, statute',[213] while James W. Morris, in his English rendition of Ja'far b. Manṣūr al-Yaman's *Kitāb al-'Ālim wa 'l-Ghulām*, deploys such terms as 'accustomed way' in translating references to the *sunna* of God.[214]

However, one of the clearest definitions, which also distinguishes the term from ḥadīth, while not totally separating them, appears in the second edition of *The Encyclopaedia of Islam*:

> *Ḥadīth* (narrative, talk) with the definite article (*al-ḥadīth*) is used for Tradition, being an account of what the Prophet said or did, or of his tacit approval of something said or done in his presence ... [While] *Sunna* (custom) refers to a normative custom of the Prophet or of the early community.[215]

The term *sunna* in the Qur'ān is associated mostly with God's action rather than that of the Prophet Muḥammad.[216] Thus God has punished unbelievers in the past (e.g. Q.8:38, Q.33:62, Q. 35: 43), and this is His *Sunna* or constant practice. The *sunnat Allāh* (practice of God) (see e.g. Q.33:38) is a powerful Qur'ānic motif.

The preferred word for 'the practice of the Prophet' in the Qur'ān is *uswa*:[217]

> Ye have indeed
> In the Apostle of God
> A beautiful pattern (of conduct) ... [218]
>
> *La-qad kāna lakum*
> *fī rasūl Allāh*
> *uswat^{un} ḥasanat^{un}...*

Uswa can mean 'example, model, pattern'.[219]

It is clear that the pre-Islamic term, *sunna*, which originally meant 'customary action', together with the divine model cited above, was transferred at a later date under al-Shāfi'ī (767–820) to the idea of the customary, good action of the Prophet[220] and, later still, came to represent 'the all-encompassing concept orthodoxy, which is still in use today' and 'any laudable precedent'.[221] And, under al-Shāfi'ī, *sunna* became the second major source of law.[222]

The terms *sunna* and ḥadīth have a certain fluidity, but both technical terms have become virtually synonymous. Strictly speaking, 'where the term *ḥadīth* refers to a document, the term *sunna* refers to the usage described in such a document'.[223] Both may be rendered as 'tradition/Tradition'.

The observance by the Islamic *umma* (community) of the *sunna* is the *imitatio Muhammadis*.[224] Put another way (of which the great ṣūfī philosopher Ibn al-'Arabī (1165–1240) himself might have approved![225]), the ḥadīth is the bezel (*faṣṣ*) which holds or enshrines the *sunna*.

As a *sign*, then, the term *sunna* in Islamic Arabic signals at least four major areas of discourse, as may be seen from the above discussions: it alerts us via the Qur'ān to *Divine* custom and precedent; it reminds us of *jāhilī* (pre-Islamic) *tribal* custom and precedent; it focuses the Muslim mind from an early period on the custom and precedent of the *Prophet* Muḥammad; and it speaks of a desired 'orthodoxy' enshrined in *communal* (but by no means monolithic) custom and precedent, with all the developed and developing legal and theological implications of such established custom down the ages.

Sunna, then may be treated as an Object and a Sign, but it also belongs to the sphere of the *sacred*, in terms both of content and of respect and reverence. *Ḥadīth Nabawī* (Prophetic Ḥadīth) transmitted the record of the actions and sayings of the Prophet Muḥammad himself; *Ḥadīth Qudsī* (Sacred Ḥadīth) transmitted via Muḥammad the 'meanings' of God's own further messages over and above the formal Qur'ānic record.[226]

For Muslims, 'tradition came to be considered second in authority to the Ḳur'ān, but this was the result of a lengthy process'.[227] The ḥadīth literature was constituted and canonised by the *umma* in six major collections, of which the *Ṣaḥīḥān* of al-Bukhārī (810–70) and Muslim b. al-Ḥajjāj (817–75) achieved primary importance.[228] So important did the *sunna* or tradition become that it served under al-Shāfi'ī, the jurist who became known as the Father of Muslim Jurisprudence, not just 'to elucidate but to supplement the Qur'ān's regulations, supplying the details needed to implement divine commands' and, going beyond this, addressing 'matters quite unmentioned in the Qur'ān'.[229]

Muslim reverence for Islamic Tradition has been unswerving since the days of al-Shāfi'ī. The famous collector of traditions, al-Nawawī (1233–77), is typical in his lauding of the *sunna* as that which 'enlighten[s] spiritual guides'[230] and he includes in his collection of forty a ḥadīth (No. 28) in which the Prophet counsels: 'Verily he among you who lives [long] will see great controversy, so you must keep to my *sunna* and to the *sunna* of the rightly-guided Rashidite Caliphs' [*Fa-'alaykum bi-sunnatī wa sunna al-Khulafā' al-Rāshidīn al-Mahdiyīn*].[231]

This does not mean that the reliability and authenticity of the tradition literature has not been challenged at various times, both within and without *Dār al-Islām*. Such challenges have been perceived as malicious attempts by allegedly 'renegade' Muslims, or by Western orientalists such as Ignaz Goldziher and Joseph Schacht,[232] to undermine the *objective* reality of the content of the tradition literature, to suggest that some – or even much – of the *matn* (the content) of the tradition literature should no longer *signify* a worthy example to be followed; and to *desacralise* that which is held to be second only to the Holy Qur'ān itself in sacredness.

Now, this volume is not concerned specifically with the issue of the reliability and authenticity *per se* of every part and facet of the tradition literature. It notes, however, the way in which religious authority may be weakened, especially in the field of law, when undue reliance is placed on 'suspect' ḥadīth texts for legal articulation and implementation. While one should not press the comparison too far, the authority of *sunna* and the authority of papal encyclicals down the ages – inasmuch as both focus on, or are vehicles for, tradition/Tradition – provide an interesting field for speculation and analysis.[233]

What *is* of profound interest for this volume is the dominant role achieved in the nineteenth, twentieth and twenty-first centuries by both Qur'ān and Tradition, and the uses and abuses of *ijtihād* (independent judgement). In Christianity, Scriptural Text, tradition/ Tradition and Magisterium perform a valuable phenomenological, semiotic and sacral function. The same is true, as we have shown, for Qur'ān and *Sunna* in Islam. *The use, and interpretation, of both is vital in our analysis of what we have characterised as 'The Traditional Imagination'*.

3.4 *Neo-*Ijtihād *and Return to the* Salaf

Our survey of *sunna*, with its various definitions, distinctions and connotations, is intended to demonstrate and underline the fact that *sunna* and ḥadīth have as central a role in Islam as oral and written tradition do in Christianity. Furthermore, they can create and mould a mindset which will automatically reject innovation (*bid'a*) and, indeed, any criticism of that which is invincibly held to be sacred. Within such a mindset, the historico-literary critical approach beloved of modern Biblical exegesis will have no place; rather, a fundamentalist traditionalism which *may* espouse a scriptural literalism, whether in Qur'ān or ḥadīth, may flourish.

It was recognised from the early days of Islam that the Qur'ān required *tafsīr*, exegesis; and many of the best Muslim minds down the ages have set themselves to explain and contextualise the sacred text. And context is vital to real understanding.[234] 'Even so, mysteries remain.'[235] Robert Irwin goes on to explain:

> Faced with the challenge of modernity, many Muslims today, rather than accommodate themselves to the age-old fudges that have prevailed in so many Muslim societies, have resorted instead to a kind of textual puritanism. Instead of referring to the way things were done in, say, colonial Morocco, or Ottoman Turkey, or, much further back, under the Abbasid caliphs, they prefer to return to the ' simple truths' of the Koran. The Koran, however, is not simple, and in many centres in Britain, Pakistan and elsewhere the

standard of training in the basic tenets of Islam, including the meaning and context of the Koran, is staggeringly poor. Naive literal readings are soldered onto modern preoccupations with the menaces of Zionism, globalisation and feminism, and this third-rate religious education is one of the things that fuels fundamentalist violence.[236]

For a pietist of such a traditionalist persuasion, the message of a ḥadīth/*sunna*, rather than its *historicity*, is the bedrock. And the sound *isnād*, chain of authorities, for that pietist is the formal guarantee of Islamic authenticity.[237]

The ḥadīth corpus has also been propagated, explicated and used in a manner akin to the usage of the Qur'ān at the hands of *its* fundamentalist and literalist exegetes. Thus, anyone who doubts the authenticity of a single ḥadīth in the *Ṣaḥīḥ* collection of al-Bukḥārī lays himself open to ridicule, condemnation and worse by fundamentalists and even by many of a more open or moderate persuasion.[238] Such partisans of *all* ḥadīths, even if the latter clearly contradict the Qur'ān itself,[239] manifest attitudes akin to those of pre-Vatican II Catholic Christians, or modern US Baptist fundamentalists, who steadfastly refused to use, even countenance, a historico-critical approach to sacred scripture. For the fundamentalist Muslim, textual *presence* in the *Ṣaḥīḥ* of al-Bukhārī was sufficient; for the fundamentalist Christian, the surface word of Scripture, often regardless of context or etymology or difficulty in translation, sufficed.

Traditional Islamic exegesis has never had – and could not tolerate – an exegete of the sublime boldness of the demythologising Lutheran theologian, Rudolf Bultmann (1884–1976). Bultmann was most famous in Biblical scholarly circles for his work on New Testament hermeneutics and his endeavour to 'demythologise' the New Testament: his great idea was that 'the mythological framework of the NT must be interpreted to expose the understanding of human life contained in it.[240] For a far less ambitious literary enterprise with regard to the Qur'ān, Dr Nāṣir Aḥmad Abū Zayd, an academic who used to teach at Cairo University, was condemned, towards the end of the twentieth century, by the conservative Egyptian '*ulamā*' and judiciary; he was forced to flee from Egypt with his wife.[241]

Even those like Professor Fazlur Rahman (1919–88), who, in *Islam and Modernity: Transformation of an Intellectual System*,[242] argued 'for the need to distinguish Quranic principles from their application in specific historical settings',[243] received a liberal dose of opprobrium and opposition from many 'pre- Enlightenment' fundamentalist Muslims.[244]

This is not to say that innovatory *tafsīr* was not possible and that all such exegesis was stifled down the centuries. The traditional engine for such exegesis was *ijtihād*, now to be labelled neo-*ijtihād*.

The second edition of *The Encyclopaedia of Islam* defines *ijtihād* thus:

> Literally 'exerting oneself' … the technical term in Islamic law, first, for the use of individual reasoning in general and later, in a restricted meaning, for the use of the method of reasoning by analogy …[245]

And Professor Mohammad Hashim Kamali proclaims that, after the Qur'ān and the *Sunna*, 'ijtihād is the most important source of Islamic law'.[246]

Inspired by Ibn Taymiyya (1263–1328), Salafī groups have rejected the mode of exegesis generated by the four Sunnī law schools (*madhāhib*)[247] known literally as 'imitation' (*taqlīd*); in effect, this involved the application of 'case law' from the past to present circumstances. They have felt free to espouse a new, wide-ranging and often radical *ijtihād*.[248] Purification of the faith has been the inspiration and the challenge.[249] This movement was sometimes, but not always, anti-intellectual,[250] an apparent paradox in the light of its espousal of the exegetical tool of *ijtihād*.

In the context of an essay on 'Muslim Culture and Reform in 18th-century South Asia', Jamal Malik had this to say; his remarks have a contemporary and wide-ranging applicability:

> The invitation to appropriate God's message individually and independently through the revealed text certainly meant, on the one hand, the emancipation of the self from immediate and direct ties of authority, and, on the other hand, the reconstruction of Islamic society by laypersons, something that harked back to early Muhammadan times. This was *ijtihâd* in the widest sense, and it expressed a desire for newness. However, the past to which they referred was not conceived in terms of a heroic era that would return. Instead, it was envisaged as a political and social utopia, which was to be lived and translated into reality. Thus, memory was to be transferred into powerful expectation. The recurring rituals around the *hadîth* were proven devices to monumentalise this expectation. Needless to say, this sort of re-discovery of tradition stood in contrast to the traditionally bound compliance with state/law and the dependence on authority – *taqlîd*. *Taqlîd* lived on jurisprudence and philosophical theology, based on logic. This logic was, again, a logic of the administration, that is the logic of the state, where philosophical theology and law flourished.[251]

The preoccupation with sources of authority, the debate over whether the 'gates of *ijtihād*' ever actually closed (as the classical doctrine proclaimed, but for which there is no real evidence[252]), the desire to return to a purified form of Islam and the rejection of *taqlīd* all led the 'reformers' (who, at the same time, believed, they were upholding a 'great tradition') to give a new currency to the word *ijtihād*.[253] The reforming founder of the Sanūsiyya Order of ṣūfīs, Muḥammad b. 'Alī al-Sanūsī (?1787–1869), who took the *salaf* as his model, refused to accept that the door of *ijtihād* had closed. For him, '*ijtihād* [was] a process that must be continuous and never-ending.'[254]

One of the chief architects and proponents of what became known as 'neo-*ijtihād*' was the Egyptian jurist and Chief Muftī Muḥammad 'Abduh (1849–1905). 'As early as 1898 … [he] had advocated the reinterpretation of the principles embodied in the divine revelation as a basis for legal reform.'[255]

It was not just legal reform that 'Abduh believed was necessary. As the Chair of an administrative Council set up to implement reforms at the Azhar, he 'improved the living conditions of the students, reorganised the libraries, reformed the administration, tightened up teaching regulations, and lengthened the university year'.[256] The curriculum was enlarged with modern subjects 'in addition to the traditional sciences'.[257]

By the time that the great blind Egyptian writer Ṭāhā Ḥusayn came to study at the Azhar, Muḥammad ʿAbduh was held in high esteem, indeed awe:

> [The students] would talk about the Imam [Muḥammad ʿAbduh] himself, discussing his extraordinary qualities [*wa-sayastaʿidūna mā kānū yasmaʿūna min nawādirihi*], recalling his judgements on the sheikhs, or theirs on him, and repeating the crushing replies with which he used to silence questioners or objectors and make them a laughing stock to their fellows.[258]

Muḥammad ʿAbduh was born in an Egyptian Delta village in 1849. At the age of 13, he began his studies at the Aḥmadī Mosque in Tanta, which proved to be a somewhat fraught and bewildering experience for the adolescent boy because of its antique pedagogical method, which relied so much on rote learning. Later, he studied at al-Azhar in Cairo between 1869 and 1877, graduating as a ʿ*Ālim* (Diplomate) and starting a teaching career at the Azhar. From 1871, he came under the influence of the revolutionary pan-Islamist[259] Jamāl al-Ḍin al-Afghānī (1839–97). After the failure of ʿUrabī Pasha's revolt in 1882, in which he was implicated, ʿAbduh was exiled from Egypt. He stayed in Beirut for a while and then joined al-Afghānī in Paris, cooperating on the publication of the periodical *al-ʿUrwa al-Wuthqā* (*The Strongest Link*).

The Khedive permitted him to return to Egypt in 1888, and thereafter his rise was swift. He was made Grand Muftī of Egypt in 1899, and he could now attempt to put into practice ideas which he had developed in exile in Beirut. He firmly believed, for example, that

> those who were being trained as government officials should be taught logic and philosophy, doctrine with emphasis on the rational proofs of its truth and an exhortation to avoid dissension between the different rites, ethics with the same emphasis on its rational basis and a study of the exemplary lives of the *salaf*, and religious history.[260]

Albert Hourani has stressed how ʿAbduh made a clear distinction in his writings between the simple – and reasonable – immutable doctrines of Islam, which have been preserved and passed down by the *salaf*, on the one hand, and mutable law and 'social morality' on the other.[261]

In his famous *Risālat al-Tawḥīd* (*The Theology of Unity*), Muḥammad ʿAbduh draws attention to the Qur'ān's espousal of reason and its rejection of slavish credulity: 'Well is it said that traditionalism can have evil consequences as well as good and may occasion loss as well as conduce to gain. It is a deceptive thing, and though it may be pardoned in an animal is scarcely seemly in man.'[262]

Reason in Islam has been liberated from the enslavement of *taqlīd*, 'blind imitation'.[263] And many have followed in ʿAbduh's footsteps: his espousal of *talfīq*, the 'piecing together' of views from the different Schools of Law to form a coherent legal doctrine, has received a favourable reception in several quarters.[264] If one *must* follow a particular School of Law (*madhhab*), it should not be done blindly. It is best to stick to the Qur'ān and *Sunna*. These were the responses of Taha Alalwani, President of the Graduate School of Islamic and Social Sciences, Leesburg, Virginia, when asked whether it was '*wājib* [compulsory] to adhere completely to a particular *madhhab* instead of picking and choosing from amongst the four schools?'[265] Examples of the use of *talfiq* in modern Arab legal codes, pointed out by Wael B. Hallaq, include the Egyptian Law of Testamentary Disposition (1946) and the Sudanese Judicial Circular No: 53.[266]

It is an apparent – but not a real – paradox, then, that 'return to tradition' and 'the purity of early Islam', for the *salaf*, requires and embraces a rejection of 'traditionalism', at least in the guise of *taqlīd*, and a rejection of rigid adherence to the four Sunnī Schools of Law, the *madhāhib*. To change means to go behind the *madhāhib*, 'to return to the examples of the first Muslim community'.[267] As Wael B. Hallaq stressed: 'The Salafī movement, which stressed the need to reinterpret Islamic teachings with direct reference to the Qur'ān and the *Sunnah*, particularly called for abandoning *taqlīd* in favour of *ijtihād*'.[268]

The various groups frequently characterised as *salafī* are by no means monolithic or possessed of an absolutely identical religious, political or cultural identity.[269] Nonetheless, they may often be said to share certain features in common: they reject *taqlīd* and foster the use of *ijtihād*; they reject the traditional classical interpretation of the Qur'ān and *Sunna* as enshrined in the four *madhāhib*; there is no need to interpret the Qur'ān in an esoteric fashion. It is only a return to the purity of early Islam, that of the Prophet and the foundational generations of Muslims, the *Salaf al-Ṣāliḥ* (the Pious Ancestors), that will guarantee real Islamic reform.[270]

It is both interesting and instructive that in contemporary, twenty-first century Medina – sometimes perceived as the most *salafī* of modern cities – the volumes entitled *Bidāyat al-Mujtahid wa Nihāyat al-Muqtaṣid* (loosely translated as *The Distinguished Jurist's Primer*)[271] written by the great mediaeval Spanish Muslim jurist, Chief Judge and philosopher Abū 'l-Walīd Muḥammad b. Aḥmad Ibn Rushd (1126–98),[272] have a particular popularity and prominence among several modern Medinan scholars.[273] Ibn Rushd was a Mālikī qāḍī, and here we find him achieving a degree of popularity in the heart of Ḥanbalī Wahhābī-land!

However, this phenomenon becomes clearer when one examines Ibn Rushd's methodology in this great work, whose title might more literally be rendered *The Beginning of the Independent Jurist and the End of the Mere Adherent to Precedent*, and which took twenty years to write.[274] Greg Noakes tells us:

> Eschewing partisan polemic, Ibn Rushd goes beyond quoting the Maliki position on various legal questions. Instead, he tackles each issue by first describing the areas of agreement among the *madhhabs*, then outlining the points disputed by the various scholars, and finally discussing the reasons for these differences. What emerges is a detailed exposition of the principles of Islamic law, their use in each school of jurisprudence, and their practical application in the daily lives of Muslims.[275]

In this text, Ibn Rushd argues powerfully in favour of *ijtihād*. He maintains that one of the strengths of *Bidāyat al-Mujtahid* is that the student can become a *mujtahid*, an independent interpreter of the law, provided that he also has sufficient knowledge of Arabic language, Arabic grammar and the foundations of Islamic jurisprudence (*uṣūl al-fiqh*).[276] In Ibn Rushd's view, mere memorisation of the plentiful minutiae of jurisprudence does not make the best jurisprudent (*faqīh*). The latter needs to be equipped with a proper set of intellectual tools – and clearly, for Ibn Rushd, that includes the capacity for discrimination and, thus, *ijtihād*. Otherwise, one is like a cobbler with many shoes but without the ability to *make* such shoes:[277] 'It is obvious that the person who has a large number of shoes will (some day) be visited by one whose feet the shoes do not fit. He will then go back to the cobbler who will make shoes that are suitable for his feet.'[278]

The *Salafī* espousal of *ijtihād* was thoroughly grounded in early Isamic history and tradition. One notes, for example, the approval of *ijtihād* famously expressed by the Prophet Muḥammad himself in his dialogue with Mu'ādh b. Jabal when the latter was sent by the Prophet to Yemen as a judge. Mu'ādh indicated that, in the absence of a clear ruling in either the Qur'ān or the *Sunna*, he would deploy *ijtihād*.[279] And the enthusiasm for this most useful of legal, linguistic and sociological of tools was continued, *inter alia*, with Mālik b. Anas,[280] the Ḥanbalī School[281] and Ibn Taymiyya.[282]

The *Salafī* preoccupation with the practice of *al-Salaf al-Ṣāliḥ* has a truly ancient pedigree. Loosely, it runs as follows: Aḥmad b. Ḥanbal (780–855)[283] > Ibn Taymiyya (1263–1328) > Muḥammad Ibn 'Abd al-Wahhāb (1703–92)[284] > Jamāl al-Dīn al-Afghānī (1839–97) > Muḥammad 'Abduh (1849–1905) > Sayyid Quṭb (1906–66) > modern, disparate *Salafī* movements and groups.[285] It is powerful chain of authorities (*isnād*) indeed! If the *Salaf al-Ṣāliḥ* are the original 'progenitors', then the luminaries listed here assume just as powerful a significance in terms of transmission, propagation and influence. Indeed, they are recognise as being among the very *salaf* themselves.[286] And *return to the salaf*, return to the ancient proof texts of Islam – Qur'ān and *Sunna* – gave the partisans of ancient tradition a greater rather than a lesser freedom, freeing them from the shackles of *taqlīd* and fostering an *ijtihād* all the more powerful for its venerable textual sources.[287]

Of all the figures mentioned in the above chain, perhaps that of Sayyid Quṭb is one of the most significant for the development of the *Salafī* movements in the twentieth and twenty-first centuries. This is not so much because of any implementation of *ijtihād* that he might have undertaken as for his rigid adherence to the sacred text of the Qur'ān. Quṭb spent his life striving to return Islam to the way of the *Salaf*.[288] For, in his view, the lands of Islam had reverted to a state of degeneration and ignorance.[289]

Sayyid Quṭb Ibrāhīm Ḥusayn Shādhilī was born on 9 October 1906 in a village near Asyut in Upper Egypt. It is said that he had become a *ḥāfiẓ* (memoriser of the whole Qur'ān) by the age of 10. In 1933, he graduated with a BA in arts education from Dār al-'Ulūm in Cairo, and, from 1933 to 1951, he worked for the Ministry of Education.[290]

In 1948, the Ministry sent him to the USA to study Western pedagogy. Here he gained an MA; but, while admiring the US economy and science, he 'was appalled by its racism, sexual permissiveness and pro-Zionism'.[291] He wrote:

> In America new gods are worshipped, which are thought to be the aim

of human existence – the god of property, the god of pleasure, the god of fame, the god of productivity! Thus it is that in America men cannot find themselves, for they cannot find the purpose of their existence The same is true of other states of ignorance, where similar gods are worshipped, and people cannot find the true God.[292]

On his return to Egypt, he joined the Muslim Brotherhood (*al-Ikhwān al-Muslimūn*) and was one of those who supported the Free Officers' coup in 1952. Falling out with the Nasserist regime, he was sentenced to fifteen years in prison in July 1955. Released in May 1964, he was re-arrested in August 1965 and charged with terrorism. On 29 August 1966, he was executed, a martyr in the view of many of his followers.[293] The *jāhilī* society which he had so much, and so frequently, condemned had taken its revenge:[294]

In his *Ma'ālim* (1964) Qutb writes that Islam knows only two types of society, the Islamic and the *Jahili*. In the first society Islam is applied fully while in the second it is not … Although in his work on social justice he does not use the term *al-jahili*, Qutb does charge Egyptian society with being un-Islamic. He says: 'Islamic society today is not Islamic in any true sense (*laysa Islamiyan bi-halin min al-ahwal*).We have already quoted a verse from the Qur'ān which cannot in any way be honestly applied today: 'Whoever does not judge by what Allah has revealed is an unbeliever'. In our modern society we do not judge by what Allah has revealed; the basis of our economic life is usury; our laws permit rather than punish oppression; the poor tax is not obligatory; and is not spent in the requisite ways. We permit the extravagance and the luxury which Islam prohibits; we allow the starvation and the destitution of which the messenger once said: "Whatever people anywhere allow a man to go hungry, they are outside the protection of Allah, the Blessed and the Exalted".'[295]

Akhavi stresses that Quṭb 'is not an advocate of the majesty of human reason'.[296] The message of the Qur'ān was there in the sacred text for all to see. Islam was 'a timeless body of ideas and practices'.[297] Akhavi concludes:

Ultmately, Quṭb's worldview rests on a manifest ahistoricity. He is not interested in a historically grounded analysis of the development of law in Islam, for example. Rather, one finds repeated references to the primary sacred texts, overwhelmingly the Qur'ān, and to a much lesser extent the *ḥadīths*. Quṭb does not acknowledge that Qur'ānic and *ḥadīth* texts might not be self-evident and that, as they are interpreted over the centuries, people might come to different conclusions as to their meanings.[298]

This reading of Quṭb makes him one of the most literalist interpreters and, almost, more '*salaf*' than the later partisans of the *Salaf al-Ṣāliḥ*.

His views were expressed in a plethora of written works. Two of the best known, and most important, are his extensive multi-volume commentary on the Qur'ān, *Fi Ẓilāl al-Qur'ān* (*In the Shade of the Qur'ān*)[299] and his political tract *Ma'ālim fi 'l-Ṭarīq*

(*Signposts on the Road*).[300] The first was completed during his prison years;[301] the latter was used by his prosecutors while he was on trial for his life in 1965.[302]

Robert Irwin sees Sayyid Quṭb as 'the father of modern Islamist fundamentalism'.[303] For him, Quṭb is a proto-Usama b. Laden. But this is perhaps to exaggerate Quṭb's role. It is a truism that there are many kinds of what is termed 'Islamism' and many kinds of what is glibly and loosely termed 'Islamic fundamentalism'. The true significance of Quṭb is his *sacrolexis*, his 'sacred textualisation'. He was in love with the sacred text of the Qur'ān; for him there was no other solution or guide to life and its manifold problems. In his adherence and fidelity to the Text, he thus provides a sublime model for all contemporary *salafī* movements.

Sayyid Quṭb did not reject the use of *ijtihād*, but for him it was somewhat circumscribed in that it could only be done within the framework of general Islamic principles and the specific absence of an authoritative text (*naṣṣ*).[304] His preferred *mujtahid* of first resort is the Islamic ruler[305] ruling in accord with God's law. The first five editions of Quṭb's *al-ʿAdāla al-Ijtimāʿiyya* (*Social Justice*) appear to accept that the Gate of *Ijtihād* had actually been closed and required to be reopened while the last edition argues for a continued historical evolution of Islamic law.[306]

Quṭb proclaims that:

> When a Muslim society in fact exists, the field will be wide open for *ijtihād* and the application of the laws of this religion, in this society, and the crucial factor in our acceptance or rejection of any development [i.e. by *ijtihād*] will be that we test it by the basic idea of Islam and its general spirit.[307]

The foundation stones of *salafī*, and *salafī*-inspired, dogmatic positions or general tendencies are clearly visible among *salaf*, and sometimes non-*salaf*, groups today. Four interrelated aspects stand out in particular: the deployment of an often visceral or, at least, tendentious *ijtihād*; the emphasis on text, textuality and proof-texts; the emphasis on purity and purification; and a consequent tendency towards a kind of Islamic 'puritanism' or asceticism. Of course, not all are present or true in all cases. However, the first two may generally be said to go hand in hand, imbued by the third, and manifesting the fourth.

Bunt has noted that

> there has been a tendency among some so-called reformers to suggest that *ijtihād* could provide a key to any transformation process, incorporating a casting off of selective 'anachronistic' interpretations of Islam, and invoking instead a recognition of certain interpretations of Islamic principles, deemed as '*purifying*' existing belief-frameworks within Muslim communities.[308]

In this emphasis on purification, one is vividly reminded of the mediaeval philolophers who went under the name of the Brethren of Purity (Ikhwān al-Ṣafā')[309] as well as the suicide flyers of '9/11'.

Thus, by way of purifying Islam of 'much misinformation [which] has been published regarding the picture of Muslims and Islam towards science',[310] *ijtihād* has been deployed to unveil the Qur'ān's perceived concurrence with – indeed, foreshadowing of – modern theories of embryology,[311] geology,[312] oceanography[313] and astronomy.[314] Here, in this kind of interpretation, is no anti-Galileo-type shrinking from the manifest and irrefutable phenomena of science, no clash of revelation and science, but a bold emphasis on the idea that modern science and ancient revelation in the shape of the Qur'ān are utterly congruent and compatible: 'The Qur'aan [*sic*],' according to Abdullah M. al-Rehaili, 'which was revealed 14 centuries ago mentioned facts that are only recently discovered by proven scientists.'[315] It is the text which provides the evidence[316] and the interpretation of that text (*ijtihād*) which harmonises it with modern science, thus 'purifying' Islam of the idea that it is anti-science.

The case of embryology is of particular interest. We may firstly note the content of verses 12–14 of *Sūra* 23, the *Sūra of the Believers* (*Sūrat al-Mu'minīn*):

> Man We did create
> From a quintessence (of clay)
> Then We placed him
> As (a drop of) sperm [*nuṭfa*]
> In a place of rest
> Firmly fixed
> Then We made the sperm
> Into a clot of congealed blood [*'alaqa*];
> Then of that clot We made
> A (foetus) lump [*muḍgha*]; Then We
> Made out of that lump
> Bones and clothed the bones
> With flesh; then We developed
> Out of it another creature.
> So blessed be God,
> The Best to create.[317]

I. A. Ibrahim, in his commentary on these verses, notes the three meanings of *'alaqa* in Arabic: '(1) leech, (2) suspended thing, and (3) blood clot'.[318] He considers that the scientific development of the embryo is reflected in these three meanings and that Qur'ānic embryology continues to reflect modern science, with the Qur'ānic movement of the embryo from the *'alaqa* to the *muḍgha* stage.[319]

Our second brief case study is taken from the field of music and singing and concerns the antique debate in Islam about the permissibility of both. The theme has been tackled at length in the work by the Muslim Canadian scholar Abu Bilal Mustafa al-Kanadi (1950–89), significantly entitled *The Islamic Ruling on Music and Singing, in Light of the Quraan, the Sunnah and* [I emphasise] *the Consensus of Our Pious Predecessors*.[320] The work is heavily textual.

Al-Kanadi notes in his Preface that the whole question about 'the legality of music and singing in the Islamic Shari'ah ... is an issue which is hotly debated among individuals and scholars in Isamic societies of our present day'.[321] Al-Kanadi's method is to examine both Qur'ān and ḥadīth before moving to an examination of the views of '*the pious predecessors of the Islamic* ummah'.[322] His conclusions are stark: apart from a few exceptions,[323] singing (*ghinā'*) is prohibited, especially when accompanied by musical instruments;[324] dancing accompanied by musical instruments is forbidden;[325] 'the profession of music, singing, dancing and instrument making and selling are all forbidden'.[326] Al-Kanadi proclaims that 'it is the duty of a Muslim that he avoid listening to music and singing in so far as it is within his power and jurisdiction (e.g. in his home, office, car etc.)'.[327]

This Canadian scholar's method, as we have already observed, is closely textual. He examines, for example, verse 6 of the thirty-first *Sūra* of the Qur'ān, *Sūra Luqmān*:

> But there, among men,
> Those who purchase idle tales [*lahw^a 'l-ḥadīth*]
> Without knowledge (or meaning),
> To mislead (men) from the Path
> Of God and throw ridicule
> (On the Path): for such
> There will be a humiliating
> Penalty.[328]

The Arabic phrase *laḥw^a 'l-ḥadīth* has been interpreted by some of the Muslim exegetes as 'singing and listening to songs'.[329] Al-Kanadi admits that this interpretation is not conclusive but, if one combines the evidence of the relevant verses of the Qur'ān with the ḥadīth literature, then the prohibitions become clearer: 'Contrary to the commonly-held belief, there are a number of authentic narratives from the prophetic *sunnah* which clearly point to the indisputable fact that music, instruments, singing to accompaniment etc. are objects prohibited by the Islamic *shari'ah*'.[330] Only *taqlid* (literally, 'imitation') leads the misinformed to regard all such narrations as *weak* (*ḍa'īf*) or forged (*mawḍu'*).[331]

The final evidence for the prohibition on music, for al-Kanadi, is to be derived from the *salaf*.[332] Their views reinforce the already very clear prohibition established by the Qur'ān and the *sunna*.[333]Al-Kanadi insists:

> One of the attributes of sound Islamic methodology is the reference to the views and positions held by the pious predecessors of the Islamic *ummah* and the respectful consideration with which one approaches them.[334]

And if some later scholars differed from the *salaf*, then the former were guilty of deviation.[335]

We have here, then, an interpretation of a range of texts – Qur'ān, ḥadīth and others – which aims to purify Islam of actions and speech which might give rise to sexual excitation or lewdness.[336] The result is a fundamentally ascetical stance with regard to such matters which bears comparison with the ascetical tendencies which developed in other areas in the early Christian Church.[337] The emphasis is on the *Text*, with primacy being given to the Qur'ānic Text, and then a specific interpretation of that text resulting in a prohibitory *ijtihād*, and *asceticism*. Clothing that prohibition is the garb of *purity* or purification. That which might give rise to uncontrolled or unrestrained sexuality is to be eschewed: the fabric and control of the *umma* depend upon it.

Mary Douglas, in her seminal work *Purity and Danger*,[338] noted that 'for us sacred things and places are to be protected from defilement. Holiness and impurity are at opposite poles.'[339] Because music and singing, for the *salafī* 'cast of mind', introduced the *possibility* of consequent sin and defilement, they were to be eschewed, indeed prohibited, except in very clearly defined circumstances such as the unaccompanied chant (*tajwīd*) of the Qur'ān.

Our third and final case study, designed to illustrate what I will term 'the *salafī* paradigm of textual intent and purification', linking and interrelating text, *ijtihād*, purity and asceticism, lies in the field of *taṣwīr*. *Taṣwīr* in Arabic, according to one modern dictionary, may be translated as 'drawing, sketching; representation, portrayal, depiction; illustration; painting; photography'.[340] The Islamic debate on the licitness, or otherwise, of *taṣwīr* ranges widely and embraces related matters such as the use of videos and watching television.

The early Islamic ban on the representation of the human form derives specifically from the ḥadīth literature rather than from the Qur'ān.[341] Oleg Grabar succinctly reminds us that, in the Qur'ān 'there is nothing similar to the concise strength of Exodus 20.4: "Thou shalt not make unto thee any graven images or any likeness of anything that is in heaven or that is in the earth beneath or that is in the water under the earth".'[342]

It is true that only God is a *muṣawwir*, a 'fashioner', as Grabar translates, noting that the word also means 'painter'.[343] Hans Wehr has the following translations for this word: 'former' 'shaper', 'creator', 'photographer' and 'illustrator'.[344] Yusuf Ali, by contrast, prefers the (almost Neoplatonic!) 'Bestower of Forms':

> He is God, the Creator [*al-Khāliq*]
> The Evolver,
> The Bestower of Forms
> (Or Colours) [*al-Muṣawwir*].
> To Him belong
> The Most Beautiful Names.[345]

However, the Qur'ān also portrays the jinn building *tamāthīl* for Sulaymān.[346] Yusuf Ali translates *tamāthīl* as 'images';[347] Grabar notes the ambiguity and wide semantic range of the word, while translating as 'statues';[348] A. J. Arberry's translation of the Qur'an also says 'statues';[349] while finally, Wehr's Dictionary notes that *timthāl* (pl. *tamāthīl*) also means 'a sculptural image'.[350]

What the Qur'ān *actually prohibits* is the *worship* of idols (*aṣnām*):[351]

> Lo! Abraham said
> To his father Āzar:
> 'Takest thou idols [*aṣnām*] for gods?
> For I see thee
> And thy people
> In manifest error.'[352]

However, early Islam's major fear was the spectre of all that might contradict, or *seem to contradict*, the central Islamic doctrine of Allāh as the sole Creator of everything *ex nihilo*, and the equally important doctrine of the Oneness of God (*tawḥīd*). So the ḥadīth literature came into its own.

Oleg Grabar gives us several examples, including this: 'Those who will be most severely punished on the Day of Judgement are the murderer of a Prophet, one who has been put to death by a Prophet, one who leads men astray without knowledge, and a maker of images or pictures'.[353]

What is clear from this brief analysis is the emphasis on *text* and the deployment of text, in this case ḥadīth, to support a particular attitude or chosen stance: the purity, or purification, of the doctrines of *creatio ex nihilo* and *tawḥid* demanded an absolute concentration on Allāh as *al-Khāliq* (The Creator) and *al-Wāḥid* (The One); all that might remotely or tangentially seem to infringe or dilute these central tenets of the Islamic faith was to be ruthlessly purged. An ascetical, rigid, almost Pharisaical deployment of apposite ḥadīth became a major adjunct to the fight against polytheism and potential polytheism.

In our own age, those who have chosen to follow what they perceive to be the example of the *salaf* have been similarly textual in their interpretations and legal rulings (*fatāwā*). It is acknowledged by scholars that the subject of *taṣwīr* has been a subject of controversy since the early days of Islam.[354] This is because of the potential dangers, to which we have already alluded, of *shirk* (polytheism) and imitating God in His creative activities.[355]

In his book, *The Islamic Ruling Concerning At-Tasweer*, Abu Muhammad Abdur-Ra'uf Shakir, a New York convert to Islam in a 1975, firstly presents, in a heavily textual manner, twenty-one famous aḥadīth concerning *taṣwīr* and its prohibition, drawn from the most famous of the collectors of Traditions like al-Bukhārī and Muslim.[356] This is followed by three contemporary commentaries,[357] including those of the famous blind Shaykh 'Abd al-'Azīz ibn Bāz (1912–99), the former Grand Muftī of Saudi Arabia;[358] although the latter was known to have belonged to the Ḥanbalī School of Islamic jurisprudence, it was insisted, *in a very salafī way*, that 'his legal verdicts [were] based on the evidences from Qur'an and Sunnah' for which, as a renowned jurist, traditionist (*muḥaddith*) and scholar, he was entitled to apply his own personal *ijtihād*.[359]

Shakir's book concludes with a section clarifying and correcting what he perceives are the mistakes in the works of Shaykh Yūsuf al-Qaraḍāwī,[360] followed by a selection of Islamic legal rulings.[361] The Appendices cover such topics as the avoidance of doubtful matters[362] and 'the problem and dangers of television'.[363]

Shakir's conclusion, drawn from the classical ḥadīth literature, is that *taṣwīr*, TV, photography and sculpture are prohibited by Islam.[364] He does not attempt to interpret the more difficult data in the Qur'ān such as those verses which concern Sulaymān, the jinn and the *tamāthīl*.[365] 'Twisted *ijtihād*' is to be condemned,[366] and Shakir feels free to deploy others' *ijtihād* which seeks to correct and overturn that of more liberal scholars like al-Qaraḍāwī, who in his writings proclaimed that some types of *taṣwīr* like photography, were permitted (*mubāḥ*).[367] The ultimate arbiters for Shakir in matters of *taṣwīr* and its prohibition must be the *salaf* and their *sunna*, except where such *salaf* have 'deviated'.[368]

To conclude: our three case studies of science, music and *taṣwīr* show clearly that the purification of Islam for contemporary *salafis* demands, *inter alia*, a return to the example and teachings of the first *salaf* via the fourfold engine of text, *ijtihād*, purity and asceticism. Tradition means a return to the *salaf*. And any advance towards the achievement of what is perceived to be true Islam has to embrace the doctrine of *Return*. That Return will yield inspiration, example and foci for *ijtihād*.[369]

3.5 *Tradition, Purification, Kénōsis and Return*

Modernity, then, for the contemporary *salafī* embraces tradition and the past; the truly modern *salafī* is one who is in love with the past. And, as we have stressed, the key *leitmotiv* which animates the spirit of the *salafiyya* is Return. In the light of this, it is useful to survey and analyse how the 'modernist' debate in Islam has run in general.

It is a mixed and multi-faceted picture. The following paragraphs provide snapshots. Some harmonise neatly with the underlying positions of the diverse *salafī* groups. Others do not. Coherence and uniformity should not – indeed, cannot – be posited of 'modernity' in Islam today.

Paradox is sometimes inherent in a given stance or movement. For example, modern Nigeria has seen the emergence of a society called the Society for the Removal of Innovation and the Reinstatement of Tradition. Its Hausa name is Yan Izala, and it is called *Jamā'at Izālat al-Bid'a wa Iqāmat al-Sunna* in Arabic. Its adherents' proclaimed intention, explicit in the name of the Society, is the extirpation of all innovations and a *return* to the *Sunna* of the Prophet Muḥammad.[370] However, Ousame Kane has perspicaciously argued that Yan Izala has been a major force for modernity in Northern Nigeria and that its ideology, though Wahhābī in orientation and infused with few attempts at positive *ijtihād*, has attempted to free certain 'lower-ranking' peoples from the classical traditions and values of the Islamic African *umma*.[371]

Politics may also be at the heart of the matter. In February 2002, President Pervez Musharraf of Pakistan made a blistering attack on modern Muslims. He berated their lack of enlightenment and their backwardness. The latter was due, he suggested, to the way that Muslims had involved themselves in 'fratricidal conflicts'. He perceived that the Islamic world was 'living in darkness' and that Islam 'had been left behind the developed world because [it] had not invested in education and technology'. He called for the Islamic *umma* to participate in an act of 'collective self-criticism'. All this, of course, roused the anger of his politico-religious 'fundamentalist' opponents, who vowed to bring him down.[372]

Antecedents to Musharraf's self-flagellation, and his diagnosis of modern Islam's ills, are not difficult to find. Over a century ago, Jamāl al-Dīn al-Afghānī (1838/9–1897) suggested just such a self-reevaluation. Islam could have a universal appeal once again if he, al-Afghānī, 'could show that the essence of Islam was the same as that of modern rationalism'.[373]

The challenges for contemporary Islam are manifest and manifold, they are, *inter alia*, political, religious and sociological. They include the questions of exclusion or inclusion, integration or assimilation, pluralism, the role of minorities, the function and process of *ijtihād*, the licitness or otherwise of violence for religio-political ends and the status of women.[374] Parvez Manzoor holds, presciently, that the crisis of modernity today 'is a crisis not of power but of meaning'.[375] For him,

> the delegitimation of modernity at the level of doctrine has undoubtedly opened a new intellectual space and created a different agenda for a dialogue between modernists and others, within the civilisation of Islam as well as between Islam and the West.[376]

For Soumaya Ghanoushi, in the great debate about modernity and the role of *ijtihād*, the solutions are clear: 'Ijtihad is the source of Islam's dynamism and flexibility'.[377] But fundamental questions of meaning remain: should one be talking about whether Islam and modernity are compatible, or whether certain diverse *interpretations* of Islam and modernity are compatible?[378] The challenge, or challenges, of modernism and modernity (as we have seen in Western Christianity during the reign of Pope Pius X (reg. 1903–14) and his anti-Modernist Encyclical *Pascendi Gregis* of 8 September 1907[379]) appeared to many to undermine the very fabric of the Islamic faith and to reject, or even destroy, centuries of accumulated wisdom, tradition and interpretation which, because they were ancient, had become canonical.

It is no accident that the Arabic word often used for 'heresy' or 'heretical dogma' is *bidʿa*, which fundamentally means 'innovation'.[380] In a sense, we hark back here to an ancient pre-Islamic paradigm where that which was customary in the tribe was right.[381] Ancient custom, ancient tradition, reconstituted in Prophetic *Sunna*,[382] abhorred innovation. The challenge, then, for modernism and modernity is that they should be perceived as part of a continuity, rather than an epistemic break of Foucault-like proportions.[383] For the Roman Catholic Church under Pius X, Modernism, defined specifically as 'the synthesis of all heresies' (*cumulatio omnium haeresium*)[384] represented a radical epistemic break with the beloved continuities inherent in the Apostolic Tradition, which was accepted as having been handed down from the earliest times. Pius X abhorred the Modernists for their 'innovations',[385] particularly the perceived heretical doctrinal interpretations; his engines or weapons of choice were condemnation, the recommendation to study scholastic philosophy, and censorship.[386] His final prescription for 'all clergy, pastors, confessors, preachers, religious superiors, and professors in philosophical-theological seminaries' was the Anti-Modernist Oath (*Sacrorum Antistitum*) on 1 September 1910.[387]

Islam too, at various times, has abhorred the innovations implicit in aspects of modernity and modernism. *Its* remedy or weapon of choice, apart from condemnation, has been the deployment of *ijtihād*, or, as it has sometimes been termed, neo-*ijtihād*. This may be neatly defined in quasi-psychological terms as a 'coping mechanism' by which to face the onslaught of the complexities of the modern age. By contrast, Pius X would never have tolerated a Catholic species of *ijtihād*. Two particular – now classical – examples of *ijtihād* as legal tool and 'coping mechanism' in modern times stand out: they are briefly surveyed here by way of conclusion to this section.

The Tunisian Law of Personal Status of 1957 outlawed divorce (*ṭalāq*) in any arena but a court of law, proclaiming : 'Any divorce outside a court of law is devoid of legal effect'.[388] No longer could a husband simply declare three times to his wife that she was divorced for that divorce to be valid and binding. The new Tunisian legislation was based on the application of *ijtihād* to the following Qur'ānic verse:

If ye fear a breach
Between them twain,
Appoint (two) arbiters,
One from his family,
And the other from hers;
If they wish for peace,
God will cause
Their reconciliation:
For God hath full knowledge,
And is acquainted
With all things. (Q.4:35)[389]

In reinterpreting this verse, the reformers argued that, in the mid-twentieth century, only a properly constituted court of law was competent to arbitrate in the case of potential divorce. Divorce in itself constituted a prime contemporary example of potential 'breach' between spouses.[390] By this ruling, the sanctity of the sacred text of the Qur'ān was upheld, since it was reinterpreted not overthrown, and yet the law was harmonised with contemporary need and reason.

The same Statute, *The Tunisian Law of Personal Status of 1957*, also banned polygamy, again by the judicious application of *ijtihād*. And again, the sacred text was respected by being reinterpreted rather than being ignored or overthrown. The relevant Qur'ānic verse was the following:

If ye fear that ye shall not
Be able to deal justly
With the orphans,
Marry women of your choice,
Two, or three, or four:
But if ye fear that ye shall not
Be able to deal justly (with them),
Then only one, or (a captive)
That your right hands possess.
That will be more suitable,
To prevent you
From doing injustice. (Q.4:3)[391]

In other words, polygamy is permitted but co-wives are to be treated with absolute equality in all respects.[392] The reason for the revelation (*sabab al-nuzūl*) of the particular *sūra*, The *Sūra of the Women* (*Sūrat al-Nisā'*), in which this verse occurs was the aftermath of the Battle of Uḥud (AD 625), a battle fought by the Prophet Muḥammad with his supporting Medinans, against their opponents from Mecca, at Uḥud, a hill which lay to the west of Medina. Militarily, the battle was a draw; but more than seventy Muslims were killed, resulting in many Muslim orphans and widows.[393]

Tunisia, however, decided that polygamy was no longer appropriate in the twentieth century and legislated accordingly, reinterpreting the above-cited 'verse of equality' as being impossible to apply in contemporary society. As Coulson notes:

> It is evident from the Qur'ān ... that equal treatment of co-wives is a legal condition of the right of polygamy. It is equally evident that in the circumstances of present-day society such equality of treatment, to the mutual satisfaction of the spouses, is in practice impossible. And with the failure of the condition the right dependent upon it must also lapse. On this ground the [Tunisian Law of Personal Status] tersely declares: 'Polygamy is prohibited'.[394]

It is clear that the motor or catalyst for such forms of *ijtihād* was the need for change in the light of contemporary society. It is equally clear that reformers, whether of a traditionalist or 'modernist' persuasion, have always known how to use the tools of Islamic jurisprudence to implement such change and to subvert a seemingly over-rigid or fossilised judicial present. One thinks, for example, of the mediaeval deployment of legal stratagems (*ḥiyal*) by the Ḥanafī and Mālikī Schools of Law and others.[395] As Coulson again notes: 'The Islamic *ḥiyal* are simply legal trickery, with the blatant purpose of circumventing an established rule of the substantive law'.[396]

Of course, the *ḥiyal* are not to be identified with *ijtihād*. They are only cited here to illustrate the fact that change is – and always was – possible in Islamic law. Reform is possible. Reform via *return* to *tradition* is also possible. I will leave the last word on the subject to the neat and wise summation of Professor David Waines:

> Writing from different legal, regional perspectives and historical contexts, Ibn Rushd [1126–98] and Ibn Taymiyya [1263–1328] were both engaged in and with a developing, authoritative juristic culture; for each, the past and present formed a continuous reality that nonetheless accommodated differences and changes in emphasis and direction.[397]

Continuity was and is both possible and real in Islam. But, for the *Salaf*, the key engine or catalyst of change and reform was a *return to tradition/Tradition*. To extend the metaphor, the fuel which powers that engine is *ijtihād*.

Ijtihād has been a guiding principle of Shīʿī law from the early days. 'Every Twelver believer, according to the dominant Usuli school, is required to follow the dictates of a living *mujtahid*.'[398] In the excellent seminal work which perhaps comes closest to the comparative methodology adopted in my own volume, Bill and Williams's *Roman Catholics and Shiʿi Muslims*, there are identified a number of 'striking structural similarities' between Shiʿi Islam and Roman Catholicism.[399] These include 'a transcendent martyr who is part of a holy family'[400] (i.e. Jesus Christ and Imām al-Ḥusayn),[401] 'a powerful mother figure'[402] (i.e. the Virgin Mary and Sayyida Fāṭima),[403] redemptive suffering and martyrdom together with a cult of saints/Imāms,[404] a shared love of mysticism,[405] and a religio-political interest[406] sometimes resulting in an uneasy tension between the authoritarian head of Church/Shīʿa and the authoritarian Head of State. And, of course, authority is of the essence in many of the debates of both Sunnī/Shīʿite Islam and Roman Catholic Christianity. The last main chapter of Bill and Williams's volume is entitled 'Authority, Justice and the Modern Polity'.[407] And, since our own work is as much concerned with Sunnism as it is with Shīʿism, it is this chapter which is perhaps most relevant to much of what has been said above.

This is not to say that many of the other 'striking structural similarities' identified between Shīʿa Islam and Roman Catholicism do not exist between Sunnī Islam and Roman Catholicism as well. They clearly do, especially in such areas as mysticism and religio-political interests. However, what I want to stress here is the mutual emphasis on authority and authoritarian figures in Sunnī and Shīʿite Islam on the one hand, and in Christianity on the other, whether in the form of caliphs, imāms, āyatullāhs, bishops or popes. It is salutary to consider that at least one author believes that '*Humanae Vitae* [Pope Paul VI's Encyclical against artificial forms of birth control] is about authority', not sex.[408]

The other principal area of shared debate, apart from authority and authenticity, is that of *umma* and community: this is a dominant theme in both Islam and Christianity. Indeed, Bill and Williams insist that 'in Catholic piety, the church and the community of the faithful are equivalent to the Islamic *umma*'.[409]

This volume has been written from a comparative perspective although it is not intended to be a *mere* exercise in comparative religion despite the powerful element of that methodology in what has gone before. It has attempted to make connections by means of the triple sieve of object, sign and the sacred. A dominant *leitmotiv* has been that of tradition and sometimes 'traditionalism'. The distinction between the two is acknowledged here,[410] although the two have sometimes been conflated above and treated as one where the case seemed to warrant it.

To use an antique terminology, is Islam an orthodoxy or an orthopraxy?[411] Islamic theology insists that it is both, although we may, for both times past as well as the present, wish to speak loosely of several 'orthodoxies' and several 'orthopraxies'. As we shall suggest shortly, these antique vocabularies are not necessarily helpful, and new terminologies may be more appropriate to the twenty-first century.

To reiterate, Islam is not a 'protestant' religion of justification by faith alone. In Q.57:7, for example, the believer is urged to believe in God and in God's Prophet Muḥammad, and to be charitable. The Five pillars of Islam incorporate belief (*shahāda*) and charity (*zakāt*).[412] The following short ḥadīth drawn from the corpus of al-Nawawī neatly illustrates the intimate relation between faith and deed:

> Let him who believes in Allah and the Last Day either speak good or keep silent, and let him who believes in Allah and the Last Day be generous to his neighbour, and let him who believes in Allah and the Last Day be generous to his guest.[413]

However, those Islamic deeds are diverse, diffuse and multifarious in their political, cultural and social articulation. The old vocabularies of 'orthodoxy' and 'heterodoxy', implying as they do a fundamental monolithic perspective from which all else proceeds, and by which all divergence may be measured, are no longer appropriate. We have suggested earlier that new vocabularies may be deployed by which to clothe and articulate the sacred in twenty-first-century Islam.

From all that has preceded in this volume, we suggest by way of conclusion that there are four fundamental paradigms to be derived from our material. The derivation of these paradigms is not intended to be an artificial exercise in the creation of models for their own methodological sake. A paradigm should illuminate and extend the material from which it is formed. It is hoped that the following four will do just that.

Paradigm One may be termed the *Neo-cycle of Tradition*. This is a basic attempt to 'reclothe' or even 're-invent' a community – in the case of Islam, the *umma* – in a more 'traditional' or 'traditionalist' guise in order to access the fundamentally sacred. The process may be viewed in some ways as a species of classical Ibn Khaldūnesque circle.[414] There is a prophetic grounding (Buddha, Jesus, Paul, Muḥammad) which yields an oral and written tradition/Tradition. This, in turn, with the passing of the years, is given a liberal/modern/Modernist slant or *tafsīr*, after which an animated reaction emerges: there is an attempt to return to that early tradition/Tradition, to the *salaf* in the case of Islam, to the days before the Second Vatican Council in the case of traditionalist Catholicism. On the one hand, the fruits of modernity are perceived as pernicious and thus denied; on the other hand, modernity is embraced by reinterpreting it, or reclothing it, as tradition/Tradition. Thus is the 'antique sacred' accessed and reasserted for a modern age.

It is not for one moment suggested, of course, that all Muslims, or all Roman Catholics for that matter, adopt this paradigm of *prophetic grounding > written and oral tradition > liberalism/Modernism > Return to the* Salaf. This volume attempts to trace only one tendency among several.

Paradigm Two is the *Paradigm of Purification*. Mary Douglas has well articulated the links between purity, purification, ritual and religion:[415] 'Sacred things and places are to be protected from defilement. Holiness and impurity are at opposite poles.'[416]

We noted earlier the emphasis by the '9/11' suicide bombers on ritual purity. And this emphasis on ritual, religious and, indeed, intellectual purity has been articulated down the ages by groups as diverse as orthodox Jews, Sadducees, Manichees, Cathars,[417] Jansenists,[418] Wahhābīs, Salafīs and Lefebvrists. For many, a departure from the tradition/Tradition(s) of the Fathers or the ancestors was a pollution or, to use the Islamic term, an innovation (*bid'a*). The required remedy was the purificatory 'fire' of a Return: a return to the tradition of the *salaf* for Muslims, a return to the pre-Vatican age for Lefebvrists. The paradigm then, simply expressed was Purification > Tradition > Neo-Catharoi of Islam and Christianity. And that purification could operate, in the most extreme cases as we have seen, *usque ad mortem* in the ritual suicide bombings of '9/11', in contemporary Palestine and elsewhere.

Our *Paradigm Three* is the *Paradigm of Kénōsis*, the Greek word for 'emptying'. Many of the attempts to access the truly sacred have been via the route of a return to tradition and the consequent 'emptying' of all that is perceived as 'modern' or 'liberal' in faith, society, custom and ritual. This is as true of the Lefebvrists as it is of the contemporary Islamic *salafis* of diverse orientations. The apparently monolithic orthopraxies of a bygone age, especially where liturgy is involved, have had an insidious appeal and beckoned the anti-modernists/Modernists of all faiths with a siren lure. This is akin to the exclusivist paradigm beloved of historians of religious plurality. Its opposite, of course, is the inclusivist paradigm which prefers to stress not orthodoxies or orthopraxies but rather the diversity and at least partial truth to be found in all forms of *sacrovalence* (sacred worth), *sacrolexis* (sacred reading, *lectio divina*) and *sacropraxis* (sacred practice).[419]

Finally, there is our *Paradigm Four*, the *Paradigm of Return*. This embraces many elements of the three paradigms which we have already derived and identified. In fact, it would be true to say that there are many Paradigms of Return. They range from the Plotinian doctrine of Neoplatonic emanation, in which the Soul yearns to return to the One[420] through the Qur'ānic acknowledgement that we all come from God and must ultimately return to Him,[421] to the contemporary *Salafī*/Lefebvrist paradigm of God > Prophet > Tradition > Infidelity/Modernism > Reform via Return > Tradition > Sacred > God > Final Judgement.

On this sublime paradigmatic journey, numerous questions and some ironies arise: for example, the *salafī* Muslim will embrace *ijtihād* wholeheartedly; the Lefebvrist Christian will reject its Christian equivalent if that equivalent represents an unrestrained reinterpretation of doctrine or morals. Return for the Lefebvrist means a return to an ancient interpretation; return for the *salafī* can mean a redeployment or reinterpretation of an ancient norm or *sunna* suitable to the modern age. *The Tunisian Law of Personal Status* provides a distinguished example.

Both Muslim and Christian fundamentalists have, at various times, attempted to grasp the sacred by diverse routes which have sometimes disregarded the roles of historical and contemporary context. This volume has explored and analysed the quest for the sacred via the path of tradition/Tradition in two of the world's major religions, focusing mainly on *Salafī* Islam but also using Roman Catholic Lefebvrist Christianity as a prime point of comparison. Both *Salafī*s and Lefebvrists have clothed the *objects* of their worship and liturgy with the vocabulary of rectitude – orthodoxy, orthopraxy – rather than the vocabulary of the sacred – sacrovalence, sacrolexis, sacropraxis – proposed above. In so doing, they have sometimes risked obscuring the very *signs* of the *sacred*, which their traditionalism was designed to guard and reveal, behind a veil of controversy.

The Vatican II document *Nostra Aetate*, promulgated on 28 October 1965, solemnly proclaimed that nothing that was true and holy in the world's religions was to be rejected.[422] While *Nostra Aetate* did not seek to conceal its Roman Catholic view of what it believed to be the 'right' doctrinal path – its own *ṣirāṭ al-mustaqīm*, to use the Arabic terminology – it was at pains to stress the existence of the sacred in all religion as well as the concept of one human community.[423] This is, of course, a concept with considerable resonance for Islam, overlapping and embracing as it does the Muslim notion of *umma*.

Tradition, and return to tradition/Tradition, may be one route to the Sacred, but it is not the only one. For both Islam and Christianity, the Sacred may be achieved by community, *umma*. Notions of community may transform that which is merely profane; and, as Eliade has shown us, we may define the sacred in one way as 'the opposite of the profane'.[424]

This volume has examined the idea of Islam and the Traditional Imagination, using the triple lens of *object*, *sign* and the *sacred* as a sieve whereby to achieve greater clarity in our analysis. It has derived and identified four distinct, but interrelated, paradigms from the evidence deployed in the Islamic and Christian texts and materials which we have studied. Behind all, indeed, veiled from all, lies the Shadow of the Divine Sacred in both Islam and Christianity.

This volume has surveyed what Eliade terms the *hierophany*, or act of manifestation, of the Sacred.[425] The Qur'ān notes: 'We will show them Our signs on the horizons and in themselves'.[426] This single verse embraces phenomena (horizons, themselves), semiotics (signs) and, above all, The Sacred (We, Our = Allāh). It also underpins the entire Tradition of Islam; and, in this way, the traditional textuality of Islam uncovers a direct route to the Sacred and the Divine.

For the believer of any faith, man lives 'in a sacralized cosmos'.[427] The traditions/Traditions whereby that sacralised cosmos is imperfectly articulated and realised may lead to the Sacred. They are not *necessarily* coterminous with that Sacred in either Islam or Christianity.

NOTES

Chapter 1: Preparation for a Threefold Sieve

1. Samuel P. Huntington, *The Clash of Civilizations and the Remaking of World Order* (London and New York: Touchstone Books, 1998), esp. pp. 209–18.
2. For Kosovo, see Miranda Vickers, *Between Serb and Albanian: A History of Kosovo* (London: Hurst, 1998). For a survey and analysis of this, 'Europe's last war of the millennium', see Bronwen Maddox et al., 'The Times in the Balkans: The 80 Days War', *Times*, 15 July 1999, pp. 43–50.
3. See John Esposito, *The Islamic Threat: Myth or Reality?*, 2nd edn (New York and Oxford: Oxford University Press, 1992, 1995).
4. A much misused, and abused, word which should be used with caution. Justo Lacunza Balda notes: 'A variety of labels are given to the different manifestations of Islam in modern times, particularly when they have to do with a resolute search for political power. Among the most common labels in use are *fundamentalism*, *radicalism* and *revivalism*. Such definitions of Islam, or for the sake of the argument of any other religion, are at times conducive to such generalisations that often people are led into a state of instant confusion. The tendency to generalise about people, countries and religions is a fashionable exercise of our age', in A. J. Lane, 'What is Radical Islam? One Answer', *Encounter (Documents for Muslim–Christian Understanding)* 216 (June–July 1995), p. 1.
5. See Norman Daniel, *Islam and the West: The Making of an Image* (Edinburgh: Edinburgh University Press, 1960, 1966); Ian Richard Netton, 'Neo-Orientalists on a New Crusade: Hope, Renewal and Salvation', *Al-Masāq: Islam and the Medieval Mediterranean*, 10 (1998), pp. 33–56; Jack G. Shaheen, *Arab and Muslim Stereotyping in American Popular Culture* (Washington, DC: Georgetown University Press, 1997).
6. James A. Bill and John Alden Williams, *Roman Catholics and Shi'i Muslims: Prayer, Passion and Politics* (Chapel Hill and London: University of North Carolina Press, 2000), p. 143.
7. I use the word 'grounded' here in a theological sense. See, for example, the usage of the word in the writings of the medieval Dominican friar and mystic, Meister Eckhart (c. 1260–1327/8). He wrote: 'As surely as the Father in his simple nature bears the Son naturally, just as surely He bears him in the inmost recesses of the spirit, and *this* is the inner world. Here God's ground is my ground and my ground is God's ground', M. O'C. Walshe

(ed. and trans.), *Meister Eckhart: Sermons and Treatises*, 3 vols (London: Watkins, 1979, 1981, 1985), p. 117, 13b cited in Richard Woods, *Eckhart's Way*, The Way of the Christan Mystics (London: Darton, Longman & Todd, 1987), p. 58, see n. 45.

8. See Julian Baldick, 'Among the Friends of God', *Times Literary Supplement*, 26 September 1986, p. 1,073.
9. See N. J. Coulson, *A History of Islamic Law*, Islamic Surveys 2 (Edinburgh: Edinburgh University Press, 1964).
10. See Baldick, 'Among the Friends of God'.
11. See, for example, Yasin Dutton, *The Origins of Islamic Law: The Qur'an, the Muwaṭṭa' and Madinan Amal*, Culture and Civilization in the Middle East (Richmond: Curzon, 1999).
12. Roger Joseph, 'The Semiotics of the Islamic Mosque', *Arab Studies Quarterly*, 3:3, p. 286.
13. Aziz al-Azmeh, *Islams and Modernities* (London and New York: Verso, 1993).
14. Vartan Gregorian, *Islam: A Mosaic Not a Monolith* (Washington, DC: Brookings Institution Press, 2003), p. 112 and passim.
15. See Gary R. Bunt, *Islam in the Digital Age: E-Jihad, Online Fatwas and Cyber Islamic Environments*, (London and Sterling, VA: Pluto Press, 2003); and idem, *Virtually Islamic: Computer-Mediated Communication and Cyber Islamic Environments*, Religion, Culture, and Society series (Cardiff: University of Wales Press, 2000).
16. See Bunt, *Islam in the Digital Age*, p. 1.
17. Peter Mandaville, 'Digital Islam: Changing the Boundaries of Religious Knowledge?', *ISIM Newsletter* [Newsletter of the International Institute for the Study of Islam in the Modern World, Leiden], 2 (March 1999), p. 1. See Bunt, *Virtually Islamic*, esp. pp. 1–3; idem, *Islam in the Digital Age*, esp. pp. 67–90, 135–66, 167–83.
18. George Baramki Azar, 'The Digital Middle East', *Aramco World*, 47:6 (November–December 1996), p. 2. See Bunt, *Virtually Islamic*, pp. 37–65.
19. See Mandaville, 'Digital Islam', passim.
20. Ibid., p. 1.
21. Ibid.; see Bunt, *Virtually Islamic*, pp. 5, 20.
22. Mandaville, 'Digital Islam', p. 1.
23. Ibid.
24. Ibid., p. 23.
25. Ibid.
26. Ibid.
27. Ibid.
28. Ibid.
29. See, for example, the discussion of modernity in the context of modern state development within the Middle East, specifically the United Arab Emirates, in Ebrahim Rashed, *The Impacts of Western Modernity upon Identity in an Islamic Society: A Case Study of the United Arab Emirates with Special Reference to the Impact of Media and Technology upon Identity*, unpublished Ph.D. thesis, University of Wales (School of Journalism, Media and Cultural Studies, Cardiff), 2000; see esp. pp. 18–30 for a survey of definitions of 'modernity', and 'identity'.
30. Muqtedar Khan, 'Muslim Women: Caught in the Crossfire', *Arabies Trends*, 25 (November 1999), p. 70 (my italics).
31. Charles Tripp, 'Can Islam Cope with Modernity? (review of Ali Rahnema, *An Islamic Utopian: A Political Biography of Ali Shari'ati*; John Cooper, Ronald L. Nettler and Mohamed Mahmoud (eds), *Islam and Modernity: Muslim Intellectuals Respond*; and Bassam Tibi, *The Challenge of Fundamentalism: Political Islam and the New World Disorder*), in *Times Literary Supplement*, 23 April 1999, p. 6.

32. Ibid.
33. Ibid.; see also Albert Hourani, *Arabic Thought in the Liberal Age 1798–1939* (Cambridge: Cambridge University Press, 1983, 1988), esp. pp. 40–67.
34. See A. J. Arberry, *Revelation and Reason in Islam* (London: George Allen & Unwin, 1957).
35. Tripp, 'Can Islam Cope with Modernity?', p. 6.
36. M. Ali Lakhani, 'Editorial', *Sacred Web: A Journal of Tradition and Modernity*, 1 (July 1998), pp. 7–8 (my italics).
37. Ibid., p. 7.
38. Frithjof Schuon, 'Tradition and Modernity', *Sacred Web*, 1 (July 1998), p. 19.
39. Ibid., pp. 21, 26.
40. Seyyed Hossein Nasr, 'Frithjof Schuon (1907–1998)', *Sacred Web*, 1 (July 1998), p. 16 .
41. Table of Contents, *Sacred Web*, 2 (December 1998), p. 6.
42. David Appelbaum, 'The Moment of Modernity', *Sacred Web*, 2 (December 1998), p. 90.
43. Ibid.; see also René Descartes, *Meditations on First Philosophy* (1641) in idem, *Meditations and Other Metaphysical Writings*, trans. with intro. by Desmond M. Clarke (London: Penguin Books, 2003), p. 18. For the original Latin, see Renati Descartes, *Meditationes de Prima Philosophia* (Paris: Michael Soly, 1641).
44. Appelbaum, 'The Moment of Modernity:', pp. 91–2; see also p. 93. For a response to Appelbaum's arguments, see William W. Quinn, 'Response to David Appelbaum's "The Moment of Modernity"', *Sacred Web*, 2 (December 1998), pp. 95–100, esp. his references to the *sophia perennis* (p. 96). See also José Segura, 'On Descartes' "Stop"', *Sacred Web*, 3 (June 1999), pp. 11–14.
45. See, for example, Linda Woodhead and Paul Heelas (eds), *Religion in Modern Times: An Anthology*, Religion and Modernity series (Oxford: Blackwell, 2000); Paul Heelas (ed.), *Religion, Modernity and Postmodernity*, Religion and Modernity series (Oxford: Blackwell, 1998); David Smith, *Hinduism and Modernity*, Religion and Modernity series (Oxford: Blackwell, 2002).
46. Abrar Ahmad Islahi, 'OIC Islamic Fiqh Academy's 11th Session', *The Muslim World League Journal*, 26:10 (January–February 1999), p. 19.
47. Ibid., p. 18.
48. Georges Khalil, 'The Working Group Modernity and Islam', *ISIM Newsletter*, 2 (March 1999), p. 36.
49. Ibid.
50. Ibid.
51. See above, n. 36.
52. See above, n. 47.
53. For Islam and globalisation, see *The Muslim World League Journal*, 30:3 (Rabi al-Awwal 1423/May 2002), esp. pp. 12–17 ('King Fahd Urges Muslims to Face Challenges of Globalization') pp. 18–23 ('4th General Islamic Conference') and pp. 24–32 ('4th General Islamic Conference: Calls for Application of Shar'iah'). See also J. Meuleman, *Islam in the Era of Globalization: Muslim Attitudes Towards Modernity and Identity* (London: RoutledgeCurzon, 2002).
54. Islahi, 'OIC Islamic Fiqh Academy's 11th Session', p. 19.
55. Ibid.
56. Abdou Filali-Ansary, 'The Debate on Secularism in Contemporary Societies of Muslims', *ISIM Newsletter*, 2 (March 1999), p. 6.
57. Ibid.
58. Ibid.
59. Ibid.

60. Ibid.
61. Chris Morris, 'Headscarf MP warns off army', *The Guardian*, 4 May 1999 (my italics). We may compare the situation in Turkey with the 2003–4 crackdown in France on the wearing of the headscarf in the classroom. See Hannah Godfrey, 'Schools' bid for headscarf ban widens French divide', *Observer*, 15 June 2003, p. 22. For further references see n. 150.
62. Morris, 'Headscarf MP'.
63. See John Freely, *Istanbul: The Imperial City* (Harmondsworth: Penguin Books, 1996), pp. 296–8.
64. Ibid., p. 299.
65. Ibid., pp. 299–300.
66. Ibid., p. 300.
67. Anthony Giddens, 'Why we still look forward to the past' [The 1999 Reith Lectures, no. 3: Tradition], *Observer*, 25 April 1999, p. 31.
68. Ibid.
69. See Charles Kurzman, 'Liberal Islam: Not a Contradiction in Terms', *ISIM Newsletter*, 2 (March 1999), p. 41; see also p. 43.
70. Ibid., p. 41.
71. Ibid.
72. Ibid.
73. See E. Tyan, art. 'Djihād', *EI*², vol. 2, pp. 538–40; see also James Turner Johnson and John Kelsay (eds), *Cross, Crescent and Sword: The Justification and Limitation of War in Western and Islamic Tradition*, Contributions to the Study of Religion, no. 27 (New York, Westport, CT and London: Greenwood Press, 1990); John Kelsay and James Turner Johnson (eds), *Just War and Jihad: Historical and Theoretical Perspectives on War and Peace in Western and Islamic Traditions*, Contributions to the Study of Religion, no. 28 (New York, Westport, CT and London: Greenwood Press, 1991); Esposito, *The Islamic Threat*; idem, *Unholy War: Terror in the Name of God* (Oxford: Oxford University Press, 2003); Gilles Kepel, *Jihad: The Trail of Political Islam* (Cambridge, MA: Harvard University Press, 2002); M. J. Akbar, *The Shade of Swords* (London: Routledge, 2003); Bernard Lewis, *What Went Wrong? The Clash Between Islam and Modernity in the Middle East* (London: Orion Books, Phoenix, 2002); Jason Burke, *Al-Qaeda: Casting a Shadow of Terror* (London and New York: I. B. Tauris, 2003). For more fantastic interpretations, see John Gray, *Al-Qaeda and What It Means to be Modern* (London: Faber, 2003). Rosemary Righter (*Times*: T2, 16 July 2003, p. 28) characterises the latter volume as an 'irritating polemic, long on assertion and short on evidence'.
74. See Peter Marsden, *The Taliban: War, Religion and the New Order in Afghanistan* (London and New York: Zed Books, 1998); see also Dietrich Reetz, 'Islamic Activism in Central Asia and the Pakistan Factor', *Journal of South Asian and Middle Eastern Studies*, 23:1 (Fall 1999), pp. 1–37, esp. pp. 2–5; Hafeez Malik, 'Taliban's Islamic Emirate of Afghanistan: Its Impact on Eurasia', in ibid., pp. 65–78; Peter L. Bergen, *Holy War, Inc.: Inside the Secret World of Osama bin Laden* (London: Weidenfeld & Nicolson, 2001); Martin Ewans, *Afghanistan: A New History*, 2nd edn (London and New York: RoutledgeCurzon, 2002), p. 26 and passim.
75. For Khomeini, see Baqer Moin, *Khomeini: Life of the Ayatollah* (London and New York: I. B. Tauris, 1999).
76. For the whole debate about apostasy, and especially classical attitudes as expressed in the Qur'ān, ḥadīth and *fiqh*, see Timothy Michael Wake Green, *Factors Affecting Attitudes to Apostasy in Pakistan*, unpublished MA dissertation, University of London, SOAS, 1998, esp. ch. 2, pp. 5–12.

77. See K. N. Pandita, 'Intricate Roots of Theo-Fascist Ideology', *Asian Affairs*, 36 (October 1999), pp. 19–10.
78. 9/11 is analysed in Eliadean terms at the very end of this chapter.
79. Abd al-Hakim Murad, 'Islamic Spirituality: the forgotten revolution', www:file:///D|ashari/nuhhakim/ahk/fgtnrevo.htm [printed 7/3/99].
80. Pandita, 'Intricate Roots', p. 9.
81. See Richard Lloyd Parry, 'Islam rises over Indonesia', *Independent on Sunday*, 24 October 1999, p. 21.
82. Ibid.
83. Ibid.
84. Ibid.
85. Ibid.
86. Ibid.
87. Ibid.
88. Mujiburrahman, 'Islam and Politics in Indonesia: The Political Thought of Abdurrahman Wahid', *Islam and Christian–Muslim Relations*, 10:3 (1999), p. 339.
89. Ibid., p. 339, citing R. William Liddle, 'Islam and politics in late new order' (Jakarta, paper presented at the Conference on Religion and Society in Southeast Asia, 29–30 May 1995, unpublished), p. 7.
90. Mujiburrahman, 'Islam and Politics in Indonesia', p. 339.
91. Ibid., p. 340.
92. Ibid.
93. Ibid.
94. Ibid.
95. Ibid., p. 341.
96. See Ṭāhā Ḥusayn, *Al-Ayyām* (3 vols in 1, Cairo: Dār al-Ma'ārif, n.d.), vol. 3, esp. pp. 79–146; Kenneth Cragg (trans.), *A Passage to France: The Third Volume of the Autobiography of Ṭāhā Ḥusain*, in Taha Hussein, *The Days: His Autobiography in Three Parts*, trans. E. H. Paxton, Hilary Wayment and Kenneth Cragg (Cairo: The American University in Cairo Press, 1997), esp. pp. 322–87. See also Pierre Cachia, *Ṭāhā Ḥusayn: His Place in the Egyptian Literary Renaissance* (London: Luzac, 1956), esp. pp. 55–8.
97. See Mujiburrahman, 'Islam and Politics in Indonesia', p. 341.
98. Ibid.; see Ṭāhā Ḥusayn, *Al-Ayyām* (Cairo: Dār al-Ma'ārif, n.d.), vol. 2; Hilary Wayment (trans.), *The Stream of Days: A Student at the Azhar* (Cairo: Al–Maaref, 1943); see Cachia, *Ṭāhā Ḥusayn*, pp. 17–52.
99. See Ṭāhā Ḥusayn, *Al-Ayyām*, vol. 3, p. 119; Cachia, *Ṭāhā Ḥusayn*, p. 55.
100. Mujiburrahman, 'Islam and Politics in Indonesia', p. 341.
101. See ibid.
102. See Ṭāhā Ḥusayn, *Al-Ayyām* (Cairo: Dār al-Ma'ārif, 1971), vol. 1, pp. 3ff; Cachia, *Ṭāhā Ḥusayn*, p. 45.
103. See V. S. Naipaul, *Beyond Belief: Islamic Excursions Among the Converted Peoples* (London: Little, Brown, 1998), pp. 27, 31.
104. See Cachia, *Ṭāhā Ḥusayn*, pp. 64–5; Parry, 'Islam rises over Indonesia', p. 21. While Gus Dur became President of Indonesia in 1999, Ṭāhā Ḥusayn was Minister of Education in the Egyptian Wafdist government from 1950 to 1952.
105. Mujiburrahman, 'Islam and Politics in Indonesia', p. 341.
106. Wayment (trans.), *The Stream of Days*, p. 199; Ḥusayn, *Al-Ayyām*, vol. 2, p. 174; Cachia, *Ṭāhā Ḥusayn*, pp. 49–50.
107. Mujiburrahman, 'Islam and Politics in Indonesia', p. 341.

108. See Ṭāhā Ḥusayn, *Al-Ayyām*, vol. 2, p. 181; Cachia, *Ṭāhā Ḥusayn*, p. 52.
109. Cachia, *Ṭāhā Ḥusayn*, p. 49.
110. Mujiburrahman, 'Islam and Politics in Indonesia', p. 341.
111. Ibid.
112. Ibid., p. 342.
113. Ibid.
114. Ibid., p. 343.
115. Ibid.
116. Ibid., p. 345.
117. Ibid.
118. Ibid., p. 346.
119. Ibid. For more on this subject, see R. Hefner, *Civil Islam: Muslims and Democratization in Indonesia*, Princeton Studies in Muslim Politics (Princeton, NJ: Princeton University Press, 2000). See also D. Porter, *Managing Politics and Islam in Indonesia* (London: RoutledgeCurzon, 2002).
120. Mujiburrahman, 'Islam and Politics in Indonesia', p. 347.
121. Ibid., p. 348.
122. Ibid.
123. Ibid. For Abdurrahman Wahid and pluralism, see Hefner, *Civil Islam*, pp. 160–3.
124. Cachia, *Ṭāhā Ḥusayn*, p. 87.
125. Ibid.
126. Ibid., p. 92.
127. Ibid., p. 94.
128. Ibid., p. 98.
129. 'Megawati will bring dignity, perhaps even stability', *Independent: The Tuesday Review*, 24 July 2001, p. 3.
130. 'Megawati's challenge', *Times*, 24 July 2001, p. 15.
131. Catherine Philip, 'Sukarno's daughter claims birthright', *Times*, 24 July 2001, p. 12.
132. Idem, 'Two Presidents condemn Jakarta to double jeopardy', in ibid.; see also Richard Lloyd Parry, 'Indonesia has a new president, only the old one won't accept that', *Independent*, 24 July 2001, p. 3. For a full-scale biography of Abdurrahman Wahid, see Greg Barton, *Abdurrahman Wahid: Muslim Democrat, Indonesian President: A View from the Inside* (Sydney: University of New South Wales Press, 2002).
133. See V. S. Naipaul, *Among the Believers: An Islamic Journey* (London: André Deutsch, 1981), esp. pp. 277–361.
134. See idem, *Beyond Belief*, esp. pp. 7–140.
135. See, for example, ibid., pp. 114–15.
136. Ibid.
137. See, for example, ibid., pp. 123–4, 3.
138. Idem, *Among the Believers*, p. 279.
139. Ibid.; see also p. 294.
140. Ibid., pp. 284, 279, 308.
141. Ibid., p. 308.
142. See ibid. and pp. 326–7.
143. See idem, *Beyond Belief*, p. 39. For Naipaul's encounters and conversations with Gus Dur, see Naipaul, *Among the Believers*, pp. 301–4, and idem, *Beyond Belief*, pp. 26–40.
144. See N. Ayubi, *Political Islam: Religion and Politics in the Arab World* (London: Routledge, 1993), pp. 3, 120 cited in Ammar Fadzil, *The Concept of Ḥukm in the Qur'ān*, unpublished Ph.D. thesis, University of Edinburgh, 1999, p. 223.

145. See above n. 118.
146. See Pope John Paul II, *Ecclesia in Europa* [Post-Synodal Apostolic Exhortation] (London: CTS, 2003), pp. 42–4.
147. See, for example, the opposite of the attitude expressed above in Marcel Lefebvre, *Against the Heresies* (Kansas City: Angelus Press, 1997), p. 200.
148. Jørgen Nielsen, *Muslims in Western Europe*, 2nd edn (Edinburgh: Edinburgh University Press, 1995).
149. Ibid., pp. 152–3ff.
150. See 'Laicité', voile: les questions clés', *Le Figaro*, 8 December 2003, pp. 1, 8–9; 'L'appel commun des Eglises chrétiennes contre une loi sur le voile', *Le Monde*, 9 December 2003, pp. 1, 10; Jon Henley, 'France to ban pupils' religious dress', *Guardian*, 12 December 2003, p. 17; Charles Bremner, 'Muslim girls face scarf ban at French schools', *Times*, 12 December 2003, p. 20; idem, 'Chirac bans use of Muslim headscarf in all state schools', *Times*, 18 December 2003, p. 20; Paul Webster, 'Chirac calls on MPs to ban headscarves', *Guardian*, 18 December 2003; Madeleine Bunting, 'Secularism goes mad', *Guardian*, 18 December 2003, p. 25; Alain Woodrow, 'Tricolour versus the scarf', *The Tablet*, 3 January 2004, pp. 6–7. See also Anthony Browne, 'Belgians call for headscarf ban', *Times*, 19 January 2004, p. 21. See, finally, François Burgat, 'Veils and Obscuring Lenses', in John L. Esposito and François Burgat (eds), *Modernizing Islam: Religion in the Public Sphere in the Middle East and Europe* (London: Hurst, 2003), esp. pp. 31–4; Jocelyne Cesari, 'Muslim Minorities in Europe: The Silent Revolution', in ibid., p. 267.
151. Nielsen, *Muslims in Western Europe*, p. 154.
152. The Runnymede Trust, *Islamophobia: A Challenge for Us All* (London: The Runnymede Trust Commission on British Muslims and Islamophobia, 1997).
153. Nielsen, *Muslims in Western Europe*, p. 155.
154. See *The Tablet*, 29 September 2001, p. 1,385.
155. See Nielsen, *Muslims in Western Europe*, p. 156.
156. The first is edited from the University of Birmingham's Centre for the Study of Islam and Christian–Muslim Relations (CSIC); the latter two are the product of the Pontifical Institute of Arabic and Islamic Studies (PISAI) in Rome.
157. See Nielsen, *Muslims in Western Europe*, pp. 158–64; Ian Richard Netton, *Text and Trauma: An East–West Primer* (Richmond: Curzon Press, 1996), esp. pp. 19–41, 84–9, 122–5, 131–5.
158. Nielsen, *Muslims in Western Europe*, p. 169.
159. Christopher Walker, 'Religious divide in a holy dispute', *Times Weekend*, 15 May 1999, p. 17.
160. Ibid. The tomb of one of the warriors of the great Ṣalāḥ al-Dīn, whose name is Shihāb al–Dīn, is alleged to be near the church.
161. Sam Kiley, 'Clerics revolt over mosque in Nazareth', *Times*, 5 November 1999.
162. Anubha Charan, 'Ayodhya: Digging Up India's Holy Places', *History Today*, 54:1 (January 2004), p. 4. See also Christian W. Troll, 'Islam and Pluralism in India', *Encounter*, 220 (December 1995), esp. p. 22; Trevor Fishlock, 'Holy town at heart of quarrel about nation's future', *Times*, 28 February 2002, p. 19; Catherine Philip, 'Muslim fire raiders kill 57 Hindus in train', ibid., p. 19. For another focal point of conflict ('the destruction of the 14th-century mosque at Chrar-e-Sharief in Kashmir'), see Mukhtar Ahmed and Tim McGirk, 'Historic mosque destroyed in new Kashmir violence', *Independent*, 12 May 1995.
163. Cathy Scott-Clark and Adrian Levy, 'Beyond Belief', *Sunday Times Magazine*, 24 January 1999, pp. 29–36, esp. p. 30.

164. Ibid., p. 30.
165. Ibid., pp. 31–2.
166. Michael Binyon, 'Religious conflicts take growing toll', *Times*, 4 January 2000, p. 14.
167. Ibid.
168. See Phil Reeves, 'Profile: Ariel Sharon: Israel's danger man', *Independent: Weekend Review*, 28 October 2000, p. 5.
169. John W. Kiser, *The Monks of Tibhirine: Faith, Love and Terror in Algeria* (New York: St. Martin's Press, 2002), p. 245; repr. Dom Christian de Chergé, 'The Testament of Dom Christian de Chergé', *White Fathers – White Sisters*, 348 (October–November 1999), pp. 11–12.
170. Kiser, *Monks of Tibhirine*, p. 246.
171. See the *Times* leader entitled 'Islam's Luther' with its sub-heading 'Khomeini's shadow still clouds the Muslim world': *Times*, 11 February 1999.
172. Ibid.; for the continuing influence of Khomeini in Iran after his death, see, for example, Michael Theodoulou, 'Thousands march for the Ayatollah', *Times*, 15 July 1999.
173. See Theodoulou, 'Thousands march'. For a major biography and orientation, see Baqer Moin, *Khomeini: Life of the Ayatollah* (London and New York: I. B. Tauris, 1999).
174. 'Islam's Luther', *Times*, 11 February 1999.
175. For the development of some of these ideas see, *inter alia*, D. Harvey, *The Priest and the King* (London: I. B. Tauris, 1998); D. Johnston and C. Sampson, *Religion: The Missing Dimension of Statecraft* (Oxford: Oxford University Press, 1994); J. Casanova, *Public Religions in the Modern World* (Chicago: University of Chicago Press, 1994). I am grateful to Dr Philip Lewis for drawing these titles to my attention. See also Netton, *Text and Trauma*, esp. pp. 87–9.
176. 'Islam's Luther', *Times*, 11 February 1999.
177. Ibid.
178. Moin, *Khomeini*, p. 313.
179. 'Islam's Luther', *Times*, 11 February 1999.
180. E. Theodore Backmann, art. 'Lutheranism', in Nicholas Lossky et al. (eds), *Dictionary of the Ecumenical Movement* (Geneva: WCC Publications and London: Council of Churches for Britain and Ireland, 1991), p. 642.
181. See, for example, his powerful sermon on the birthday of the Prophet Muḥammad's daughter Fāṭima, on 27 October 1964, recorded in Moin, *Khomeini*, pp. 122–7, esp. p. 126.
182. See Eamon Duffy, *The Stripping of the Altars: Traditional Religion in England c. 1400–c. 1580* (New Haven, CT and London: Yale University Press, 1992), p. 379.
183. Moin, *Khomeini*, p. 128; G. R. Elton, *Reformation Europe 1517–1559*, The Fontana History of Europe (London and Glasgow: Collins, 1964), pp. 51–2.
184. For references, see Netton, *Text and Trauma*, pp. 89, 110 n. 171.
185. Elton, *Reformation Europe*, pp. 55–6.
186. See ibid., pp. 186–97.
187. See ibid., pp. 197–209.
188. See ibid., p. 180, 184–5. His full name was Gaetano di Thiene, co-founder of the Theatines, a new religious order comprising clergy and laity who worked within the world and rejected the enclosure characteristic of the old monastic way of life.
189. See Diarmaid MacCulloch, *Reformation: Europe's House Divided 1490–1700* (London: Allen Lane, 2003), pp. 410–17.
190. See, for example, Ian Richard Netton, *Allāh Transcendent: Studies in the Structure and Semiotics of Islamic Philosophy, Theology and Cosmology* (London and New York: Routledge,

1989; repr. Richmond: Curzon Press, 1994).
191. See, for example, Ernest Gellner, *Postmodernism, Reason and Religion* (London and New York: Routledge, 1992).
192. See above, n. 3.
193. Princeton, NJ: Princeton University Press, 1957, 1966.
194. London and Sydney: Croom Helm, 1982, repr. 1984.
195. Modern Middle East series, no. 1 (Austin and London: University of Texas Press, 1976, 1981).
196. New Haven, CT and London: Yale University Press, 1968. (This was reprinted as a Phoenix Book, Chicago and London: University of Chicago Press, 1971.) All references are to the Yale 1968 edition.
197. See above, n. 133.
198. See above, n. 103.
199. Huntington, *Clash of Civilizations*, p. 111.
200. Ibid.
201. Ibid.
202. Ibid., p. 121.
203. Samuel P. Huntington, 'The Clash of Civilizations', *Foreign Affairs*, 72:3 (Summer 1993), pp. 22–8; Esposito, *The Islamic Threat*, pp, 195, 267 n. 25.
204. Esposito, *The Islamic Threat*, p. 195; Huntington, *The Clash of Civilizations*, p. 13.
205. Bernard Lewis, 'The Roots of Muslim Rage', *Atlantic Monthly* (September 1990), pp. 47–60; Esposito, *The Islamic Threat*, pp. 195, 297 n. 25.
206. Esposito, *The Islamic Threat*, p. 195 (my emphasis).
207. Ibid., p. 194; see also pp. 195–8.
208. Ibid., p. 207.
209. Ibid., pp. 3–6.
210. Ibid., pp. 7–24.
211. Ibid., pp. 188–253.
212. Ibid., pp. 25–46.
213. Ibid., pp. 47–76.
214. Ibid., pp. 77–118.
215. Ibid., pp. 119–87.
216. Edinburgh: Edinburgh University Press, 1960, 1966.
217. Edinburgh: Edinburgh University Press, 1966.
218. Cited on the back cover of the Oxford paperback edition of Esposito's *Islamic Threat*, 2nd edn (1995).
219. Esposito, *The Islamic Threat*, p. xix.
220. Ibid., pp. 7–8, 23.
221. Ibid., p. 250.
222. For more on this particular Orientalist paradigm, see Ian Richard Netton, 'Neo-Orientalists on a New Crusade: Hope, Renewal and Salvation', *Al-Masāq: Islam and the Medieval Mediterranean*, 10 (1998), pp. 33–56; see also Mustafa al-Azam, 'Orientalists and the Qur'an', *Muslim World League Journal* (Muharram 1422/April 2001), pp. 13–18.
223. Esposito, *The Islamic Threat*, p. xix (my emphasis).
224. Ibid., p. xvi.
225. Ibid., p. xix.
226. Ibid., p. 5.
227. Ibid.; see also p. 14.

228. Ibid., p. 14.
229. Cantwell Smith, *Islam in Modern History*, p. v.
230. Ibid.
231. Ibid., p. vi.
232. Ibid.
233. For the teaching of that Council on Ecumenism, and Inter-Faith matters, see the *Decree on Ecumenism* (*Unitatis Redintegratio*) of 21 November 1964, reprinted in English in Austin Flannery (ed.), *Vatican Council II: The Conciliar and Post-Conciliar Documents*, 1988 rev. edn (Dublin: Dominican Publications, Leominster: Fowler Wright Books and New Town, NSW, Australia: E. J. Dwyer, 1988), vol. 1, pp. 452–73; and the *Declaration on the Relation of the Church to Non-Christian Religions* (*Nostra Aetate*) of 28 October 1965 in ibid., pp. 738–49, esp., with reference to Islam, Sect. 3, pp. 739–40.
234. Cantwell Smith, *Islam in Modern History*, pp. 3–40.
235. Ibid., p. 39.
236. Ibid., pp. 39–40.
237. See ibid.
238. See Ian Richard Netton, art. 'Umayyads', in idem, *A Popular Dictionary of Islam* (Richmond: Curzon, 1997), p. 253; Bernard Lewis, *The Arabs in History*, Hutchinson University Library (London: Hutchinson, 1968), p. 64; idem, *The Middle East: 2000 Years of History from the Rise of Christianity to the Present Day*, History of Civilisation (London: Weidenfeld & Nicolson, 1995), p. 65. For a succinct appraisal of the Umayyad dynasty, see Clifford Edmund Bosworth, *The New Islamic Dynasties: A Chronological and Genealogical Manual* (Edinburgh: Edinburgh University Press, 1996), pp. 3–5.
239. In his Preface to *Islam in Modern History*, p. v.
240. Ibid., p. 41.
241. Ibid., p. 49.
242. Ibid., p. 48.
243. Ibid., p. 49.
244. See ibid., p. 50 citing al-Afghānī's use of Q.13:11: 'Verily never will God change the condition of a people until they change it themselves' (trans. Abdullah Yusuf Ali, *The Holy Qur'an: Text, Translation and Commentary* (Kuwait: Dhāt al-Salāsil, 1984), p. 606).
245. See Albert Hourani, *Arabic Thought in the Liberal Age 1798–1939* (Cambridge: Cambridge University Press, reissue with new preface, 1983, 1988), esp. pp. 109–10; al-Afghānī and Muḥammad 'Abduh, *Al-'Urwa al-Wuthqā*, 2 vols (Beirut: Maṭba'a al-Tawfīq, 1328/1910); ibid. (Beirut: Dār al-Kātib al-'Arabī, 1970). The latter was originally published in Paris in eighteen weekly issues (13 March to 17 October 1884). It was the official organ of a society called Jam'iyyat al-'Urwa al-Wuthqā.
246. Cantwell Smith, *Islam in Modern History*, p. 69.
247. Ibid., p. 85.
248. Ibid., pp. 88–9.
249. Ibid., pp. 93–160.
250. Ibid., pp. 161–205.
251. Ibid., pp. 206–55.
252. Ibid., pp. 256–91.
253. Ibid., pp. 292–6.
254. Ibid., p. 292.
255. Ibid., pp. 297–308.
256. Ibid., p. 297.
257. Ibid.

258. Gilsenan, *Recognizing Islam*, p. 22, see also pp. 1–11.
259. Ibid., pp. 22–6.
260. Ibid., pp. 27–54.
261. Ibid., pp. 55–74.
262. Ibid., pp. 75–94.
263. Ibid., pp. 95–115.
264. Ibid., pp. 116–41. For concepts of purity, compare the classic work by Mary Douglas, *Purity and Danger: An Analysis of the Concepts of Pollution and Taboo* (London and New York: Routledge, repr. 1996).
265. Gilsenan, *Recognizing Islam*, pp. 142–63, 215–50.
266. Ibid., pp. 164–91, 192–214; see also Jean Holm (ed.), *Sacred Place*, Themes in Religious Studies series (London and New York: Pinter, 1994).
267. Gilsenan, *Recognizing Islam*, pp. 215–50.
268. Ibid., pp. 251–68.
269. Ibid., p. 269.
270. The *Observer* cited on the back cover of the paperback edition of ibid.
271. See Gilsenan, *Recognizing Islam*, pp. 21–2.
272. London: Collins, 1979.
273. Gilsenan, *Recognizing Islam*, p. 22.
274. Raban, *Arabia Through the Looking Glass*, p. 15.
275. Oxford: Blackwell, 2000.
276. Ibid., p. ix.
277. Ibid., p. 2.
278. See, for example, his *Nuer Religion* (Oxford: Clarendon Press, 1956; repr. Oxford: Oxford University Press, 1974).
279. See Bowie, *Anthropology of Religion*, pp. 222–7; see also E. E. Evans-Pritchard, *Witchcraft, Oracles and Magic among the Azande* (Oxford: Clarendon Press, 1937; abridged version, 1976); idem, *Man and Woman among the Azande* (London: Faber, 1974).
280. E. E. Evans-Pritchard, *Theories of Primitive Religion* (Oxford: Oxford University Press, 1972 [originally published 1965]), p. 17, cited in Bowie, *Anthropology of Religion*, pp. 4–5.
281. Bowie, *Anthropology of Religion*, pp. 38–69.
282. Ibid., pp. 70–90.
283. Ibid., pp. 91–117.
284. Ibid., pp. 93–7.
285. Ibid., pp. 118–50.
286. Ibid., pp. 151–89.
287. Ibid., pp. 190–218.
288. Ibid., pp. 219–58.
289. See above, n. 264.
290. Gilsenan, *Recognizing Islam*, pp. 95–115.
291. Bowie, *Anthropology of Religion*, p. 16.
292. Ibid.
293. Ibid., p. 31 n. 16.
294. Ibid.
295. Ibid.
296. Gilsenan, *Recognizing Islam*, p. 16.
297. Ibid., pp. 29, 47–8.
298. Ibid., p. 75.

299. Ibid., pp. 75–94.
300. Ibid., p. 77.
301. Ibid., p. 82.
302. Ibid., p. 91.
303. Ibid., pp. 95–115.
304. Ibid., p. 99.
305. Ibid., p. 115.
306. Back cover, paperback edn, Eickelman, *Moroccan Islam.*
307. Ibid., p. xiii.
308. Ibid., p. 6.
309. Ibid., pp. 11–12; see also p. 161.
310. Ibid., p. 12.
311. Ibid.
312. Ibid., p. 6; see also p. 15–64.
313. Ibid., pp. 65–8.
314. Ibid., pp. 89–154.
315. Ibid., pp. 155–82.
316. Ibid., p. 158.
317. Ibid., pp. 183–237.
318. Ibid., p. 237.
319. Ibid.
320. Geertz, *Islam Observed*, p. ix.
321. Ibid., p. ix.
322. Ibid., pp. x–xi.
323. Ibid., p. xi.
324. Ibid., pp. 4, x.
325. Ibid., p. 4.
326. Ibid.
327. Ibid., p. 9.
328. Ibid., p. 12.
329. Ibid., p. 13.
330. Ibid., p. 15.
331. Ibid., p. 16.
332. Ibid., p. 25.
333. Ibid., pp. 25–54.
334. Ibid., p. 54.
335. Ibid., p. 62.
336. Ibid., p. 104.
337. Robert W. Hefner, *Civil Islam: Muslims and Democratization in Indonesia*, Princeton Studies in Muslim Politics (Princeton, NJ and Oxford: Princeton University Press, 2000), p. 28.
338. Ibid., p. xix. For a map of 'The Seeds of Religious Strife in Indonesia', see the *Times*, 15 October 2002, p. 4.
339. See 'Brilliant – even if he says so himself: Profile: V. S. Naipaul', *Sunday Times*, 14 October 2001, p. 19; Dalya Alberge, 'Reclusive author expresses delight at Nobel Prize', *Times*, 12 October 2001, p. 15.
340. Robert McCrum, 'Inimitable and truly great', *Observer Review*, 14 October 2001, p. 18.
341. Jason Cowley, 'Scornful outsider who made a new homeland in literature', *Times*, 12 October 2001, p. 15.

342. Ibid.
343. *Among the Believers*, pp. 7–80.
344. Ibid., pp. 81–209.
345. Ibid., pp. 211–76.
346. Ibid., pp. 277–361.
347. Ibid., pp. 363–99.
348. Ibid., p. 399.
349. Ibid., pp. 398–9.
350. Ibid., p. 15.
351. Ibid., pp. 16–17.
352. Ibid., p. 16.
353. Ibid., p. 80.
354. Ibid., p. 168.
355. Ibid., pp. 270–1.
356. Ibid., pp. 250–1.
357. Ibid., p. 361.
358. *Beyond Belief*, p. 1.
359. Ibid., p. 2.
360. Ibid., p. 3.
361. Ibid., pp. 5–140. The N-250 was a new aeroplane designed by an aerospace company owned by the Indonesian Minister for Research and Technology (see ibid., pp. 8–9, 22–3).
362. Ibid., pp. 141–259.
363. Ibid., pp. 261–381.
364. Ibid., pp. 383–437.
365. Ibid., p. 140.
366. Ibid., p. 259.
367. Ibid., p. 381.
368. Ibid., p. 414.
369. Ibid., pp. 26–9.
370. See Ibn Baṭṭūṭa, *Riḥlat Ibn Baṭṭūṭa*, (Beirut: Dār Ṣādir/Dār Bayrūt, 1964).
371. Pankaj Mishra, '*Commentary*: A dream of order: Naipaul, India and Islamic fervour', *Times Literary Supplement*, 2 November 2001, p. 18.
372. Ibid.
373. Ibid.
374. Ibid.
375. Compare Netton, *Text and Trauma*, pp. 115–30.
376. See idem, 'Arabia and the Pilgrim Paradigm of Ibn Baṭṭūṭa: A Braudelian Approach', in idem, *Seek Knowledge: Thought and Travel in the House of Islam* (Richmond: Curzon Press, 1996), p. 114. For Braudel, see his three volumes *Civilization matérielle, économie et capitalisme (XVe–XVIIIe siècle)* (Paris: Librairie Armand Colin, 1979) and idem, *La Méditerranée et le monde méditerranéen à l'époque de Philippe II* (Paris: Librairie Armand Colin, 1949; 2nd rev. edn 1966). The latter was trans. by Siân Reynolds, *The Mediterranean and the Mediterranean World in the Age of Philip II*, 2 vols (London: Collins, 1972).
377. Barry Smith and David Woodruff Smith (eds), 'Introduction', in idem (eds), *The Cambridge Companion to Husserl* (Cambridge: Cambridge University Press, 1995), p. 7.
378. Paul Ricoeur, *Husserl: An Analysis of His Phenomenology*, trans. Edward G. Ballard and Lester E. Embree, Northwestern University Studies in Phenomenology of Existential Philosophy (Evanston, IL: Northwestern University Press, 1967), p. 3.

379. George Nakhnikian, 'Introduction', in Edmund Husserl, *The Idea of Phenomenology*, trans. William P. Alston and George Nakhnikian (The Hague: Nijhoff, 1964), p. ix.
380. Ibid., p. x.
381. See his *Logical Investigations* [*Logische Untersuchungen*], trans. J. N. Findlay (New York: Humanities Press, 1970), p. 262, cited in David Bell, *Husserl*, The Arguments of the Philosophers series (London and New York: Routledge, 1990, 1995), p. 86. For the original German, see the Husserliana edition of Husserl's Collected Works, vol. xix/1–2: *Logische Untersuchungen: Zweiter Band: Untersuchungen zur Phänomenologie und Theorie der Erkenntnis*, ed. U. Panzer, 2 vols (The Hague: Nijhoff, 1984).
382. Ricoeur, *Husserl*, p. 202.
383. Ibid.
384. Jaakko Hintikka, 'The Phenomenological Dimension', in Smith and Smith (eds), *The Cambridge Companion to Husserl*, p. 78.
385. Smith and Smith, 'Introduction', in idem (eds), *The Cambridge Companion to Husserl*, pp. 8–9.
386. Ibid., p. 1.
387. Nakhnikian, 'Introduction', in Husserl, *The Idea of Phenomenology*, p. ix.
388. Ibid., p. xiii; see also Husserl's actual text, pp. 34, 38.
389. Ricoeur, *Husserl*, p. 10.
390. Husserl, *The Idea of Phenomenology*, pp. 6, 45.
391. Nakhnikian, 'Introduction', in Husser1, *The Idea of Phenomenology*, p. xvii.
392. Hintikka, 'The Phenomenological Dimension', pp. 79, 101.
393. Nakhnikian, 'Introduction', in Husserl, *The Idea of Phenomenology*, p. xviii; see also Husserl's actual text, pp. 10, 48, 50, 55–6, 59–60.
394. Martin Heidegger, *Being and Time*, trans. Joan Stambaugh (Albany, NY: State University of New York Press, 1996), p. 34. See also Robert Sokolowski, *Introduction to Phenomenology* (Cambridge: Cambridge University Press, 2000), p. 217.
395. Heidegger, *Being and Time*, p. 24.
396. Ibid., p. 27.
397. Ibid., pp. 24, 30.
398. Ibid., p. 31.
399. Ibid., p. 34.
400. Ibid., p. 31.
401. Sokolowski, *Introduction to Phenomenology*, p. 211.
402. Ibid., p. 227.
403. Ibid., p. 209.
404. Ibid., p. 31.
405. Ibid., p. 22.
406. Ibid., pp. 25, 27.
407. Ibid., pp. 27–8.
408. Ibid., p. 48.
409. Ibid., p. 49.
410. Ibid., pp. 177–84.
411. 'Husserl, Heidegger and Modern Existentialism: Dialogue with Hubert Dreyfus', in Bryan Magee, *The Great Philosophers: An Introduction to Western Philosophy* (London: BBC Books, 1987), p. 255.
412. See Maurice Merleau-Ponty, *Phénoménologie de la perception* (Paris: Gallimard, 1945); trans. C. Smith, *The Phenomenology of Perception* (London: Routledge, 1962).
413. See Maya Jaggi, 'Profile: Umberto Eco: Signs of the Times', *The Guardian: Review*, 12

October 2002, pp. 20–3.

414. Umberto Eco, *Il nome della rosa* (Milan: Bompiani, 1980); trans. William Weaver, *The Name of the Rose* (New York: Harcourt Brace Jovanovich, 1983; London: Secker & Warburg, 1983; Pan/Picador, 1984). For an accessible range of essays on *The Name of the Rose*, see Teresa De Lauretis, 'Gaudy Rose: Eco and Narcissism', in Rocco Capozzi (ed.), *Reading Eco: An Anthology*, Advances in Semiotics (Bloomington and Indianapolis: Indiana University Press, 1997), pp. 239–55; David H. Richter, 'The Mirrored World: Form and Ideology in *The Name of the Rose*', in ibid., pp. 256–75; Thomas Sebeok, 'Give Me Another Horse', in ibid., pp. 276–82.
415. Umberto Eco, *Il pendolo di Foucault* (Milan: Bompiani, 1988); trans. William Weaver, *Foucault's Pendulum* (New York: Harcourt Brace Jovanovich, 1989; London: Secker & Warburg, 1989). For essays on *Foucault's Pendulum*, see Peter Bondanella, 'Interpretation, Overinterpretation, Paranoid Interpretation and *Foucault's Pendulum*', in Capozzi (ed.), *Reading Eco*, pp. 285–99; Theresa Coletti, 'Bellydancing: Gender, Silence and the Women of *Foucault's Pendulum*', in ibid., pp. 300–11; Linda Hutcheon, 'Irony-clad Foucault', in ibid., pp. 312–27; Lois Parkinson Zamora, 'The Swing of the Pendulum: Eco's Novels', in ibid., pp. 328–47.
416. Umberto Eco, *L'isola del giorno prima* (Milan: Bompiani, 1994); trans. William Weaver, *The Island of the Day Before* (New York and San Diego: Harcourt Brace Jovanovich, 1995; London: Secker & Warburg, 1995; Minerva/Mandarin, 1996. For essays on *The Island of the Day Before*, see Norma Bouchard, 'Whose "Excess of Wonder" Is It Anyway? Reading Eco's Tangle of Hermetic and Pragmatic Semiosis in *The Island of the Day Before*', in Capozzi (ed.), *Reading Eco*, pp. 350–61; Claudia Miranda, '"*Dove*" is the Dove?', in ibid., pp. 362–86; Rocco Capozzi, 'Intertextuality, Metaphors and Metafiction as Cognitive Strategies in *The Island of the Day Before*', in ibid., pp. 387–403.
417. Umberto Eco, *Baudolino* (Milan: Bompiani, 2000); trans. William Weaver, *Baudolino* (London: Secker & Warburg, 2002).
418. Umberto Eco, *Travels in Hyperreality: Essays*, trans. William Weaver (London: Picador edn, Pan Books in association with Secker & Warburg, 1987; first published in the UK by Secker & Warburg in 1986 under the title *Faith in Fakes*).
419. Umberto Eco, *Serendipities* (London, Phoenix, 1999).
420. Umberto Eco, *Kant and the Platypus: Essays on Language and Cognition*, trans. Alastair McEwen (New York: Harcourt Brace & Company, 2000).
421. Lois Parkinson Zamora, 'The Swing of the "Pendulum": Eco's Novels', in Capozzi (ed.), *Reading Eco*, p. 328.
422. See Terence Hawkes, *Structuralism and Semiotics*, New Accents (London: Methuen, 1977, 1985), p. 124.
423. See Peter Pericles Trifonas, *Umberto Eco and Football*, Postmodern Encounters (Cambridge: Icon Books; USA: Totem Books, 2001).
424. See Umberto Eco, *Semiotics and the Philosophy of Language* (London: Macmillan Press, 1984). See also idem, *Mouse or Rat? Translation as Negotiation* (London: Weidenfeld & Nicolson, 2003).
425. Art. 'Semiotics', in Alan Bullock and Oliver Stallybrass (eds), *The Fontana Dictionary of Modern Thought*, new and rev. edn by Alan Bullock and Stephen Trombley assisted by Bruce Eadie (London: Fontana Press, HarperCollins Publishers, 1988), p. 769.
426. Art. 'Semiology', in ibid., p. 769.
427. Paul Cobley and Litza Jansz, *Introducing Semiotics* (Cambridge: Icon Books, 1999), p. 4.
428. Hawkes, *Structuralism and Semiotics*, p. 125.
429. See his posthumous (1916) *Cours de linguistique générale*, trans. W. Baskin, *Course in*

General Linguistics (Glasgow: Fontana, 1974); also trans. R. Harris, *Course in General Linguistics* (London: Duckworth, 1983). See also Jonathan Culler, *Saussure*, Fontana Modern Masters (London: Fontana, Collins, 1976, 1985).

430. See Charles Hartshorne, Paul Weiss and A. W. Burks (eds), *The Collected Papers of Charles Sanders Peirce*, 8 vols (Cambridge, MA: Harvard University Press, 1931–58).
431. Umberto Eco, *A Theory of Semiotics*, Advances in Semiotics (Bloomington and London: Indiana University Press, 1976).
432. See *La struttura assente* (Milan: Bompiani, 1968) and *Le forme del contenuto* (Milan: Bompiani, 1971).
433. Hawkes, *Structuralism and Semiotics*, pp. 179–80. For a further critique of Eco's *A Theory of Semiotics*, see John Deely, 'Looking Back on *A Theory of Semiotics*: One Small Step for Philosophy, One Giant Leap for the Doctrine of Signs', in Capozzi (ed.), *Reading Eco*, pp. 82–110.
434. Eco, *Theory of Semiotics*, p. 3.
435. Ibid.
436. Ibid., pp. 3–31.
437. Ibid., pp. 32–47.
438. Ibid., pp. 48–150.
439. Ibid., pp. 151–313.
440. Ibid., pp. 314–18.
441. Ibid., p. 317.
442. See Cobley and Jansz, *Introducing Semiotics*, pp. 158–62; Umberto Eco, 'Unlimited Semiosis and Drift: Pragmaticism vs "Pragmatism"', in idem, *The Limits of Interpretation*, Advances in Semiotics (Bloomington and Indianapolis: Indiana University Press, 1990), pp. 22–43.
443. Cobley and Jansz, *Introducing Semiotics*, p. 158.
444. Ibid., p. 162; see also Umberto Eco, *The Role of the Reader: Explorations in the Semiotics of Texts*, Advances in Semiotics (Bloomington and London: Indiana University Press, 1979), esp. pp. 191–8 (in the chapter entitled 'Peirce and the Semiotic Foundations of Openness: Signs as Texts and Texts as Signs'). For more on the concept of 'interpretant', see Michael Riffaterre, 'The Interpretant in Literary Semiotics', in Capozzi (ed.), *Reading Eco*, pp. 173–84.
445. See Umberto Eco, ' An Author and His Interpreters', in Capozzi (ed.), *Reading Eco*, p. 60.
446. Cited on back of paperback edn, *The Name of the Rose*, Picador edn (my italics).
447. Eco, *The Name of the Rose*, trans. Weaver, Picador edn, p. 396.
448. Zamora 'The Swing of the "Pendulum"', p. 329.
449. Ibid., p. 329.
450. Ibid.
451. Ibid., p. 330.
452. Richter, 'The Mirrored World', p. 257.
453. Ibid .
454. Q.17:12; trans. Yusuf Ali, *The Holy Qur'an*, pp. 1,302–3; compare Q.41:53.
455. Mircea Eliade (ed.-in-chief), Charles J. Adams et al. (eds), *The Encyclopedia of Religion*, 16 vols (New York: Macmillan, 1987; London: Collier Macmillan, 1987).
456. See, for example, Joseph M. Kitagawa and Charles H. Long (eds), with the collaboration of Jerald C. Brauer and Marshall G. S. Hodgson, *Myths and Symbols: Studies in Honor of Mircea Eliade* (Chicago and London: University of Chicago Press, 1969), esp. pp. 417–33 ('Bibliography of Mircea Eliade'). Given the date of publication of this

Festschrift, and Eliade's own date of death, this Bibliography is, of course, incomplete. See also John A. Saliba, *'Homo Religiosus' in Mircea Eliade: An Anthropological Evaluation*, Supplementa ad Numen, Altera Series: Dissertationes Ad Historiam Religionum Pertinentes, vol. 5 (Leiden: E. J. Brill, 1976).

457. See Mircea Eliade, *A History of Religious Ideas, 2: From Gautama Buddha to the Triumph of Christianity* (Chicago and London: University of Chicago Press, 1982), p. iv.
458. Thomas J. J. Altizer, *Mircea Eliade and the Dialectic of the Sacred* (Philadelphia: Westminster Press, 1963), p. 16 cited in Mircea Popescu, 'Eliade and Folklore' in Kitagawa and Long (eds), *Myths and Symbols*, p. 81 n. 2.
459. 'Curriculum Vitae' in Kitagawa and Long (eds), *Myths and Symbols*, p. 415.
460. Saliba, 'Homo Religiosus', pp. 102–3.
461. Ibid., p. 2.
462. Ibid., p. 103.
463. Ibid.
464. See Mircea Eliade, *A History of Religious Ideas, 1: From the Stone Age to the Eleusinian Mysteries* (London: Collins, 1979); *2: From Gautama Buddha to the Triumph of Christianity* (Chicago and London: University of Chicago Press, 1982), pp. 3–43 ('The Religions of Ancient China'); *3: From Muhammad to the Age of Reforms* (Chicago and London University of Chicago Press, 1985), pp. 62–84 ('Muhammad and the Unfolding of Islam'), pp. 113–51 ('Muslim Theologies and Mystical Traditions').
465. Saliba, 'Homo Religiosus' p. 103.
466. Ibid.
467. Ibid., p. 104.
468. Ibid., p. 30.
469. Ibid.
470. Ibid., p. 33.
471. Ibid.
472. Ibid., p. 38.
473. Ibid., p. 57.
474. Mircea Eliade, *Patterns in Comparative Religion*, trans. Rosemary Sheed (London and New York: Sheed & Ward, 1958).
475. Eliade, *History of Religious Ideas*, 1, p. xiv; see also p. xiii.
476. Ibid., p. xiii.
477. *Patterns in Comparative Religion*, p. 459.
478. Saliba, 'Homo Religiosus', p. 48.
479. Ibid., p. 176. See also Jean Holm (ed.) with John Bowker, *Sacred Place*, Themes in Religious Studies series (London: Pinter, 1994, 2000) and B. Kedar (ed.), *Sacred Space: Shrine, City, Land* (London: Palgrave; New York: New York University Press, 1998).
480. Eliade, *Patterns in Comparative Religion*, p. 17.
481. Ibid., p. 30.
482. Ibid., p. xi.
483. Mircea Eliade, Čarţile populaire in literatura românească', *Revista Fundaţilor Regale*, 6 (1939), p. 137, cited and trans. in Popescu, 'Eliade and Folklore', in Kitagawa and Long (eds), *Myths and Symbols*, p. 87.
484. Popescu, 'Eliade and Folklore', p. 87.
485. Eliade, *Patterns to Comparative Religion*, pp. 440ff.
486. See Dietrich von Hildebrand, 'In Defence of the Old Liturgy', *Inside the Vatican* (February 2004), pp. 34–7; Cardinal Alfredo Ottaviani and Cardinal Antonio Bacci, 'The Ottaviani Intervention: Rome, September 25, 1969', in ibid., pp. 38–49.

487. For a general orientation on, and introduction to, this apocalyptic event, see Jenny Baxter and Malcolm Downing (eds), *The Day That Shook the World: Understanding September 11th* (London: BBC Worldwide Ltd, 2001) and Simon Reeve, *The New Jackals: Ramzi Yousef, Osama bin Laden and the Future of Terrorism* (London: André Deutsch, 1999); see also Jim Lynch (ed.), *9/11 One Year Later: A Nation Remembers*, Special Commemorative Edition (Boca Raton, FL:American Media Inc., 2002).
488. Joanna Walters and John Arlidge, 'Focus: Fear in the Air: Tailspin', *Observer*, 18 November 2001, p. 21 (my italics).
489. See above, n. 73. See also Q.2:190–3, Q.9:20 and Rudolph Peters, *Jihad in Classical and Modern Islam*, Princeton Series on the Middle East (Princeton: Markus Wiener Publishers, 1996); also Ahmed Rashid, *Jihad: The Rise of Militant Islam in Central Asia*, A World Policy Institute Book (New Haven, CT and London: Yale University Press, 2002).
490. Mircea Eliade, *The Sacred and the Profane: The Nature of Religion*, trans. Willard R. Trask (San Diego, New York and London: Harcourt Brace & Co., 1959, 1987) .
491. Ibid., p. 11.
492. Ibid., p. 10.
493. Ibid., p. 13.
494. Ibid., pp. 12–13.
495. Ibid., p. 13.
496. Ibid., p. 12.
497. Ibid.
498. Ibid.
499. Ibid., p. 17.
500. Ibid., pp. 20–65. For the theme of sacred space, see also Holm and Bowker (eds), *Sacred Place*; Kedar (ed.), *Sacred Space: Shrine, City, Land*; Juan Cole, *Sacred Space and Holy War: The Politics, Culture and History of Shi'ite Islam* (London: I. B. Tauris, 2002); Barbara Daly Metcalf (ed.), *Making Muslim Space in North America and Europe* (Berkeley: University of California Press, 1996); and review of this last in *Journal of Semitic Studies*, 46:1 (Spring 2001), pp. 195–7.
501. Eliade, *The Sacred and the Profane*, pp. 68–113; see also 'Allama Tabataba'i, Jassim M. Hussain and Abdulaziz A. Sachedina, 'Messianism and the Mahdi', in Seyyed Hossein Nasr, Hamid Dabashi and Seyyid Vali Reza Nasr (eds), *Expectation of the Millennium: Shi'ism in History* (Albany, NY: State University of New York Press, 1989), esp. pp. 42–3, which deal with the 'sacred time' of the rule of the Mahdī and the *raj'a*.
502. Eliade, *The Sacred and the Profane*, pp. 116–59.
503. Ibid., pp. 162–213.
504. See also Evan Thomas, 'Cracking the Terror Code', *Newsweek*, 138:16 (15 October 2001), p. 55.
505. For the significance and context of this day, see John B .Teeple, *Timelines of World History* (London: Dorling Kindersley, 2002), pp. 286–7.
506. *History of Religious Ideas*, 3, pp. 62–84, 113–51.
507. A. J. Arberry (trans.), *The Koran Interpreted*, 2 vols (London: Allen & Unwin; New York: Macmillan, 1955).
508. W. Montgomery Watt, *Muhammad at Mecca* (Oxford: Oxford University Press, 1953).
509. Tor Andrae, *Mohammed: The Man and His Faith* (London: George Allen & Unwin, 1936).
510. Eliade, *History of Religious Ideas*, 3 [hereafter referred to as Eliade, *Religious Ideas* 3], p. 62.

511. J. B. Sykes (ed.), *The Concise Oxford Dictionary of Current English*, 6th edn (Oxford: Clarendon Press, 1976), p. 778 s.v. 'otiose'.
512. D. P. Simpson, *Cassell's New Latin–English, English–Latin Dictionary*, 3rd edn (London: Cassell, 1964), p. 418 s.v. *otiosus* (my emphasis).
513. Eliade, *Religious Ideas* 3, p. 64.
514. Ibid., p. 62.
515. Ibid., p. 63.
516. Ibid., pp. 64, 68. See Netton, *Text and Trauma*, esp. pp. 84–7.
517. Eliade, *Religious Ideas* 3, p. 64.
518. Ibid., pp. 64–5.
519. Ibid., p. 65.
520. Ibid., p. 66.
521. Ibid.
522. Ibid., pp. 67–8.
523. Ibid., pp. 67–88.
524. Ibid., pp. 70–1 (my emphasis).
525. Ibid., p. 70.
526. Ibid., p. 77.
527. Ibid., p. 78.
528. Ibid., p. xii.
529. Ibid., pp. 113–51.
530. Ibid., p. 125.
531. Ibid., p. 125.
532. Ibid., p. 150.
533. *Guardian*, Wednesday 12 September 2001, p. 1; see also *Yorkshire Evening Post*, Wednesday 12 September 2001, p. 1 and *Sunday Times: Special 24-Page Supplement: America at War*, Sunday 16 September 2001, p. 1.
534. *Guardian*, Wednesday 12 September 2001, p. 4.
535. Ibid., pp. 6–7. For *later* headlines and reactions, see *inter alia Guardian*, Thursday 13 September 2001, p. 1 ('US rallies the West for attack on Afghanistan'); *Al-Ḥayāt*, Thursday 13 September 2001, p. 1 ('*Al-taḥqīq yataqaddam bi-sur'a wa taḥāluf duwalī yasta'idd li-ḥarb 'alā al-irhāb*'); *Yorkshire Post*, Thursday 13 September 2001, p. 1 ('Wasteland USA'); *Independent*, Thursday 13 September 2001, p. 1 ('The American dream in ruins'); *Times*, Thursday 13 September 2001, p. 1 ('Good will prevail over evil'). See also Robert Lowry, 'Apocalypse Now', *Trends: The International Magazine on Arab Affairs*, 47 (November 2001), pp. 28–30.
536. *Yorkshire Post*, Wednesday 12 September 2001, p. 1.
537. *Yorkshire Post*, Section B, Wednesday 12 September 2001, p. 1.
538. *Al-Quds al-'Arabī*, Wednesday 12 September 2001, p. 1. *The Guardian*: G2 of Thursday 13 September 2001 provided a two-page spread illustrating the headlines of thirty-seven newspapers around the world (see pp. 12–13).
539. See Richard Woods, 'When death came out of a blue sky', *Sunday Times: Special 24-Page Supplement: America at War*, Sunday 16 September 2001, p. 7 citing Nostradamus, Century Six, Quatrain 97. For the original source of this quatrain, see Nostradamus in the edn of Peter Lemesurier, *Nostradamus: The Illustrated Prophecies* (Alresford, Hants: John Hunt Publishing Ltd, 2003), pp. 246–7, which, however, does not link this question with 9/11 in the commentary.
540. Severin Carrell and Andrew Gumbel, 'Murders of Asian men in US heighten fears of revenge attacks', *Independent*, Monday 17 September 2001, p. 8.

541. See, for example, Ian Herbert, 'In the mosques of Bradford, the anger is directed towards America', *Independent*, Thursday 13 September 2001, p. 13; Matthew Beard, 'Hijackers should be made martyrs, says London cleric', in ibid.; Gary Younge, 'How could they cheer?', *Guardian*: G2, Thursday 13 September 2001, pp. 6–7. The contemporary literature desperately tried to understand this new phenomenon. See, *inter alia*, Fareed Zakaria, 'The Roots of Rage', *Newsweek*, 138:16 (15 October 2001), pp. 24–45 (The cover of this edition of *Newsweek* bore the caption: 'Why They Hate America'); Gareth Smyth, 'Earthly Wisdom', *Trends: The International Magazine on Arab Affairs*, 46 (October 2001), pp. 18–19; John Bulloch, 'The Roots of Terror', in ibid., pp. 22– 3; Fred Halliday, *Two Hours that Shook the World: September 11, 2001: Causes and Consequences* (London: Saqi Books, 2001).
542. See A. J. Wensinck and B. Lewis, art. 'Ḥadjdj', *EI*², vol. 3, pp. 31–8; I. R. Netton, art. 'Riḥla', *EI*², vol. 8, p. 528.
543. See Ben Macintyre, 'Slaughterhouse of the religions', *Times* 2, 3 December 2001, pp. 2–4.
544. Ibid., p. 2.
545. William Blake, 'Milton', in Peter Butter (ed.), *William Blake*, Everyman's Poetry 3 (London, J. M. Dent, 1996), p. 85, lines 13–16.
546. Ibid., line 8.
547. The first editions of many of Jubrān's English works had their publication in New York. See C. Nijland, art. 'Jubrān, Jubrān Khalīl', in Julie Scott Meisami and Paul Starkey (eds), *Encyclopedia of Arabic Literature*, 2 vols (London and New York: Routledge, 1998), vol. 1, pp. 415–16. For a full life, see K. S. Hawi, *Khalil Gibran: His Background, Character and Works* (Beirut: Arab Institute for Research and Publishing, 1972).
548. See Giles Foden, 'Bin Laden: the former CIA "client" obsessed with training pilots', *Guardian*, Thursday 13 September 2001, p. 9; Philip Smucker, 'Militant is revered by dispossessed Arabs', *Daily Telegraph*, Thursday 13 September 2001, p. 8; Christopher Dickey and Daniel McGinn, 'Meet the bin Ladens', *Newsweek*, 138:16 (15 October 2001), pp. 63–4; Peter Bergen, 'How Bin Laden controls his international web of terror', *Sunday Times: Special 24-Page Supplement: America at War*, Sunday 16 September 2001, p. 20.
549. Macintyre, 'Slaughterhouse of the religions', p. 3.
550. Ibid. (my emphasis).
551. Clive Holes, 'A word in your ear, Tony, learn a little Arabic', *Times*, 23 October 2001, p. 16.
552. Ibid.; see also Netton, 'Neo-Orientalists on a New Crusade', esp. p. 33.
553. Adel Darwish, 'Same old jibes and polemics', *Times* 2, 21 September 2001, p. 24; see also Michael Binyon, 'Careless word stirs hatred in Muslims', *Times*, 21 September 2001, p. 4.
554. Jonathan Phillips, 'Why a crusade will lead to a jihad', *Independent*, *The Tuesday Review*, 18 September 2001, p. 5.
555 J. J. G. Jansen, art. 'Uṣūliyya 2. In Modern Islamic theologico-political parlance', *EI*², vol. 10, p. 938.
556. Idem, *The Dual Nature of Islamic Fundamentalism* (London and Ithaca, New York: C. Hurst & Co., 1997), p. xvi, cited in ibid.
557. K. N. Pandita, 'Intricate Roots of Theo-Fascist Ideology', *Asian Affairs*, 36 (October 1999), p. 9.
558. Scott Thomas, 'Can the West and Islam live together?', *The Tablet* (6 October 2001), p. 1,397.
559. Ibid.

560. Robert Irwin, 'Is this the man who inspired Bin Laden?', *Guardian: Thursday*: G2, l November 2001, pp. 8–9. See Adnan Musallam, *Sayyid Qutb: The Emergence of the Islamicist 1939–1950* (Jerusalem: Palestinian Academic Society for the Study of International Affairs, 1990).
561. Irwin, 'Is this the man ...?" p. 8.
562. Ibid., p. 8.
563. Sayyid Quṭb, *Fi Ẓilāl al-Qur'ān*, 20 vols in 10, 1st and 2nd edns (Cairo: Dār Iḥyā' al-Kutub al-'Arabiyya, 1952–9); 20 vols in 8, rev. edn (Beirut: Dār al-Ma'rifa/Dār Iḥyā' al-Turāth al-'Arabī, 1971); 6 vols, rev. edn (Beirut: Dār al-Shurūq, 1973–4).
564. Irwin, 'Is this the man ...?', p. 9.
565. See Ben Macintyre, 'Rituals reflect a battle to the death', *Times*, 28 September 2001, p. 13.
566. See Bowie, *Anthropology of Religion*, p. 73.
567. See Leviticus 15:19; trans. Henry Wansbrough (gen. ed.), *The New Jerusalem Bible* (London: Darton, Longman & Todd, 1985), p. 154.
568. See Levicus 15:24.
569. *New Jerusalem Bible*, p. 153 n.15a (my emphasis).
570. Q.2:222, trans. Yusuf Ali, *The Holy Qur'an*, pp. 87–8. See also Marwān Ibrāhīm al-Kaysī, *Morals and Manners in Islam: A Guide to Islamic Ādāb* (Leicester: The Islamic Foundation, 1994), pp . 62, 122, 123.
571. Douglas, *Purity and Danger*, pp. 2–3.
572. Ibid., p. 7.
573. W. Lloyd Warner, A *Black Civilization* (New York: Harper & Brothers, 1937), p. 394 cited in Bowie, *Anthropology of Religion*, p. 97.
574. Adam Robinson, *Bin Laden: Behind the Mask of the Terrorist* (Edinburgh and London: Mainstream, 2001), p. 233.
575. See above, nn. 73, 489.
576. Michael Gove, 'How moralists justify fighting the good fight', *Times*, 26 September 2001, p. 7.
577. See St Thomas Aquinas, *Summa Theologiae*, 2a, 2ae, q40 arts 1–3, cited in Ronald Preston, 'Christian Ethics', in Peter Singer (ed.), A *Companion to Ethics*, Blackwell Companions to Philosophy no. 2 (Oxford: Blackwell, 2005), p. 98.
578. Gove, 'How moralists justify fighting the good fight', p. 7.
579. Michael Quinlan, 'The Just War litmus test', *The Tablet*, 13 October 2001, p. 1,451.
580. Ibid.
581. Robert Fisk, 'Hypocrisy, hatred and the war on terror', *Independent: The Thursday Review*, 8 November 2001, p. 5.
582. Michael Steinberger, 'So, are civilisations at war?', *Observer*, 21 October 2001, p. 28. See also an extension by Samuel P. Huntington of his original thesis to the domain of Mexican immigration. Huntington claims that the USA is being transformed into a two-peoples, two-cultures (Hispanic and Anglo), two-languages (Spanish and English) nation. See Samuel P. Huntington, *Who Are We? America's Crisis of National Identity* (London: Free, 2004). For further discussion of the issues see James Bone, 'Hispanic invasion will split US, says Harvard academic', *Times*, 22 March 2004, p. 33.
583. Steinberger, 'So, are civilisations at war?', p. 28.
584. Ibid.
585. Ibid.
586. Thomas Meyer, 'A fundamental fallacy:', *Times Higher*, 9 November 2001, p. 15. See also Fred Halliday, *Islam and the Myth of Confrontation* (London and New York, I. B. Tauris, 1994).

587. Meyer, 'A fundamental fallacy', p. 15.
588. Ibid.
589. Sheikh Hamdan bin Zayed, 'Don't throw away your chance in the Middle East, Mr Blair. There won't be many more', *Times*, 2 June 2003.
590. Edward W. Said, *Orientalism* (London: Penguin Books, 1995; first published by Routledge & Kegan Paul, 1978).
591. See Netton, 'Neo-Orientalists on a New Crusade', pp. 33–56, esp. pp. 39–41 for a critique of Said's *Orientalism*.
592. James Bone, 'Still fighting for our survival', *Times: T2*, 12 March 2002, p. 6.

Chapter 2: Orthodoxy and Heterodoxy

1. H. A. R. Gibb, *Mohammedanism: An Historical Survey*, 2nd edn, The Home University Library of Modern Knowledge 197, (London, New York and Toronto: Oxford University Press, 1953, 1964), p. 13 (my emphases).
2. Ibid., pp. 107–26.
3. Ibid., p. 107.
4. Ibid., p. 108.
5. Ibid.
6. Ibid., p. 110.
7. Ibid., pp. 118–19.
8. Ibid., pp. 124.
9. Gilsenan, *Recognizing Islam*, p. 31. See also pp. 30–3.
10. Ibid., p. 33.
11. Timothy Ware, *The Orthodox Church*, new edn (London: Penguin Books. 1993), p. 8.
12. Ibid.
13. Ibid., p. 2.
14. J. B. Sykes (ed.), *The Concise Oxford Dictionary of Current English*, 6th edn (Oxford: Clarendon Press, 1979), p. 776 s.v. 'orthodox'.
15. Ibid., p. 505 s.v. 'heterodox'.
16. N. S. Doniach (ed.) *The Concise Oxford English–Arabic Dictionary of Current Usage* (Oxford: Oxford University Press, 1982), p. 266 s.v. 'orthodoxy'.
17. Ibid., s.v. 'orthodoxy'.
18. See Hans Wehr, *A Dictionary of Modern Written Arabic*, 2nd printing (Wiesbaden: Otto Harrassowitz; London: George Allen & Unwin, 1966), p. 433 s.v. 'sunna', p. 503 s.v. 'ṣaḥīḥ'. See also N. J. Coulson, *A History of Islamic Law*, Islamic Surveys 2 (Edinburgh: Edinburgh University Press, 1964), esp. p. 39 for 'sunna'.
19. A. Popovic and G. Veinstein (eds), *Les orders mystiques dans l'Islam: cheminements et situation actuelle*, Recherches d'histoire et de sciences sociales 13 (Paris: Éditions de l'École des Hautes Études en Sciences Sociales, 1985), p. 7 (my emphasis).
20. Marc Gaborieau, 'Les orders mystiques dans le sous-continent indien', in Popovic and Veinstein (eds), *Les orders mystiques*, p. 105.
21. Baldick, 'Among the friends of God'. p. 1,073.
22. Ibid.; see also Gilles Veinstein, 'Un essai de sythèse', in Popovic and Veinstein (eds), *Les orders mystiques*, pp. 293–309.
23. See Romans 13:1–2, cited in *Catechism of the Catholic Church* (London: Geoffrey Chapman, 1994), pp. 416–17 # 1899; see also ibid., p. 482 # 2234 ff.; Q.4:59.
24. Hans Urs Von Balthasar, *The Glory of the Lord: A Theological Aesthetics, volume VI: Theology: The Old Covenant*, trans. Brian McNeil and Erasmo Leiva-Merikakis, ed. John

Riches (Edinburgh: T. & T. Clark, 1991), p. 218. For Hans Urs Von Balthasar as a theologian, see John O'Donnnell, *Hans Urs Von Balthasar*, Outstanding Christian Thinkers (London: Geoffrey Chapman, 1992); see also Aidan Nichols, *The World Has Been Abroad: A Guide Through Balthasar's Aesthetics* (Edinburgh: T. & T. Clark, 1998) and idem, *No Bloodless Myth: A Guide through Balthasar's Dramatics* (Edinburgh: T. & T. Clark, 2000).

25. Von Balthasar, *The Glory of the Lord*, vol vi, p. 217.
26. Ibid.
27. Ibid.
28. Bernard Sesboüé, art. 'Authority', in Nicholas Lossky et al. (eds), *Dictionary of the Ecumenical Movement* (Geneva: WCC Publications; London: Council of Churches for Britain and Ireland, 1991), p. 69.
29. Ibid.
30. See, for example, Muḥammad Abū Zahra, *Uṣūl al-Fiqh* (Cairo: Dār al-Fikr al-'Arabī, 1377/1958), pp. 207, 215; and al-Ghazālī, *al-Mustaṣfā min 'Ilm al-Uṣūl* (Cairo: al-Maktaba al-Tijāriyya, 1356/1937), vol. 1, pp. 139–40. I am indebted to Mohammad Hashim Kamali, *Principles of Islamic Jurisprudence*, rev. edn (Cambridge: Islamic Texts Society, 1991), pp. 248, 265 n. 9 and 267, 281 n. 2 for the last two references.
31. Sesboüé, art. 'Authority', p. 70.
32. See Ikhwān al–Ṣafā', *Rasā'il Ikhwān al-Ṣafā'* (Beirut: Dār Ṣādir/Dār Bayrūt, 1957), vol. 4, p. 17; see also Yāqūt al-Rūmī, *Mu'jam al-Buldan* (Beirut: Dār Ṣādir, 1977), vol. 3, pp. 414–15 s.v. 'Ṣiffīn'.
33. See Michel Foucault, *The Order of Things: An Archaeology of the Human Sciences* (London: Tavistock Publications, 1970).
34. Peter Heather, 'The Pope, the Emperor and the Legacy of Ancient Rome', *Folio* (Summer 2003), p. 7.
35. See Alexis Kniazeff, art. 'Schism' in Lossky et al. (eds), *Dictionary of the Ecumenical Movement*, p. 901; and Alasdair Heron, art. 'Filioque' in ibid., pp. 423–4. See also Timothy Ware [Bishop Kallistos of Diokleia], *The Orthodox Church*, pp. 43–72 esp. p. 44.
36. See Ware, *The Orthodox Church*, p. 60. See also Rosemary Morris, 'Northern Europe invades the Mediterranean 900–1200', in George Holmes (ed.), *The Oxford Illustrated History of Medieval Europe* (Oxford and New York: Oxford University Press, 1988, 1996), p. 234 for an initial summary orientation on the Fourth Crusade. For a recent and more extended account, see Jonathan Phillips, *The Fourth Crusade and the Sack of Constantinople* (London: Jonathan Cape, 2004). See also n. 45 below.
37. See Ludwig Ott, *Fundamentals of Catholic Dogma*, ed. James Canon Bastible (Rockford, IL: Tan Books, 1974), pp. 63–4.
38. Heather, 'The Pope, the Emperor and the Legacy of Ancient Rome', pp. 7–8.
39. There is a massive literature on the subject of the Reformation. See, first and foremost, Diarmaid MacCulloch, *Reformation: Europe's House Divided 1490–1700* (London: Penguin Books, Allen Lane, 2003). Thereafter see the equally magisterial volume by Eamon Duffy, *The Stripping of the Altars: Traditional Religion in England c.1400–c.1580* (New Haven, CT and London: Yale University Press, 1992). See also G. R. Elton, *Reformation Europe 1517–1559*, The Fontana History of Europe (London and Glasgow: Collins, 1964); idem, *England Under the Tudors* (London: The Folio Society, 1997).
40. See Ware, *The Orthodox Church*, pp. 58–9.
41. Jonathan Phillips, 'The Latin East 1098–1291', in Jonathan Riley-Smith (ed.), *The Oxford Illustrated History of the Crusades* (Oxford and New York: Oxford University Press, 1995). p. 131.
42. Steven Runciman, *A History of the Crusades Volume 3: The Kingdom of Acre and the Later*

Crusades (London: The Folio Society, 1994; 1st publ. Cambridge University Press, 1954), pp. 91–111.

43. Ibid., p. 104.
44. Ibid., p. 109.
45. Ibid., pp. 110–11 (my emphases). A fundamental primary source for the Fourth Crusade is Geoffroi de Villehardouin, *La Conquête de Constantinople*, ed. and trans. E. Faral, Les Classiques de l'histoire de France au Moyen Age 18–19, 2 vols (Paris: Société d'Édition 'Les Belles Lettres', 1938–39); ibid., trans. M. R. B. Shaw, 'The Conquest of Constantinople', in M. R. B. Shaw (trans.), *Chronicles of the Crusades* (London: Penguin Books, 1963), pp. 29–160. (Geoffrey died in AD 1212/13.) Among the huge quantity of new research on the subject of the Fourth Crusade, to which we refer in our text, are the following important works: Edgar H. McNeal and Robert Lee Wolff, 'The Fourth Crusade', in Kenneth M. Setton (gen. ed.), *A History of the Crusades, volume 2: The Later Crusades, 1189–1311*, ed. Robert Lee Wolff and Harry W. Hazard (Madison, Milwaukee and London: University of Wisconsin Press, 1969), pp. 153–85; M. Angold, *The Fourth Crusade: Event and Context* (London: Longman, 2004); D. E. Queller and T. F. Madden, *The Fourth Crusade: The Conquest of Constantinople* (Philadelphia: University of Pennsylvania Press, 1997); A. J. Andrea, *Contemporary Sources for the Fourth Crusade* (Leiden: E. J. Brill, 2000). See, finally, Carole Hillenbrand, *The Crusades: Islamic Perspectives* (Edinburgh: Edinburgh University Press, 1999) for a magnificent and highly authoritative account of the whole crusading era which draws powerfully on the Islamic sources.
46. Sesboüé, 'Authority', p. 71.
47. Ibid.
48. Ibid.
49. Ibid.
50. *Catechism of the Catholic Church*, p. 206 # 890.
51. *Lumen Gentium* # 25 in Austin Flannery (ed.), *Vatican Council II: The Conciliar and Post Conciliar Documents*, rev. edn (Dublin: Dominican Publications; Leominster: Fowler Wright Books; New Town, NSW, Australia: E. J. Dwyer, 1988), p. 380.
52. See Sesboüé, 'Authority', p. 72; see also *Catechism of the Catholic Church*, pp. 25–7 # 80–93; Ott, *Fundamentals*, pp. 4ff.
53. J. N. D. Kelly, *Early Christian Doctrines*, 5th rev. edn (London: Adam & Charles Black, 1977), p. 417.
54. Norman Davies, *Europe: A History* (London: Pimlico, 1997), p. 232; J. N. D. Kelly, *The Oxford Dictionary of Popes* (Oxford: Oxford University Press, 1988, 1996), pp. 43–5. Finally, for a musicological gloss, see Ian Wood, 'History and Legend in Verdi's Attila', in Royal Opera House, [Programme for] *Attila 2001/2* (London: Royal Opera House Covent Garden, 2002), p. 21.
55. Kelly, *Early Christian Doctrines*, p. 417.
56. Frederic W. Farrar, *The Early Days of Christianity* (London, Paris and Melbourne: Cassell & Co., 1897), pp. 593–4 (Appendix: Excursus 1: 'The Asserted Primacy of St Peter').
57. Q.1:6.
58. W. Montgomery Watt, *Islamic Philosophy and Theology: An Extended Survey*, 2nd edn (Edinburgh: Edinburgh University Press, 1985), p. 4.
59. Trans. R. Knox, *The Holy Bible* (London: Burns & Oates/Macmillan, 1960). For one of innumerable books on the papacy, see Eamon Duffy, *Saints and Sinners: A History of the Popes* (London: Goodliffe Neale, 1999). For the Petrine succession, see, *inter alia*, Hans Urs Von Balthasar, *The Office of Peter and the Structure of the Church* (San Francisco: Ignatius Press, 1986); Scott Butler, Norman Dahlgren and David Hess, *Jesus, Peter and*

the Keys: A Scriptural Handbook on the Papacy (Goleta, CA: Queenship Publishing, 1996); Stephen K. Ray, *Upon this Rock: St Peter and the Primacy of Rome in Scripture and the Early Church*, Modern Apologetics Library (San Francisco: Ignatius Press, 1999); see also Russell Shaw, *Papal Primacy in the Third Millennium* (Huntington, IN: Our Sunday Visitor Publishing Division, 2000).

60. See Francis A. Sullivan, *Salvation Outside the Church? Tracing the History of the Catholic Response* (London: Geoffrey Chapman, 1992), p. 6, 18–20ff.; Peter M. J. Stravinskas, *Salvation Outside the Church?* (Huntington, IN: Our Sunday Visitor Publishing Division, 2002), esp. pp. 11–29.
61. 'Extra ecclesiam, nulla salus', *Christian Order*, 42:10 (October 2001), pp. 501–2; Sullivan, *Salvation Outside the Church?*, pp. 5–6.
62. Sullivan, *Salvation Outside the Church?*, esp. pp. 123ff.; see also Anglican–Roman Catholic International Commission [ARCIC II] *Salvation and the Church: An Agreed Statement*, with Commentary and Study Guide by M. Cecily Boulding and Timothy Bradshaw (London: Church House Publishing/Catholic Truth Society, 1987–9); Mikka Ruokanen, *The Catholic Doctrine of Non-Christian Religions According to the Second Vatican Council*, Studies in Christian Mission, vol. 7, (Leiden, New York and Cologne: E. J. Brill, 1992), esp. pp. 92–103.
63. Among numerous works of interest on the Avignon Papacy, see firstly, by way of orientation, Geoffrey Barraclough, *The Medieval Papacy*, Library of European Civilisation (London: Thames & Hudson, 1968, repr. 1992), esp. pp. 142–64. See, then, S. Menache, *Clement V*, Cambridge Studies in Medieval Life and Thought: Fourth Series 36 (Cambridge: Cambridge University Press, 2002); D. Wood: *Clement VI: The Pontificate and Ideas of an Avignon Pope*, Cambridge Studies in Medieval Life and Thought: Fourth Series 13 (Cambridge: Cambridge University Press, 2002). Clement V, the first Avignon Pope, reg. 1305–14; Clement VI reg. 1342–52.
64. See John Cornwall, *Hitler's Pope: The Secret History of Pius XII* (London: Viking, 1999). For a 'detailed rebuttal' of this volume, see Peter Gumpel, 'Cornwall's Pope', *Christian Order*, 42:2 (February 2001), pp. 73–86; see also Pierre Blet, *Pius XII and the Second World War According to the Archives of the Vatican* (Herefordshire: Gracewing, 1999); Ralph McInerny, *The Defamation of Pius XII* (South Bend, IN: St Augustine's Press, 2001); Ronald J. Rychlak, 'Pius XII and the Holocaust' [Letters to the Editor], *Times Literary Supplement*, 15 March 2002.
65. See *Catechism of the Catholic Church*, p. 353 # 1577; Rupert Shortt, 'Counting the world as dust' [Review of John Cornwall's *Breaking Faith: The Pope, the People and the Future of Catholicism* (London: Viking, 2001)], *Times Literary Supplement*, 29 March 2002, p. 3.
66. See Joseph Cardinal Ratzinger and Tarcisio Bertone (Congregation for the Doctrine of the Faith), *Declaration: 'Dominus Jesus': On the Unicity and Salvific Universality of Jesus Christ and the Church* (London: Catholic Truth Society, 2000); Shortt, 'Counting the world as dust', p. 3; see also [Interview with] Joseph Ratzinger in *L'Osservatore Romano*, 8 October 2000 [= excerpts from an earlier interview with the *Frankfurter Allegmeine*]; William Clements, 'The Declaration "Dominus Jesus"', *Together in Christ* [Diocesan Bulletin for Christian Unity, Archdiocese of Southwark: Christian Unity Commission], 20:62 (February 2002), pp. 11–13.
67. Ratzinger and Bertone, *Dominus Jesus*, p. 28 # 22; see also ibid., p. 22 # 17; Shortt, 'Counting the world as dust', p. 3.
68. See John Cornwall, 'Winter of the patriarch', *Sunday Times: News Review*, 23 December 2001, p. 2.
69. Ibid. See also idem, *Breaking Faith*.

70. Idem, 'Winter of the patriarch', p. 2. See Martin E. Marty and R. Scott Appleby (eds), *Fundamentalisms Observed*, The Fundamentalism Project vol. 1 (Chicago and London: University of Chicago Press, 1991, 1994), esp. chapters 1–5.
71. Sesboüé, 'Authority', p. 73.
72. Ibid.
73. (My emphases), ARCIC, 'Authority in the Church II (Windsor 1981)', in idem, *The Final Report* (London: CTS/SPCK, 1982), p. 88. See also ARCIC, *The Gift of Authority: Authority in the Church III* (An Agreed Statement by the Anglican–Roman Catholic International Commission [ARCIC]), (London: CTS; Toronto: Anglican Book Centre; New York: Church Publishing Inc., 1999), esp. pp. 42–3.
74. Maurice Wiles, *Archetypal Heresy: Arianism through the Centuries* (Oxford: Clarendon Press, 1996), p. 4.
75. E. P. Sanders, *The Historical Figure of Jesus* (London: Penguin Books, Allen Lane, 1993), p. xiii.
76. Rowan Williams, *Arius: Heresy and Tradition* (London: Darton, Longman & Todd, 1987), pp. 29–30.
77. Ibid., p. 31.
78. See ibid., pp. 32–41.
79. Ibid., p. 40.
80. Ibid., pp. 41, 45.
81. Ibid., pp. 48–9.
82. Ibid., pp. 67–70.
83. Ibid., pp. 70–1.
84. Ibid., pp. 74–81.
85. Ibid., p. 82.
86. Wiles, *Archetypal Heresy*, p. 7.
87. Ibid.
88. Kelly, *Early Christian Doctrines*, pp. 227ff.; see Williams, *Arius*, pp. 96–7.
89. Athanasius, *De Sententia Dionysii*: 2, in H. G. Opitz (ed.) *Athanasius Werke* (Berlin and Leipzig: W. De Gruyter, 1934), ii.1; English trans. cited in Wiles, *Archetypal Heresy*, p. 8 n. 19; see also ibid., pp. 10–26.
90. Williams, *Arius*, p. 109. For the credal documents of Arius and Arianism, see ibid., pp. 246–56.
91. Kate Cooper, 'From Bethlehem to Byzantium', *Times Literary Supplement*, 29 March 2002, p. 9 [a review of Henry Chadwick's *The Church in Ancient Society: From Galilee to Gregory the Great* (Oxford: Oxford University Press: 2001)]. See also R. A. Markus, 'The persecuted sect that captured the Roman Empire', *The Tablet*, 9 March 2002, pp. 14–15.
92. Kelly, *Early Christian Doctrines*, p. 45.
93. Ibid., p. 47.
94. See Ibid., p. 231; see also Wiles, *Archetypal Heresy*, p. 1.
95. See Kelly, *Early Christian Doctrines*, p. 231.
96. See Williams, *Arius*, pp. 67–8.
97. Wiles, *Archetypal Heresy*, p. 6.
98 Williams, *Arius*, p. 2.
99. Kelly, *Early Christian Doctrines*, p. 45.
100. See ibid., pp. 231–7.
101. See Wiles, *Archetypal Heresy*, p. 6.
102. Ibid., p. 1.

103. Ibid., p. 3. See also p. 2. For a translation of the Greek into English, see Kelly, *Early Christian Doctrines*, p. 232; see also *Catechism of the Catholic Church*, pp. 46–8.
104. Williams, *Arius*, p. 1.
105. Kelly, *Early Christian Doctrines*, p. 231.
106. Ibid.
107. See ibid., pp. 233, 237.
108. See ibid., pp. 237–238.
109. See ibid., pp. 238, 251; see also Wiles, *Archetypal Heresy*, pp. 32–8.
110. B. J. Kidd, *A History of the Church to* AD 461, 3 vols (Oxford: Clarendon Press, 1922), vol. 2, p. 242 cited in Wiles, *Archetypal Heresy*, p. 32 n. 17.
111. See David Whitton, 'The Society of Northern Europe in the High Middle Ages', in Holmes (ed.), *Oxford Illustrated History of Medieval Europe*, pp. 141, 156; see also K. F. Morrison, 'Canossa. A Revision', *Traditio*, 18 (1962), pp. 121–48; I. S. Robinson, 'Pope Gregory VII, the princes and the *pactum*', *English Historical Review*, 94 (1979), pp. 721–56.
112. See Frank Barlow, *Thomas Becket* (London: Folio Society, 2002; 1st publ. London: Weidenfeld & Nicolson, 1986), esp. pp. 109ff.
113. Daniel H. Williams, 'Ambrose, Emperors and Homoians in Milan: The First Conflict over a Basilica', in Michael R. Barnes and Daniel H. Williams (eds), *Arianism after Arius: Essays on the Development of the Fourth-Century Trinitarian Conflicts* (Edinburgh: T. & T. Clark, 1993), p. 127.
114. See ibid., pp. 127–46.
115. Williams, *Arius*, p. 234.
116. Ibid.; Wiles, *Archetypal Heresy*, pp. 4–5.
117. Wiles, *Archetypal Heresy*, pp. 4–5.
118. Williams, *Arius*, p. 156.
119. Ibid., p. 230.
120. Ibid., p. 175.
121. Ibid., pp. 232–3.
122. Ibid., p. 231.
123. Ibid., p. 1.
124. Barnes and Williams (eds), *Arianism after Arius*, p. xiii ('Introduction').
125. See Epiphanius, *Panarion haer*. 69.1.1–2.1, trans. in P. R. Amidon, *The Panarion of St Epiphanius, Bishop of Salamis: Selected Passages* (Oxford: Oxford University Press, 1990), p. 261, cited in Barnes and Williams (eds), *Arianism after Arius*, p. xiii n. 1.
126. Wiles, *Archetypal Heresy*, p. 5.
127. Robert C. Gregg, 'Foreward' in idem (ed.), *Arianism: Historical and Theological Reassessments: Papers from the Ninth International Conference on Patristic Studies* (September 5–10, 1983, Oxford, England), Patristic Monograph Series, no. 11 (Cambridge, MA: Philadelphia Patristic Foundation, 1985), p. iii.
128. See Wiles, *Archetypal Heresy*, pp. 4–7.
129. Williams, *Arius*, p. 233.
130. The best source for the life of St Augustine is his own *Confessions*: the original Latin text will be found in the bilingual Loeb edition: William Watts (trans.), *Augustine: Confessions*, Loeb Classical Library, 2 vols (Cambridge, MA and London: Harvard University Press, 1999, 2000). For a good English translation, see Henry Chadwick (trans.), *Saint Augustine: Confessions* (Oxford: Oxford University Press, 1991), For an excellent, and very lucid, introduction to the life and works of Augustine, see Henry Chadwick, *Augustine: A Very Short Introduction* (Oxford: Oxford University Press,

2001). For a more popular account, see Garry Wills, *St Augustine* (London: Phoenix, Orion Books, 2000).

131. Chadwick (trans.), *Saint Augustine: Confessions*, p. xiii; idem, *Augustine: A Very Short Introduction*, p. 1; Wills, *Saint Augustine*, pp. 1–2.
132. S. *Augustini Confessionum*, Liber II cap. III (5): trans. Chadwick, *Saint Augustine: Confessions*, p. 26. The Loeb Latin–English edn provides Book and Chapter divisions; Chadwick's translation provides an extra *paragraph* division of each Book, in parentheses. I have added these paragraph references to my primary Latin citation of the text in each case. See also Chadwick, *Augustine: A Very Short Introduction*, p. 8; Wills, *Saint Augustine*, pp. 3–30.
133. S. *Augustini Confessionum*, Liber I cap. XIII (20): trans. Chadwick, *Saint Augustine: Confessions*, p. 15 [hereafter referred to as 'trans. Chadwick']; Chadwick, *Augustine: A Very Short Introduction*, p. 8 [hereafter referred to as 'Chadwick, *Introduction*']; Wills, *Saint Augustine*, p. 9 [hereafter referred to as 'Wills, *Augustine*'].
134. S. *Augustini Confessionum*, Liber II cap. II (4) to cap. III (7).
135. Chadwick, *Introduction*, p. 11; Wills, *Augustine*, p. xvii.
136. Wills, *Augustine*, p. xvii.
137. S. *Augustini Confessionum*, Liber IV cap. II (2); trans. Chadwick, p. 53.
138. S. *Augustini Confessionum*, Liber II cap. III (6); trans. Chadwick, pp. 26–7. See Wills, *Augustine*, pp. xvii–xix.
139. Wills, *Augustine*, p. 10.
140. S. *Augustini Confessionum*, Liber II cap. IV (9); trans. Chadwick, pp. 28–9.
141. S. *Augustini Confessionum*, Liber II cap. VI (12); trans. Chadwick, pp. 30–1.
142. See MacCulloch, *Reformation*, pp. 115–16.
143. S. *Augustini Confessionum*, Liber VI cap. XV (25); trans. Chadwick, p. 109; idem, *Introduction*, p. 16; Wills, *Augustine*, p. 41; Eleonore Stump and Norman Kretzmann (eds), *The Cambridge Companion to Augustine* (Cambridge: Cambridge University Press, 2001) [hereafter referred to as CCA], pp. 1, 18.
144. Trans. Chadwick, 'Introduction', p. xvi.
145. See ibid., see also Chadwick, *Introduction*, p. 16; Wills, *Augustine*, p. 41.
146. See above, n. 145.
147. See trans. Chadwick, p. xvi.
148. Ibid.; see also Chadwick, *Introduction*, p. 16.
149. Edmund Hill, 'Comment: St Augustine's two vocations', *New Blackfriars*, 67:793–4 (July–August 1986), p. 302.
150. James J. O'Donnell, 'Augustine: his time and lives', in CCA, p. 23.
151. Hill, 'Comment', p. 302.
152. S. *Augustini Confessionum*, Liber VI cap XV (25); trans. Chadwick, p. 109.
153. Jostein Gaarder, *Vita Brevis: A Letter to St Augustine* (London: Phoenix, Orion Books, 1998, 2000).
154. Idem, *Sophie's World: A Novel about the History of Philosophy*, trans. Paulette Moller (London: Phoenix House 1995); originally published in Norwegian under the title *Sofies Verden* (Oslo: H. Aschehoug & Co. (W. Nygaard), 1991).
155. Gaarder, *Vita Brevis*, p. 13.
156. See ibid., p. 11.
157. Ibid., p. 159.
158. See Mary Grey, 'Augustine and the Legacy of Guilt', *New Blackfriars*, 70:832 (November 1989), p. 478.
159. Ibid., p. 480.

160. Ibid., p. 481.
161. Ibid., p. 483.
162. Trans. Chadwick, 'Introduction', p. ix.
163. 'Augustine and the Legacy of Guilt', p. 478.
164. Wills, *Augustine*, p. xvi.
165. Ibid., p. xiv.
166. Ibid., p. xv.
167. Ibid.
168. D. P. Simpson, *Cassell's New Latin–English/English–Latin Dictionary*, 3rd edn (London: Cassell, 1964), p. 132 s.v. 'confiteor'.
169. See Chadwick, *Introduction*, p. 27; Wills, *Augustine*, p. 46.
170. S. *Augustini Confessionum*, Liber VIII cap. VI (13); trans. Chadwick, p. 141.
171. S. *Augustini Confessionum*, Liber VIII cap VIII (19–20); trans. Chadwick, pp. 146–7.
172. S. *Augustini Confessionum*, Liber IX cap. II (4); trans. Chadwick, p. 157.
173. S. *Augustini Confessionum*, Liber IX cap. IV (7); trans. Chadwick, p. 159. See also S. *Augustini Confessionum*, Liber IX cap II (2).
174. Francis Thompson, author of the famous Victorian poem *The Hound of Heaven*, lived from 1859 to 1907. See *The Hound of Heaven* (Portland, ME: T. B. Mosher, 1917).
175. See section 2.4.2 of this volume.
176. See S. *Augustini Confessionum*, Liber IX cap. III (5) to cap. IV (8); trans. Chadwick, pp. 158–60; idem, *Introduction*, p. 28; Wills, *Augustine*, pp. 49–56.
177. See Abū Ḥāmid al-Ghazālī, *al-Munqidh min al-Ḍalāl*, 2nd edn, [Arabic text with] French trans., ed. Farid Jabre (Beirut: Commission Libanaise pour la Traduction des Chefs d'Oeuvre, 1969). The work was translated into English by W. M. Watt in *The Faith and Practice of al-Ghazālī*, Ethical and Religious Classics of East and West (London: George Allen & Unwin, 1953, 1970), pp. 19–85.
178. S. *Augustini Confessionum*, Liber VIII cap. VIII (19); trans. Chadwick, pp. 146–7; see idem, *Introduction*, pp. 27–8.
179. S. *Augustini Confessionum*, Liber IX cap. V (13) to cap. VI (14); trans. Chadwick, pp. 163–4; idem, *Introduction*, p. 28; Wills, *Augustine*, p. 58; O'Donnell, 'Augustine: his time and lives', p. 18.
180. See Wills, *Augustine*, pp. 66–7.
181. See trans. Chadwick, 'Introduction', p. xi; Wills, *Augustine*, p. 67; Chadwick, *Introduction*, p. 58.
182. Trans. Chadwick, 'Introduction', p. xi; idem, *Introduction*, p. 68; Wills, *Augustine*, p. 81.
183. Paul Parvis, 'On the Function of Heresy', *New Blackfriars*, 70:824 (February 1989), p. 97.
184. Ibid., p. 98.
185. Ibid., pp. 103–4.
186. Elaborated most fully in the *De Civitate Dei*; see following note.
187. See, for example, Augustine, *De Genesi contra Manichaeos*, ed. D. Weber, CSEL 91 (Vienna: Verlag der Österreichischen Akademie der Wissenschaften, 1988); idem, *De Civitate Dei*, Libri I–X, ed. B. Dombart and A. Kalb, Corpus Christianorum Series Latina (CCSL) 47 (Turnhout: Brepols, 1955); idem, *De Civitate Dei*, Libri XI–XXII, ed. B. Dombard and A. Kalb, CCSL 48 (Turnhout: Brepols, 1955). The Latin text is also available in the Loeb bilingual seven volume edition; this is the Latin edition to which reference will be made in my own volume here: George E. McCracken et al. (trans.), *Augustine: The City of God Against the Pagans*, Loeb Classical Library, 7 vols

(Cambridge, MA and London: Harvard University Press, 1957–72; some vols printed by William Heinemann at various times. For another translation into English, see Augustine, *Concerning the City of God Against the Pagans*, trans. Henry Bettenson with introduction by John O'Meara (London: Penguin Books, 1984) [hereafter referred to as '*City of God*', trans. Bettenson'].

188. John O'Meara, 'Introduction' to *City of God*, trans. Bettenson, p. ix.
189. Ibid.
190. See Wills, *Augustine*, pp. 29, 33; Chadwick, *Introduction*, pp. 12–16; Scott MacDonald, 'The Divine Nature', in CCA, pp. 73–5.
191. S. *Augustini Confessionum*, Liber III cap. VI (10); trans. Chadwick, p. 40 esp. n. 15.
192. Kelly, *Early Christian Doctrines*, pp. 13–14.
193. S. *Augustini Confessionum*, Liber III cap. IV (7–8); trans. Chadwick, pp. 38–9.
194. S. *Augustini Confessionum*, Liber III cap. III (6); trans. Chadwick, p. 38.
195. S. *Augustini Confessionum*, Liber III cap. III (6); trans. Chadwick, p. 38.
196. MacDonald, 'The Divine Nature', p. 75.
197. Ibid., pp. 83–4.
198. S. *Augustini Confessionum*, Liber III cap. VIII (15); trans. Chadwick, p. 46.
199. S. *Augustini Confessionum*, Liber VIII cap. VII (11); trans. Chadick, p. 119. See also idem, *Introduction*, p. 89.
200. Chadwick, *Introduction*, pp. 29–30.
201. Augustine, *De Ordine*, ii, 26–7, cited in Chadwick, *Introduction*, p. 30.
202. Chadwick, *Introduction*, p. 38.
203. Augustine, 'Letter 133: Augustine to Marcellinus (411)', in E. M. Atkins and R. J. Dodaro (eds), *Augustine: Political Writings*, Cambridge Texts in the History of Political Thought (Cambridge: Cambridge University Press, 2001), p. 63.
204. Augustine, 'Letter 153: Augustine to Macedonius (413/414)', in ibid., p. 80.
205. Quoted in 'Letter 153' in ibid., p. 82.
206. Paul Weithman, 'Augustine's Political Authority', in CCA, pp. 237–8.
207. 'Letter 133: Augustine to Marcellinus (411)', in Atkins and Dodaro (eds), *Augustine: Political Writings*, pp. 61–3.
208. Ibid.
209. Augustine, *City of God*, Liber XIX cap. XIV: Loeb edn, vol. 6, pp. 184, 186 (Latin text), 185, 187 (English trans.). The trans. cited here is from *City of God*, trans. Bettenson, p. 874.
210. See Chadwick, *Introduction*, pp. 84–5; Wills, *Augustine*, pp. 104–9; Atkins and Dodaro (eds), *Augustine: Political Writings*, p. xxxvii.
211. Ibid.
212. John O'Meara, 'Introduction', to *City of God*, trans. Bettenson, p. x.
213. Ibid., p. ix.
214. Ibid.
215. Ibid., p. 10.
216. See Augustine, *City of God*, Liber I cap. III: Loeb edn, vol. 1, pp. 18, 20, 22, 24 (Latin text), pp. 19, 21, 23, 25, (English trans.).
217. See Wills, *Augustine*, p. 144.
218. See above, Chapter 1, nn. 383, 384, 385.
219. See above ibid. n. 398.
220. See, for example, Geoffrey Wainwright, art. 'Church', in Lossky et al. (eds), *Dictionary of the Ecumenical Movement*, pp. 159–67; *Catechism of the Catholic Church*, pp. 173–222 # 751–972 (Art. 9: 'I Believe in the Holy Catholic Church'); *Lumen Gentium* [The

Dogmatic Constitution on the Church: Second Vatican Council: 21 November 1964], in Flannery (ed.), *Vatican Council II: The Conciliar and Post-Conciliar Documents*, pp. 350–426.

221. Steven G. Mackie, art. 'Church as Institution', in Lossky et al. (eds), *Dictionary of the Ecumenical Movement*, p. 173.
222. See *Catechism of the Catholic Church*, pp. 176–7 # 763–6.
223. Mackie, art. 'Church as Institution', p. 172; see also J.–M. R. Tillard, art. 'Koinonia', in Lossky et al. (eds), *Dictionary of the Ecumenical Movement*, pp. 568–74.
224. See Tillard, art. 'Koinonia', p. 568.
225. H. G. Liddell, *An Intermediate Greek–English Lexicon*, Founded upon the 7th edn of Liddell and Scott's *Greek–English Lexicon* (Oxford: Clarendon Press, 1968), pp. 440–1 s.v. 'koinōnía'.
226. Tillard, art. 'Koinonia', p. 569.
227. ARCIC, *The Final Report, Windsor, September 1981* (London: SPCK/CTS, 1982), p. 5.
228. Ibid., pp. 5–6.
229. Q.2:143.
230. *The Penny Catechism* (Libertyville, IL: Prow Books/Franciscan Marytown Press, 1982), p. 44 no. 249 (my emphases). For a basic commentary on the elementary definition, see A Priest [= A. N. Gilbey], *We Believe* (Valletta: Progress Press, 1983), esp. pp. 141–2.
231. Herbert McCabe, *The Teaching of the Catholic Church: A New Catechism* (London: CTS, 1985), p. 15 no. 68 (my emphasis).
232. *Catechism of the Catholic Church*, p. 249 # 1084.
233. Ott, *Fundamentals*, p. 325.
234. Augustine, *City of God*, Liber X cap. V: Loeb edn, vol. 3, p. 268 (Latin text), p. 269 (English trans.).
235. Ott, *Fundamentals*, p. 326.
236. *Catechism of the Catholic Church*, p. 258 # 1127.
237. Ibid., p. 258 # 1128; see also Ott, *Fundamentals*, pp. 329–30.
238. *Catechism of the Catholic Church*, pp. 263–4 # 1146–52.
239. Hans Urs Von Balthasar, *The Glory of the Lord: A Theological Aesthetics, volume 1: Seeing the Form*, trans. Erasmo Leiva-Merikakis, ed. Joseph Fessio and John Riches (Edinburgh: T. & T. Clark, 1989), p. 198.
240. Ibid., pp. 199, 204.
241. Robert S. Corrington, *A Semiotic Theory of Theology and Philosophy* (Cambridge: Cambridge University Press, 2000), p. 105.
242. *Catechism of the Catholic Church*, p. 255 # 1113, p. 256 # 1117, p. 276 # 1210; see also Ott, *Fundamentals*, pp. 326, 338–9; *The Book of Common Prayer* (Oxford: Oxford University Press; London: Geoffrey Cumberlege, n.d.), pp. 686–7: 'Articles of Religion', Art. XXV: 'There are two Sacraments ordained of Christ our Lord in the Gospel, that is to say, Baptism and the Supper of the Lord'. The same article accepts these two as 'effectual signs' but denies that the other five have 'any visible sign or ceremony ordained of God'.
243. See *Catechism of the Catholic Church*, p. 255 # 1113.
244. Ibid., p. 173 # 752.
245. Ibid., p. 308 # 1369.
246. 'Intercommunion also involves issues relating to authority and to the mutual recognition of ministry': this statement is drawn from 'Eucharistic Doctrine: Elucidation (1979)' in ARCIC, *The Final Report*, p. 25 no. 25. See *Catechism of the Catholic Church*, p. 316 # 1398 –1401.

247. Cormac Murphy-O'Connor and Mark Santer (eds), *Church as Communion: An Agreed Statement by the Second Anglican–Roman Catholic International Commission* (London: Church House Publishing/CTS, 1991), p. 19 no. 24. The text quoted is copyright © Cormac Murphy-O'Connor and Mark Santer, 1991. Bishop [now Cardinal] Murphy-O'Connor and Bishop Santer were the Co-Chairmen of ARCIC II.
248. ARCIC, 'Introduction' to *The Final Report*, p. 7 # 7.
249. See above Chapter 1, nn. 425, 427.
250. See above Chapter 1, n. 434.
251. See above Chapter 1, n. 441.
252. *Catechism of the Catholic Church*, pp. 255–6 # 1114, p. 276 # 1210.
253. See above (this Chapter), n. 234.
254. Eco, *The Name of the Rose*, trans. Weaver, Picador edn, p. 396.
255. See Ott, *Fundamentals*, p. 159. For some popular devotions to the Sacred Heart of Jesus, see Gabriel Denis, *The Reign of Jesus Through Mary*, trans. Andrew Somers, 6th edn (England: The Montfort Fathers, 1958), esp. pp. 291–2 ('Memorare to Our Lady of the Sacred Heart'), pp. 307–10 ('Litany of the Sacred Heart of Jesus').
256. See, for one modern example, among many discussions, Binyamin Abrahamov, 'Faḫr al-Dīn al-Rāzī on the Knowability of God's Essence and Attributes', *Arabica*, 49:2 (2002), pp. 204–30.
257. Ott, *Fundamentals*, p. 159.
258. 'Preface' to *Gravissimum Educationis* [The Declaration on Christian Education: Second Vatican Council: 28 October 1965], in Flannery (ed.), *Vatican Council II: The Conciliar and Post-Conciliar Documents*, p. 725,
259. Ibid., p. 736 # 11.
260. Ibid., p. 737 ('Conclusion').
261. *Catechism of the Catholic Church*, p. 25 # 80.
262. Sykes (ed.), *Concise Oxford Dictionary*, 6th edn, p. 992 s.v. 'sacred'.
263. Ninian Smart, *Dimensions of the Sacred: An Anatomy of the World's Beliefs* (London: HarperCollins, 1996), pp. 8–11, see also pp. 12–14.
264. Ibid., p. 92.
265. See, for example, David Torevell, *Losing the Sacred: Ritual, Modernity and Liturgical Reform* (Edinburgh: T. & T. Clark, 2000).
266. *Dimensions of the Sacred*, p. 298.
267. Ibid.
268. *Catechism of the Catholic Church*, p. 176 # 763.
269. See Butler et al., *Jesus, Peter and the Keys*, p. 199; Peter Denley, 'The Mediterranean in the Age of the Renaissance 1200–1500', in Holmes (ed.), *Oxford Illustrated History of Medieval Europe*, pp. 273–5, 279.
270. See Von Balthasar, *The Office of Peter*, pp. 256–7.
271. See *Catechism of the Catholic Church*, p. 192 # 827. See also the various articles in *Discourse*, 23 (June 2002). The sex-abuse scandal in the USA in 2002 precipitated the resignation of the Cardinal Archbishop of Boston, Bernard Law (see 'Boston hopes for change after Cardinal's resignation', *The Tablet* 21/28 December 2002, pp. 46–9), as well as 'persistent media reports that [Cardinal Cormac Murphy-O'Connor of Westminster] was negligent in dealing with cases concerning paedophile priests in his former diocese of Arundel and Brighton' (see 'Cardinal takes on the media' in ibid., pp. 54–5). No prosecutions were brought in the latter case.
272. For lyrical and musical dimensions of the Heloise and Abelard tale, see David Wulstan, '*Novi modulaminis melos*: the music of Heloise and Abelard', *Plainsong and Medieval*

Music, 11:1 (April 2002), pp. 1–23; Constant J. Mews, 'Heloise and liturgical experience at the Paraclete', in ibid., pp. 25–35; Juanita Feros Ruys, '*Planctus magis quam cantici*: the generic significance of Abelard's *planctus*', in ibid., pp. 37–44.

273. See Jean Holm (ed.), *Sacred Place*, esp. ch. 2: Douglas Davies, 'Christianity', pp. 33–61. For an Islamic contrast, see Saphinaz-Amal Naguib, 'Aesthetics of Islamic Spaces in Norway', *ISIM Newsletter*, no. 10 (July 2002), p. 13.
274. John O'Meara, 'Introduction' to *City of God*, trans. Bettenson, p. ix.
275. Ibid., pp. viii–ix.
276. Ian Richard Netton, *A Popular Dictionary of Islam* (London: Curzon, 1992), p. 112 s.v. 'Ibn Khaldūn'.
277. Trans. Franz Rosenthal, *Ibn Khaldûn: The Muqaddimah*, 2nd edn (London: Routledge & Kegan Paul, 1967), vol. 1, p. 297. For the Arabic text, see Ibn Khaldūn, *al-Muqaddima* (Cairo: al-Maktaba al-Tijāriyya al-Kubrā, n.d.), p. 146.
278. Elton, *Reformation Europe 1517–1559*, pp. 83, 190.
279. See ibid., pp. 79–80.
280. Ibid.
281. See, for example, Q.2:23; see also al-Ṭabarī, *Tafsīr al-Ṭabarī: Jāmi' al-Bayān 'an Ta'wīl Āy al-Qur'ān*, ed. Ṣalāḥ 'Abd al-Fattāḥ al-Khālidī (Damascus: Dār al-Qalam; Beirut: Dār al-Shāmiyya, 1998), vol. 1, p. 18 and pp. 157–60 (Commentary on Q.2:23); trans. in J. Cooper (ed. and trans.), *The Commentary on the Qur'ān by Abū Ja'far Muḥammad B. Jarīr al-Ṭabarī* (Oxford: Oxford University Press, 1989), vol. 1, pp. 7, 167.
282. Al-Ṭabarī, *Jāmi' al-Bayān*, vol. 1, p. 15; trans. Cooper, *Commentary*, vol. l, p. 5.
283. Al-Ṭabarī, *Jāmi' al-Bayān*, vol. 1, p. 18 ; trans. Cooper, vol. 1, p. 7.
284. Q.37:102–7.
285. See Q.2:124, al-Ṭabarī, *Jāmi' al-Bayān*, vol. 1, pp. 431–4 (commentary on Q.2:124).
286. See Q.2:34, al-Ṭabarī, *Jāmi' al-Bayān*, vol. 1, pp. 190–3 (commentary on Q.2:34).
287. Al-Ṭabarī, *Jāmi' al-Bayān*, vol, 1, pp. 192–3; trans. Cooper, *Commentary*, vol. 1, p. 242.
288. Q.4:59; trans. Yusuf Ali, *The Holy Qur'an*, p. 198.
289. Wehr, *Dictionary of Modern Written Arabic*, 2nd printing, p. 314 s.v. 'dhū'. See *Tafsīr al-Jalālayn* (Beirut: Dār al-Ma'rifa, n.d.), s.v. 'Sūrat al-Nisā' v. 59.
290. See Yusuf Ali (trans.), *The Holy Qur'an*, p. 198 n. 580.
291. Ibid.
292. Ibid.
293. Q.3:14.
294. Q.7:157.
295. Q.3:110.
296. Q.31:17.
297. Q.3:104. See Michael Cook, *Commanding Right and Forbidding Wrong in Islamic Thought* (Cambridge: Cambridge University Press, 2000), p. 13.
298. Q.3:104.
299. See Cook, *Commanding Right*, esp. pp. 13–31.
300. Ibid., p. 31.
301. Khaled Abou El Fadl, *Speaking in God's Name: Islamic Law, Authority and Women* (Oxford: Oneworld, 2001), p, 82 n. 169, p. 57; Cook, *Commanding Right*, passim.
302. 'Abd al-Qādir al-Jīlānī, *al-Ghunya li-Ṭālibī Ṭarīq al-Ḥaqq* (Beirut: Dār al-Kutub al-'Ilmiyya, 1997), 1, pp. 110–17 cited in Abou El Fadl, *Speaking in God's Name*, p. 82 n. 169. See also Cook, *Commanding Right*, pp. 129–38, 598–9.
303. Q.1:6; trans. Yusuf Ali, *The Holy Qur'an*, p. 15. See al-Ṭabarī, on this verse, *Jāmi' al-Bayān*, vol. 1, pp. 80–6; see also *Tafsīr al-Jalālayn*, s.v. 'Sūrat al-Fātiḥa', vv. 6–7.

304. Q.15:1.
305. Q.37:23; see also Jane Idleman Smith and Yvonne Yazbeck Haddad, *The Islamic Understanding of Death and Resurrection* (Albany, NY: State University of New York Press, 1981), esp. pp. 78–80. For another usage of *ṣirāṭ*, see Ikhwān al-Ṣafā', *Rasā'il*, vol. 4, p. 25,
306. Muhammad Abdel Haleem, *Understanding the Qur'an: Themes and Style* (London and New York: I. B. Tauris, 1999), pp. 19–21.
307. Ibid., p. 21.
308. See Ibn al-Haytham, *Kitāb al-Munāẓarāt*, p. 128 (Arabic text) [final passage written by Ḥasan b. Nūḥ al-Bharuchī] in Wilferd Madelung and Paul E. Walker (eds and trans.), *The Advent of the Fatimids: A Contemporary Shi'i Witness: An [Arabic] Edition and English Translation of Ibn al-Haytham's Kitāb al-Munāẓarāt*, Institute of Ismaili Studies: Ismaili Texts and Translations Series, 1 (London and New York: I. B. Tauris in assoc. with the Institute of Ismaili Studies, London, 2000); for the English trans., see p. 175 and also nn. 192–3 on the same page.
309. Ibn al-Haytham, *Kitāb al-Munāẓarāt*, p. 127 (Arabic text), p. 173 (English trans.).
310. A. J. Arberry (trans.), *The Koran Interpreted*, 2 vols (London: Allen and Unwin; New York: Macmillan, 1971), vol. 1, p. 283.
311. Trans. Yusuf Ali, *The Holy Qur'an*, p. 644.
312. Ibn al-Haytham, *Kitāb al-Munāẓarāt*, pp. 29–30 (Arabic text); p. 85 (English trans.).
313. Ibid.
314. Ibid., p. 127 (Arabic text); p. 174 (English trans.).
315. Ibid., p. 174 (English trans.).
316. Ibid., pp. 127–8 (Arabic text).
317. See al-Ghazālī, *al-Munqidh min al-Ḍalāl*, ed. Farīd Jabr (Beirut: Commission Libanaise pour la Traduction des Chefs-d'Oeuvre, 1969), pp. 28, 33; trans. W. Montgomery Watt, *The Faith and Practice of al-Ghazālī*, Ethical and Religious Classics of East and West, no. 8 (London: Allen & Unwin, 1953, 1970), pp. 44, 52.
318. Al-Ghazālī, *al-Munqidh*, p. 31; trans. Watt, *Faith and Practice*, pp. 48–9. See also al-Ghazālī, *al-Qisṭās al-Mustaqīm*, ed. Victor Chelhot (Beirut: Imprimerie Catholique, 1959), p. 79; trans. D. P. Brewster, *al-Ghazali: The Just Balance [al-Qisṭās al-Mustaqīm]* (Lahore: Sh. Muhammad Ashraf, 1978), p. 69.
319. Al-Ghazālī, *al-Munqidh*, p. 29; trans. Watt, *Faith and Practice*, p. 46.
320. See al-Ghazālī, *al-Qisṭās al-Mustaqīm*, passim.
321. See E. Tyan, art. 'Djihād', *EI*², vol. 2, pp. 538–40, esp. p. 538. See also Rudolph Peters, *Jihad in Classical and Modern Islam: A Reader*, Princeton Series on the Middle East (Princeton: Markus Wiener Publishers, 1996), p. 1.
322. Tyan, art. 'Djihād', p. 538.
323. Al-Nawawī, *Forty Hadith [Matn al-Arba'īn al-Nawawiyya]*, trans. Ezzedin Ibrahim and Denys Johnson-Davies, bilingual Arabic–English edn (Damascus: The Holy Koran Publishing House, 1977), p. 47 (Arabic text), p. 46 (English trans.),
324. Tyan, art. 'Djihād', p. 538.
325. Ibid.
326. Ibid., p. 539. See also Peters, *Jihad in Classical and Modern Islam*, p. 4.
327. *Al-Muwatta of Imam Malik ibn Anas: The First Formulation of Islamic Law*, trans. Aisha Abdurrahman Bewley, The Islamic Classical Library (London and New York: Kegan Paul International, 1989), p. 182; for the Arabic text, see Mālik b. Anas, *Kitāb al-Muwaṭṭa'* (Beirut: Dār al-Kitāb al-'Arabī, 1996), part 1, p. 300 no. 45. For a wide range of other views, see Peters, *Jihad in Classical and Modern Islam*.

328. Haleem, 'War and Peace in the Qur'ān', in idem, *Understanding the Qur'an*, p. 60.
329. Ibid., p. 61 (my emphases).
330. Tyan, art. 'Djihād', p. 538.
331. Haleem, 'War and Peace in the Qur'ān', pp. 59–70. See 'The Christian view', *Times*, 21 January 2003: 'The principles of the just war, *jus ad bellum*, were outlined by St Augustine in the 5th century and by St Thomas Aquinas in the 13th ... [Modern theory includes the following points]: There is a just cause; War is waged by a proper authority; It is waged with correct intent; There is a reasonable chance of success; Total good outweighs total evil; It is a last resort; It is waged with a final aim of peace.' To these might be added the principle of proportionality.
332. Peters, *Jihad in Classical and Modern Islam*, p. 2.
333. Haleem, *Understanding the Qur'an*, p. 65.
334. Ibid., pp. 65–6.
335. See Peters, *Jihad in Classical and Modern Islam*, p. 169.
336. Tyan, art. 'Djihād', p. 539.
337. See Haleem, *Understanding the Qur'an*, p. 60.
338. See Fred M. Donner, 'The Sources of Islamic Conceptions of War', in Kelsay and Johnson (eds.), *Just War and Jihad*, p. 32.
339. Donner, 'Sources of Islamic Conceptions of War', pp. 47, 65 n. 75. See also Richard C. Martin, 'The Religious Foundations of War, Peace and Statecraft in Islam', in Kelsay and Johnson (eds), *Just War and Jihad*, pp. 91–117, and Abdulaziz A. Sachedina, 'The Development of Jihad in Islamic Revelation and History', in Johnson and Kelsay (eds), *Cross, Crescent and Sword*, pp. 35–50; Peters, *Jihad in Classical and Modern Islam*, p. 2. For some further classical views, see al-Sarakhsī, *Kitāb al-Mabsūṭ* (Cairo: Maṭba'a al-Sa'āda, 1906), vol. 10 s.v. 'Kitāb al-Siyyar'; Ibn Taymiyya, *Mukhtaṣar al-Fatāwā al-Miṣriyya*, comp. Badr al-Dīn Abī 'Abdullāh b. 'Alī al-Ḥanbalī (Gujjran Wala, Pakistan: Dār al-Nashr al-Kutub al-Islāmiyya, 1977) s.v. 'Kitāb al-Jihād'.
340. C. Brockelmann, art. 'Al-Māwardī', *EI²*, vol. 6, p. 869. See also Asma Afsaruddin, *Excellence and Precedence: Medieval Islamic Discourse on Legitimate Leadership*, Islamic History and Civiliation Studies and Texts, 36 (Leiden, Boston, MA and Cologne: E. J. Brill, 2002).
341. Hamilton A. R. Gibb, 'Al-Mawardi's Theory of the Caliphate', in idem, *Studies on the Civilization of Islam*, ed. Stanford J. Shaw and William R. Polk (London: Routledge & Kegan Paul, 1962), p. 151.
342. Muhammad Qamaruddin Khan, 'Al-Māwardī', in M. M. Sharif (ed.), *A History of Muslim Philosophy*, 2 vols (Wiesbaden: Otto Harrassowitz, 1963), vol. 1, p. 719. See also Hanna Mikhail, *Politics and Revelation: Māwardī and After* (Edinburgh: Edinburgh University Press, 1995), Appendix A, pp. 59–60.
343. Khan, 'Al-Māwardi', pp. 731, 720.
344. Mikhail, *Politics and Revelation*, p. xxxi.
345. See Gibb, 'Al-Mawardi's Theory of the Caliphate', pp. 151–4.
346. Ibid., pp. 153, 165 n. 10.
347. Khan, 'Al-Māwardi', p. 720. See also Afsaruddin, *Excellence and Precedence*, p. 144.
348. Erwin, I. J. Rosenthal, *Political Thought in Medieval Islam: An Introductory Outline* (Cambridge: Cambridge University Press, 1968), p. 27; Afsaruddin, *Excellence and Precedence*, p. 144; Gibb, 'Al-Mawardi's Theory of the Caliphate', pp. 152–3.
349. Al-Māwardī, *al-Aḥkām al-Sulṭāniyya* (Beirut: Dār al-Kitāb al-'Arabī, 1994), p. 27. All translations from this Arabic text are mine.
350. See ibid.

351. Ibid.,
352. Ibid., p. 29. See also Afsaruddin, *Excellence and Precedence*, p. 272.
353. Al-Māwardī, *al-Aḥkām*, pp. 29–30.
354. Ibid., p. 30.
355. Ibid., pp. 31–2.
356. Ibid., pp. 31–2.
357. See ibid., pp. 51–2. See also Khan, 'Al-Māwardī', pp. 726–7.
358. Rosenthal, *Political Thought*, p. 36.
359. Al-Māwardī, *al-Aḥkām*, p. 53 (my emphasis on 'Obedience').
360. Ibid., pp. 53–4ff.
361. Ibid., pp. 61–71. See also Mikhail, *Politics and Revelation*, pp. 26–7.
362. Al-Māwardī, *al-Aḥkām*, pp. 72–8.
363. Ibid., p. 78. See also Gibb, 'Al-Mawardi's Theory of the Caliphate', pp. 162–4.
364. See Asadullah Yate's Foreword to Al-Māwardī, *al-Aḥkām as-Sultaniyyah: The Laws of Islamic Governance*, trans. Asadullah Yate (London: TA-HA Publishers, 1996), p. 6.
365. Netton, *Popular Dictionary of Islam*, pp. 177–8 s.v. 'Muḥtasib'.
366. Cl. Cahen and M. Talbi, art. 'Ḥisba', *EI*[2], vol. 3, pp. 485–6.
367. Ibid., p. 486.
368. Ibid., p. 487.
369. Ibid.
370. Wehr, *Dictionary of Modern Written Arabic*, 2nd printing, p. 175 s.v. 'ḥasaba u (ḥasb ...)'; see also J. G. Hava, *Al-Farā'id Arabic–English Dictionary* (Beirut: Dār al-Mashriq, 1970), p. 122 s.v. 'ḥasaba o ḥasb'.
371. Hava, *Al-Farā'id*, p. 123 s.v. 'ḥisba'.
372. Al-Māwardī, *al-Aḥkām*, trans. Yate, p. 337.
373. Cook, *Commanding Right*, esp. pp. xii, 344, 448.
374. For example, on the inside of the title page of Denis, *Reign of Jesus Through Mary*, we find the following rubric: 'Nihil Obstat: Josephus A. Carroll, *Censor Theol. Deput*'; and on the inside of the title page of Thomas À Kempis, *The Imitation of Christ* (London: Burns & Oates, n.d.) we read: 'Nihil Obstat: Arthur J. Scanlan: *Censor librorum*'.
375. Canon Law Society of Great Britain and Ireland, *The Code of Canon Law* (London: Collins, 1983), p. 255, Canon 1430 (my emphasis).
376. Ibid., p. 255, Canon 1435.
377. See al-Māwardī, *al-Aḥkām*, pp. 392ff.
378. Noel J. Coulson, *Conflicts and Tensions in Islamic Jurisprudence*, Publications of the Center for Middle Eastern Studies, no. 5 (Chicago and London: University of Chicago Press, 1969), pp. 66–7.
379. Malcolm Vale, 'The Civilization of Courts and Cities in the North: 1200–1500', in Holmes (ed.), *Oxford Illustrated History of Medieval Europe*, p. 331.
380. Cook, *Commanding Right*, pp. 344–5.
381. Al-Māwardī, *al-Aḥkām*, p. 391.
382. Ibid., pp. 391–2. See also Mikhail, *Politics and Revelation*, p. 25.
383. Al-Māwardī, *al-Aḥkām*, p. 413.
384. Ibid., p. 27.
385. See ibid., pp. 53–4.
386. See ibid., pp. 61ff.
387. See ibid., pp. 62–3.
388. See, for example, ibid., p. 146. See also Mikhail, *Politics and Revelation*, pp. 24–5.
389. Al-Māwardī, *al-Aḥkām*, pp. 79–112.

390. Ibid., pp. 113–28.
391. See ibid., pp. 79–112.
392. See ibid., pp. 79, 113.
393. See ibid., p. 59.
394. Ibid., p. 113.
395. Ibid., p. 118.
396. Ibid., p. 124.
397. Ibid., pp. 79. 113.
398. Ibid., p. 84.
399. Ibid., pp. 113–14.
400. Ibid., p. 120.
401. Ibid., pp. 121–2.
402. Ibid., p. 124; Q.5:36, trans. Yusuf Ali, *The Holy Qur'an*, pp. 252–3.
403. Al-Māwardī, *al-Aḥkām*, pp. 126–8.
404. See Gibb, 'Al-Māwardī's Theory of the Caliphate', p. 153.
405. See Afsaruddin, *Excellence and Precedence*, p. 272.
406. See W. Montgomery Watt, *Islamic Philosophy and Theology: An Extended Survey*, pp. 48–52.
407. Netton, *Popular Dictionary of Islam*, pp. 185–6 s.v. 'Muʿtazila'. See also J. R. T. M. Peters, *God's Created Speech: A Study in the Speculative Theology of the Muʿtazilî Qâḍî l-Quḍât Abû l-Ḥasan ʿAbd al–Jabbār bn Aḥmad al-Hamadânî* (Leiden: E. J. Brill, 1976), p. 5; Binyamin Abrahamov, *Islamic Theology: Traditionalism and Rationalism* (Edinburgh: Edinburgh University Press, 1998), pp. 34–40.
408. For example, see al-Ashʿarī, *Maqālāt al-Islāmiyyīn [Die dogmatischen Lehren der Anhaenger des Islam]*, ed. Helmut Ritter, Bibliotheca Islamica 1a (Istanbul: Maṭbaʿat al-Dawla [Devlet Matbaasi]; Konstantinopel: Staatsdruckerei, 1929–30), pp. 290–7, esp. pp, 290–1; *idem*, *al-Ibāna ʿan Uṣūl al-Diyāna* (Beirut: Dār al-Kitāb al-ʿArabī, 1985), pp. 13ff., 18.
409. Netton, *Popular Dictionary of Islam*, p. 41 s.v. 'Al-Ashʿarī Abū 'l-Ḥasan ʿAlī b. Ismāʿīl'.
410. Watt, *Islamic Philosophy and Theology: An Extended Survey*, p. 46.
411. Ibid.
412. George F. Hourani, *Islamic Rationalism: The Ethics of ʿAbd al-Jabbār* (Oxford: Clarendon Press, 1971), p. 10.
413. Peters, *God's Created Speech*, p. 5.
414. Richard C. Martin and Mark R. Woodward with Dwi S. Atmaja, *Defenders of Reason in Islam: Muʿtazilism from Medieval School to Modern Symbol* (Oxford: Oneworld, 1997), p. 18. See also Majid Fakhry, *A History of Islamic Philosophy*, 2nd edn (London: Longman; New York: Columbia University Press, 1983), p. 47.
415. Harry Austryn Wolfson, *The Philosophy of the Kalam*, Structure and Growth of Philosophic Systems from Plato to Spinoza IV (Cambridge, MA and London: Harvard University Press, 1976), p. 30.
416. Cook, *Commanding Right*, p. 196.
417. Ibid., p. 204.
418. Ibid., pp, 224–6.
419. Ibid., pp. 215–16.
420. Al-Ashʿarī, *Maqālāt*, pp. 290–7; idem, *al-Ibāna*, pp. 41ff.
421. See Djamel E. Kouloughli, 'L'Influence Muʿtazilite sur la Naissance et le Développement de la Rhétorique Arabe', *Arabic Sciences and Philosophy*, 12 (2002), esp. p. 223 n. 13.
422. H. Laoust, art. 'Aḥmad B. Ḥanbal', *EI*², vol. 1, pp. 272–7. See also Nimrod Hurvitz, *The Formation of Ḥanbalism: Piety into Power*, Culture and Civilization in the Middle East

(London: RoutledgeCurzon, 2002),

423. Laoust, art. 'Aḥmad B. Ḥanbal', p. 273. For a profound and extended theological discussion of the doctrines of an Uncreated and a Created Qur'ān, see Wolfson, *Philosophy of the Kalam*, pp. 235–303.
424. See C. E. Bosworth (trans. and ed.), *The History of al-Ṭabarī (Ta'rīkh al-rusul wa 'l-mulūk): Volume XXXII: The Reunification of the 'Abbāsid Caliphate*, Bibliotheca Persica (Albany, NY: State University of New York Press, 1987) [hereafter referred to as Bosworth–Ṭabarī, *Reunification*], pp. 3, 129 n. 383.
425. See al-Ṭabarī , *Ta'rīkh al-rusul wa 'l-mulūk*, ed. M. J. de Goeje [under title *Annales quos scripsit Abu Djafar Mohammed Ibn Djarir At-Tabari*] (Leiden: E. J. Brill, 1964), Photomechanical reprint [hereafter referred to as al-Ṭabarī, *Ṭa'rīkh*], Tertia Series 2, pp. 1,112–16; Bosworth–Ṭabarī, *Reunification*, pp. 199–204.
426. Al-Ṭabarī, *Ta'rīkh*, Tertia Series 2, pp. 1,116–22; Bosworth–Ṭabarī, *Reunification*, pp. 204–10.
427. Al-Ṭabarī, *Ta'rīkh*, Tertia Series 2, pp. 1,122–32; Bosworth–Ṭabarī, *Reunification*, pp. 210–21.
428. Trans. Bosworth–Ṭabarī, *Reunification*, pp. 221; al-Ṭabarī, *Ta'rīkh*, Tertia Series, 2, p. 1,131.
429. Al-Ṭabarī, *Ta'rīkh*, Tertia Series 2, pp. 1,133–40; Bosworth–Ṭabarī, *Reunification*, pp. 222–31.
430. Al-Ṭabarī, *Ta'rīkh*, Tertia Series 2, p. 1,136; Bosworth–Ṭabarī, *Reunification*, pp. 225.
431. See C. E. Bosworth (trans. and ed.), *The History of al-Ṭabarī (Ta'rīkh al-rusul wa 'l-mulūk): Volume XXXIII: Storm and Stress along the Northern Frontiers of the 'Abbāsid Caliphate*, Bibliotheca Persica (Albany, NY: State University of New York Press, 1991) [hereafter referred to as Bosworth–Ṭabarī, *Storm and Stress*], pp. xvi, 1–2; al-Ṭabarī, *Ta'rīkh*, Tertia Series 2, p. 1,164–5. See also Hurvitz, *Formation of Ḥanbalism*, pp. 132–44.
432. See Hurvitz, *Formation of Ḥanbalism*, pp. 133–5.
433. Cook, *Commanding Right*, pp. 112–13.
434. M. A. Shaban, *Islamic History: A New Interpretation 2: A.D. 750–1055 (A.H. 132–448)* (Cambridge, Cambridge University Press, 1976), p. 54 (my emphases).
435. See Watt, *Islamic Philosophy and Theology: An Extended Survey*, p. 50.
436. Martin et al., *Defenders of Reason in Islam*, pp. 12–13.
437. See John Henry Newman, *Apologia Pro Vita Sua*, ed. Martin Svaglic (Oxford: Clarendon Press, 1967); ed. Ian Ker, Penguin Classics (London: Penguin Books, 1994, repr. 2004). For a major biography of Newman, see Ian Ker, *John Henry Newman: A Biography* (Oxford: Clarendon Press, 1988).
438. Al-Ghazālī, *al-Munqidh*, p. 15. See also Michael E. Marmura, 'Ghazali and Ash'arism Revisited', *Arabic Sciences and Philosophy*, 12 (2002), pp. 94ff.
439. Al-Ghazālī, *al-Munqidh*, p. 15.
440. Ibid., p. 16.
441. Ibid., p. 20.
442. Ibid., p. 35.
443. Ibid., p. 28.
444. Ibid., p. 29.
445. Ibid., p. 30.
446. Ibid., p. 31; trans. Watt, *Faith and Practice*, pp. 48–9.
447. Trans. Yusuf Ali, *The Holy Qur'an*, p. 704.
448. Trans. Brewster, *The Just Balance*, p. 5; al-Ghazālī, *al-Qisṭās*, p. 43.
449. Trans. Brewster, *The Just Balance*, p. 11; al-Ghazālī, *al-Qisṭās*, p. 46.

450. Trans. Brewster, *The Just Balance*, p. 95; al-Ghazālī, *al-Qisṭās*, p. 93.
451. See al-Ghazālī, *al-Qisṭās*, pp. 78ff., 100, trans. Brewster, *The Just Balance*, pp. 67, 109–10.
452. Trans. Brewster, *The Just Balance*, p. 110; al-Ghazālī, *al-Qisṭās*, p. 100.
453. Farouk Mitha, *Al-Ghazālī and the Ismailis: A Debate on Reason and Authority in Medieval Islam*, Ismaili Heritage series, 5 (London and New York: I. B. Tauris in assoc. with the Institute of Ismaili Studies, 2001), pp. 2–3. For the Arabic text, see al-Ghazālī, *Faḍā'iḥ al-Bāṭiniyya wa Faḍā'il al-Mustaẓhiriyya*, ed. ʿAbd al-Raḥmān Badawī (Cairo: al-Dār al-Qawmiyya li 'l-Ṭibāʿa wa 'l-Nashr, 1964). The lengthy title of this work is often abbreviated to *Kitāb al-Mustaẓhirī* (see Mitha, *Al-Ghazālī and the Ismailis*, p. xv).
454. *Kitāb al-Mustaẓhirī*, p. 274, trans. and cited in Mitha, *Al-Ghazālī and the Ismailis*, pp. 73, 112 n. 119.
455. Mitha, *Al-Ghazālī and the Ismailis*, p. 73.
456. *Kitāb al-Mustaẓhirī*, p. 275, trans. and cited in Mitha, *Al-Ghazālī and the Ismailis*, pp. 73, 112 n. 122.
457. See Mitha, *Al-Ghazālī and the Ismailis*, p. 45.
458. See ibid., p. 99.
459. See the discussion of authority in ibid., pp. 95–102.
460. See, especially, the 'History' section of G. Rentz, art. 'Djazīrat al ʿArab', *EI*², vol. 1, pp. 533–56; see also Strabo, *The Geography of Strabo* [bilingual edn], trans. Horace Leonard Jones, Loeb Classical Library (London: William Heinemann; Cambridge, MA: Harvard University Press, 1966), vol. VII, esp. pp. 346, 348 (Greek), 347, 349 (English trans.), 16.4.19; Pliny, *Natural History/Naturalis Historia*, [bilingual edn], trans. H. Rackham, Loeb Classical Library (London: William Heinemann; Cambridge, MA: Harvard University Press, 1968), vol. IV, esp. pp 36–62 (Latin), 37–63 (English trans.) = Bk XII, xxx–xlii; Wilfred H. Schoff (trans.), *The Periplus of the Erythraean Sea* (New Delhi: Oriental Books Reprint Corporation, 1974: repr. of 1912 edn published by Longmans, Green & Co., New York), esp. pp. 30–1 and passim; G. W. B. Huntingford (trans.), *The Periplus of the Erythraean Sea*, Hakluyt Society Second Series no. 151 (London: The Hakluyt Society, 1980), esp. pp. 33–4 and passim; Brian Doe, *Southern Arabia*, New Aspects of Antiquity (London: Thames & Hudson, 1971); Nigel Groom, *Frankincense and Myrrh: A Study of the Arabian Incense Trade*, Arab Background Series (London and New York: Librairie du Liban, 1981); St John Simpson (ed.), *Queen of Sheba: Treasures from Ancient Yemen* (London: British Museum Press, 2002). For the ancient languages of South Arabia, see Karolus Conti Rossini (ed.), *Chrestomathia Arabica Meridionalis Epigraphica* (Rome: Istituto Per L'Oriente, 1931).
461. W. Montgomery Watt, *Muhammad, Prophet and Statesman* (London: Oxford University Press, 1967), p. 236.
462. Ibid., p. 215; see Q.30:1–4.
463. Trans. Ismail Poonawala, *The History of al-Ṭabarī (Ta'rīkh al-rusul wa 'l-mulūk): Volume IX: The Last Years of the Prophet*, Bibliotheca Persica (Albany, NY: State University of New York Press, 1990) [hereafter referred to as Poonawala–Ṭabarī, *Last Years*], p. 185. See al-Ṭabarī, *Ta'rīkh*, Prima Series 4, p. 1,817.
464. Q.34:15–17. For this dam, see Conti Rossini, *Chrestomathia*, p. 73 (CIH 541).
465. See Netton, *Popular Dictionary of Islam*, pp. 215–6 s.v. 'al-Rūm'.
466. Q.2:143; trans. Yusuf Ali, *The Holy Qur'an*, pp. 57–8.
467. Mitha, *Al-Ghazālī and the Ismailis*, pp. 99–100.
468. Q.82:1–4, trans. Yusuf Ali, *The Holy Qur'an*, p. 1,699.
469. See Q.18:47, 99.
470. See Ian Richard Netton, *Ṣūfī Ritual: The Parallel Universe*, Curzon Sufi series (Richmond:

Curzon Press, 2000), pp. 119–20.

471. See Q.54:52–3, Q.84:7–11.
472. See Q.20:109; see also Netton, *Popular Dictionary of Islam*, pp. 100–1 s.v. 'Ḥawḍ'.
473. Q.3:110.
474. Al-Nawawī, *Forty Hadith*, pp. 29, 31 (Arabic text), 28, 30 (English trans.).
475. Hammudah Abdalati, *Islam in Focus* (Kuwait: International Islamic Federation of Student Organizations, 1981), p. 10.
476. Gilsenan, *Recognizing Islam*, pp. 15–16.
477. See above Chapter 1, n. 393.
478. See Coulson, *Conflicts and Tensions*, pp. 20–1; see also J. Schacht, art. 'Ikhtilāf', *EI*², vol. 3, pp. 1,061–2.
479. Coulson, *Conflicts and Tensions*, p. 21.
480. Verse 43 of the first version of Edward Fitzgerald, *The Rubaiyat of Omar Khayyam* (London: The Folio Society, 1970, 7th imp. 1986) (my emphases). See W. Montgomery Watt, *The Formative Period of Islamic Thought* (Edinburgh: Edinburgh University Press, 1973), p. 3.
481. See Eco, *Theory of Semiotics*, pp. 6–7.
482. Idem, *The Name of the Rose*, p. 396.
483. For example, see Q.2:164, Q.3:190, Q.17:12, Q.41:53.
484. Q.2:164, trans. Yusuf Ali, *The Holy Qur'an*, p. 64.
485. Q.73:4, trans. Yusuf Ali, *The Holy Qur'an*, p. 1,633.
486. Q.17:82, trans. Yusuf Ali, *The Holy Qur'an*, p. 718.
487. Q.29:50–1, trans. Yusuf Ali, *The Holy Qur'an*, p. 1,043.
488. See Netton, *Ṣūfī Ritual*, pp. 103–23, 123–7, 130–6.
489. See ibid.
490. See al-Nawawī, *Forty Hadith*, pp. 28–33.
491. Genesis 1:31, trans. Knox.
492. Richard J. Clifford and Roland E. Murphy, 'Genesis' in R. E. Brown et al (eds), *The New Jerome Biblical Commentary* (London: Geoffrey Chapman, 1990), p. 11.
493. Q.32:7, trans. Yusuf Ali, *The Holy Qur'an*, p. 1,093.
494. Wehr, *Dictionary of Modern Written Arabic*, 2nd printing, p. 178 s.v. 'ḥasan'.
495. Arberry, *The Koran Interpreted*, vol. 2, p. 117.
496. For example, see Q.15:85, Q.16:3, Q.44:39, Q.45:22, Q.46:3.
497. For example, see Q.6:95–9.
498. For example, see Q.6:99.
499. For example, see Q.2:164.
500. See Q.36:37–40.
501. See Q.88:17–20.
502. Q.41:53. This is one of the classic themes of the Qur'ān. For much more on this theme, see Ian Richard Netton, art. 'Nature as Signs', in Jane Dammen McAuliffe (gen. ed.), *Encyclopaedia of the Qur'an*, 5 vols (Leiden and Boston, MA: E. J. Brill, 2003), vol. 3, pp. 528–36.
503. Wehr, *Dictionary of Modern Written Arabic*, 2nd printing, p. 263 s.v. 'da'wa'. For other definitions, see E. Tyan, 'Da'wa', *EI*², vol. 2, pp. 168–72.
504. Tyan, art. 'Da'wa', p. 168.
505. See Q.40:50.
506. See Q.29:47–51; see also Q.40:1–4.
507. See Decree on the Church's Missionary Activity, *Ad Gentes*, 7 December 1965, nn 11, 13 cited in Alfred Agius (comp.), *Interfaith Dialogue: The Teaching of the Catholic Church*

(London: Catholic Communications Service for the Committee for Other Faiths of the Catholic Bishops' Conference of England and Wales, 2002), p. 10.

508. Pope John Paul II, 'To the Delegation of the World Islamic Call Society, Rome, 15th January 1990' cited in Agius (comp.), *Interfaith Dialogue*, p. 43.
509. Ibid.
510. See Netton, *Popular Dictionary of Islam*, p. 124 s.v. 'Irtidād'.
511. See *Unitatis Redintegratio* [Decree on Ecumenism: Second Vatican Council: 21 November 1964], # 11 in Flannery (ed.), *Vatican Council II: The Conciliar and Post-Conciliar Documents*, p. 462.
512. See Ratzinger and Bertone, *Dominus Jesus*, passim but esp. p. 28 # 22.
513. M.Afr. is an abbreviation for 'Missionary of Africa', the more modern name for a Roman Catholic missionary order originally known as the White Fathers (WF), founded by the Archbishop of Algiers, Cardinal Charles Lavigerie, in 1868 for the evangelisation of Africa. See Peter Finn, *History of the Priory, Bishop's Waltham* (Winchester: Hedera Books, 2002), p. 13.
514. 'Optimism on the Christian–Muslim Front; Papal Appeal for Peace; Vatican "note" on Politics': e-mail record of interview between Michael Fitzgerald and NCR, 28 December 2002: transmitted from David J. Goergen on 17 January 2003 (mafrgbpt@btinternet.com) to Peter D. Smith (mafrgb@ukonline.co.uk) [hereafter referred to as 'Optimism'], p. 2
515. Ibid., pp. 3–4.
516. Ibid., p. 4.
517. Ibid., p. 6.
518. Ibid.
519. Ibid., pp. 6–7.
520. See ibid.
521. U. Rubin, art. 'Sā'a: 3. In Eschatology', *EI*², vol. 8, p. 656.
522. Ibid., pp. 656–7. See also Smith and Haddad, *Islamic Understanding of Death and Resurrection*, pp. 65–70, 125–31, 145–6.
523. Al-Bukhārī, *Mukhtaṣar Ṣaḥīḥ al-Bukhārī* [dual Arabic–English text], comp. Zayn al-Dīn Aḥmad b. 'Abd al-Laṭīf al-Zubaydī, trans. Muḥammad Muḥsin Khān (Riyadh: Maktaba Dār al-Salām, 1994), p. 1,022: *Kitāb al-Fitan*, ch. 9, no. 2,196
524. Ibid., pp. 1,022–3: *Kitāb al-Fitan*, Ch. 10, no. 2,198.
525. Trans. Yusuf Ali, *The Holy Qur'an*, p. 1,337.
526. See Helmut Gätje, *The Qur'ān and its Exegesis: Selected Texts with Classical and Modern Muslim Interpretations* (London and Henley: Routledge & Kegan Paul, 1976). p. 129; al-Bayḍāwī, *Tafsīr al-Bayḍāwī al-Musammā Anwār al-Tanzīl* (Beirut: Dār al-Kutub al-'Ilmiyya, 1999), vol. 2, p. 376.
527. Q.46:13–14, trans. Yusuf Ali, *The Holy Qur'an*, p. 1,369.
528. Q.4:124, trans. Yusuf Ali, *The Holy Qur'an*, p. 219.
529. Q.7:50–1, trans. Yusuf Ali, *The Holy Qur'an*, pp. 353–4.
530. Q.36:63, trans. Yusuf Ali, *The Holy Qur'an*, p. 1,184.
531. Q.39:71–2, trans. Yusuf Ali, *The Holy Qur'an*, p. 1,258. For more on the semiotic features of Heaven, Hell and other eschatological phenomena, see Smith and Haddad, *Islamic Understanding of Death and Resurrection*, passim but esp. pp. 63–97. See also Netton, art. 'Nature as Signs'.
532. Q.89:28, trans. Yusuf Ali, *The Holy Qur'an*, p. 1,735.
533. For example, see al-Mas'ūdī, *Murūj al-Dhahab*, ed. Barbier de Meynard and Pavet de Courteille, rev. Charles Pellat, Section des Études Historiques, 11 (Beirut: Publications

de L'Université Libanaise, 1973), vol 4, p. 243 quoting Q.89:27–30.

534. Wehr, *Dictionary of Modern Written Arabic*, 2nd printing, p. 655 s.v. 'ma'ād'.
535. See A. S. Tritton, art. 'Ākhira', *EI*², vol. 1, p. 325; Smith and Haddad, *Islamic Understanding of Death and Resurrection*, pp. 6–9. See also al-Ghazālī, *Iḥyā' 'Ulūm al-Dīn*, 5 vols (Beirut: Dār al-Ma'rifa, n.d.) vol. 4, pp. 448ff.
536. Wehr, *Dictionary of Modern Written Arabic*, 2nd printing, p. 655 s.v. 'ma'ād'.
537. See, for example, Plotinus, *Enneads*, VI.9.9, in A. H. Armstrong (ed. and trans.), *Plotinus: Enneads*, 7 vols (Cambridge, MA: Harvard University Press; London: Heinemann, 1988), vol. 7, pp. 335ff. [Loeb bilingual edn].
538. Yusuf Ali, *The Holy Qur'an*, p. 354 n. 1,029, commenting on Q.7:51.
539. *Tafsīr al-Jalālayn* (Beirut: Dār al-Ma'rifa, 1981–2), *tafsīr* of Q.7:51.
540. See W. Montgomery Watt, *Muslim Intellectual: A Study of al-Ghazali* (Edinburgh: Edinburgh University Press, 1971), pp. 147, 180.
541. Al-Ghazālī, *al-Munqidh*, p. 49; trans. Watt, *Faith and Practice*, p. 75.
542. See above, nn. 534, 535.
543. See above, Chapter 1, n. 492.
544. See Sykes, *Concise Oxford Dictionary of Current English*, 6th edn, p. 1,026 s.v. 'secular'.
545. N. S. Doniach (ed.), *The Concise Oxford English–Arabic Dictionary of Current Usage* (Oxford: Oxford University Press, 1982), p. 344 s.v. 'sacred'.
546. Wehr, *Dictionary of Modern Written Arabic*, 2nd printing, p. 747 s.v. 'muqaddas'.
547. Ibid.
548. See, *inter alia*, Macintyre, 'Slaughterhouse of the religions', pp. 2–4; Bernard Wasserstein, *Divided Jerusalem: The Struggle for the Holy City* (London: Profile, 2002); M. Dumper, *The Politics of Sacred Space: The Old City of Jerusalem in the Middle East Conflict* (London: Lynne Rienner Publishers, 2002).
549. Wehr, *Dictionary of Modern Written Arabic*, 2nd printing, p. 747 s.v. 'muqaddas'.
550. Q.15:1; trans. Yusuf Ali, *The Holy Qur'an*, p. 636.
551. See, for example, the Arabic title page of the Yusuf Ali edn and trans. of the Qur'ān referred to throughout this volume.
552. See above, n. 264.
553. Wehr, *Dictionary of Modern Written Arabic*, 2nd printing, pp. 171–2 s.v. 'ḥarām'.
554. See Cyril Glassé, *The Concise Encyclopaedia of Islam* (London: Stacey International, 1989), p. 148 s.v. 'Ḥarām'. See also Lamin Sanneh, 'Sacred and Secular in Islam', *ISIM Newsletter*, no. 10 (July 2002), p. 6.
555. Sanneh, 'Sacred and Secular in Islam', p. 6.
556. See above, Chapter 1, n. 13.
557. Antony Black, *The History of Islamic Political Thought from the Prophet to the Present* (Edinburgh: Edinburgh University Press, 2001), pp. 311–12.
558. Sanneh, 'Sacred and Secular in Islam', p. 6.
559. See Bernard Lewis, *The Arabs in History*, Hutchinson University Library (London: Hutchinson, 1968), p. 64, esp. the quotation from al-Ṭabarī's, *Ta'rikh*; idem, *The Middle East: 2000 Years of History from the Rise of Christianity to the Present Day*, History of Civilisation series (London: Weidenfeld & Nicolson, 1995), p. 65; Black, *History of Islamic Political Thought*, pp. 18–19.
560. G. E. von Grunebaum, *Classical Islam: A History 600–1258* (London: Allen & Unwin, 1970), p. 200.
561. Sanneh, 'Sacred and Secular in Islam', p. 6.
562. Ibn Khaldūn, *al-Muqaddima*, p. 208; trans. Rosenthal, *Ibn Khaldûn: The Muqaddimah*, vol. 1, p. 427 cited in Sanneh, 'Sacred and Secular in Islam', p. 6.

563. Acts of the Apostles 15:1–2, 6–7; trans. Knox (my emphases).
564. Ibid., 15:7–29.
565. Richard J. Dillon, 'Acts of the Apostles' in R. E. Brown et al. (ed), *New Jerome Biblical Commentary*, p. 751; see also Joseph A. Fitzmyer, 'Paul', in ibid., p. 1,335.
566. Raymond E. Brown, Carolyn Osiek and Pheme Perkins, 'Early Church', in ibid., p. 1,342.
567. Ibid., p. 1,341.
568. See Hugh Kennedy, *The Prophet and the Age of the Caliphates: The Islamic Near East from the Sixth to the Eleventh Century*, A History of the Near East (London and New York: Longman, 1986), pp. 77–81. See also M. A. Shaban, *Islamic History A.D. 600–750 (A.H. 32): A New Interpretation* (Cambridge: Cambridge University Press, 1971), pp. 71–8.
569. Coulson, *Conflicts and Tensions*, p. 21.

Chapter 3: The Flight to Tradition

1. Sykes (ed.), *Concise Oxford Dictionary of Current English*, p. 1,229 s.v. 'tradition'.
2. D. P. Simpson, Cassell's *New Latin–English, English–Latin Dictionary*, 3rd edn (London: Cassell, 1964), p. 609. s.v. 'trādo'.
3. Lossky et al. (eds), *Dictionary of the Ecumenical Movement*, p. 1,013 s.v. 'Tradition and Traditions'. In this substantial and illuminating article (pp. 1,013–18) the author, Kallistos Ware, surveys the different usages of the word.
4. Ibid., p. 1,017.
5. Herbert McCabe, *The Teaching of the Catholic Church: A New Catechism of Christian Doctrine* (London: CTS, 1985), p. 14 # 63.
6. Ibid., p. 24 # 78.
7. Ibid., p. 25 # 82.
8. David Brown, *Tradition and Imagination: Revelation and Change* (Oxford: Oxford University Press, 1999), p. 1.
9. Ibid., pp. 25, 61.
10. Ibid., p. 104.
11. Joseph A. Fitzmyer, 'Pauline Theology' in R. E. Brown et al. (eds), *New Jerome Biblical Commentary*, p. 1,386.
12. Ibid.
13. Anthony Giddens, 'Why we still look forward to the past', *Observer*, 25 April 1999, p. 31.
14. See, for example, the diatribe by John Cornwall, 'Winter of the patriarch', *Sunday Times: News Review*, 23 December 2001, p. 2; see also idem, *The Pope in Winter: The Dark Face of John Paul II's Papacy* (London: Penguin Books, Viking, 2004), passim.
15. Peter Ackroyd, *The Life of Thomas More* (London: Vintage, 1999), p. 394. See also G. R. Elton, *England Under the Tudors*, A History of England (London: The Folio Society, 1997), p. 139.
16. Eamon Duffy, *The Stripping of the Altars: Traditonal Religion in England c. 1400–c.1580* (New Haven, CT and London: Yale University Press, 1992), p. 381.
17. See Elton, *England Under the Tudors*, p. 298.
18. Ibid., p. 300.
19. John Henry Newman, *Certain Difficulties Felt by Anglicans in Catholic Teaching*, 2 vols (London: Longmans, Green & Co., c. 1890), vol. 2, p. 261 cited in Ian Ker, *Newman and the Fullness of Christianity* (Edinburgh:. T. & T. Clark, 1993, 1998), p. 79 n. 87.

20. Martin E. Marty and R. Scott Appleby (eds), *Fundamentalisms Observed*, The Fundamentalism project (Chicago and London: University of Chicago Press, 1994), p. ix.
21. Yves M.-J. Congar, *Tradition and Traditions* (San Diego: Basilica Press; Needham Heights, MA: Simon & Schuster, 1997 [repr. of London: Burns & Oates edn 1966]).
22. For a discussion of authorship, see Charles Homer Giblin, 'The Second Letter to the Thessalonians' in R. E. Brown et al. (eds), *New Jerome Biblical Commentary*, pp. 871–2.
23. 2 Thess. 2:14, cited by Jeff Cavins as v. 15 in his Foreword to Congar's *Tradition and Traditions*, p. 1: my emphasis. The translation here is by Knox, *The Holy Bible: The New Testament*, p. 216.
24. Giblin, 'The Second Letter to the Thessalonians', p. 873.
25. See Mark 7:1–14.
26. See Congar, *Tradition and Traditions*, p. 348.
27. Ibid., p. 23; see also pp. 177, 244.
28. Cavins, Foreword to ibid., p. 2.
29. Ibid.
30. Cavins, Foreword to ibid., p. 3.
31. Ibid. See also main text, pp. 19, 157, 287ff.
32. Congar, *Tradition and Traditions*, pp. 414, 422.
33. Ibid., p. 422.
34. See N. J. Coulson, *A History of Islamic Law*, Islamic Surveys no. 2 (Edinburgh: Edinburgh University Press, 1964) , pp. 57–9.
35. See Congar, *Tradition and Traditions*, pp. 86–7.
36. Cavins, Foreword to ibid., pp. 1–2.
37. Congar, *Tradition and Traditions*, p. 140.
38. Ibid., p. 466.
39. See Pius X, *Encyclical Letter 'Pascendi Gregis' … On the Doctrines of the Modernists* [hereafter referred to as *Pascendi Gregis*] (London: Burns & Oates, 1907, repr. Long Prairie: The Neumann Press, 1983), p. 48.
40. Ibid.; see also Ian Richard Netton, *Text and Trauma: An East–West Primer* (Richmond: Curzon, 1996), pp. 91–3.
41. See Netton, *Text and Trauma*, pp. 91–3.
42. *Pascendi Gregis*, p. 54.
43. See ibid., pp. 18–19.
44. See Netton, *Text and Trauma*, p. 92.
45. For the text of this decree, see Michael Davies, *Partisans of Error: St Pius X Against the Modernists* (Long Prairie: The Neumann Press, 1983), Appendix 2, pp. 94–102.
46. For a traditionalist evaluation and commentary, see Marcel Lefebvre, *Against the Heresies* (Kansas City: Angelus Press, 1997), pp. 213–41.
47. 'The Oath Against Modernism', in Davies, *Partisans of Error*, Appendix 2, p. 104.
48. Ibid., p. 105.
49. Ibid., p. 104.
50. Ibid., p. 106.
51. See Brown, *Tradition and Imagination*, pp. 44ff.
52. 'The Oath Against Modernism', in Davies, *Partisans of Error*, Appendix 2, p. 106.
53. Ibid., pp. 106– 7.
54. Netton, *Text and Trauma*, p. 94.
55. Ibid., p. 94.
56. See Pierre Blet, *Pius XII and the Second World War: According to the Archives of the Vatican* (Herefordshire: Gracewing, 1999); Ralph McInerny, *The Defamation of Pius XII* (South

Bend, IN: St Augustine's Press, 2001); Carol Rittner and John K. Roth (eds), *Pope Pius XII and the Holocaust* (London and New York: Leicester University Press, 2002); John Cornwall, *Hitler's Pope: The Secret History of Pius XII* (Harmondsworth: Viking Penguin Books, 1999); Peter Gumpel, 'Cornwall's Pope', *Christian Order* (February 2001), pp. 73–86.

57. Carol Rittner and John K. Roth, 'A Chronology about Pope Pius XII and the Holocaust', in Rittner and Roth (eds), *Pope Pius XII*, pp. 15–39; McInerny, *Defamation*, pp. 1, 9, 21; Eamon Duffy, *Saints and Sinners: A History of the Popes*, 2nd edn (New Haven, CT and London: Yale University Press, Yale Nota Bene Book, 2002), pp. 341–55; J. N. D. Kelly, *The Oxford Dictionary of Popes* (Oxford: Oxford University Press, 1996), pp. 318–20 s.v. 'Pius XII'; Puis XII, *Encyclical Letter of Pius XII: Promotion of Biblical Studies (Divino Afflante Spiritu)* (Boston, MA: Pauline Books & Media, repr. n.d.) [hereafter referred to as *DAS*].
58. W. Montgomery Watt, *Muhammad, Prophet and Statesman* (London: Oxford University Press, 1961, 1967), p. 231.
59. See above, n. 56.
60. See Michael R. Marrus, 'Pius XII and the Holocaust: Ten Essential Themes', in Rittner and Roth (eds), *Pope Pius XII*, pp. 46–7.
61. Cornwall, *Hitler's Pope*, pp. x, 360, 268 and passim.
62. McInerny, *Defamation*, pp. x–xi.
63. Cornwall, *Hitler's Pope*, p. 357; Susan Zuccotti, 'Pope Pius XII and the Rescue of Jews during the Holocaust: Examining Commonly Held Assertions', in Rittner and Roth (eds), *Pope Pius XII*, p. 212.
64. McInerny, *Defamation*, pp. 117, 120.
65. Ronald J. Rychlak, 'Pius XII and the Holocaust', Letters to the Editor, *Times Literary Supplement*, 15 March 2002.
66. Carol Rittner, 'What Kind of Witness?', in Rittner and Roth (eds), *Pope Pius XII*, pp. 269–70.
67. See Marrus, 'Pius XII and the Holocaust', pp. 44–5.
68. Ibid., pp. 45–6.
69. See Thomas à Kempis, *The Imitation of Christ* (London: Burns & Oates, n.d.); Eva Fleischner, 'The Spirituality of Pius XII', in Rittner and Roth (eds), *Pope Pius XII*, p. 125.
70. Fleischner, 'The Spirituality of Pius XII', pp. 125–6.
71. Ibid., pp. 127–8.
72. Ibid., pp. 128–30.
73. See Marrus, 'Pius XII and the Holocaust', p. 47; Cornwall, *Hitler's Pope*, pp. 3, 210–15.
74. See, for example, McInerny, *Defamation*, passim; Blet, *Pius XII*, passim.
75. See Sergio I. Minerbi, 'Pius XII: A Reappraisal', in Rittner and Roth (eds), *Pope Pius XII*, p. 95.
76. Quotation by Kilian McDonnell OSB on back jacket cover of Blet, *Pius XII*. See also McInerny, *Defamation*, p. 116.
77. See McInerny, *Defamation*, pp. 115–16; Rittner and Roth, 'Chronology', pp. 28–9; Blet, *Pius XII*, pp. 214–15. But see Cornwall, *Hitler's Pope*, pp. 301–2.
78. McInerny, *Defamation*, pp. 116–17; Blet, *Pius XII*, pp. 215–18.
79. Congar, *Tradition and Traditions*, p. 65.
80. Ibid., pp. 69–77.
81. Ibid., pp. 79–80.
82. Ibid., p. 82.

83. Alexa Suelzer and John S. Kselman, 'Modern Old Testament Criticism', in R. E. Brown et al. (eds), *New Jerome Biblical Commentary*, p. 1,114. See also John S. Kselman and Ronald D. Witherup, 'Modern New Testament Criticism', in ibid., p. 1,131.
84 Suelzer and Kselman, 'Modern Old Testamen Criticism', p. 1,115; see also Kselman and Witherup, 'Modern New Testament Criticism', pp. 1,131–2.
85. Suelzer and Kselman, 'Modern Old Testament Criticism', pp. 1,115–17.
86. Ibid., p. 1,121. See also Kselman and Witherup, 'Modern New Testament Criticism', p. 1,136.
87. Ibid.
88. See Kselman and Witherup, 'Modern New Testament Criticism', pp. 1,137–39.
89. Ibid., p. 1,126.
90. Ibid.
91. Raymond E. Brown and Thomas Aquinas Collins, 'Church Pronouncements', in Brown et al. (eds), *New Jerome Biblical Commentary*, p. 1,167.
92. Ibid., p. 1,168.
93. Ibid., p. 1,169. See Leo XIII, *Encyclical Letter of Pope Leo XIII: On the Study of Sacred Scripture (Providentissimus Deus)* (Boston, MA: Pauline Books and Media, n.d.) [hereafter referred to as *PD*].
94. Brown and Collins, 'Church Pronouncements', p. 1,169.
95. *PD*, p. 8.
96. Ibid., p. 12.
97. Ibid., p. 15.
98. Ibid.
99. Ibid., p. 16.
100. Ibid., pp. 16–17.
101. Ibid., p. 18.
102. Ibid., p. 22.
103. Ibid., p. 23.
104. Ibid., p. 24.
105. See ibid., pp. 25–7.
106. Ibid., p. 26.
107. Ibid., p. 29.
108. Ibid., pp. 29–30.
109 Brown and Collins, 'Church Pronouncements', p. 1,170; see Pius X, *Pascendi Gregis*.
110. Cornwall, *Hitler's Pope*, p. 337; for the text of *Humani Generis*, see Pius XII, *Humani Generis: Some False Opinions which Threaten to Undermine Catholic Doctrine* (Boston, MA: Pauline Books and Media, 1992) [hereafter referred to as *HG*].
111. Brown and Collins, 'Church Pronouncements', p. 1,167.
112. Ibid.
113. Ibid., p. 1,170.
114. Ibid.
115. *DAS*, pp. 6–8.
116. Ibid., p. 12.
117. Ibid., p. 14.
118. Ibid., p. 21.
119. Ibid., pp. 23–4.
120. Ibid., p. 27.
121. Cornwall, *Hitler's Pope*, p. 337.
122. See ibid., pp. 270–1, 318, 329; see also John Hogue, *The Last Pope: The Decline and Fall*

of the Church of Rome: The Prophecies of St Malachy for the New Millennium (Shaftesbury: Element, 1998), pp. 255–66.

123. See above, n. 39.
124. Cornwall, *Hitler's Pope*, p. 337.
125. Brown and Collins, 'Church Pronouncements', p. 1,171.
126. *HG*, p. 1.
127. Ibid., pp. 1ff.
128. Ibid., pp. 3–16.
129. Ibid., pp. 5–11.
130. Ibid., pp. 7–9.
131. Ibid., p. 9.
132. Ibid., pp. 11–14.
133. Ibid., pp. 14–16.
134. Ibid., p. 9.
135. See Fleischner, 'The Spirituality of Pius XII', p. 124.
136. Peter Hebblethwaite, *John XXIII: Pope of the Century* (London and New York: Continuum, 2000), p. 1. For a summary introduction to the life of John XXIII, see Kelly, *Oxford Dictionary of Popes*, pp. 320–2 s.v. 'John XXIII', and Duffy, *Saints and Sinners*, pp. 355–64.
137. Hebblethwaite, *John XXIII*, p. 3.
138. Ibid., p. 145. See also Geoffrey Barraclough, *The Medieval Papacy*, Library of European Civilisation (London: Thames & Hudson, 1968, repr. 1992), pp. 177–8; Kelly, *Oxford Dictionary of Popes*, pp. 237–59 s.v. 'John (XXIII) (antipope)'; Duffy, *Saints and Sinners*, p. 170.
139. See Pope John XXIII, *Journal of a Soul* (London: Geoffrey Chapman, 1965).
140. 'Chronology 1881–1963', in John XXIII, *Journal of a Soul*, pp. xxxvii–xl; Hebblethwaite, *John XXIII*, pp. 9–24.
141. 'Chronology 1881–1963', in John XXIII, *Journal of a Soul*, p. xi; Hebblethwaite, *John XXIII*, p. 24.
142. 'Chronology 1881–1963', in John XXIII, *Journal of a Soul*, pp. xliii–xlv; Hebblethwaite, *John XXIII*, pp. 39–55.
143. 'Chronology 1881–1963', in John XXIII, *Journal of a Soul*, p. xlvii; Hebblethwaite, *John XXIII*, pp. 70–81.
144. 'Chronology 1881–1963', in John XXIII, *Journal of a Soul*, p. xlix; Hebblethwaite, *John XXIII*, pp. 96–116.
145. 'Chronology 1881–1963', in John XXIII, *Journal of a Soul*, p. li; Hebblethwaite, *John XXIII*, pp. 117–31.
146. 'Chronology 1881–1963', in John XXIII, *Journal of a Soul*, p. liii; Hebblethwaite, *John XXIII*, pp. 132–45.
147. John XXIII, *Journal of a Soul*, pp. 326; see also Hebblethwaite, *John XXIII*, p. 161, whose English translation of the *Journal* paragraph differs slightly.
148. See Hebblethwaite, *John XXIII*, pp. 129, 158, 164, 169, 200, 206, 210. See also Philip Trower, *Turmoil and Truth: The Historical Roots of the Modern Crisis in the Catholic Church* (Oxford: Family Publications; San Francisco: Ignatius Press, 2003), pp. 11ff.
149. Debora Mazza, *The Pocket Oxford Italian Dictionary* (Oxford and New York: Oxford University Press, 2000), p. 9 s.v. *aggiornamento*.
150. See above, n. 148.
151. Press conference held by Archbishop of Birmingham (England) Patrick Dwyer, on 23 October 1967, *Documentation Catholique*, 1967, col. 2,072, cited in Didier Bonneterre,

The Liturgical Movement from Dom Guéranger to Annibale Bugnini, or The Trojan Horse in the City of God (Kansas City: Angelus Press, 2002), p. 94.

152. See above, n. 39.
153. Bonneterre, *Liturgical Movement*, p. 95.
154. Hebblethwaite, *John XXIII*, p. 223. See also Trower, *Turmoil and Truth*, pp. 10, 16.
155. Hebblethwaite, *John XXIII*, p. 133.
156. See Kselman and Witherup, 'Modern New Testament Criticism', in R. E. Brown et al. (eds), *New Jerome Biblical Commentary*, p. 1,142; Brown and Collins, 'Church Pronouncements', in ibid., p. 1,169; Ware, 'Tradition and Traditions', in Lossky et al. (eds), *Dictionary of the Ecumenical Movement*, pp. 1,015–16.
157. Ware, 'Tradition and Traditions', p. 1,015.
158. Ibid.
159. *Dei verbum*, ch. 2 # 9, in Austin Flannery, *Vatican Council II: The Conciliar and Post-Conciliar Documents*, Vatican Collection Volume 1 (Dublin: Dominican Publications; Leominster: Fowler Wright Books; New Town, NSW: E. J. Dwyer, rev. edn 1988), p. 755 [hereafter referred to as *DV*].
160. Ibid.; see Brown and Collins, 'Church Pronouncements', p. 1,169.
161. Ware, 'Tradition and Traditions', p. 1,016.
162. *DV*, ch. 2 # 10, p. 755.
163. Ibid., p. 756.
164. Ware, 'Tradition and Traditions', p. 1,016.
165. For Marcel Lefebvre, his ideas, teaching and movement, see Marcel Lefebvre, *Against the Heresies* (Kansas City: Angelus Press, 1997) and idem, *I Accuse the Council* (Dickinson, TX: Angelus Press, 1982); see also Michael Davies, *Apologia Pro Marcel Lefebvre*, 3 vols (Kansas City: Angelus Press, 1979); idem, *Cranmer's Godly Order* (Kansas City: Angelus Press, 1976); idem, *Pope John's Council* (Kansas City: Angelus Press, 1976); idem, *Pope Paul's New Mass* (Kansas City: Angelus Press, 1980); F. Laisney, *Archbishop Lefebvre and the Vatican* (Kansas City: Angelus Press, 1989); Charles P. Nemeth, *The Case of Marcel Lefebvre* (Kansas City: Angelus Press, 1994).
166. See Kelly, *Early Christian Doctrines*, pp. 233, 243 and Index s.v. 'Athanasius'.
167. William D. Dinges, 'Roman Catholic Traditionalism and Activist Conservatism in the United States', in Marty and Appleby (eds), *Fundamentalisms Observed*, p. 97.
168. Ibid.
169. Ibid., p. 66.
170. Ibid., pp. 74–8. Among the many traditionalist defences of Marcel Lefebvre's life and work, especially with reference to the excommunication and the Society of St Pius X, are the following: François Pivert, *Schism or Not? The 1988 Episcopal Consecrations of Archbishop Marcel Lefebvre* (Kansas City: Angelus Press, 1995, 2003); Angelus Press (ed.), *Is Tradition Excommunicated? A Collection of Independent Studies* (Kansas City: Angelus Press, 1993, 2003); Fathers of Holy Cross Seminary [Goulburn, Australia] (eds), *Most Asked Questions About the Society of Saint Pius X* (Kansas City: Angelus Press, 1997, 2001). Finally, see Marcel Lefebvre's own *Open Letter to Confused Catholics* (Kansas City: Angelus Press, 1987, 2001).
171. Dinges, 'Roman Catholic Traditionalism', in Marty and Appleby (eds), *Fundamentalisms Observed*, p. 78.
172. See ibid., p. 67. For the ongoing debate, see *Mass of Ages: Magazine of the Latin Mass Society*, no. 136 (May 2003), passim.
173. Dinges, 'Roman Catholic Traditionalism', p. 81.
174. Franz Schmidberger [Superior General of the Priestly Society of Saint Pius X and

successor of Marcel Lefebvre], 'Preface' to Lefebvre, *Against the Heresies*, p. xi.

175. Lefebvre, *Against the Heresies*, p. xiv.
176. See ibid., pp. 23–38.
177. See ibid., pp. 307–29.
178. Ibid., pp. xx–xxi (my emphasis).
179. Ibid., p. xxi.
180. Ibid., p. xxi.
181. Ibid., pp. 210–20.
182. See ibid., pp. 198–9.
183. See ibid., pp. 204–5.
184. Idem, *I Accuse the Council*, p. 99.
185. Idem, *Against the Heresies*, pp. 214–41.
186. Ibid., pp. 103, 240, 303–4, 284–6. See also idem, *I Accuse the Council*, passim.
187. Idem, *Against the Heresies*, p. 218.See Francis A. Sullivan, *Salvation Outside the Church? Tracing the History of the Catholic Response* (London: Geoffrey Chapman, 1992); Peter M. J. Stravinskas, *Salvation Outside the Church?* (Huntington, IN: Our Sunday Visitor Publishing Division, 2002); John M. Rist, 'The Status of "Extra Ecclesiam Nulla salus"', [Letter to] *Catholic Herald*, 27 December 2002.
188. Back cover of paperback edn of Lefebvre, *Against the Heresies*.
189. Kelly, *Early Christian Doctrines*, pp. 35–9.
190. Rembert Weakland, 'The right road for the liturgy', *The Tablet*, 2 February 2002, pp. 10–11, 12. See also Klaus Gamber, *The Reform of the Roman Liturgy* (San Juan Capistrano: Una Voce Press, 1993).
191. See David Torevell, *Losing the Sacred: Ritual, Modernity and Liturgical Reform* (Edinburgh: T&T Clark, 2000), p. xiii.
192. Pope John Paul II, *Ecclesia in Europa* [Post-Synodal Apostolic Exhortation] (London: CTS, 2003), # 70, p. 52; see also # 73, p. 53.
193. See Joseph A. Gribbin, [Letter to] *Catholic Times*, 26 January 2003. (The Rite is more accurately referred to as the Roman Rite contained in the Roman Missal of 1962.)
194. See Torevell, *Losing the Sacred*, passim.
195. Ibid., p. 159.
196. Ibid.
197. Ibid., p. 160.
198. Denis Crouan, *The Liturgy Betrayed* (San Francisco: Ignatius Press, 2000; trans. Marc Sebanc from the original French edn entitled *La Liturgie confisquée: Lettre ouverte aux évêques et à tous ceux qui trahissent la liturgie conciliaire* (Paris: Pierre Téqui, 1997), pp. 15–16.
199. Ibid., p. 32.
200. *Sacrosanctum Concilium* in Flannery (ed.), *Vatican Council II: The Conciliar and Post-Conciliar Documents*, pp. 1–40; see also Crouan, *The Liturgy Betrayed*, passim; and idem, *The Liturgy After Vatican II: Collapsing or Resurgent?* (San Francisco: Ignatius Press, 2001; trans. Marc Sebanc from the original French edn entitled *La Liturgie après Vatican II:Effondrement ou redressement?* (Paris: Pierre Téqui, 1999), pp. 41–3.
201. Idem, *The Liturgy Betrayed*, pp. 32–3, 61–5.
202. Idem, *The Liturgy After Vatican II*, p. 93.
203. Q.2:196, trans. Yusuf Ali, *The Holy Qur'an*, pp. 77–8.
204. See Ian Richard Netton, *Ṣūfī Ritual: The Parallel Universe* (Richmond: Curzon Press, 2000), pp. 116–23.
205. See Lefebvre, *Against the Heresies*, pp. 222–3. See also the collection of articles in

Christian Order, 43:3 (March 2002), esp. Brian W. Harrison, 'On Rewriting the Bible' (pp. 155–78); Peter Grace, 'The Flight from Biblical Truth' (pp. 179–87); and James P. Kelleher, 'Historico-critical Sedition' (pp. 188–95).

206. See above, n. 57.
207. Lefebvre, *Against the Heresies*, p. 58.
208. Crouan, *The Liturgy After Vatican II*, p. 93.
209. See Alfred Latham-Koenig, 'Earthquake in Rome', [Letter to] *The Tablet*, 9 November 2002, p. 16, in which it is noted that Cardinal de Lubac, a *peritus* at Vatican II, later 'stigmatised some of the most regrettable drifts from the spirit of the Council, *such as a disregard for tradition*, which the Council had exalted' (my emphasis); and John Beaumont, 'The Society of St Pius X *is* in schism with the Church', [Letter to] *Catholic Herald*, 24 January 2003, in which Beaumont, having cited various alleged acts of disobedience by the Society of St Pius X, asks: 'Is this really how one should witness *to tradition and the Pope*' (my emphasis).
210. 'Glossary', in Aisha Abdurrahman Bewley (trans.), *Al-Muwatta of Imam Malik ibn Anas: The First Formulation of Islamic Law,* The Islamic Classical Library (London: Kegan Paul International, 1989), p. 435.
211. Wehr, *Dictionary of Modern Written Arabic*, 2nd printing, p. 433 s.v. '*sunna*'.
212. Cook, *Commanding Right and Forbidding Wrong*, pp. 33, 52.
213. A. J. Wensinck, art. 'Sunna', in H. A. R. Gibb and J. H. Kramers (eds), *Shorter Encyclopaedia of Islam* (Leiden: E. J. Brill; London: Luzac, 1961) [hereafter referred to as *EIS*], p. 552.
214. James W. Morris, *The Master and the Disciple: An Early Islamic Spiritual Dialogue*, A New Arabic Edition and English Translation of Ja'far b. Manṣūr al-Yaman's *Kitāb al-'Ālim wa 'l-Ghulām*, Ismaili Texts and Translations Series, 3 (London and New York: I. B. Tauris in association with the Institute of Ismaili Studies, London, 2001), pp. 71 (English trans.), 6 (Arabic text).
215. J. Robson, art. 'Ḥadīth', *EI*², vol. 3, p. 23.
216. G. H. A. Juynboll, art. 'Sunna', *EI*², vol. 9, p. 879.
217. See Q.33:21 cited in Juynboll, art. 'Sunna', p. 879.
218. Q.33:21, trans. Yusuf Ali, *The Holy Qur'an*, p. 1,109.
219. Wehr, *Dictionary of Modern Written Arabic*, 2nd printing, p. 18 s.v. '*uswa, iswa*'.
220. See John Burton, *An Introduction to the Ḥadīth*, Islamic Surveys (Edinburgh: Edinburgh University Press, 1994), pp. x, xx and passim; idem, *The Sources of Islamic Law: Islamic Theories of Abrogation* (Edinburgh: Edinburgh University Press, 1990, repr. 2003), p. 10.
221. Juynboll, art. 'Sunna', pp. 878–9. See also Wensinck, art. 'Sunna', *EIS*, p. 552; Coulson, *History of Islamic Law*, pp. 39–57, 240 (s.v. '*sunna*').
222. See Coulson, *History of Islamic Law*, p. 57.
223. See Burton, *Introduction to the Ḥadīth*, pp. ix, 50.
224. Wensinck, art. 'Sunna', *EIS*, p. 552
225. See his *Fuṣūṣ al-Ḥikam*, ed. A. E. Affifi (Beirut, Dār al-Kitāb al-'Arabī, n.d. repr. from the Cairo: al-Ḥalabī edn of 1946).
226. See J. Robson, art. 'Ḥadīth Ḳudsī', *EI*², vol. 3, pp. 28–9. Robson notes that the largest collection of this type of ḥadīth is the 858-strong collection in Muḥammad al-Madanī [al-Madyanī] [died AD 1476], *Itḥāfāt al-Saniyya fi 'l-Aḥādīth al-Qudsiyya* (Hyderabad, 1905). See also Akbarally Meherally, *Myths and Realities of Hadith: A Critical Study* (Burnaby, Canada: Mostmerciful.com Publishers, 2001), pp. 23–4.
227. Robson, art. 'Ḥadīth', *EI*², vol. 3, p. 23.

228. These two compilations have been republished many times down the centuries. For modern printed versions, see the multi-volume set of al-Bukhārī, *Ṣaḥīḥ al-Bukhārī*, ed. Muḥammad Muḥsin Khān, 3rd rev. edn (Chicago: Kazi Publications, 1979); idem, *Mukhtaṣar Ṣaḥīḥ al-Bukhārī*, ed. Muḥammad Muḥsin Khān (Riyad: Maktaba Dār al-Salām, 1994); Muslim, *Ṣaḥīḥ* (Beirut: Dār Ibn Ḥazm, 1995).
229. Burton, *Introduction to the Ḥadīth*, p. 180.
230. Al-Nawawī, *Matn al-Arbaʿīn al-Nawawiyya/Forty Ḥadīth*, p. 19 (Arabic text), p. 18 (English trans.).
231. Ibid., p. 95 (Arabic text), p. 94 (English trans.).
232. See Burton, *Introduction to the Ḥadīth*, pp. 180–1; Ignaz Goldziher, *Muslim Studies (Muhammedanische Studien)*, ed. S. M. Stern, trans. C. R. Barber and S. M. Stern, 2 vols (London: Allen & Unwin, 1967, 1971); Joseph Schacht, *An Introduction to Islamic Law*, (Oxford: Clarendon Press, 1964, 1966); idem, *The Origins of Muhammadan Jurisprudence* (Oxford: Clarendon Press, 1950, 1967); see also Alfred Guillaume, *The Traditions of Islam: An Introduction to the Study of the Hadith Literature* (Beirut: Khayats, 1966); Akbarally Meherally, *Myths and Realities of Hadith: A Critical Study* (Burnaby, Canada: Mostmerciful.com Publishers, 2001); ʿAbd al-Munʿim Ṣāliḥ al-ʿAlī al–Izzī, *Difāʿ ʿan Abī Hurayra* (Dubai: Maṭbaʿa Kāẓim, 1984).
233. For this debate, see Daniel Brown, *Rethinking Tradition in Modern Islamic Thought*, Cambridge Middle East Series, no. 5 (Cambridge University Press, 1999), esp. pp. 80–107.
234. See Robert Irwin, 'Ramadan Nights' [= review of *The Koran*, trans. N. F. Dawood (London: Penguin Books, 2003)], *London Review of Books*, 7 August 2003, p. 27.
235. Ibid.
236. Ibid.
237. See Burton, *Introduction to the Ḥadīth*, pp. 180–1.
238. See Meherally, *Myths and Realities*, p. 42.
239. Ibid., pp. 83–4.
240. Kselman and Witherup, 'Modern New Testament Criticism', p. 1,138.
241. See Netton, *Text and Trauma*, pp. 83–4. John L. Esposito and François Burgat (eds), *Modernizing Islam: Religion in the Public Sphere in the Middle East and Europe* (London: Hurst, 2003) contains two important articles which refer to the Abū Zayd affair: François Burgat, 'Veils and Obscuring Lenses', esp. p. 30, and Baudouin Dupret, 'A Return to the Shariah? Egyptian Judges and Referring to Islam', esp. pp. 126, 137–8. See finally Fauzi M. Najjar, 'Islamic Fundamentalism and the Intellectuals: The Case of Naṣr Ḥāmid Abū Zayd', *British Journal of Middle Eastern Studies*, 27:2 (November 2000), pp. 177–200.
242. Chicago: University of Chicago Press, 1984.
243 Brown, *Tradition and Imagination*, p. 151 n. 128; see also Wael B. Hallaq, *A History of Islamic Legal Theories: An Introduction to Sunnī Uṣūl al-Fiqh* (Cambridge: Cambridge University Press, 1997, 1999), p. 244.
244. Brown, *Tradition and Imagination*, p. 152; Hallaq, *History of Islamic Legal Theories*, pp. 254, 262.
245. J. Schacht and D. B. MacDonald, art. 'Idjtihād', *EI*², vol. 3, pp. 1,026–7.
246. Mohammad Hashim Kamali, *Principles of Islamic Jurisprudence*, rev. edn (Cambridge: Islamic Texts Society, 1991), p. 366. For an excellent, deep-rooted analysis of *ijtihād*, including such matters as value, proof, conditions, procedure, the *ijtihād* of the Prophet and his companions, truth and fallacy of *ijtihād*, and classification and restrictions, see ibid., pp. 366–94.
247. Schacht and MacDonald, art. 'Idjtihād', p. 1,027.
248. See Fazlur Rahman, 'Islam: Challenges and Opportunities', in Alford T. Welch and

Pierre Cachia (eds), *Islam: Past Influence and Present Challenge* (Edinburgh: Edinburgh University Press, 1979), esp. pp. 317, 319–20. See also Brown, *Rethinking Tradition*, p. 30.

249. Schacht and MacDonald, art. 'Idjtihād', p. 1,027.
250. See Rahman, 'Islam', pp. 317–18.
251. Jamal Malik, 'Muslim Culture and Reform in 18th-Century South Asia', *Journal of the Royal Asiatic Society*, 3rd series, 13:2 (July 2003), p. 231.
252. See Wael B. Hallaq, art. 'Ijtihād', in John L. Esposito (ed.), *The Oxford Encyclopaedia of the Modern Islamic World* (New York and Oxford: Oxford University Press, 1995), vol. 2, p. 180.
253. See Bunt, *Islam in the Digital Age*, p. 129; see also Schacht and MacDonald, art. 'Idjtihād', p. 1,026; Wael B. Hallaq, *Authority, Continuity and Change in Islamic Law* (Cambridge: Cambridge University Press, 2001), pp. 24–56, esp. p. 56 n. 143; Coulson, *History of Islamic Law*, esp. pp. 202–17; M. B. Hooker, *Indonesian Islam: Social Change through Contemporary Fatāwā*, Southeast Asia Publications series (Asian Studies Association of Australia in association with Crows Nest, NSW: Allen & Unwin; Honolulu: University of Hawai'i Press, 2003), p. 232.
254. Knut S. Vikør, 'Opening the Maliki School: Muhammad. B. 'Ali al-Sanusi's Views on the Madhhab', *Journal of Libyan Studies*, 1:1 (Summer 2000), p. 7.
255. Coulson, *History of Islamic Law*, p. 202. See also Albert Hourani, *Arabic Thought in the Liberal Age 1798–1939* (Cambridge: Cambridge University Press, 1988), pp. 130–60; Elie Kedourie, *Afghani and 'Abduh: An Essay on Religious Unbelief and Political Activism in Modern Islam* (London: Frank Cass, 1966).
256. Hilary Wayment (trans.), Introduction to Ṭahā Hussein, *The Stream of Days: A Student at the Azhar*, in Hussein, *The Days*, p. 101.
257. Ibid.
258. Trans. Wayment, *The Stream of Days*, p. 127; for the Arabic text, see Ṭahā Ḥusayn, *al-Ayyām* (Cairo: Dār al-Ma'ārif, 1939), vol. 2, p. 33.
259. Hourani, *Arabic Thought in the Liberal Age*, p. 108.
260. Ibid., p. 154. Details of 'Abduh's life are drawn from ibid., pp. 130–60. See also Kedourie, *Afghani and 'Abduh, passim.*
261. Albert Hourani, *A History of the Arab peoples* (London: Faber, 1991), p. 308. See Rashīd Riḍā, *Ta'rīkh al-Ustādh al-Imām al-Shaykh Muḥammad 'Abduh*, 3 vols (Cairo: Maṭba'a al-Manār, 1931), p. 11, cited in ibid., p. 498 n. 5.
262. Muḥammad 'Abduh, *Risālat a1-Tawḥīd* (Limassol, Cyprus: al Jaffan wa 'l-Jabī; Beirut: Dār al-Ḥazm, 2001), p. 79; trans. Isḥāq Musa'ad and Kenneth Cragg, *The Theology of Unity* (London: Allen & Unwin, 1966), pp. 39–40.
263. 'Abduh, *Risālat al-Tawḥīd*, pp. 208–9; trans. Musa'ad and Cragg, *Theology of Unity*, pp. 126–7.
264. See Bunt, *Islam in the Digital Age*, p. 177; Hallaq, *History of Islamic Legal Theories*, p. 261.
265. Bunt, *Islam in the Digital Age*, p. 177.
266. Hallaq, *History of Islamic Legal Theories*, p. 210.
267. Bunt, *Islam in the Digital Age*, p. 128.
268. Hallaq, art. 'Ijtihād', p. 181; see also Khaled Abou El Fadl, *Speaking in God's Name: Islamic Law, Authority and Women* (Oxford: Oneworld, 2001), p. 174; and D. I. Sesay (trans.), 'MWL Organizes Islamic Seminar on Ijtehad', *The Muslim World League Journal*, 32:4–5 (June–July 2004), pp. 11–15.
269. See Brown, *Rethinking Tradition*, p. 149 n. 31.

270. Ibid., pp. 30–1; see also Schacht and MacDonald, art. 'Idjtihad', p. 1,027; Gavin Picken, art. 'Salafis (al-Salafiyya)', in Ian Richard Netton (ed.), *Encyclopaedia of Islamic Civilization and Religion* (London and New York: Routledge, 2006); E. Chaumont, art. 'al-Salaf wa 'l-Khalaf', *EI*², vol. 8, p. 900; P. Shinar and W. Ende, art. 'Salafiyya', *EI*², vol. 8, pp. 900–9.
271. Ibn Rushd, *Bidāyat al-Mujtahid wa Nihāyat al-Muqtaṣid*, ed. ʿAbd al-Ḥalīm Muḥammad ʿAbd al-Ḥalīm and ʿAbd al-Raḥmān Ḥasan Maḥmūd, 2 vols (Beirut: Dār Iḥyāʾ al-Turāth al-ʿArabī, 1992); trans. Imran Ahsan Khan Nyazee with Review by Mohammad Abdul Rauf, *The Distinguished Jurist's Primer*, Great Books of Islamic Civilization, 2 vols (Reading: Garnet, 1994–6, 2000).
272. For Ibn Rushd, see the magisterial article by R. Arnaldez, 'Ibn Rushd', *EI*², vol. 3, pp. 909–20. See also Ibn Rushd, *Tahāfut al-Tahāfut*, ed. Sulaymān Dunyā, Dhakhāʾir al-ʿArab, no. 37, 2 vols (Cairo: Dār al-Maʿārif, 1969–71).
273. Personal communication to the author from Dr Gavin Picken after a visit by the latter to Medina in 2003. See also Sesay (trans.), 'MWL Organizes Islamic Seminar on Ijtehad'.
274. Guy Noakes, 'Ibn Rushd the Jurist', *Saudi Aramco World*, 54:3 (May–June 2003), p. 13.
275. Ibid.
276. Ibn Rushd, *Bidāyat al-Mujtahid*, vol. 2, pp. 249, 500; Nyazee (trans.), *Distinguished Jurist's Primer*, vol. 2, pp. 232, 468; see also *Bidāyat*, vol. 2, pp. 594ff; Nyazee (trans.), *Distinguished Jurist's Primer*, vol. 2, pp. 553 ff.
277. Ibn Rushd, *Bidāyat al-Mujtahid*, vol. 2, p. 249; Nyazee (trans.), *Distinguished Jurist's Primer*, vol. 2, pp. 232–3; Noakes, 'Ibn Rushd the Jurist', p. 13.
278. Nyazee (trans.), *Distinguished Jurist's primer*, vol. 2, p. 233; Ibn Rushd, *Bidāyat al-Mujtahid*, vol. 2, p. 249.
279. See Abū Dāwūd, *Sunan*, trans. Aḥmad Ḥasan (Lahore: Ashraf Press, 1984), vol. 3, p. 109, *Ḥadīth* no. 1,038 cited in Kamali, *Principles of Islamic Jurisprudence*, pp. 217–18. For the original Arabic, see Abū Dāwūd, *Sunan Abī Dāwūd*, 4 parts in 2 vols (Beirut: Dār al-Fikr, 1980s), vol. 2: pt 3, p. 303, *Ḥadīth* no. 3,592.
280. See Bewley (trans.), *Al-Muwatta*, p. 359 # 43.5; for the original Arabic, see Mālik b. Anas, *Kitāb al-Muwaṭṭaʾ*, pt 2, p. 203.
281. See Brown, *Rethinking Tradition*, p. 20.
282. See D. B. MacDonald, art. 'Idjtihād', *EIS*, p. 158.
283. See Nimrod Hurvitz, *The Formation of Ḥanbalism: Piety into Power*, Culture and Civilization in the Middle East (London: RoutledgeCurzon, 2002).
284. See Muḥammad ibn ʿAbd al-Wahhāb, *Kitāb al-Tawḥīd* (Jedda: Maktaba al-ʿIlm, 1991); trans. Compilation and Research Department, Dar-us-Salām [under the title *Kitab at-Tawhid*] (Riyad: Dār al-Salām li 'l-Nashr, 1996). See also Muḥammad ibn ʿAbd al-Wahhāb, *al-Qawāʿid al-Arbaʿa*, Arabic text (pp. 18–22) with English trans. (pp. 23–8), in Abu Ammaar Yasir Qadhi, *An Explanation of Muḥammad Ibn ʿAbdul-Wahhab's Four Principles of Shirk* (Birmingham: al–Hidaayah Publishing, 2002).
285. See Emad Eldin Shain, art. 'Salafīyah', in Esposito (ed.), *Oxford Encyclopaedia of the Modern Islamic World*, vol. 3, pp. 463–9.
286. Ibid., p. 463.
287. Ibid., p. 465.
288. Sayyid Quṭb, *In the Shade of the Qurʾān*, trans. M. A. Salahi and A. A. Shamis (London: MWH London Publishers, 1979), vol. 30, p. xiii (Introduction).
289. Ibid., pp. 53, 331. For the Arabic text, see Sayyid Quṭb, *Fī Ẓilāl al-Qurʾān*, vol. 6: pt 26–30 (Beirut: Dār al-Shurūq, n.d.), pt 30, pp. 3,830–1, 3,992.

290. Shahrough Akhavi, art. 'Quṭb, Sayyid', in Esposito (ed.), *Oxford Encyclopaedia of the Modern Islamic World*, vol. 3, p. 400. For Sayyid Quṭb's childhood, see his autobiography, *Ṭifl min al-Qarya* (Cairo: Dār al-Shurūq, 1946); ed. and trans. with an intro. by John Calvert and William Shepard under the title *A Child from the Village*, Middle East Literature in Translation (Syracuse: Syracuse University Press, 2004).
291 Akhavi, art. 'Quṭb, Sayyid', p. 401. See also Adnan Musallam, *Sayyid Qutb: The Emergence of the Islamicist 1939–1950* (Jerusalem: Palestinian Society for the Study of International Affairs, 1990), esp. pp. 103–6.
292. Sayyid Quṭb, *This Religion of Islam (hadha 'd-din)* (Damascus: Holy Koran Publishing House, 1977), p. 26. For the Arabic, see idem, *Hādhā al-Dīn* (Cairo: Dār al-Qalam, 1962), p. 26.
293. Akhavi, art. 'Quṭb, Sayyid', pp. 401–2.
294. See ibid, p. 402.
295. Musallam, *Sayyid Quṭb*, p. 102, referring to Sayyid Quṭb, *Ma'ālim fī 'l-Ṭarīq* (Beirut: Dār al-Shurūq, n.d., repr. of Cairo edn of 1964), pp. 105–6; and citing Sayyid Quṭb, *Social Justice in Islam*, trans. John B. Hardie (New York: Octagon Books, 1980), pp. 227–8. See Sayyid Quṭb, *al-'Adāla al-Ijtimā'iyya fī 'l-Islām*, 6th edn (Beirut: Dār al-Shurūq, 1975), passim.
296. Akhavi, art. 'Quṭb, Sayyid', p. 402.
297. Ibid.
298. Ibid., p. 403.
299. Sayyid Quṭb, *Fī Ẓilāl al-Qur'ān*, 20 vols in 10, 1st and 2nd edns (Cairo: Dār Iḥyā' al-Kutub al-'Arabiyya, 1952–9); 20 vols in 8, rev. edn (Beirut: Dār al-Ma'rifa and Dār Iḥyā' al-Turāth al-'Arabī, 1971); 6 vols, rev. edn (Beirut: Dār al-Shurūq, 1973–4).
300. See above, n. 295.
301. Robert Irwin, 'Is this the man who inspired Bin Laden?', *Guardian Thursday: G2*, 1 November 2001, p. 8.
302. Akhavi, art. 'Quṭb, Sayyid', p. 401. See also Roxanne Euben, 'West's lessons in decadence fuel the making of a martyr', *Times Higher Education Supplement*, l August 2003, p. 18.
303. Irwin, 'Is this the man who inspired Bin Laden?', p. 8.
304. See Quṭb, *Al-'Adāla al-Ijtimā'iyya*, 6th edn, p. 245; trans. in William E. Shepard, *Sayyid Quṭb and Islamic Activism: A Translation and Critical Analysis of Social Justice in Islam*, Social, Economic and Political Studies of the Middle East and Asia, vol. 54 (Leiden, New York and Cologne: E. J. Brill, 1996), p. 278 para. 33; see also pp. xxxv–xxxvi, xlii (Introduction).
305. See Quṭb, *Al-'Adāla al-Ijtimā'iyya*, p. 245. See also Shepard (trans.), *Sayyid Quṭb and Islamic Activism*, above.
306. Shepard (trans.), *Sayyid Quṭb and Islamic Activism*, p. xlix. For the various Arabic editions of Quṭb, *al-'Adāla al-Ijtimā'iyya*, see the Bibliography (Primary Sources) below.
307. Quṭb, *Al-'Adāla al-Ijtimā'iyya*, 6th edn, p. 264; trans. Shepard, *Sayyid Quṭb*, p. 296 para. 105, see also p. l.
308. Bunt, *Islam in the Digital Age*, pp. 130–1 (my emphasis).
309. See Ikhwān al-Ṣafā', *Rasā'il*, 4 vols (Beirut: Dār Ṣādir/Dār Bayrūt, 1957), passim; see also Netton, *Muslim Neoplatonists*.
310. Abdullah M. al-Rehaili (comp.), *This is the Truth: Newly Discovered Scientific Facts Revealed in the Qur'an and Authentic Hadeeth*, 2nd edn (Mecca: Muslim World League; Riyad: Alharamain Islamic Foundation, 1998), p. e.
311. Ibid., pp. 4–22.

312. Ibid., pp. 33–41.
313. Ibid., pp. 42–51.
314. Ibid., pp. 52–8.
315. Ibid., p. 7.
316. Ibid., p. 62; see also I. A. Ibrahim, *A Brief Illustrated Guide to Understanding Islam*, 2nd edn (Houston, TX: Darussalam Publishers, 1997), esp. pp. 5–31.
317. Q.23:12–14, trans. Yusuf Ali, *The Holy Qur'an*, pp. 875–6.
318. Ibrahim, *Brief Illustrated Guide to Understanding Islam*, p. 6.
319. Ibid., pp. 6–10. See also al-Rehaili, *This is the Truth*, pp. 3–22.
320. 2nd edn (Jedda: Bilal M. al-Kanadi & Brothers, 1998, first publ. 1985).
321. Ibid., p. iii.
322. Ibid., p. iv (my emphasis).
323. See ibid., pp. 67–8.
324. Ibid.
325. Ibid., p. 68.
326. Ibid., pp. 68–9.
327. Ibid., p. 69.
328. Q.31:6; trans. Yusuf Ali, *The Holy Qur'an*, pp. 1,080–1.
329. Al-Kanadi, *Islamic Ruling*, p. 9.
330. Ibid., p. 13.
331. Ibid.
332. Ibid., pp. 27–40.
333. Ibid., p. 27.
334. Ibid.
335. Ibid., p. 40.
336. Ibid., pp. 68–9.
337. See, for example, Bowie, *Anthropology of Religion*, pp. 82–5.
338. Mary Douglas, *Purity and Danger: An Analysis of the Concepts of Pollution and Taboo* (London and New York: Routledge, repr. 1996).
339. Ibid., p. 7.
340. Wehr, *Dictionary of Modern Written Arabic*, 2nd printing, p. 530 s.v. '*taṣwīr*'.
341. See Oleg Grabar, *The Formation of Islamic Art* (New Haven, CT and London: Yale University Press, 1973, 1977), esp. pp. 75ff., 86.
342. Ibid., p. 83.
343. Ibid., p. 84.
344. Wehr, *Dictionary of Modern Written Arabic*, 2nd printing, p. 530 s.v. '*muṣawwir*'.
345. Q.59:24, trans. Yusuf Ali, *The Holy Qur'an*, p. 1,529.
346. Q.34:13. See Grabar, *Formation*, pp. 81–2.
347. Q.34:13, trans. Yusuf Ali, *The Holy Qur'an*, p. 1,137.
348. Grabar, *Formation*, p. 81.
349. Arberry, *The Koran Interpreted*, vol. 2, p. 132.
350. Wehr, *Dictionary of Modern Written Arabic*, 2nd printing, p. 892.
351. Grabar, *Formation*, p. 83.
352. Q.6:74, trans. Yusuf Ali, *The Holy Qur'an*, p. 309.
353. Grabar, *Formation*, p. 86. For the original Arabic, see Aḥmad b. Ḥanbal, *al-Musnad*, 1/407 no. 3,867, cited in Abu Muhammad Abdur-Ra'uf Shakir, *The Islamic Ruling Concerning At-Tasweer* (Philadelphia: Zakee Muwwakkil Books & Articles; South Orange, NJ: CWP Publishing & Distribution, 1998), pp. 52–3 n. 92; see also ibid., p. 52. Aḥmad b. Ḥanbal's *Musnad* in Arabic is available in a 6-vol Beirut edn published

in 1389/1969 by Dār al-Fikr.

354. Shakir, *Tasweer*, p. 3.
355. Ibid., p. 12.
356. Ibid., pp. 17–84.
357. Ibid., pp. 85–121.
358. Ibid., pp. 85–105. Shaykh ʿAbd al-ʿAzīz ibn Abdallāh Ibn Bāz was blind from the age of 20.
359. See ibid., pp. 251–2.
360. See Yūsuf al-Qaraḍāwī, *Kitāb al-Ḥalāl wa ʾl-Ḥarām fi ʾl-Islām*, 12th edn (Beirut: al-Maktab al-Islāmī, 1978).
361. Shakir, *Tasweer*, pp. 122–215.
362. Ibid., pp. 218–25
363. Ibid., pp. 226–41.
364. See ibid., pp. 17ff.. 216ff. and passim.
365. Q.34:13.
366. See Shakir, *Tasweer*, p. 140.
367. Ibid., p. 122.
368. Ibid., pp. 202–3, 15.
369. See art. 'Salafiyyah', in Cyril Glassé, *The Concise Encyclopaedia of Islam* (London: Stacey International, 1989), p. 344. See also Shepard (trans.), *Sayyid Quṭb and Islamic Activism*, p. xiii.
370. See Ousmane Kane, *Muslim Modernity in Postcolonial Nigeria: A Study of the Society for the Removal of Innovation and Reinstatement of Tradition*, Islam in Africa, vol. 1 (Leiden and Boston, MA: E. J. Brill, 2003), esp. p. 232.
371. Ibid., pp. 232, 239.
372. Zahid Hussain, 'Musharraf condemns "backward Muslims"', *Times*, 18 February 2002, p. 20.
373. Hourani, *Arabic Thought in the Liberal Age*, p. 123. See also Jamāl al-Dīn al-Afghānī, *Al-Radd ʿalā ʾl-Dahriyyīn* (Cairo: Dār al-Karnak, 1960s), passim.
374. Mansoor al-Jamri (ed.), 'Addressing contemporary challenges with a new vision', *Islam 21*, 23 (June 2000), p. 1.
375. Parvez Manzoor, 'Postmodernism: A Symptom of the Crisis of Modernism', in ibid., pp. 2ff.
376. Ibid.
377. Islam 21 Forum, 'Debating Modernism and "ijtihad" in Islam', *Islam 21*, 23 (June 2000), p. 13.
378. Martin van Bruinessan, 'ISIM Workshop: Muslim Intellectuals and Modern Challenges', *ISIM Newsletter*, no. 5 (June 2000), p. 5.
379. See Pius X, *Pascendi Gregis*, passim.
380. See Wehr, *Dictionary of Modern Written Arabic*, 2nd printing, p. 46 s.v. '*bidʿa*'.
381. See Coulson, *History of Islamic Law*, p. 10.
382. Ibid., pp. 42–3.
383. See Michel Foucault, *The Order of Things: An Archaeology of the Human Sciences* (London: Tavistock Publications, 1970); idem, *The Archaelogy of Knowledge* (London: Tavistock Publications, 1972).
384. Pius X, *Pascendi Gregis*, p. 48; see also Michael Davies, *Partisans of Error: St Pius X Against the Modernists*, (Long Prairie, MN: The Neumann Press, 1983), pp. xiii, 1.
385. 'It is abundantly clear how great and how eager is the passion of such men [the Modernists] for innovation': Pius X, *Pascendi Gregis*, p. 46.

386. Ibid., pp. 56ff.
387. For the text of Pius X's 'Oath Against Modernism', see Davies, *Partisans of Error*, pp. 104–7.
388. Coulson, *Conflicts and Tensions*, pp. 48–9, 92; idem, *History of Islamic Law*, p. 211.
389. Trans. Yusuf Ali, *The Holy Qur'an*, p. 191.
390. Coulson, *History of Islamic Law*, p. 211.
391. Trans. Yusuf Ali, *The Holy Qur'an*, p. 179.
392. See ibid., n. 509.
393. See Netton, *Popular Dictionary of Islam*, pp. 251, 194 s.vv. 'Uḥud, Battle of', 'al-Nisā''.
394. Coulson, *Conflicts and Tensions*, p. 94; see also idem, *History of Islamic Law*, p. 210; Hallaq, *History of Islamic Legal Theories*, p. 211. Hallaq dates the Tunisian Statute to 1956 rather than 1957 as in Coulson. Hallaq also laments the lack of 'cohesive legal methodology' in this kind of what he calls 'quasi-*ijtihād*' (ibid., p. 211).
395. See Hallaq, *History of Islamic Legal Theories*, pp. 173, 185, 186, 187.
396. Coulson, *Conflicts and Tensions*, p. 87; see also pp. 88–91; idem, *History of Islamic Law*, pp. 100, 139–42; J. Schacht, art. 'Ḥiyal', EI^2, vol. 3, pp. 510–13.
397. David Waines, 'Religion and Modernity: Reflections on a Modern Debate', *ISIM Newsletter*, no. 12 (June 2003), p. 29.
398. James A. Bill and John Alden Williams, *Roman Catholics and Shi'i Muslims: Prayer, Passion and Politics* (Chapel Hill and London: University of North Carolina Press, 2002), p. 98. For a variety of other perspectives, particularly theological and spiritual, on Catholic and Shi'a engagement, see the collection of papers in Anthony O'Mahony, Wulstan Peterburs and Mohammad Ali Shomali (eds), *Catholics and Shi'a in Dialogue: Studies in Theology and Spirituality* (London: Melisende, 2004).
399. Bill and Williams, *Roman Catholics and Shi'i Muslims*, p. 47.
400. Ibid.
401. Ibid., pp. 47–50.
402. Ibid., p. 47.
403. Ibid. pp. 50–5.
404. Ibid., pp. 63–74, 55–62.
405. Ibid., pp. 75–92.
406. Ibid., pp. 93–116.
407. Ibid., pp. 117–41.
408. Ibid., p. 127.
409. Ibid., p. 110. See Keith Ward, *Religion and Community* (Oxford: Clarendon Press, 2000), passim but esp. pp. 31–52.
410. See Trower, *Turmoil and Truth*, p. 38.
411. For the implications and ramifications of this term, see Hans Urs Von Balthasar, *Theo-Drama: Theological Dramatic Theory, volume One: Prolegomena*, trans. Graham Harrison (San Francisco: Ignatius Press, 1988), esp. pp. 31–4.
412. See al-Nawawī, *Matn al-Arba'īn al-Nawawiyya*, p. 29 (*Ḥadīth* no. 2, the famous *Ḥadīth* of Jibrīl).
413. Ibid., p. 60 (English text), p. 61 (Arabic text) (*Ḥadīth* no. 15).
414. See Ibn Khaldūn, *The Muqaddimah: An Introductionn to History*, trans. Franz Rosenthal, (London: Routledge & Kegan Paul, 1958, 2nd corrected edn 1967), vol. 2, esp. pp. 124–37. For the Arabic text, see Ibn Khaldūn, *al-Muqaddima*, pp. 294–311.
415. Douglas, *Purity and Danger*.
416. Ibid., p. 7.
417. See Malcolm Barber, *The Cathars: Dualist Heretics in Languedoc in the High Middle Ages*,

The Medieval World (Harlow: Pearson Education and Longman, 2000).

418. See D. Van Kley, *The Jansenists and the Expulsion of the Jesuits from France 1757–1765* (New Haven, CT: Yale University Press, 1975).
419. See Harold Kasimow, 'Modern Muslim Perceptions of Judaism and Christianity', *Interreligious Insight: A Journal of Dialogue and Engagement*, 2:4 (October 2004), pp. 30–7. See also *Nostra Aetate* (Declaration on the Relation of the Church to Non-Christian Religions, 28 October 1965), # 2 in Flannery (ed.), *Vatican Council II: The Conciliar and Post-Conciliar Documents*, p. 739: 'The Catholic Church rejects nothing of what is true and holy in these religions'.
420. See Plotinus, *Enneads*, III.8.8, IV.4.4, IV.7.10, IV.8.8; Dominic J. O'Meara, *Plotinus: An Introduction to the Enneads* (Oxford: Clarendon Press, 1993), pp. 103–6 ('The Return to the One'). See also A. C. Lloyd, *The Anatomy of Neoplatonism* (Oxford: Clarendon Press, 1990), pp. 123–4. Lloyd P. Gerson, *Plotinus*, The Arguments of the Philosophers (London and New York: Routledge, 1994), p. 203 notes: 'The central notion of Plotinus' philosophy of religion is that of return (*epistrophé*). All creation is disposed by nature to return to the source whence it came, in so far as it is is able.' See also ibid., pp. 61–2.
421. See Q.96:8.
422. *Nostra Aetate*, # 2, p. 739. See above, n. 419.
423. Ibid., # 1, p. 738.
424. Eliade, *The Sacred and the Profane*, p. 10.
425. Ibid., p. 11.
426. Q.41:53; trans. Arberry, *The Koran Interpreted*, vol. 2, p. 191.
427. Eliade, *The Sacred and the Profane*, p. 17.

BIBLIOGRAPHY OF WORKS CITED

Primary Sources

Arabic, French, Greek, Hebrew, Latin, Persian, Provençal and Sabaean sources are listed here. Translations from these texts are also included in this section.

ʿAbduh, Muḥammad, *Risālat al-Tawḥīd*, (Limassol, Cyprus: al-Jaffan wa 'l-Jabī; Beirut: Dār al-Ḥazm, 2001); trans. Ishāq Musaʿad and Kenneth Cragg, *The Theology of Unity* (London: Allen & Unwin, 1966); *see* al-Afghānī, Jamāl al-Dīn and Muḥammad ʿAbduh.

Abū Dāwūd, *Sunan Abī Dāwūd*, 4 parts in 2 vols (Beirut: Dār al-Fikr, 1980s) vol. 2, pt 3; trans. Aḥmad Ḥasan, *Abū Dāwūd: Sunan* (Lahore: Ashraf Press, 1984), vol. 3.

Abu Zahra, *Uṣul al-Fiqh* (Cairo: Dār al-Fikr al-ʿArabī, 1377/1958).

al-Afghānī, Jamāl al-Dīn, *al-Radd ʿalā 'l-Dahriyyīn* (Cairo: Dār al-Kamah, 1960s).

al-Afghānī, Jamāl al-Dīn and Muḥammad ʿAbduh, *al ʿUrwa al-Wuthqā*, 2 vols (Beirut: Maṭbaʿat al-Tawfīq, 1910; Beirut: Dār al-Kātib al ʿArabī, 1970).

Amidon, P. R., *The Panarion of St Epiphanius, Bishop of Salamis: Selected Passages* (Oxford: Oxford University Press, 1990).

Aquinas, St Thomas, *Summa Theologiae*, 61 vols (London: Blackfriars in conjunction with Eyre Spottiswoode; New York: McGraw-Hill Book Co., 1963–81).

al-Ashʿarī, *al-Ibāna ʿan Uṣūl al-Diyāna* (Beirut: Dār al-Kitāb al-ʿArabī, 1985).

al-Ashʿarī, *Maqālāt al-Islāmiyyīn [Die dogmatischen Lehren der Anhaenger des Islam]*, ed. Helmut Ritter, Bibliotheca Islamica 1a (Istanbul: Maṭbaʿat at al-Dawla [Devlet Matbaasi]; Konstantinopel: Staatsdruckerei, 1929–30).

Athanasius, *De Sententia Dionysii*: *see* Opitz (ed.), *Athanasius Werke*.

Atkins, E. M. and R. K. Dodaro (eds), *Augustine: Political Writings*, Cambridge Texts in the History of Political Thought (Cambridge: Cambridge University Press, 2001).

Augustine, St, *Confessions*:

Henry Chadwick (trans.), *Saint Augustine: Confessions* (Oxford: Oxford University Press, 1991).

William Watts (trans), *Augustine: Confessions*, Bilingual Latin–English edn, Loeb Classical Library, 2 vols (Cambridge, MA and London: Harvard University Press, 1999, 2000).

Augustine, St, *De Civitate Dei*:
Henry Bettenson (trans.), *Concerning the City of God Against the Pagans* (London: Penguin Books, 1984).
B. Dombart and A. Kalb (eds), *De Civitate Dei*, Libri I–X, *Corpus Christianorum Series Latina* (CCSL) 47 (Turnhout: Brepols, 1955); Libri XI–XXII, *CCSL* 48 (Turnhout: Brepols, 1955).
George E. McCracken et al. (trans.), *Augustine: The City of God Against the Pagans*, Bilingual Latin–English edn, Loeb Classical Library, 7 vols (Cambridge, MA and London: Harvard University Press, 1957–72 [some volumes printed by William Heinemann at various times]).

Augustine, St, *De Genesi contra Manichaeos*, ed. D. Weber, *CSEL* 91 (Vienna: Verlag der Österreichischen Akademie der Wissenschaften, 1988).

Augustine, St, *De Ordine*: *see* Secondary Sources s.v. Chadwick, *Augustine: A Very Short Introduction*.

Augustine, St, 'Letter 133: Augustine to Marcellinus (411)' *see* Atkins and Dodaro (eds), *Augustine*.

Augustine, St, 'Letter 153: Augustine to Macedonius (413/414)' *see* Atkins and Dodaro (eds), *Augustine*.

Augustine, St *see* Atkins and Dodaro (eds), *Augustine*.

al-Bayḍāwī, *Tafsīr al-Bayḍāwī al-Musammā Anwār al-Tanzīl* (Beirut: Dār al-Kutub al-ʿIlmiyya, 1999), vol. 2.

Bible:
R. Knox (trans.), *The Holy Bible* (London: Burns & Oates/Macmillan, 1960).
Henry Wansbrough (gen. ed. and trans.), *The New Jerusalem Bible* (London: Darton, Longman & Todd, 1985).

Bosworth, C. E. (trans. and ed.) *see under* al-Ṭabarī.

al-Bukhārī, *Mukhtaṣar Ṣaḥīḥ al-Bukhārī* [dual Arabic–English text], comp. Zayn al-Dīn Aḥmad b. ʿAbd al-Laṭīf al-Zubaydī, trans. Muḥammad Muḥsin Khān (Riyad: Maktaba Dār al-Salām, 1994).

al-Bukhārī, *Ṣaḥīḥ al-Bukhārī*, ed. Muḥammad Muḥsin Khān, 3rd rev. edn (Chicago: Kazi Publications, 1979).

Cragg, Kenneth *see under* ʿAbduh, Muḥammad; Ḥusayn [Hussein], Ṭāhā.

De Villehardouin, Geoffroi, *La Conquête de Constantinople*, ed. and trans. E. Faral, Les Classiques de l'Histoire de France au Moyen Age 18–19, 2 vols (Paris: Société d'Édition 'Les Belles Lettres', 1938–9); trans. M. R. B. Shaw, 'The Conquest of Constantinople', in M. R. B. Shaw (trans.), *Chronicles of the Crusades* (London: Penguin Books, 1963).

Descartes, Renati, *Meditationes de Prima Philosophia* (Paris: Michael Soly, 1641); Desmond M. Clarke (trans. with intro.), René Descartes: *Meditations and Other Metaphysical Writings* (London: Penguin Books, 2003).

Doniach, N. S (ed.), *The Concise Oxford English–Arabic Dictionary of Current Usage* (Oxford: Oxford University Press, 1982).

Eckhart, Meister *see* M. O'C. Walshe.

Epiphanius, *Panarion haeri*: *see* Amidon, *Panarion*.

Gätje, Helmut (trans.), *The Qur'ān and Its Exegesis: Selected Texts with Classical and Modern Muslim Interpretations* (London and Henley: Routledge & Kegan Paul, 1976).

al-Ghazālī, Abū Ḥamīd, *Faḍā'iḥ al-Bāṭiniyya wa Faḍā'il al-Mustaẓhiriyya*, ed. ʿAbd al-Rahmān Badawī (Cairo: al-Dār al-Qawmiyya li 'l-Ṭibāʿa wa 'l-Nashr, 1964); partly trans.in Farouk Mitha, *Al-Ghazālī and the Ismailis: A Debate on Reason and Authority in Medieval Islam*, Ismaili Heritage Series, 5 (London and New York: I. B. Tauris in association with the Institute of Ismaili Studies, 2001).

al-Ghazālī, Abū Ḥamīd, *Iḥyā' 'Ulūm al-Dīn*, 5 vols (Beirut: Dār al-Ma'rifa, n.d.), vol. 4.

al-Ghazālī, Abū Ḥamīd, *al-Munqidh min al- Ḍalāl*, 2nd edn, Arabic text with French trans. ed. Farid Jabre (Beirut: Commission Libanaise pour la Traduction des Chefs d'Oeuvre, 1969); trans. W. M. Watt, *The Faith and Practice of al-Ghazālī*, Ethical and Religious Classics of East and West (London: George Allen & Unwin, 1953, 1970).

al-Ghazālī, Abū Ḥamīd, *al-Mustaṣfā min 'Ilm al-Usūl* (Cairo: al-Maktaba al-Tijāriyya, 1356/1937), vol. I.

al-Ghazālī, Abū Ḥamīd, *al-Qisṭās al-Mustaqīm*, ed. Victor Chelhot (Beirut: Imprimerie Catholique, 1959); trans. D. P. Brewster, *al-Ghazālī: The Just Balance [al-Qisṭās al-Mustaqīm]* (Lahore: Sh. Muhammad Ashraf, 1978).

Hava, J. G., *Al-Farā'id Arabic–English Dictionary* (Beirut: Dār al-Mashriq, 1970).

al-Ḥayāt, Thursday 13 September 2001.

Ḥusayn [Hussein], Ṭāhā: *al-Ayyām*:

al-Ayyām, 3 vols in 1 (Cairo: Dār al-Ma'ārif, n.d.)

al-Ayyām, vol. 1 (Cairo: Dār al-Ma'ārif, 1971).

al-Ayyām, vol. 2 (Cairo: Dār al-Ma'ārif, 1939).

E. H. Paxton, Hilary Wayment and Kenneth Cragg (trans.), *The Days: His Autobiography in Three Parts* (Cairo: The American University in Cairo Press, 1997).

Hilary Wayment (trans.), *The Stream of Days: A Student in the Azhar* (Cairo: Dār al-Maaref, 1943).

Ibn 'Abd al-Wahhāb, *Kitāb al-Tawḥīd* (Jedda: Maktaba al-'Ilm, 1991); trans. Compilation and Research Department, Da-us-Salam [under the title *Kitab at-Tawhid*] (Riyad: Dār al-Salām 'l-Nashr, 1996).

Ibn 'Abd al-Wahhāb, *al-Qawā'id al-Arb'a*, [bilingual Arabic–English text]: Abu Ammaar Yasir Qadhi, *An Explanation of Muḥammad Ibn 'Abdul-Wahhab's Four Principles of Shirk* (Birmingham: al-Hidaayah Publishing, 2002).

Ibn al-'Arabi, *Fuṣūṣ al-Ḥikam*, ed. A. E. I. Affifi (Beirut: Dār al-Kitāb al 'Arabī, repr. from the Cairo: al-Ḥalabī edn of 1946).

Ibn Baṭṭūṭa, *Riḥlat Ibn Baṭṭūṭa* (Beirut: Dār Ṣādir/Dār Bayrūt, 1964).

Ibn Ḥanbal, Aḥmad, *Musnad*, 6 vols (Beirut: Dār al-Fikr, 1389/1969).

Ibn al-Haytham, *Kitāb al-Munāẓarāt*: Wilferd Madelung and Paul E. Walker (eds and trans.), *The Advent of the Fatimids: A Contemporary Shī'ī Witness: An [Arabic] Edition and English Translation of Ibn al-Haytham's* Kitāb al-Munaẓarāt, Institute of Ismaili Studies: Ismaili Texts and Translation Series, 1 (London and New York: I. B. Tauris in association with the Institute of Ismaili Studies, 2000).

Ibn Khaldūn, *al-Muqaddima* (Cairo: al-Maktaba al-Tijāriyya al-Kubrā, n.d.); trans. Franz Rosenthal, *Ibn Khaldûn: The Muqaddimah*, 2nd edn, 3 vols (London: Routledge & Kegan Paul, 1958, 1967). _

Ibn Rushd, *Bidāyat al-Mujtahid wa Nihāyat al-Muqtaṣid*, ed. 'Abd al-Ḥalīm Muḥammad 'Abd al-Ḥalīm and 'Abd al-Raḥman Ḥasan Maḥmūd, 2 vols (Beirut: Dār Iḥyā' al-Turāth al-'Arabī, 1992); trans. Imran Ahsan Khan Nyazee with Review by Mohammad Abdul Raof, *The Distinguished Jurists' Primer*, Great Books of Islamic Civilization, 2 vols (Reading: Garnet, 1994–6, 2000).

Ibn Rushd, *Tahāfut al-Tahāfut*, ed. Sulaymān Dunyā, Dhakhā'ir al-'Arab, 37, 2 vols (Cairo: Dār al-Ma'ārif, 1969–71).

Ibn Taymiyya, *Mukhtaṣar al-Fatāwā al-Miṣriyya*, comp. Badr al-Dīn Abī 'Abdullāh b. 'Alī al-Ḥanbalī (Gujjran Wala, Pakistan: Dār al-Nashr al-Kutub al-Islāmiyya, 1977).

Ikhwān al-Ṣafā' *Rasā'il Ikhwān al-Ṣafā'* 4 vols (Beirut: Dār Ṣādir/Ḍār Bayrūt, 1957).

al 'Izzi, 'Abd al-Mun'im Ṣāliḥ al-'Alī, *Difā' 'an Abī Hurayra* (Dubai: Maṭba'a Kāẓim, 1984).

Jalālayn, *Tafsīr al-Jalālayn* (Beirut: Dār al-Ma'rifa, 1981–2).
al-Jīlānī, 'Abd al-Qādir, *al-Ghunya li-Ṭalibī Ṭarīq al-Ḥaqq* (Beirut: Dār al-Kutub al-'Ilmiyya, 1997).
Khayyām, 'Umar: Edward Fitzgerald (trans.), *The Rubaiyat of Omar Khayyam* (London: The Folio Society, 1970, 7th imp. 1986).
Liddell, H. G., *An Intermediate Greek–English Lexicon*, founded upon the 7th edn of Liddell and Scott's Greek–English Lexicon (Oxford: Clarendon Press, 1968).
al-Madanī [al-Madyanī], Muḥammad, *Itḥāfāt al-Saniyya fī 'l-Aḥādīth al-Qudsiyya* (Hyderabad, 1905).
Madelung, Wilferd and Paul E. Walker *see under* Ibn al-Haytham.
Mālik b. Anas, *Kitāb al-Muwaṭṭa'* (Beirut: Dār al-Kitāb al-'Arabī, 1996); trans. Aisha Abdurrahman Bewley, *Al-Muwatta of Imam Malik ibn Anas: The First Formulation of Islamic Law*, The Islamic Classical Library (London and New York: Kegan Paul International, 1989).
al-Mas'ūdī, *Murūj al-Dhahab*, ed. Barbier de Meynard and Pavet de Courteille, rev. Charles Pellat, Section des Études Historiques XI (Beirut: Publications de l'Université Libanaise, 1973), vol. 4.
al-Māwardī, *al-Aḥkām al-Sulṭāniyya* (Beirut: Dār al-Kitāb al-'Arabī, 1994); trans. Asadullah Yate, *Al-Ahkam as-Sultaniyyah: The Laws of Islamic Governance* (London: TA-HA Publishers, 1996).
Mitha, Farouk *see under* al-Ghazālī.
Morris, James *see under* al-Yaman.
Muslim, *Ṣaḥīḥ* (Beirut: Dār Ibn Ḥazm, 1995).
al-Nawawī, *Matn al-Arba'īn al-Nawawiyya/Forty Hadith*, bilingual Arabic–English edn, trans. Ezzedin Ibrahim and Denys Johnson-Davies (Damascus: The Holy Koran Publishing House, 1977).
Nostradamus: *Nostradamus: The Illustrated Prophecies*, ed. Peter Lemesurier (Alresford: John Hunt, 2003).
Nyazee, Imran Ahsan Khan *see under* Ibn Rushd.
Opitz, H. G. (ed.), *Athanasius Werke* (Berlin and Leipzig: W. de Gruyter, 1934).
Paxton, E. H. *see under* Ḥusayn [Hussein], Ṭāhā.
Periplus:
G W. B. Huntingford (trans.), *The Periplus of the Erythraean Sea*, Hakluyt Society Second Series no. 151 (London: The Hakluyt Society, 1980).
Wilfred H. Schoff (trans.), *The Periplus of the Erythraean Sea* (New Delhi : Oriental Books Reprint Corporation, 1974: repr. of 1912 edn published by New York: Longmans, Green & Co.).
Pliny, *Natural History/Naturalis Historia*, trans. H. Rackham, bilingual Latin–English edn, Loeb Classical Library, 7 vols (London: William Heinemann; Cambridge, MA: Harvard University Press, 1968), vol. 4
Plotinus, A. H. Armstrong (ed. and trans), *Plotinus: Enneads*, bilingual Greek–English edn, Loeb Classical Library, 7 vols (Cambridge, MA: Harvard University Press; London: William Heinemann, 1988).
Poonawala, Ismail (trans. and ed.) *see under* al-Ṭabarī.
al-Qaraḍāwī, Yūsuf, *Kitāb al-Ḥalāl wa 'l-Ḥarām fī 'l-Islām*, 12th edn (Beirut: al-Maktab al-Islāmī, 1978).
al-Quds al-'Arabī, Wednesday 12 September 2001.
Qur'ān:
Abdullah Yusuf Ali (trans. and comment.), *The Holy Qur'ān: Text, Translation and Commentary* (Kuwait: Dhāt al-Salāsil, 1984).

A. J. Arberry (trans.), *The Koran Interpreted*, 2 vols (London: Allen and Unwin; New York: Macmillan, 1955).
Quṭb, Sayyid *see* Sayyid Quṭb.
Riḍā, Rashīd, *Ta'rīkh al-Ustādh al-Imām al Shaykh Muḥammad 'Abduh*, 3 vols (Cairo: Maṭba'at al-Manār, 1931).
Rosenthal, Franz *see under* Ibn Khaldūn.
Rossini, Karolus Conti (ed.), *Chrestomathia Arabica Meridionalis Epigraphica* [Sabaean with Latin index (Rome: Istituto Per L'Oriente, 1931).
al-Sarakhsī, *Kitāb al-Mabsūṭ* (Cairo: Maṭba'at al-Sa'ada, 1906), vol. 10.
Sayyid Quṭb, *al-'Adāla*:
al-'Adalā al-Ijtimā'iyya fī 'l-Islām, 6th edn (Beirut: Dār al-Shurūq, 1975).
John B. Hardie (trans.) (New York: Octagon Books, 1980).
William E. Shepard (trans.), *Sayyid Qutb and Islamic Activism: A Translation and Critical Analysis of Social Justice in Islam*, Social, Economic and Political Studies of the Middle East and Asia, vol. 54 (Leiden, New York and Cologne: E. J. Brill, 1996).
The various Arabic editions of Quṭb's *al-'Adāla al-Ijtimā'iyya* are as follows:
1st edn: Cairo: Maktabat Miṣr [1949].
2nd edn: Cairo: Maktabat Miṣr [1950].
3rd edn: Cairo: Sharikat al-Ṭab'a wa 'l-Ṣiḥāfa li 'l-Ikhwān al-Muslimīn, 1952.
4th edn: Ibid., 1954.
5th edn: Cairo: Dār Iḥyā' al-Kutub al-'Arabiyya, 1377/1958.
6th edn: Cairo: Maṭba'at 'Isa Bābī 'l-Ḥalabī, 1383/1964, repro Beirut: Dār al-Shurūq, 1974, 1981.
Sayyid Quṭb, *Fi Ẓilāl al-Qur'ān*, 20 vols in 10, 1st and 2nd edns (Cairo: Dār Iḥyā' al-Kutub al-'Arabiyya, 1952–9); 20 vols in 8, rev. edn (Beirut: Dār al-Ma'rifa and Dār Iḥyā' al-Turāth al 'Arabī, 1971); 6 vols, rev edn (Beirut: Dār al-Shurūq, 1973–4); vol. 6: pts 26–30 (Beirut: Dār al-Shurūq, n.d.; M. A. Salahi and A. A. Shamis (trans.), *In the Shade of the Qur'ān* (London: MWH Publishers, 1979), vol. 30.
Sayyid Quṭb, *Hādhā al-Dīn* (Cairo: Dār al-Qalam, 1962), trans. *This Religion of Islam (hadha 'd-din)* (Damascus: Holy Koran Publishing House, 1977).
Sayyid Quṭb, *Ma'ālim fī 'l-Ṭarīq* (Beirut: Dār al-Shurūq, nd, repr. of Cairo edn of 1964).
Sayyid Quṭb, *Ṭifl min al-Qarya* (Cairo: Dār al-Shurūq, 1946); ed. and trans. John Calvert and William Shepard, *A Child from the Village*, Middle East Literature in Translation (Syracuse, NY: Syracuse University Press, 2004).
Shaw, M. R. B., *Chronicles of the Crusades see under* De Villehardouin.
Simpson, D. P., *Cassell's New Latin–English, English–Latin Dictionary*, 3rd edn (London: Cassell, 1964).
Strabo, *The Geography of Strabo*, trans. Horace Leonard Jones, bilingual Greek–English edn, Loeb Classical Library (London: William Heinemann; Cambridge, MA: Harvard University Press, 1966), vol. 7.
al-Ṭabarī: *Ta'rīkh/History*
al-Ṭabarī: *Ta'rīkh al-rusul wa 'l-mulūk*, ed. M, J. de Goeje [under title *Annales quos scripsit Abu Djafar Mohammed Ibn Djarir At-Tabari*] (Leiden: E. J. Brill, 1964), Photomechanical reprint; Tertia Series 2 [trans. Bosworth, *Reunification, see below*]; Prima Series 4 [trans. Poonawala, *Last Years, see below*].
C. E. Bosworth (trans. and ed.), *The History of al-Ṭabarī (Ta'rīkh al-rusul wa 'l-mulūk)*: Volume XXXII: *The Reunification of the 'Abbasid Caliphate*, Bibliotheca Persica (Albany, NY: State University of New York Press, 1987).
C. E. Bosworth (trans. and ed.), *The History of al-Ṭabarī (Ta'rīkh al-rusul wa 'l-mulūk)*:

Volume XXXIII: *Storm and Stress along the Northern Frontiers of the 'Abbasid Caliphate*, Bibliotheca Persica (Albany, NY: State University of New York Press, 1991).

Ismail Poonawala (trans. and ed.), *The History of al-Ṭabarī (Ta'rīkh al-rusul wa 'l-mulūk): Volume IX: The Last Years of the Prophet*, Bibliotheca Persica (Albany, NY: State University of New York Press, 1990).

al-Ṭabarī, *Tafsīr al-Ṭabarī: Jāmi' al-Bayān 'an Ta'wīl Āy al-Qur'ān*, ed. Ṣalāḥ 'Abd al Fattāḥ al-Khālidī (Damascus: Dār al-Qalam; Beirut: Dār al-Shāmiyya, 1998), vol. 1; trans. J. Cooper (ed. and trans.), *The Commentary on the Qur'ān by Abū Ja'far Muḥammad b. Jarīr al-Ṭabarī* (Oxford: Oxford University Press, 1989), vol. 1.

Thomas À Kempis, *The Imitation of Christ* (London: Burns & Oates, n.d.).

Walshe, M. O'C. (ed. and trans.), *Meister Eckhart: Sermons and Treatises*, 3 vols (London: Watkins, 1979, 1981, 1985).

Watt, W. M. *see under* al-Ghazālī.

Wayment, Hilary *see under* Ḥusayn [Hussein], Ṭāhā.

Wehr, Hans, *A Dictionary of Modern Written Arabic*, 2nd printing (Wiesbaden: Otto Harrassowitz; London: George Allen & Unwin, 1966).

al-Yaman, Ja'far b. Manṣūr: James W. Morris, *The Master and the Disciple: An Early Islamic Spiritual Discourse*, A New Arabic Edition and English Translation of *Ja'far b. Mansur al-Yaman's Kitāb al-'Ālim wa 'l-Ghulām*, Ismaili,Texts and Translations Series, 3 (London and New York: I. B. Tauris in association with the Institute of Ismaili Studies, London, 2001)

Yāqūt al-Rūmī, *Mu'jam al-Buldān* (Beirut: Dār Ṣādir, 1977), vol. 3.

Yate, Asadullah *see under* al-Māwardī.

Secondary Sources

Abdalati, Hammudah, *Islam in Focus* (Kuwait: International Islamic Federation of Student Organizations, 1981).

Abdel Haleem, Muhammad, *Understanding the Qur'ān: Themes and Style* (London and New York: I. B. Tauris, 1999).

Abou El Fadl, Khaled, *Speaking in God's Name: Islamic Law, Authority and Women* (Oxford: Oneworld, 2001).

Abrahamov, Binyamin, *Islamic Theology: Traditionalism and Rationalism* (Edinburgh: Edinburgh University Press, 1998)

Abrahamov, Binyamin, 'Faḥr al-Dīn al-Rāzī on the Knowability of God's Essence and Attributes', *Arabica*, 49:2 (2002), pp. 204–30.

Ackroyd, Peter, *The Life of Thomas More* (London: Vintage, 1999).

Afsaruddin, Asma, *Excellence and Precedence: Medieval Islamic Discourse on Legitimate Leadership*, Islamic History and Civilization Studies and Texts, vol. 36 (Leiden, Boston, MA and Cologne: E. J. Brill, 2002).

Agius, Alfred (comp.), *Interfaith Dialogue: The Teaching of the Catholic Church* (London: Catholic Communications Service for the Committee for Other Faiths of the Catholic Bishops' Conference of England and Wales, 2002).

Akbar, M. J., *The Shade of Swords* (London: Routledge, 2003).

Akhavi, Shahrough, 'Quṭb, Sayyid' *see* Esposito (ed.), *Oxford Encyclopaedia of the Modern Islamic World*.

Altizer, Thomas J. J., *Mircea Eliade and the Dialectic of the Sacred* (Philadelphia: Westminster Press, 1963).

Andrae, Tor, *Mohammed: The Man and His Faith* (London: George Allen & Unwin, 1936).

Andrea, A. J., *Contemporary Sources for the Fourth Crusade*, (Leiden: E. J. Brill, 2000).

Angelus Press (ed.), *Is Tradition Excommunicated? A Collection of Independent Studies* (Kansas City: Angelus Press, 1993, 2003).

Anglican–Roman Catholic International Commission [ARCIC], *The Final Report*, Windsor, September 1981 (London: CTS/SPCK, 1982).

Anglican–Roman Catholic International Commission [ARCIC], *Salvation and the Church: An Agreed Statement*, with Commentary and Study Guide by M. Cecily Boulding and Timothy Bradshaw (London: Church House Publishing/CTS, 1987–9).

Anglican–Roman Catholic International Commission [ARCIC], *The Gift of Authority: Authority in the Church III* (London: CTS; Toronto: Anglican Book Centre; New York: Church Publishing Inc., 1999).

Anglican–Roman Catholic International Commission *see also* Murphy-O'Connor and Santer (eds).

Angould, M., *The Fourth Crusade: Event and Context* (London: Longman, 2004)

Appelbaum, David, 'The Moment of Modernity', *Sacred Web: A Journal of Tradition and Modernity*, 2 (December 1998).

Arberry, A. J., *Revelation and Reason in Islam* (London: George Allen & Unwin, 1957).

Arberry, A. J. *see also* Primary Sources s.v. *Qur'ān*.

Arnaldez, R., 'Ibn Rushd', *EI²*, vol. 3.

Ayalon, Ami, *The Press in the Arab Middle East: A History* (New York and Oxford: Oxford University Press, 1995).

Ayubi, N., *Political Islam: Religion and Politics in the Arab World* (London: Routledge, 1993).

Azar, George Baramki, 'The Digital Middle East', *ARAMCO WORLD*, 47:6(November–December 1996).

al-Azmeh, Aziz, *Islams and Modernities* (London and New York: Verso, 1993).

Backmann, E. Theodore, 'Lutheranism' *see* Lossky et al. (eds), *Dictionary of the Ecumenical Movement*.

Balda, Justo Lacunza *see* Lane, A. J.

Baldick, Julian, 'Among the Friends of God', *Times Literary Supplement*, 26 September 1986.

Barber, Malcolm, *The Cathars: Dualist Heretics in Languedoc in the High Middle Ages*, The Medieval World (Harlow: Pearson Education and Longman, 2000).

Barlow, Frank, *Thomas Beckett* (London: Folio Society, 2002; first publ. London: Weidenfeld & Nicolson, 1986).

Barnes, Michael R. and David H. Williams (eds), *Arianism after Arius: Essays on the Development of the Fourth-Century Trinitarian Conflicts* (Edinburgh: T. & T. Clark, 1993).

Barraclough, Geoffrey, *The Medieval Papacy*, Library of European Civilisation (London: Thames & Hudson, 1968, repr. 1992).

Barton, Greg, *Abdurrahman Wahid: Muslim Democrat, Indonesian President: A View from the Inside* (Sydney: University of New South Wales Press, 2002).

Baxter, Jenny and Malcolm Downing (eds), *The Day that Shook the World: Understanding September 11th* (London: BBC Worldwide Ltd, 2001).

Bell, David, *Husserl*, The Arguments of the Philosophers (London and New York: Routledge, 1990, 1995).

Bergen, Peter L., *Holy War, Inc.: Inside the Secret World of Osama bin Laden* (London: Weidenfeld & Nicolson, 2001).

Bill, James A. and John Alden Williams, *Roman Catholics and Shi'i Muslims: Prayer, Passion and Politics* (Chapel Hill and London: University of North Carolina Press, 2002).

Black, Antony, *The History of Islamic Political Thought: From the Prophet to the Present* (Edinburgh: Edinburgh University Press, 2001).

Blake, William, *[Poems of] William Blake*, ed. Peter Butler, Everyman's Poetry 3 (London: J. M. Dent, 1996).

Blet, Pierre, *Pius XII and the Second World War According to the Archives of the Vatican* (Herefordshire: Gracewing, 1999).

Bondanella, Peter, 'Interpretation, Overinterpretation, Paranoid Interpretation and *Foucault's Pendulum*' *see* Capozzi (ed.), *Reading Eco.*

Bonneterre, Didier, *The Liturgical Movement from Dom Guéranger to Annibale Bugnini, or The Trojan Horse in the City of God* (Kansas City: Angelus Press, 2002).

Book of Common Prayer, The (Oxford: Oxford University Press; London: Geoffrey Cumberlege, n.d.).

Bosworth, Clifford Edmund, *The New Islamic Dynasties: A Chronological and Genealogical Manual* (Edinburgh: Edinburgh University Press, 1996).

Bosworth, Clifford Edmund *see also* Primary Sources s.v. al-Ṭabarī.

Bouchard, Norma, 'Whose "Excess of Wonder" Is It Anyway? Reading Eco's Tangle of Hermetic and Pragmatic Semiosis in *The Island of the Day Before*' *see* Capozzi (ed.), *Reading Eco.*

Bowie, Fiona, *Anthropology of Religion: An Introduction* (Oxford: Blackwell, 2000).

Bowker, John, *Sacred Place*, Themes in Religious Studies series (London: Pinter, 1994, 2000).

Braudel, Fernand, *Civilization Matérielle, Économie et Capitalisme (XVe–XVIIIe Siècle)*, 3 vols (Paris: Librairie Armand Colin, 1979).

Braudel, Fernand, *La Méditerranée et le Monde Méditerranéen à l'Epoque de Philippe II* (Paris: Librairie Armand Colin, 1949; 2nd rev. edn 1966); trans. Siân Reynolds, *The Mediterranean and the Mediterranean World in the Age of Philip II*, 2 vols (London: Collins, 1972).

Brockelmann, C., 'Al-Māwardī', *EI*^{2}, vol. 6.

Brown, Daniel, *Rethinking Tradition in Modern Islamic Thought*, Cambridge Middle East Series no. 5 (Cambridge: Cambridge University Press, 1999).

Brown, David, *Tradition and Imagination: Revelation and Change* (Oxford: Oxford University Press, 1999).

Brown, Raymond E. and Thomas Aquinas Collins, 'Church Pronouncements' *see* R. E. Brown et al. (eds), *New Jerome Biblical Commentary.*

Brown, Raymond E., Joseph A. Fitzmyer and Roland E. Murphy (eds), *The New Jerome Biblical Commentary* (London: Geoffrey Chapman, 1990).

Brown, Raymond E., Carolyn Osiek and Pheme Perkins, 'Early Church' *see* R. E. Brown et al. (eds), *New Jerome Biblical Commentary.*

Bullock, Alan and Oliver Stallybrass (eds), *The Fontana Dictionary of Modern Thought*, new rev. edn by Alan Bullock and Stephen Trombley assisted by Bruce Eadie (London: Fontana Press, HarperCollins Publishers, 1988).

Bunt, Gary R., *Virtually Islamic: Computer-Mediated Communication and Cyber Islamic Environments*, Religion, Culture and Society series (Cardiff: University of Wales Press, 2000).

Bunt, Gary R., *Islam in the Digital Age: E-Jihad, Online Fatwas and Cyber Islamic Environments* (London and Stirling, VA: Pluto Press, 2003).

Burgat, François, 'Veils and Obscuring Lenses' *see* Esposito and Burgat (eds), *Modernizing Islam.*

Burke, Jason, *Al-Qaeda: Casting a Shadow of Terror* (London and New York: I. B. Tauris, 2003).

Burton, John, *The Sources of Islamic Law: Islamic Theories of Abrogation* (Edinburgh: Edinburgh University Press, 1990; repr. 2003).

Burton, John, *An Introduction to the Ḥadīth*, Islamic Surveys series (Edinburgh: Edinburgh University Press, 1994)

Butler, Scott, Norman Dahlgren and David Hess, *Jesus, Peter, and the Keys: A Scriptural Handbook on the Papacy* (Goleta, CA: Queenship Publishing, 1996).
Cachia, Pierre, *Ṭāhā Ḥusayn: His Place in the Egyptian Literary Renaissance* (London: Luzac, 1956).
Cahen, Cl. and M. Talbi, 'Ḥisba', *EI*², vol. 3.
Canon Law Society of Great Britain and Ireland, *The Code of Canon Law* (London: Collins, 1983).
Cantwell Smith, Wilfrid, *Islam in Modern History* (Princeton, NJ: Princeton University Press, 1957, 1966).
Capozzi, Rocco, 'Intertextuality, Metaphors and Metafiction as Cognitive Strategies in *The Island of the Day Before*' *see* Capozzi (ed.), *Reading Eco.*
Capozzi, Rocco (ed.), *Reading Eco: An Anthology*, Advances in Semiotics (Bloomington and Indianapolis: Indiana University Press, 1997).
Casanova, J., *Public Religions in the Modern World* (Chicago: University of Chicago Press, 1994).
Catechism of the Catholic Church (London: Geoffrey Chapman, 1994).
Cesari, Jocelyne, 'Muslim Minorities in Europe: The Silent Revolution' *see* Esposito and Burgat (eds), *Modernizing Islam.*
Chadwick, Henry, *Augustine: A Very Short Introduction* (Oxford: Oxford University Press, 2001).
Chadwick, Henry, *The Church in Ancient Society: From Galilee to Gregory the Great* (Oxford: Oxford University Press, 2001).
Charan, Anubha, 'Ayodha: Digging up India's Holy Places', *History Today*, 54:1 (January 2004).
Chaumont, E., 'al-Salaf wa 'l-Khalaf', *EI*², vol. 8.
Christian Order, 'Extra Ecclesiam, nulla salus', *Christian Order*, 42:10 (October 2001).
Clements, William, 'The Declaration "Dominus Jesus"', *Together in Christ*, 20:62 (February 2002).
Clifford, Richard J. and Roland E. Murphy, 'Genesis' *see* R. E. Brown et al. (eds), *New Jerome Biblical Commentary.*
Cobley, Paul and Litza Jansz, *Introducing Semiotics* (Cambridge: Icon Books, 1999).
Cole, Juan, *Sacred Space and Holy War: The Politics, Culture and History of Shi'ite Islam* (London: I. B. Tauris, 2002).
Coletti, Theresa, 'Bellydancing: Gender, Silence and the Women of *Foucault's Pendulum*' *see* Capozzi (ed.), *Reading Eco.*
Congar, Yves M.-J., *Tradition and Traditions* (San Diego: Basilica Press; Needham Heights, MA: Simon & Schuster, 1997; repr. of London: Burns & Oates edn, 1966).
Constitution on the Sacred Liturgy (Sacrosanctum Concilium) see Flannery (ed.), *Vatican Council II.*
Cook, Michael, *Commanding Right and Forbidding Wrong in Islamic Thought* (Cambridge: Cambridge University Press, 2000).
Cornwall, John, *Hitler's Pope: The Secret History of Pius XII* (London: Viking, 1999).
Cornwall, John, *Breaking Faith: The Pope, the People and the Future of Catholicism* (London: Viking, 2001).
Cornwall, John, *The Pope in Winter: The Dark Face of John Paul II's Papacy* (London: Viking, 2004).
Cornwall, John *see also* Contemporary Media Sources
Corrington, Robert S., *A Semiotic Theory of Theology and Philosophy* (Cambridge: Cambridge University Press, 2000).

Coulson, N. J., *A History of Islamic Law*, Islamic Surveys 2 (Edinburgh: Edinburgh University Press, 1964).

Coulson, N. J., *Conflicts and Tensions in Islamic Jurisprudence*, Publications of the Center for Middle Eastern Studies, no. 5 (Chicago and London: University of Chicago Press, 1969).

Crouan, Denis, *La Liturgie après Vatican II: Effondrement ou redressement?* (Paris: Pierre Téqui, 1999); trans. Marc Sebane, *The Liturgy After Vatican II: Collapsing or Resurgent?* (San Francisco: Ignatius Press, 2001).

Crouan, Denis, *La Liturgie confisquée: Lettre ouverte aux évêques et tous qui trahissent la liturgie conciliaire* (Paris: Pierre Téqui, 1997); trans. Marc Sebane, *The Liturgy Betrayed* (San Francisco: Ignatius Press, 2000).

Culler, Jonathan, *Saussure*, Fontana Modern Masters (London: Fontana/Collins, 1976, 1985).

Daniel, Norman, *Islam and the West: The Making of an Image* (Edinburgh: Edinburgh University Press, 1960, 1966).

Daniel, Norman, *Islam, Europe and Empire* (Edinburgh: Edinburgh University Press, 1966).

Davies, Douglas, 'Christianity' *see* Holm (ed.), *Sacred Place*.

Davies, Michael, *Cranmer's Godly Order* (Kansas City: Angelus Press, 1976).

Davies, Michael, *Pope John's Council* (Kansas City: Angelus Press, 1976).

Davies, Michael, *Apologia Pro Marcel Lefebvre*, 3 vols (Kansas City: Angelus Press, 1979).

Davies, Michael, *Pope Paul's New Mass* (Kansas City: Angelus Press, 1980).

Davies, Michael, *Partisans of Error: St Pius X Against the Modernists* (Long Prairie: Neumann Press, 1983).

Davies, Norman, *Europe: A History* (London: Pimlico, 1997).

De Chergé, Dom Christian, 'The Testament of Dom Christian de Chergé', *White Fathers–White Sisters*, 348 (October–November 1999).

De Lauretis, Teresa, 'Gaudy Rose: Eco and Narcissism' *see* Capozzi (ed.), *Reading Eco*.

De Saussure, Ferdinand, *Cours de Linguistigue Générale*, trans. W. Baskin, *Course in General Linguistics* (Glasgow: Fontana, 1974), trans. R. Harris, *Course in General Linguistics* (London: Duckworth, 1983).

Declaration on Christian Education (Gravissimum Educationis) see Flannery (ed.), *Vatican Council II*.

Declaration on the Relation of the Church to Non-Christian Religions (Nostra Aetate) see Flannery (ed.), *Vatican Council II*.

Decree on Ecumenism (Unitatis Redintegratio) see Flannery (ed.), *Vatican Council II*.

Decree on the Church's Missionary Activity (Ad Gentes) see Agius (comp.), *Interfaith Dialogue*.

Deely, John, 'Looking Back on *A Theory of Semiotics*: One Small Step for Philosophy, One Giant Leap for the Doctrine of Signs' *see* Capozzi (ed.), *Reading Eco*.

Denis, Gabriel, *The Reign of Jesus Through Mary*, trans. Andrew. Somers, 6th edn (England: The Montfort Fathers, 1958).

Denley, Peter, 'The Mediterranean in the Age of the Renaissance, 1200-1500' *see* Holmes (ed.), *Oxford Illustrated History of Medieval Europe*.

Dillon, Richard J., 'Acts of the Apostles' *see* R. E. Brown et al. (eds), *New Jerome Biblical Commentary*.

Dinges, William D., 'Roman Catholic Traditionalism and Activist Conservatism in the United States' *see* Marty and Appleby (eds), *Fundamentalisms Observed*.

Doe, Brian, *Southern Arabia*, New Aspects of Antiquity (London: Thames & Hudson, 1971).

Dogmatic Constitution on Divine Revelation (Dei Verbum) see Flannery (ed.), *Vatican Council II*.

Dogmatic Constitution on the Church (Lumen Gentium) see Flannery (ed.), *Vatican Council II*.

Donner, Fred M., 'The Sources of Islamic Conceptions of War' *see* Kelsay and Johnson (eds), *Just War and Jihad.*

Douglas, Mary, *Purity and Danger: An Analysis of the Concepts of Pollution and Taboo* (London and New York: Routledge, repr. 1996).

Dreyfus, Hubert, 'Husserl, Heidegger and Modern Existentialism' *see* Magee, *The Great Philosophers.*

Duffy, Eamon, *The Stripping of the Altars: Traditional Religion in England c.1400-c.1580* (New Haven, CT and London: Yale University Press, 1992).

Duffy, Eamon, *Saints and Sinners: A History of the Popes* (London: Goodliffe Neale, 1999).

Dumper, M., *The Politics of Sacred Space: The Old City of Jerusalem in the Middle East Conflict* (London: Lynne Rienner Publishers, 2002).

Dupret, Baudouin, 'A Return to the Shariah? Egyptian Judges and, Referring to Islam' *see* Esposito and Burgat (eds), *Modernizing Islam.*

Dutton, Yasin, *The Origins of Islamic Law: The Qur'an, the Muwaṭṭa' and Medinan 'Amal*, Culture and Civilisation in the Middle East (Richmond: Curzon, 1999).

Eco, Umberto, 'An Author and His Interpreters' *see* Capozzi (ed.), *Reading Eco.*

Eco, Umberto, *La struttura assente* (Milan: Bompiani, 1968).

Eco, Umberto, *La forme del contenuto* (Milan: Bompiani, 1971).

Eco, Umberto, *A Theory of Semiotics*, Advances in Semiotics (Bloomington and London: Indiana University Press, 1976).

Eco, Umberto, *The Role of the Reader: Explorations in the Semiotics of Text*, Advances in Semiotics (Bloomington and London: Indiana University Press, 1979).

Eco, Umberto, *Il nome della rosa* (Milan: Bompiani, 1980); trans. William Weaver, *The Name of the Rose* (New York: Harcourt Brace Jovanovich, 1983; London: Secker & Warburg, 1983; Pan/Picador, 1984).

Eco, Umberto, *Semiotics and the Philosophy of Language* (London: Macmillan Press, 1984).

Eco, Umberto, *Travels in Hyperreality: Essays*, trans. William Weaver (London: Picador edn, Pan Books in assoc. with Secker & Warburg, 1987; first published in the UK by Secker & Warburg under the title *Faith in Fakes*).

Eco, Umberto, *Il pendolo di Foucault* (Milan: Bompiani, 1988); trans. William Weaver, *Foucault's Pendulum* (New York: Harcourt Brace Jovanovich, 1989; London: Secker & Warburg, 1989).

Eco, Umberto, *The Limits of Interpretation*, Advances in Semiotics (Bloomington and Indianapolis: Indiana University Press, 1990).

Eco, Umberto, *L'isola del giorno prima* (Milan: Bompiani, 1994); trans. William Weaver, *The Island of the Day Before* (New York and San Diego: Harcourt Brace Jovanovich 1995; London: Secker & Warburg, 1995; London: Minerva, Mandarin Paperbacks, 1996).

Eco. Umberto. *Serendipities* (London: Phoenix, 1999).

Eco, Umberto, *Baudolino* (Milan: Bompiani, 2000); trans. William Weaver, *Baudolino* (London: Secker & Warburg 2002).

Eco, Umberto, *Kant and the Platypus: Essays on Language and Cognition*, trans. Alastair McEwen (New York: Harcourt Brace & Co., 2000).

Eco, Umberto, *Mouse or Rat? Translation as Negotiation* (London: Weidenfeld & Nicolson, 2003).

Edge, Ian (ed.), *Islamic Law and Legal Theory* (Aldershot: Dartmouth Publishing Co., 1993).

Eickelman, Dale F., *Moroccan Islam: Tradition and Society in a Pilgrimage Center*, Modern Middle East Series no. 1 (Austin and London: University of Texas Press, 1976, 1981).

Eliade, Mircea, 'Čarţile populaire in literatura româneasca', *Revista Fundaţiilor Regale*, 6 (1939).

Eliade, Mircea, *Patterns in Comparative Religion*, trans. Rosemary Sheed (London and New York: Sheed &Ward, 1958).

Eliade, Mircea, *The Sacred and the Profane: The Nature of Religion*, trans. Willard R. Trask (San Diego, New York and London: Harcourt Brace & Co., 1959).

Eliade, Mircea, *A History of Religious Ideas*, 3 vols (vol. 1: London: Collins, 1979; vols 2–3: Chicago and London: University of Chicago Press, 1982, 1985).

Eliade, Mircea (ed.-in-chief), Charles J. Adams et al. (eds), *The Encyclopedia of Religion*, 16 vols (New York: Macmillan, 1987; London: Collier Macmillan 1987).

Elton, G. R., *Reformation Europe 1517–1559*, The Fontana History of Europe (London and Glasgow: Collins, 1964).

Elton, G. R., *England under the Tudors* (London: The Folio Society, 1997; first publ. London: Methuen, 1955; 3rd edn London: Routledge, 1991).

Encyclopaedia of Islam [*EI*²] ed. H. A. R. Gibb et al., 2nd edn, 12 vols, incl. Supplement (Leiden: E. J. Brill; London: Luzac [for some vols], 1960–2004).

Endress, Gerhard, *An Introduction to Islam* (Edinburgh: Edinburgh University Press, 1988).

Esposito, John, *The Islamic Threat: Myth or Reality?*, 2nd edn (New York and Oxford: Oxford University Press, 1995).

Esposito, John L. (ed.), *The Oxford Encyclopaedia of the Modern Islamic World*, 4 vols (New York and Oxford: Oxford University Press, 1995), vol. 2.

Esposito, John L. (ed.), *Oxford History of Islam* (Oxford: Oxford University Press, 1999).

Esposito, John L., *Unholy War: Terror in the Name of God* (Oxford: Oxford University Press, 2003).

Esposito, John L. and François Burgat (eds), *Modernizing Islam: Religion in the Public Sphere in the Middle East and Europe* (London: Hurst & Co., 2003).

Evans-Pritchard, E. E., *Witchcraft, Oracles and Magic Among the Azande* (Oxford: Clarendon Press, 1937, abridged version 1976).

Evans-Pritchard, E. E., *Nuer Religin* (Oxford: Clarendon Press, 1956, repr. Oxford: Oxford University Press, 1974).

Evans-Pritchard, E. E., *Theories of Primitive Religion* (Oxford: Oxford University Press, 1972 [orig. publ. 1965]).

Evans-Pritchard, E. E., *Man and Woman Among the Azande* (London: Faber, 1974).

Ewans, Martin, *Afghanistan: A New History*, 2nd edn (London and New York: Routledge-Curzon, 2002).

Fadzil, Ammar, *The Concept of Ḥukm in the Qur'ān*, unpublished Ph.D. thesis, University of Edinburgh, 1999.

Fakhry, Majid, *A History of Islamic Philosophy*, 2nd edn (London: Longman; New York: Columbia University Press, 1983).

Farrar, Frederic W., *The Early Days of Christianity* (London, Paris and Melbourne: Cassell & Co., 1897).

Fathers of Holy Cross Seminary [Goulburn, Australia] (eds), *Most Asked Questions About the Society of Saint Pius X* (Kansas City: Angelus Press, 1997, 2001).

Filali-Ansary, Abdou, 'The Debate on Secularism in Contemporary Societies of Muslims', *ISIM Newsletter*, no. 2 (March 1999).

Finn, Peter, *History of the Priory, Bishops Waltham* (Winchester: Hedera Books, 2002)

Fitzgerald, Michael and NCR, 'Optimism on the Christian–Muslim Front; Papal Appeal for Peace; Vatican "note" on Politics': Interview, 28 December 2002: e-mail record.

Fitzmyer, Joseph A., 'Paul' *see* R. E. Brown et al. (eds), *New Jerome Biblical Commentary*.

Fitzmyer, Joseph A., 'Pauline Theology, *see* R. E. Brown et al. (eds), *New Jerome Biblical Commentary*.

Flannery, Austin (ed.), *Vatican Council II: The Conciliar and Post-Conciliar Documents*, rev. edn (Dublin: Dominican Publication; Leominster: Fowler Wright Books; New Town, NSW, Australia: E. J. Dwyer, 1988), vol. 1.

Fleischner, Eva, 'The Spirituality of Pius XII' *see* Rittner and Roth (eds), *Pope Pius XII*.

Foucault, Michel, *The Order of Things: An Archaeology of the Human Sciences* (London: Tavistock Publications, 1970).

Foucault, Michel, *The Archaeology of Knowledge* (London: Tavistock Publications, 1972).

Freely, John, *Istanbul: The Imperial City* (Harmondsworth: Penguin Books, 1996).

Gaarder, Jostein, *Sofies Verden* (Oslo: H. Aschehoug & Co. (W. Nygaard), 1991); trans. Paulette Moller, *Sophie's World: A Novel about the History of Philosophy* (London: Phoenix House, 1995).

Gaarder, Jostein, *Vita Brevis: A Letter to St Augustine* (London: Phoenix, Orion Books, 1998, 2000).

Gaborieau, Marc, 'Les ordres mystiques dans le sous-continent indien' *see* Popovic and Veinstein (eds), *Les ordres mystiques*.

Gamber, Klaus, *The Reform of the Roman Liturgy* (San Juan Capistrano: Una Voce Press, 1993).

Geertz, Clifford, *Islam Observed* (New Haven, CT and London: Yale University Press, 1968; repr. as a Phoenix Book: Chicago and London: University of Chicago Press, 1971).,

Gellner, Ernest, *Postmodernism, Reason and Religion* (London and New York: Routledge, 1992).

Gerson, Lloyd P., *Plotinus*, The Arguments of the Philosophers (London and New York: Routledge, 1994).

Gibb, H. A. R., *Mohammedanism: An Historical Survey*, 2nd edn, The Home University Library of Modern Knowledge, 197 (London, New York and Toronto: Oxford University Press, 1953, 1964).

Gibb, H. A. R., *Studies on the Civilization of Islam*, ed. Stanford J. Shaw and William R. Polk (London: Routledge & Kegan Paul, 1962).

Gibb, H. A. R. *see also Encyclopaedia of Islam* [*EI*^{2}] and *Shorter Encyclopaedia of Islam* [*EIS*],

Gibb, H. A. R. and J. H. Kramers (eds), *Shorter Encyclopaedia of Islam* [*EIS*] ([Leiden: E. J. Brill; London: Luzac, 1961).

Giblin, Charles Homer, 'The Second Letter to the Thessalonians' *see* R. E. Brown et al. (eds), *New Jerome Biblical Commentary*.

Gilsenan, Michael, *Recognizing Islam: An Anthropologist's Introduction* (London and Sydney Croom Helm, 1982, repr. 1984).

Glassé, Cyril, *The Concise Encyclopaedia of Islam* (London: Stacey International, 1989).

Goldziher, Ignaz, *Muslim Studies (Muhammedanische Studien)*, ed. S. M. Stern, trans. C. R. Barber and S. M. Stern, 2 vols (London: Allen & Unwin, 1967, 1971).

Grabar, Oleg, *The Formation of Islamic Art* (New Haven, CT and London: Yale University Press, 1973, 1977).

Grace, Peter, 'The Flight from Biblical Truth', *Christian Order*, 43:3 (March 2002), pp. 179–87.

Gray, John, *Al-Qaeda and What It Means to be Modern* (London: Faber, 2003).

Green, Timothy Michael Wake, *Factors Affecting Attitudes to Apostasy in Pakistan*, unpublished MA dissertation, University of London, SOAS, 1998.

Gregg, Robert C. (ed.), *Arianism: Historical and Theological Reassessments: Papers from the Ninth International Conference on Patristic Studies* (5–10 September 1983, Oxford, England), Patristic Monograph Series, no. 11 (Cambridge, MA: Philadelphia Patristic Foundation, 1985).

Gregorian, Vartan, *Islam: A Mosaic Not a Monolith* (Washington, DC: Brookings Institution Press, 2003).

Grey, Mary, 'Augustine and the Legacy of Guilt', *New Blackfriars*, 70:832 (November 1989).

Groom, Nigel, *Frankincense and Myrrh: A Study of the Arabian Incense Trade*, Arab Background Series (London and New York: Librairie du Liban, 1981).

Guillaume, Alfred, *The Traditions of Islam: An Introduction to the Study of the Hadith Literature* (Beirut: Khayats, 1966).

Gumpel, Peter, 'Cornwall's Pope', *Christian Order*, 42:2 (February 2001).

Hallaq, Wael B., 'Was the Gate of Ijtihād Closed?', *International Journal of Middle East Studies*, 16 (1984), pp. 3–41.

Hallaq, Wael B., *A History of Islamic Legal Theories: An Introduction to Sunnī Uṣūl al-Fiqh* (Cambridge: Cambridge University Press, 1997, 1999).

Hallaq, Wael B., *Authority, Continuity and Change in Islamic Law* (Cambridge: Cambridge University Press, 2001).

Hallaq, Wael B., 'Ijtihād' *see* Esposito (ed), *Oxford Encyclopaedia of the Modern Islamic World.*

Halliday, Fred, *Islam and the Myth of Confrontation* (London and New York: I. B. Tauris, 1994).

Halliday, Fred, *Two Hours that Shook the World: September 11 2001: Causes and Consequences* (London: Saqi Books, 2001).

Harrison, Brian W., 'On Rewriting the Bible', *Christian Order*, 43:3 (March 2002), pp. 155–78.

Hartshorne, Charles, Paul Weiss and A. W. Burks (eds), *The Collected Papers of Charles Sanders Peirce*, 8 vols (Cambridge, MA: Harvard University Press, 1931–58).

Harvey, D., *The Priest and the King* (London: I. B. Tauris, 1998).

Hawi. K. S., *Khalil Gibran: His Background. Character and Works* (Beirut: Arab Institute for Research and Publishing, 1972).

Hawkes, Terence, *Structuralism and Semiotics*, New Accents (London: Methuen, 1977, 1985).

Heather, Peter, 'The Pope, the Emperor and the Legacy of Ancient Rome', *Folio* (Summer 2003).

Hebblethwaite, Peter, *John XXXIII: Pope of the Century* (London and New York: Continuum, 2000).

Heelas, Paul (ed.), *Religion, Modernity and Postmodernity*, Religion and Modernity series (Oxford: Oxford University Press, 1998).

Hefner, R., *Civil Islam: Muslims and Democratization in Indonesia*, Princeton Studies in Muslim Politics (Princeton: Princeton University Press, 2000).

Heidegger, Martin, *Being and Time*, trans. Joan Stambaugh (Albany, NY: State University of New York Press, 1996).

Hill, Edmund, 'Comment: St Augustine's two vocations' *New Blackfriars*, 67:793–4 (July–August 1986).

Hillenbrand, Carole, *The Crusades: Islamic Perspectives* (Edinburgh: Edinburgh University Press, 1999).

Hintikka, Jaakko, 'The Phenomenological Dimension' *see* Smith and Smith, *Cambridge Companion to Husserl.*

Hodgson, M. G. S., *The Venture of Islam*, 3 vols (Chicago: Chicago University Press, 1974)

Hogue, John, *The Last Pope: The Decline and Fall of the Church of Rome: The Prophecies of St Malachy for the New Millennium* (Shaftesbury: Element, 1998).

Holm, Jean (ed.) with John Bowker, *Sacred Place*, Themes in Religious Studies series (London and New York: Pinter, 1994, 2000).

Holmes, George (ed.), *The Oxford Illustrated History of Medieval Europe* (Oxford and New York: Oxford University Press, 1988, 1996).
Hooker, M. B., *Indonesian Islam: Social Change through Contemporary Fatāwā*, Southeast Asia Publications series (Asian Studies Association of Australia in association with Crows Nest, NSW: Allen & Unwin; Honolulu: University of Hawai'i Press, 2003).
Hourani, Albert, *Arabic Thought in the Liberal Age 1798–1939* (Cambridge: Cambridge University Press, 1983, 1988).
Hourani, Albert, *A History of the Arab Peoples* (London: Faber , 1991).
Hourani, George F., *Islamic Rationalism: The Ethics of 'Abd al-Jabbar* (Oxford: Clarendon Press, 1971).
Huntington, Samuel P., 'The Clash of Civilizations', *Foreign Affairs*, 72:3 (Summer 1993), pp. 22–8.
Huntington, Samuel P., *The Clash of Civilizations and the Remaking of World Order* (London and New York: Touchstone Books, 1998).
Huntington, Samuel P., *Who Are We? America's Crisis of National Identity* (London: Free, 2004).
Hurvitz, Nimrod, *The Formation of Ḥanbalism: Piety into Power*, Culture and Civilization in the Middle East (London: RoutledgeCurzon, 2002).
Husserl, Edmund, *The Idea of Phenomenology*, trans. William P. Alston and George Nakhnikian (The Hague: Martinus Nijhoff, 1964).
Husserl, Edmund, Husserliana edn of Husserl's Collected Works, vols 19:1–2: *Logische Untersuchungen: Zweite Band: Untersuchungun zur Phänomenologie und Theorie der Erkenntnis*, ed. U. Panzer, 2 vols (The Hague: Nijhoff, 1984); trans. J. N. Findlay (New York: Humanities Press, 1970).
Hutcheon, Linda, 'Irony-clad Foucault' *see* Capozzi (ed.), *Reading Eco*.
Ibrahim, I. A., *A Brief Illustrated Guide to Understanding Islam*, 2nd edn (Houston, TX: Darussalam Publishers, 1997).
Islam 21 Forum, 'Debating Modernism and "ijtihad" in Islam', *Islam 21*, 23 (June 2000).
al-Jamri, Mansour (ed.), 'Addressing contemporary challenges with a new vision', *Islam 21*, 23 (June 2000).
Jansen, J. J. G., *The Dual Nature of Islamic Fundamentalism* (London and Ithaca, NY: Hurst, 1997).
Jansen, J. J. G., 'Uṣūliyya 2. In Modern Islamic theologico-political parlance', *EI*[2], vol. 10.
John XXIII, Pope, *Journal of a Soul* (London: Geoffrey Chapman, 1965).
John Paul II, Pope, *Ecclesia in Europa* [Post-Synodal Apostolic Exhortation] (London: CTS, 2003).
Johnson, James Turner and John Kelsay (eds), *Cross, Crescent and Sword: The Justification and Limitation of War in Western and Islamic Tradition*, Contributions to the Study of Religion, no. 27 (New York, Westport, CT and London : Greenwood Press, 1990).
Johnston, D. and C. Sampson, *Religion: The Missing Dimension of Statecraft* (Oxford: Oxford University Press, 1994).
Joseph, Roger, 'The Semiotics of the Islamic Mosque', *Arab Studies Quarterly*, 3:3 (Autumn 1981).
Journal of Semitic Studies, 46:1 (Spring 2001).
Juynboll, G. H. A., 'Sunna', *EI*[2], vol. 9.
Kallistos of Diokleia, Bishop *see* Ware, Timothy.
Kamali, Mohammad Hashim, *Principles of Islamic Jurisprudence*, rev. edn (Cambridge: Islamic Texts Society, 1991).
al-Kanadi, Abu Bilal Mustafa, *The Islamic Ruling on Music and Singing, in Light of the Quraan,*

the Sunnah and the Consensus of Our Pious Predecessors, 2nd edn (Jedda: Bilal M. al-Kanadi & Brothers, 1998; first publ. 1985).

Kane, Ousmane, *Muslim Modernity in Postcolonial Nigeria: A Study of the Society for the Removal of Innovation and Reinstatement of Tradition*, Islam in Africa, vol. 1 (Leiden and Boston, MA: E. J. Brill, 2003).

Kasimow, Harold, 'Modern Muslim Perceptions of Judaism and Christianity', *Interreligious Insight: A Journal of Dialogue and Engagement*, 2:4 (October 2004).

al-Kaysī, Marwān Ibrāhīm, *Morals and Manners in Islam: A Guide to Islamic Ādāb* (Leicester: The Islamic Foundation, 1994).

Kedar, B. (ed.), *Sacred Space: Shrine, City, Land* (London: Palgrave; New York: New York University Press, 1998).

Kedourie, Elie, *Afghani and 'Abduh: An Essay on Religious Unbelief and Political Activism in Modern Islam* (London: Frank Cass, 1966).

Kelleher, James P., 'Historico-Critical Sedition', *Christian Order*, 43:3 (March 2002), pp. 188–95.

Kelly, J. D. N., *Early Christian Doctrines*, 5th rev. edn (London: A. & C. Black, 1977).

Kelly, J. D. N., *The Oxford Dictionary of Popes* (Oxford: Oxford University Press, 1988, 1996).

Kelsay, John and James Turner Johnson (eds), *Just War and Jihad: Historical and Theoretical Perspectives on War and Peace in Western and Islamic Traditions*, Contributions to the Study of Religions, no. 28 (New York, Westport, CT and London: Greenwood Press, 1991).

Kennedy, Hugh, *The Prophet and the Age of the Caliphates: The Islamic Near East from the Sixth to the Eleventh Century*, A History of the Near East (London and New York: Longman, 1986).

Kepel, Gilles, *Jihad: The Trail of Political Islam* (Cambridge, MA: Harvard University Press, 2002).

Ker, Ian, *John Henry Newman: A Biography* (Oxford: Clarendon Press, 1988).

Ker, Ian, *Newman and the Fullness of Christianity* (Edinburgh: T. & T. Clark, 1993, 1998).

Khalil, Georges, 'The Working Group Modernity and Islam', *ISIM Newsletter*, no. 2 (March 1999).

Khan, Muhammad Qamaruddin, 'al-Māwardi' *see* Sharif (ed.), *History of Muslim Philosophy*, vol. I.

Khan, Muqtedar, 'Muslim Women: Caught in the Crossfire', *Arabies Trends*, 25 (November 1995).

Kidd, B. J., *A History of the Church to AD 461*, 3 vols (Oxford: Clarendon Press, 1922).

Kiser, John W., *The Monks of Tibhirine: Faith, Love and Terror in Algeria* (New York: St. Martin's Press, 2002).

Kitagawa, Joseph M. and Charles H. Long, 'CurriculumVitae' *see* Kitagawa and Long (eds), *Myths and Symbols*.

Kitagawa, Joseph M. and Charles H. Long (eds), with the collaboration of Jerald C. Brauer and Marshall G. S. Hodgson, *Myths and Symbols: Studies in Honor of Mircea Eliade* (Chicago and London: The University of Chicago Press, 1969).

Kouloughli, Djamel E., 'L'Influence Mu'tazilite sur la Naissance et le Développement de la Rhétorique Arabe', *Arabic Sciences and Philosophy*, 12 (2002).

Kramers, J. H. *see Shorter Encyclopaedia of Islam* [*EIS*].

Kselman, John S. and Ronald D. Witherup, 'Modern New Testament Criticism' *see* R. E. Brown et al. (eds), *New Jerome Biblical Commentary*.

Kurzman, Charles, 'Liberal Islam: Not a Contradiction in Terms', *ISIM Newsletter*, no. 2 (March 1999).

Laisney, F., *Archbishop Lefebvre and the Vatican* (Kansas City: Angelus Press, 1989).

Lakhani, M. Ali, 'Editorial', *Sacred Web: A Journal of Tradition and Modernity*, 1 (July 1998).

Lakhani, M. Ali, 'Table of Contents', *Sacred Web: A Journal of Tradition and Modernity*, 2 (December 1998).

Lane, A. J., 'What is Radical Islam? One Answer.', *Encounter (Documents for Muslim–Christian Understanding)*, 216 (June–July 1995).

Laoust, H., 'Aḥmad B. Ḥanbal'. *EI*², vol. 1.

Lefebvre, Marcel, *I Accuse the Council* (Dickinson, TX: Angelus Press, 1982).

Lefebvre, Marcel, *Against the Heresies* (Kansas City: Angelus Press, 1997).

Lefebvre, Marcel, *Open Letter to Confused Catholics* (Kansas City: Angelus Press, 1987, 2001).

Leo XIII, Pope, *Encyclical Letter of Pope Leo XIII: On the Study of Sacred Scripture: Providentissimus Deus* (Boston, MA: Pauline Books and Media, n.d.).

Lewis, Bernard, *The Arabs in History*, Hutchinson University Library (London: Hutchinson, 1968).

Lewis, Bernard, 'The Roots of Muslim Rage', *Atlantic Monthly* (September 1990), pp. 47–60.

Lewis, Bernard, *The Middle East: 2000 Years of History from the Rise of Christianity to the Present Day*, History of Civilisation (London, Weidenfeld & Nicolson, 1995).

Lewis, Bernard, *What Went Wrong? The Clash Between Islam and Modernity in the Middle East* (London: Orion Books, Phoenix, 2002).

Liddle, R. William, 'Islam and politics in late new order' (Jakarta: unpublished paper presented at the *Conference on Religion and Society in Southeast Asia*, 29–30 May 1995).

Lloyd, A. C., *The Anatomy of Neoplatonism* (Oxford: Clarendon Press, 1990).

Lossky, Nicholas *et al.* (eds), *Dictionary of the Ecumenical Movement* (Geneva: WCC Publications; London: Council of Churches for Britain and Ireland, 1991).

Lynch, Jim (ed.), *9/11 One Year Later: A Nation Remembers*, Special Commemorative Edition (Boca Raton, FL: American Media Inc., 2002).

MacCulloch, Diarmaid, *Reformation: Europe's House Divided 1490-1700* (London: Allen Lane, 2003).

MacDonald, D. B., 'Idjtihād', *EIS*.

MacDonald, Scott, 'The Divine Nature' see Stump and Kretzmann (eds), CCA.

Magee, Bryan, *The Great Philosophers: An Introduction to Western Philosophy* (London: BBC Books, 1987).

Malik, Hafeez, 'Taliban's Islamic Emirate of Afghanistan: Its Impact on Eurasia', *Journal of South Asian and Middle Eastern Studies*, 23:1 (Fall 1999), pp. 65–78.

Malik, Jamal, 'Muslim Culture and Reform in 18th-Century South Asia', *Journal of the Royal Asiatic Society*, 3rd series, 13:2 (July 2003).

Mandaville, Peter, 'Digital Islam: Changing the Boundaries of Religious Knowledge', *ISIM Newsletter*, no. 2 (March 1999).

Manzoor, Parvez, 'Postmodernism: A Symptom of the Crisis of Modernism', *Islam 21*, 23 (June 2000).

Marmura, Michael E., 'Ghazali and Ash'arism Revisited', *Arabic Sciences and Philosophy*, 12 (2002).

Marrus, Michael R., 'Pius XII and the Holocaust: Ten Essential Themes' *see* Rittner and Roth (eds), *Pope Pius XII*.

Marsden, Peter, *The Taliban: War, Religion and the New Order in Afghanistan* (London and New York: Zed Books, 1998).

Martin, Richard C., 'The Religious Foundations of War, Peace and Statecraft in Islam' *see* Kelsay and Johnson (eds), *Just War and Jihad*.

Martin, Richard C. and Mark R. Woodward with Dwi S. Atmaja, *Defenders of Reason in Islam: Mu'tazilism from Medieval School to Modern Symbol* (Oxford: Oneworld, 1997).

Marty, Martin E. and R. Scott Appleby (eds), *Fundamentalisms Observed*, The Fundamentalism Project, vol. 1 (Chicago and London: University of Chicago Press, 1991, 1994).

Mazza, Debora, *The Pocket Oxford Italian Dictionary* (Oxford and New York: Oxford University Press, 2000).

McAuliffe, Jane Dammen (gen. ed.), *Encyclopaedia of the Qur'an* (Leiden and Boston, MA: E. J. Brill, 2003), vol. 3.

McCabe, Herbert, *The Teaching of the Catholic Church: A New Catechism* (London: CTS, 1985).

McInerny, Ralph, *The Defamation of Pius XII* (South Bend, IN: St Augustine's Press, 2001).

McNeal, Edgar H. and Robert Lee Wolff, 'The Fourth Crusade' *see* Setton (gen. ed.), *History of the Crusades*.

Meherally, Akbarally, *Myths and Realities of Hadith: A Critical Study* (Burnaby, Canada: Mostmerciful.com Publishers, 2001).

Meisami, Julie Scott and Paul Starkey (eds), *Encyclopedia of Arabic Literature*, 2 vols (London and New York: Routledge, 1998).

Menache, S., *Clement V*, Cambridge Studies in Medieval Life and Thought: fourth series, 36 (Cambridge: Cambridge University Press, 2002).

Merleau-Ponty, Maurice, *Phénoménologie de la Perception* (Paris: Gallimard, 1945); trans. C. Smith, *The Phenomenology of Perception* (London: Routledge, 1962).

Metcalf, Barbara Daly (ed.), *Making Muslim Space in North America and Europe* (Berkeley: University of California Press, 1996).

Meuleman, J., *Islam in the Era of Globalization: Muslim Attitudes towards Modernity and Identity* (London: RoutledgeCurzon, 2002).

Mews, Constant J., 'Heloise and liturgical experience at the Paraclete', *Plainsong and Medieval Music*, 11:1 (April. 2002).

Meyer, Thomas, 'A fundamental fallacy', *The Times Higher*, 9 November 2001.

Mikhail, Hanna, *Politics and Revelation: Māwardī and After* (Edinburgh: Edinburgh University Press, 1995).

Minerbi, Sergio I., 'Pius XII: A Reappraisal' *see* Rittner and Roth (eds), *Pope Pius XII*.

Miranda, Claudia, '"Dove" is the Dove?' *see* Capozzi (ed.), *Reading Eco*.

Mitha, Farouk, *Al-Ghazālī and the Ismailis: A Debate on Reason and Authority in Medieval Islam*, Ismaili Heritage Series, 5 (London and New York: I. B. Tauris in association with the Institute of Ismaili Studies, 2001).

Moin, Baqer, *Khomeini: Life of the Ayatollah* (London and New York: I. B. Tauris, 1999).

Morris, Rosemary, 'Northern Europe invades the Mediterranean 900-1200' *see* Holmes (ed.), *Oxford Illustrated History of Medieval Europe*.

Morrison, K. F., 'Canossa. A Revision', *Traditio*, 18 (1962).

Mujiburrahman, 'Islam and Politics in Indonesia: the Political Thought of Abdurrahman Wahid', *Islam and Christian-Muslim Relations*, 10:3 (1999).

Murata, Sachiko and William C. Chittick, *The Vision of Islam: The Foundations of Muslim Faith and Practice* (London and New York: I. B. Tauris, 1996).

Murphy-O'Connor, Cormac and Mark Santer (eds), *Church as Communion: An Agreed Statement by the Second Anglican–Roman Catholic International Commission* (London: Church House Publishing/CTS, 1991).

Musallam, Adnan, *Sayyid Qutb: The Emergence of the Islamicist 1939-1950* (Jerusalem: Palestinian Academic Society for the Study of International Affairs, 1990).

Naguib, Saphinaz-Amal, 'Aesthetics of Islamic Spaces in Norway', *ISIM Newsletter*, no. 10 (July 2002).

Naipaul, V. S., *Among the Believers: An Islamic Journey* (London: André Deutsch, 1981).

Naipaul, V. S., *Beyond Belief: Islamic Excursions Among the Converted Peoples* (London: Little,

Brown, 1998).
Najjar, Fauzi M., 'Islamic Fundamentalism and the Intellectuals: The Case of Naṣr Ḥāmid Abū Zayd', *British Journal of Middle Eastern Studies*, 27:2 (November 2000).
Nakhnikian, George, "Introduction" to Edmund Husserl, *The Idea of Phenomenology* (*see* Husserl).
Nasr, Seyyed Hossein, 'Frithjof Schuon (1907–1998)', *Sacred Web: A Journal of Tradition and Modernity*, 1 (July 1998).
Nasr, Seyyed Hossein, Hamid Dabashi and Seyyed Vali Reza Nasr (eds), *Expectation of the Millennium: Shi'ism in History* (Albany, NY: State University New York Press, 1989).
Nemeth, Charles P., *The Case of Marcel Lefebvre* (Kansas City: Angelus Press, 1994).
Netton, Ian Richard, 'Neo-Orientalists on a New Crusade: Hope, Renewal and Salvation', *Al-Masāq: Islam and the Medieval Mediterranean*, 10 (1988).
Netton, Ian Richard, *Allāh Transcendent: Studies in the Structure and Semiotics of Islamic Philosophy, Theology and Cosmology* (London and New York: Routledge, 1989; repr. Richmond: Curzon Press, 1994).
Netton, Ian Richard, 'Arabia and the Pilgrim Paradigm of Ibn Baṭṭūṭa: A Braudelian Approach' *see* Netton, *Seek Knowledge* (1996).
Netton, Ian Richard, *Seek Knowledge: Thought and Travel in the House of Islam* (Richmond: Curzon Press, 1996).
Netton, Ian Richard, *Text and Trauma: An East–West Primer* (Richmond: Curzon Press, 1996).
Netton, Ian Richard, *A Popular Dictionary of Islam* (Richmond: Curzon, 1997).
Netton, Ian Richard, *Ṣūfī Ritual: The Parallel Universe*, Curzon Sufi Series (Richmond: Curzon Press, 2000).
Netton, Ian Richard, *Muslim Neoplatonists: An Introduction to the Thought of the Brethren of Purity (Ikhwān al- Ṣafā')* (London: RoutledgeCurzon, 2002).
Netton, Ian Richard (ed.), *Encyclopaedia of Islamic Civilization and Religion* (London and New York: Routledge, 2006)
Netton, Ian Richard, 'Nature as Signs' *see* McAuliffe (gen. ed.) *Encyclopaedia of the Qur'an*, vol. 3.
Netton, Ian Richard, 'Riḥla', *EI*², vol. 8.
Newman, John Henry, *Certain Difficulties Felt by Anglicans in Catholic Teaching*, 2 vols (London: Longmans, Green & Co. c. 1890).
Newman, John Henry, *Apologia Pro Vita Sua*, ed. Martin Svaglic (Oxford: Clarendon Press, 1967); ed. Ian Ker, Penguin Classics (London: Penguin Books, 1994, repr. 2004).
Nichols, Aidan, *The World Has Been Abroad: A Guide Through Balthasar's Aesthetics* (Edinburgh: T&T Clark, 1998).
Nichols, Aidan, *No Bloodless Myth: A Guide Through Balthasar's Dramatics* (Edinburgh: T. & T. Clark, 2000).
Nielsen, Jørgen, *Muslims in Western Europe*, 2nd edn (Edinburgh: Edinburgh University Press, 1995).
Noakes, Guy, 'Ibn Rushd the Jurist', *Saudi Aramco World*, 54:3 (May–June 2003).
O'Donnell, James J., 'Augustine: his time and lives' *see* Stump and Kretzmann (eds), CCA.
O'Donnell, John, *Hans Urs Von Balthasar*, Outstanding Christian Thinkers (London: Geoffrey Chapman, 1992).
O'Mahony, Anthony, Wulstan Peterburs and Mohammad Ali Shomali (eds), *Catholics and Shi'a in Dialogue: Studies in Theology and Spirituality* (London: Melisende, 2004).
O'Meara, Dominic J., *Plotinus: An Introduction to the Enneads* (Oxford: Clarendon Press, 1993).
Ott, Ludwig, *Fundamentals of Catholic Dogma*, ed. James Canon Bastible (Rockford, IL: Tan Books, 1974).

Parvis, Paul, 'On the Function of Heresy', *New Blackfriars*, 70:824 (February 1989).

Peirce, Charles Sanders, *see* Hartshorne *et al.* (eds).

Penny Catechism, The (Libertyville, IL: Prow Books/Franciscan Marytown Press, 1982).

Peters, J. R. T. M., *God's Created Speech: A Study in the Speculative Theology of the Mu'tazilî Qâḍî l-Quḍāt Abū l-Ḥasan 'Abd al-Jabbār bn Aḥmad al-Hamaḏânî* (Leiden: E J. Brill, 1976).

Peters, Rudolph, *Jihad in Classical and Modern Islam: A Reader*, Princeton Series on the Middle East (Princeton: Markus Wiener Publishers, 1996).

Phillips, Jonathan, *The Fourth Crusade and the Sack of Constantinople* (London: Jonathan Cape, 2004).

Phillips, Jonathan, 'The Latin East 1098–1291' *see* Riley-Smith (ed.), *Oxford Illustrated History of the Crusades.*

Picken, Gavin, 'Salafīs (al-Salafiyya)' *see* Netton (ed.), *Encyclopaedia of Islamic Civilization and Religion.*

Pius X, Pope, *Encyclical Letter 'Pascendi Gregis' … On the Doctrines of the Modernists* (London Burns & Oates, 1907; repr. Long Prairie: The Neumann Press, 1983).

Pius XII, Pope, *Encyclical Letter of Pius XII: Promotion of Biblical Studies (Divino Afflante Spiritu)* (Boston, MA: Pauline Books and Media, n.d.).

Pius XII , Pope, *Humani Generis: Some False Opinions which Threaten to Undermine Catholic Doctrine* (Boston, MA: Pauline Books and Media, 1992).

Pivert, François, *Schism or Not? The 1988 Episcopal Consecrations of Archbishop Marcel Lefebvre* (Kansas City: Angelus Press, 1995, 2003).

Popescu, Mircea, 'Eliade and Folklore' *see* Kitagawa and Long (eds), *Myths and Symbols.*

Popovic, A. and G. Veinstein (eds), *Les ordres mystiques dans l'Islam: cheminements et situation actuelle*, Recherches d'Histoire et de Sciences Sociales 13 (Paris: Editions de l'École des Hautes Études en Sciences Sociales, 1985).

Porter, D., *Managing Politics and Islam in Indonesia* (London: RoutledgeCurzon, 2002).

Preston, Ronald, 'Christian Ethics' *see* Singer (ed.), *Companion to Ethics.*

Priest, A (= A. N. Gibley), *We Believe* (Valletta: Progress Press, 1983).

Queller, D. E. and T. F. Madden, *The Fourth Crusade: The Conquest of Constantinople* (Philadelphia, PA: University of Pennsylvania Press, 1997).

Quin, William W., 'Response to David Appelbaum's "The Moment of Modernity"', *Sacred Web: A Journal of Tradition and Modernity*, 2 (December 1998).

Raban, Jonathan, *Arabia Through the Looking Glass* (London: Collins, 1979).

Rahman, Fazlur, *Islam and Modernity: Transformation of an Intellectual System* (Chicago: University of Chicago Press, 1984).

Rahman, Fazlur, 'Islam: Challenges and Opportunities' *see* Welch and Cachia (eds), *Islam.*

Rashed, Ebrahim, *The Impacts of Western Modernity upon Identity in an Islamic Society: A Case Study of the United Arab Emirates with Special Reference to the Impact of Media and Technology upon Identity*, unpublished Ph.D. thesis, School of Journalism, Media and Cultural Studies, University of Wales, Cardiff, 2000.

Rashid, Ahmed, *Jihad: The Rise of Militant Islam in Central Asia*, A World Policy Institute Book (New Haven, CT and London: Yale University Press, 2002).

Ratzinger, Joseph Cardinal [*later*, from 2005, Pope Benedict XVI] and Tarcisio Bertone, *Declaration: 'Dominus Jesus': On the Unicity and Salvific Universality of Jesus Christ and the Church* (London: CTS, 2000).

Ray, Stephen K., *Upon this Rock: St Peter and the Primacy of Rome in Scripture and the Early Church*, Modern Apologetics Library (San Francisco: Ignatius Press, 1999).

Reetz, Dietrich, 'Islamic Activism in Central Asia and the Pakistan Factor', *Journal of South Asian and Middle-Eastern Studies*, 23:1 (Fall 1999).

Reeve, Simon, *The New Jackals: Ramzi Yousef, Osama bin Laden and the Future of Terrorism* (London: André Deutsch, 1999).

al-Rehaili, Abdullah (comp.), *This is the Truth: Newly Discovered Scientific Facts Recorded in the Qur'an and Authentic Hadeeth*, 2nd edn (Mecca: Muslim World League; Riyad: Alharamain Islamic Foundation, 1998).

Rentz, G., 'Djazīrat al-'Arab', *EI*², vol. 1.

Richter, David H., 'The Mirrored World: Form and Ideology in *The Name of the Rose*' *see* Capozzi (ed.), *Reading Eco*.

Ricoeur, Paul, *Husserl: An Analysis of His Phenomenology*, trans. Edward G. Ballard and Lester E. Embree, Northwestern University Studies in Phenomenology of Existential Philosophy (Evanston, IL: Northwestern University Press, 1967).

Riffaterre, Michael, 'The Interpretant in Literary Semiotics' *see* Capozzi (ed.), *Reading Eco*.

Riley-Smith, Jonathan (ed.), *The Oxford Illustrated History of the Crusades* (Oxford and New York: Oxford University Press, 1995)

Rittner, Carol, 'What Kind of Witness?' *see* Rittner and Roth (eds), *Pope Pius XII*.

Rittner, Carol and John K. Roth, 'A Chronology about Pope Pius XII and the Holocaust' *see* Rittner and Roth (eds), *Pope Pius XII*.

Rittner, Carol and John K. Roth (eds), *Pope Pius XII and the Holocaust* (London and New York: Leicester University Press, 2002).

Robinson, Adam, *Bin Laden: Behind the Mask of the Terrorist* ((Edinburgh and London: Mainstream Publishing, 2001).

Robinson, I. S., 'Pope Gregory VII, the princes and the *pactum*', *English Historical Review*, 94 (1979).

Robson, J., 'Ḥadīth', *EI*², vol. 3.

Robson, J., 'Ḥadīth Qudsī', *EI*², vol. 3.

Rosenthal, Erwin I. J., *Political Thought in Medieval Islam: An Introductory Outline* (Cambridge: Cambridge University Press, 1968).

Rubin, U., 'Sā'a: 3. In Eschatology', *EI*², vol. 8.

Runciman, Steven, *A History of the Crusades*, 3 vols (London: The Folio Society, 1994; first publ. Cambridge University Press, 1954).

Runnymede Trust, The, *Islamophobia: A Challenge for Us All* (London: The Runnymede Trust Commission on British Muslims and Islamophobia, 1997).

Ruokanen, Mikka, *The Catholic Doctrine of Non-Christian Religions According to the Second Vatican Council*, Studies in Christian Mission, vol. 7 (Leiden, New York and Cologne: E. J. Brill, 1992).

Ruys, Juanita Feros, '*Planctus magis quam cantici*: the generic significance of Abelard's *planctus*', *Plainsong and Medieval Music*, 11:1 (April 2002).

Sachedina, Abdulaziz A., 'The Development of Jihad in Islamic Revelation and History' *see* Johnson and Kelsay (eds), *Cross, Crescent and Sword*.

Said, Edward W., *Orientalism* (London: Penguin Books, 1995; first publ. Routledge & Kegan Paul, 1978).

Salhi, Zahia Smail and Ian Richard Netton (eds), *The Arab Diaspora: Voices of an Anguished Scream* (Abingdon: Routledge, 2006).

Saliba, John A., *'Homo Religiosus' in Mircea Eliade: An Anthropological Evaluation*, Supplementa ad Numen, Altera Series: Dissertationes ad Historiam Religionum Pertinentes, vol. 5 (Leiden: E. J. Brill, 1976).

Sanders, E. P., *The Historical Figure of Jesus* (London: Penguin Books, Allen Lane, 1993).

Sanneh, Lamin, 'Sacred and Secular in Islam', *ISIM Newsletter*, no. 10 (July 2002).

Schacht, J., 'Ḥiyal', *EI*², vol. 3.

Schacht, J., 'Ikhtilāf', *EI*², vol. 3.
Schacht, Joseph, *The Origins of Muhammadan Jurisprudence* (Oxford: Clarendon Press, 1950, 1967).
Schacht, Joseph, *An Introduction to Islamic Law* (Oxford: Clarendon Press, 1964, 1966).
Schacht, J. and D. B. Macdonald, 'Idjtihād', *EI*², vol. 3.
Schuon, Frithjof, 'Tradition and Modernity', *Sacred Web: A Journal of Tradition and Modernity* 1 (July 1998).
Sebeok, Thomas, 'Give Me Another Horse' *see* Capozzi (ed.), *Reading Eco.*
Segura, José, 'On Descartes' "Stop"', *Sacred Web: A Journal of Tradition and Modernity*, 3 (June 1999).
Setton, Kenneth M. (gen ed.), *A History of the Crusades, Volume II: The Later Crusades, 1189–1311*, ed. Robert Lee Wolff and Harry W. Hazard (Madison, Milwaukee and London: University of Wisconsin Press, 1969).
Shaban, M. A., *Islamic History A.D. 600–750 (A.H. 132): A New Interpretation* (Cambridge: Cambridge University Press, 1971).
Shaban, M. A., *Islamic History: A New Interpretation 2: A.D. 750–1055 (A.H. 132–448)* (Cambridge: Cambridge University Press, 1976).
Shaheen, Jack G., *Arab and Muslim Stereotyping in American Popular Culture* (Washington, DC: Georgetown University, 1977).
Shain, Emad Eldin, 'Salāfiya' *see* Esposito (ed.), *Oxford Encyclopaedia of the Modern Islamic World.*
Shakir, Abu Muhammad Abdur-Ra'uf, *The Islamic Ruling Concerning At-Tasweer* (Philadelphia: Zakee Muwwakkil Books & Articles; South Orange, NJ: CWP Publishing & Distribution, 1998).
Sharif, M. M. (ed.), *A History of Muslim Philosophy*, 2 vols (Wiesbaden: Otto Harrassowitz, 1963).
Shaw, Russell, *Papal Primacy in the Third Millennium* (Huntington, IN: Our Sunday Visitor Publishing Division, 2000).
Shinar, P. and W. Ende, 'Salafiyya', *EI*², vol. 8.
Shorter Encyclopaedia of Islam [*EIS*], ed. H. A. R. Gibb and J. H. Kramers (Leiden: E. J. Brill; London: Luzac 1961).
Simpson, St. John (ed.), *Queen of Sheba: Treasures from Ancient Yemen* (London: British Museum Press, 2002).
Singer, Peter (ed.), *A Companion to Ethics*, Blackwell Companions to Philosophy, no. 2 (Oxford: Blackwell, 2005).
Smart, Ninian, *Dimensions of the Sacred: An Anatomy of the World's Beliefs* (London: HarperCollins, 1996). ;
Smith, Barry and David Woodruff Smith (eds), *The Cambridge Companion to Husserl* (Cambridge: Cambridge University Press, 1995).
Smith, David, *Hinduism and Modernity*, Religion and Modernity series (Oxford: Blackwell, 2002).
Smith, Jane Idleman and Yvonne Yazbeck Haddad, *The Islamic Understanding of Death and Resurrection* (Albany, NY: State University of New York Press, 1981).
Sokolowski, Robert, *Introduction to Phenomenology* (Cambridge: Cambridge University Press, 2000).
Stravinskas, Peter M. J., *Salvation Outside the Church* (Huntington, IN: Our Sunday Visitor Publishing Division, 2002).
Stump, Eleonore and Norman Kretzmann (eds), *The Cambridge Companion to Augustine* [CCA] (Cambridge: Cambridge University Press, 2001).

Suelzer, Alexa and John S. Kselman, 'Modern Old Testament Criticism' *see* R. E. Brown et *al.* (eds), *New Jerome Biblical Commentary*.

Sullivan, Francis A., *Salvation Outside the Church? Tracing the History of the Catholic Response* (London: Geoffrey Chapman, 1992).

Sykes, J. B., *The Concise Oxford Dictionary of Current English*, 6th edn (Oxford: Clarendon Press, 1976).

Tabataba'i, 'Allama, Jassim M. Hussain and Abdulaziz A. Sachedina, 'Messianism and the Mahdi' *see* Nasr et al. (eds), *Expectation of the Millennium*.

Teeple, John B., *Timelines of World History* (London et al.: Dorling Kindersley, 2002).

Thompson, Francis, *The Hound of Heaven* (Portland, ME: T. B. Mosher, 1917).

Torevell, David, *Losing the Sacred: Ritual, Modernity and Liturgical Reform* (Edinburgh: T. & T. Clark, 2000).

Trifonas, Peter Pericles, *Umberto Eco and Football*, Postmodern Encounters (Cambridge: Icon Books; USA: Totem Books, 2001).

Tripp, Charles, 'Can Islam cope with modernity?', *Times Literary Supplement*, 23 April 1999.

Tritton, A. S., 'Ākhira', *EI*², vol. 1.

Troll, Christian W., 'Islam and Pluralism in India', *Encounter*, 220 (December 1995).

Trower, Philip, *Turmoil and Truth: The Historical Roots of the Modern Crisis in the Catholic Church* (Oxford: Family Publications; San Francisco: Ignatius Press, 2003).

Tyan, E., Da'wa', *EI*², vol. 2.

Tyan, E., Djihād', *EI*², vol. 2.

Vale, Malcolm, 'The Civilization of Courts and Cities in the North: 1200–1500' *see* Holmes (ed.), *Oxford Illustrated History of Medieval Europe*.

Van Kley, D., *The Jansenists and the Expulsion of the Jesuits from France, 1757–1765* (New Haven, CT : Yale University Press, 1975).

Veinstein, G., 'Un essai de synthese' *see* Popovic and Veinstein (eds), *Les ordres mystiques*.

Vickers, Miranda, *Between Serb and Albanian: A History of Kosovo* (London: Hurst, 1998).

Vikør, Knut S., 'Opening the Maliki School: Muhammad b. 'Ali al-Sanusi's Views on the Madhhab', *Journal of Libyan Studies*, 1:1 (Summer 2000).

Von Balthasar, Hans Urs, *The Office of Peter and the Structure of the Church* (San Francisco: Ignatius Press, 1986).

Von Balthasar, Hans Urs, Theo-Drama: *Theological Dramatic Theory, Volume One: Prolegomena*, trans. Graham Harrison (San Francisco: Ignatius Press, 1988).

Von Balthasar, Hans Urs, *The Glory of the Lord: A Theological Aesthetics, Volume One: Seeing the Form*, trans. Erasmo Leiva-Merikakis, ed. Joseph Fessio and John Riches (Edinburgh: T. & T. Clark, 1989).

Von Balthasar, Hans Urs, *The Glory of the Lord: A Theological Aesthetics, Volume Six: Theology: The Old Covenant*, trans. Brian McNeil and Erasmo Leiva-Merikakis, ed. John Riches (Edinburgh: T. & T. Clark, 1991).

Von Bruinessan, Martin, 'ISIM Workshop: Muslim Intellectuals and Modern Challenges', *ISIM Newsletter*, no 5 (June 2000).

Von Grunebaum, G. E., *Classical Islam: A History 600–1258* (London: Allen & Unwin, 1970)

Waines, David, *An Introduction to Islam* (Cambridge: Cambridge University Press, 1995).

Waines, David, 'Religion and Modernity: Reflections on a Modern Debate', *ISIM Newsletter*, no. 12 (June 2003).

Ward, Keith, *Religion and Community* (Oxford: Clarendon Press, 2000).

Ware, Timothy [Bishop Kallistos of Diokleia], *The Orthodox Church*, new edn (London: Penguin Books, 1993).

Warner, W. Lloyd, *A Black Civilization* (New York: Harper & Brothers, 1937).

Wasserstein, Bernard, *Divided Jerusalem: The Struggle for the Holy City* (London: Profile, 2002).
Watt, W. Montgomery, *Muhammad at Mecca* (Oxford: Oxford University Press, 1953).
Watt, W. Montgomery, *Muhammad, Prophet and Statesman* (London: Oxford University Press, 1967).
Watt, W. Montgomery, *Muslim Intellectual: A Study of al-Ghazali* (Edinburgh,: Edinburgh University Press, 1971).
Watt, W. Montgomery, *The Formative Period of Islamic Thought* (Edinburgh: Edinburgh University Press, 1973).
Watt, W. Montgomery, *Islamic Philosophy and Theology: An Extended Survey*, 2nd edn (Edinburgh: Edinburgh University Press, 1985).
Watt, W. Montgomery, *see also* Primary Sources: al-Ghazālī.
Weithman, Paul, 'Augustine's Political Authority' *see* Stump and Kretzmann (eds), CCA.
Welch, Alford T. and Pierre Cachia (eds), *Islam: Past Influence and Present Challenge* (Edinburgh: Edinburgh University Press, 1979).
Wensinck, A. J., 'Sunna' *see* Gibb and Kramers (eds), *EIS*.
Wensinck, A. J. and B. Lewis, 'Ḥadjdj', *EI*², vol. 3.
Whitton, David, 'The Society of Northern Europe in the High Middle Ages' *see* Holmes (ed.), *Oxford Illustrated History of Medieval Europe*.
Wiles, Maurice, *Archetypal Heresy: Arianism Through the Centuries* (Oxford: Clarendon Press, 1996).
Williams, David H., 'Ambrose, Emperors and Homoians in Milan: The First Conflict over a Basilica' *see* Barnes and Williams (eds), *Arianism after Arius*.
Williams, Rowan, *Arius: Heresy and Tradition* (London: Darton, Longman & Todd, 1987).
Wills, Gary, *St Augustine* (London: Phoenix, Orion Books, 2000).
Wolfson, Harry Austryn, *The Philosophy of the Kalam*, Structure and Growth of Philosophic Systems from Plato to Spinoza IV (Cambridge, MA and London: Harvard University Press, 1976).
Wood, D., *Clement VI: The Pontificate and Ideas of an Avignon Pope*, Cambridge Studies in Medieval Life and Thought, 4th series, 13 (Cambridge: Cambridge University Press, 2002).
Wood, Ian, 'History and Legend in Verdi's Attila', in Royal Opera House [Programme for] *Attila 2001/2* (London: Royal Opera House Covent Garden, 2002).
Woodhead, Linda and Paul Heelas (eds), *Religion in Modern Times: An Anthology*, Religion and Modernity Series (Oxford: Blackwell, 2000).
Woods, Richard, *Eckhart's Way*, The Way of the Christian Mystics (London: Darton, Longman & Todd, 1987).
Wulstan, David, '*Novi Modulaminis melos*: the music of Heloise and Abelard', *Plainsong and Medieval Music*, 11:1 (April 2002).
Zamora, Lois Parkinson, 'The Swing of the Pendulum: Eco's Novels' *see* Capozzi (ed.), *Reading Eco*.
Zuccotti, Susan,'Pope Pius XII and the Rescue of Jews during the Holocaust: Examining Commonly Held Assertions' *see* Rittner and Roth (eds), *Pope Pius XII*.

Contemporary Media Sources

Ahmed, Mukhtar and Tim McGirk, 'Historic mosque destroyed in new Kashmir violence', *Independent*, 12 May 1995.
Alberge, Dalya, 'Reclusive author expresses delight at Nobel Prize', *Times*, 12 October 2001.

al-Azam, Mustafa, 'Orientalists and the Qur'an', *Muslim World League Journal* (Muharram 1422/April 2001)
Beard, Matthew, 'Hijackers should be made martyrs, says London cleric', *Independent*, 13 September 2001.
Beaumont, John, 'The Society of St Pius X *is* in schism with the Church', letter to *Catholic Herald*, 24 January 2003.
Bergen, Peter, 'How Bin Laden controls his international web of Terror', *Sunday Times: Special 24-Page Supplement: America at War*, 16 September 2001.
Bin Zayed, Sheikh, 'Don't throw away your chance in the Middle East, Mr Blair. There won't be many more', *Times*, 2 June 2003.
Binyon, Michael, 'Religious conflicts take growing toll', *Times*, 4 January 2000.
Binyon, Michael, 'Careless word stirs hatred in Muslims', *Times*, 21 September 2001.
Bone, James. 'Still fighting for our survival', *Times: T2*, 12 March 2002.
Bone, James 'Hispanic invasion will split US, says Harvard academic', *Times*, 22 March 2004.
Bremner, Charles, 'Muslim girls face scarf ban at French schools', *Times*, 12 December 2003.
Bremner, Charles, 'Chirac bans use of Muslim headscarf in all state schools', *Times*, 18 December 2003.
Browne, Anthony, 'Belgians call for headscarf ban', *Times*, 19 January 2004.
Bulloch, John, 'The roots of terror', *Trends: The International Magazine on Arab Affairs*, 46 (October 2001).
Bunting, Madeleine, 'Secularism goes mad', *Guardian*, 18 December 2003.
Carrell, Severin and Andrew Gumbel, 'Murders of Asian men in US heighten fears of revenge attacks', *Independent*, 17 September 2001.
Cooper, Kate, 'From Bethlehem to Byzantium', *Times Literary Supplement*, 29 March 2002.
Cornwall, John, 'Winter of the patriarch', *Sunday Times: News Review*, 23 December 2001.
Cornwall, John *see also* Secondary Sources.
Cowley, Jason, 'Scornful outsider who made a new homeland in literature', *Times*, 12 October 2001.
Darwish, Adel, 'Same old jibes and polemics', *Times 2*, 21 September 2001.
Dickey, Christopher and Daniel McGinn, 'Meet the bin Ladens', *Newsweek*, 138:16, 15 October 2001.
Discourse, 23 (June 2002).
Euben, Roxanne, 'West's lessons in decadence fuel the making of a martyr', *Times Higher Education Supplement*, 1 August 2003.
Figaro, Le, 'Laicité, voile: les questions clés', *Le Figaro*, 8 December 2003.
Fishlock, Trevor, 'Holy town at heart of quarrel about nation's future', *Times*, 28 February 2002.
Fisk, Robert, 'Hypocrisy, hatred and the war on terror', *Independent: The Thursday Review*, 8 November 2001.
Fuden, Giles, 'Bin Laden: the former CIA "client" obsessed with training pilots', *Guardian*, 13 September 2001.
Giddens, Anthony, 'Why we still look forward to the past', The 1999 Reith Lectures, no. 3: Tradition, *Observer*, 25 April 1999.
Godfrey, Hannah, 'Schools' bid for headscarf ban widens French divide', *Observer*, 15 June 2003.
Gove, Michael, 'How moralists justify fighting the good fight', *Times*, 26 September 2001.
Gribbin, Joseph A., letter to *Catholic Times*, 26 January 2003.
Guardian, 12 September 2001; 13 September 2001; *Guardian: G2*, 13 September 2001.

Henley, Jon, 'France to ban pupils' religious dress', *Guardian*, 12 December 2003.
Herbert, Ian, 'In the mosques of Bradford, the anger is directed towards America', *Independent*, 13 September 2001.
Holes, Clive, 'A word in your ear, Tony, learn a little Arabic', *Times*, 23 October 2001.
Hussain, Zahid, 'Musharraf condemns "backward" Muslims', *Times*, 18 February 2002.
Independent, 13 September 2001.
Independent, 'Megawati will bring dignity, perhaps even stability', *Independent: The Tuesday Review*, 24 July, 2001.
Irwin, Robert, 'Is this the man who inspired Bin Laden?', *Guardian:* G2, 1 November 2001.
Irwin, Robert, 'Ramadan Nights', *London Review of Books*, 7 August 2003.
Islahi, Abrar Ahmad, 'OIC Islamic Fiqh Academy's 11th Session', *Muslim World League Journal*, 26:10 (Jan.–Feb. 1999).
Jaggi, Maya, 'Profile: Umberto Eco: Signs of the Times', *Guardian: Review*, 12 October 2002.
Kiley, Sam, 'Clerics revolt over mosque in Nazareth', *Times*, 5 November 1999.
Latham-Koenig, Alfred, 'Earthquake in Rome', letter to *The Tablet*, 9 November 2002.
Lowry, Robert, 'Apocalypse Now', *Trends: The International Magazine on Arab Affairs*, 47 (November 2001).
Macintyre, Ben, 'Rituals reflect a battle to the death', *Times*, 28 September 2001.
Macintyre, Ben, 'Slaughterhouse of the religions', *Times*: 2, 3 December 2001.
Maddox, Bronwen et al., 'The Times in the Balkans: The 80 Days War', *Times*, 15 July 1999.
Markus, R. A., 'The persecuted sect that captured the Roman Empire', *The Tablet*, 9 March 2002.
Mass of Ages: Magazine of the Latin Mass Society, 136 (May 2003).
McCrum, Robert, 'Inimitable and truly great', *Observer Review*, 14 October 2001.
Mishara, Pankaj, 'Commentary: a dream of order: Naipaul, India and Islamic fervour', *Times Literary Supplement*, 2 November 2001.
Monde Le, 'L'appel commun des Eglises chrétiennes contre une loi sur de voile', *Le Monde*, 9 December 2003.
Morris, Chris, 'Headscarf MP warns off army', *Guardian*, 4 May 1999.
Murad, Abd al-Hakim, 'Islamic Spirituality: the forgotten revolution': www:file:///D | /ashari/nuhhakim/ahk/fgtnrevo/htm
Muslim World League Journal, 30:3 (Rabi al-Awwal 1423/May 2002).
L'Osservatore Romano, 8 October 2000.
Ottaviani, Alfredo and Antonio Bacci, 'The Ottaviani Intervention: Rome, September 25 1969', *Inside the Vatican* (February 2004).
Pandita, K. N., 'Intricate Roots of Theo-Fascist Ideology', *Asian Affairs*, 36 (October 1999).
Parry, Richard Lloyd, 'Islam rises over Indonesia', *Independent on Sunday*, 24 October 1999.
Parry, Richard Lloyd, 'Indonesia has a new president, only the old one won't accept that', *Independent*, 24 July 2001.
Philip, Catherine, 'Sukarno's daughter claims birthright', *Times*, 24 July 2001.
Philip, Catherine, 'Two Presidents condemn Jakarta to double jeopardy', *Times*, 24 July 2001.
Philip, Catherine, 'Muslim fire raiders kill 57 Hindus in train', *Times*, 28 February 2002
Phillips, Jonathan, 'Why a crusade will lead to a jihad', *Independent: The Tuesday Review*, 18 September 2001.
Quinlan, Michael, 'The Just War Litmus Test', *The Tablet*, 13 October 2001.
Reeves, Phil, 'Profile: Ariel Sharon: Israel's danger man', *Independent: The Weekend Review*,28 October 2000.

Righter, Rosemary, review of John Gray, *Al-Qaeda and What It Means to be Modern*: *Times: T2*, 16 July 2003.
Rist, John M., 'The status of "Extra Ecclesiam Nulla Salus"', letter to *Catholic Herald*, 27 December 2002.
Rychlak, Ronald J., 'Pius XII and the Holocaust', letter to the Editor, *Times Literary Supplement*, 15 March 2002.
Scott-Clark, Cathy and Adrian Levy, 'Beyond belief', *Sunday Times Magazine*, 24 January 1999.
Sesay, D. I. (trans.), 'MWL Organizes Islamic Seminar on Ijtehad [*sic*]', *Muslim World League Journal*, 32: 4–5 (June–July 2004).
Shortt, Rupert, 'Counting the world as dust', *Times Literary Supplement*, 29 March 2002.
Smucker, Philip, 'Militant is revered by dispossessed Arabs', *Daily Telegraph*, 13 September 2001.
Smyth, Gareth, 'Earthly Wisdom', *Trends: The International Magazine on Arab Affairs*, 46 (October 2001).
Steinberger, Michael, 'So, are civilisations at war?', *Observer*, 21 October 2001.
Sunday Times, 'Brilliant – even if he says so himself: Profile: V. S. Naipaul', *Sunday Times*, 14 October 2001.
Sunday Times Special 24-Page Supplement: America at War, 16 September 2001.
Tablet, The, 29 September 2001.
Tablet, The, 'Boston hopes for change after Cardinal's resignation', *The Tablet*, 21–28 December 2002.
Tablet, The, 'Cardinal takes on the media', *The Tablet*, 21–28 December 2002.
Theodoulou, Michael, 'Thousands march for the Ayatollah', *Times*, 15 July 1999.
Thomas, Evan, 'Cracking the Terror Code', *Newsweek*, 138:16, 15 October 2001.
Thomas, Scott, 'Can the West and Islam live together?' *The Tablet*, 6 October 2001.
Times, 'Islam's Luther: Khomeini's shadow still clouds the Muslim world', *Times*, 11 February 1999.
Times, 'Megawati's challenge', *Times*, 24 July 2001.
Times, 13 September 2001.
Times, 'The seeds of religious strife in Indonesia', *Times*, 15 October 2002.
Times, 'The Christian view', *Times*, 21 January 2003.
Von Hildenbrand, Dietrich, 'In Defence of the Old Liturgy', *Inside the Vatican* (February 2004).
Walker, Christopher, 'Religious divide in a holy dispute', *Times Weekend*, 15 May 1999.
Walters, Joanna and John Arlidge, 'Focus: Fear in the air: Tailspin', *Observer*, 18 November 2001.
Weakland, Rembert, 'The right road for the liturgy', *The Tablet*, 2 February 2002.
Webster, Paul, 'Chirac calls on MPs to ban headscarves', *Guardian*, 18 December 2003.
Woodrow, Alain, 'Tricolour versus the scarf', *The Tablet*, 3 January 2004.
Woods, Richard, 'When death came out of a blue sky', *Sunday Times: Special 24-Page Supplement: America at War*, 16 September 2001.
Yorkshire Evening Post, 12 September 2001.
Yorkshire Post, 12 September 2001 and Section B; 13 September 2001.
Younge, Gary, 'How could they cheer?', *Guardian: G2*, 13 September 2001.
Zakaria, Fareed, 'The Roots of Rage', *Newsweek*, 138:16, 15 October 2001.

INDEX